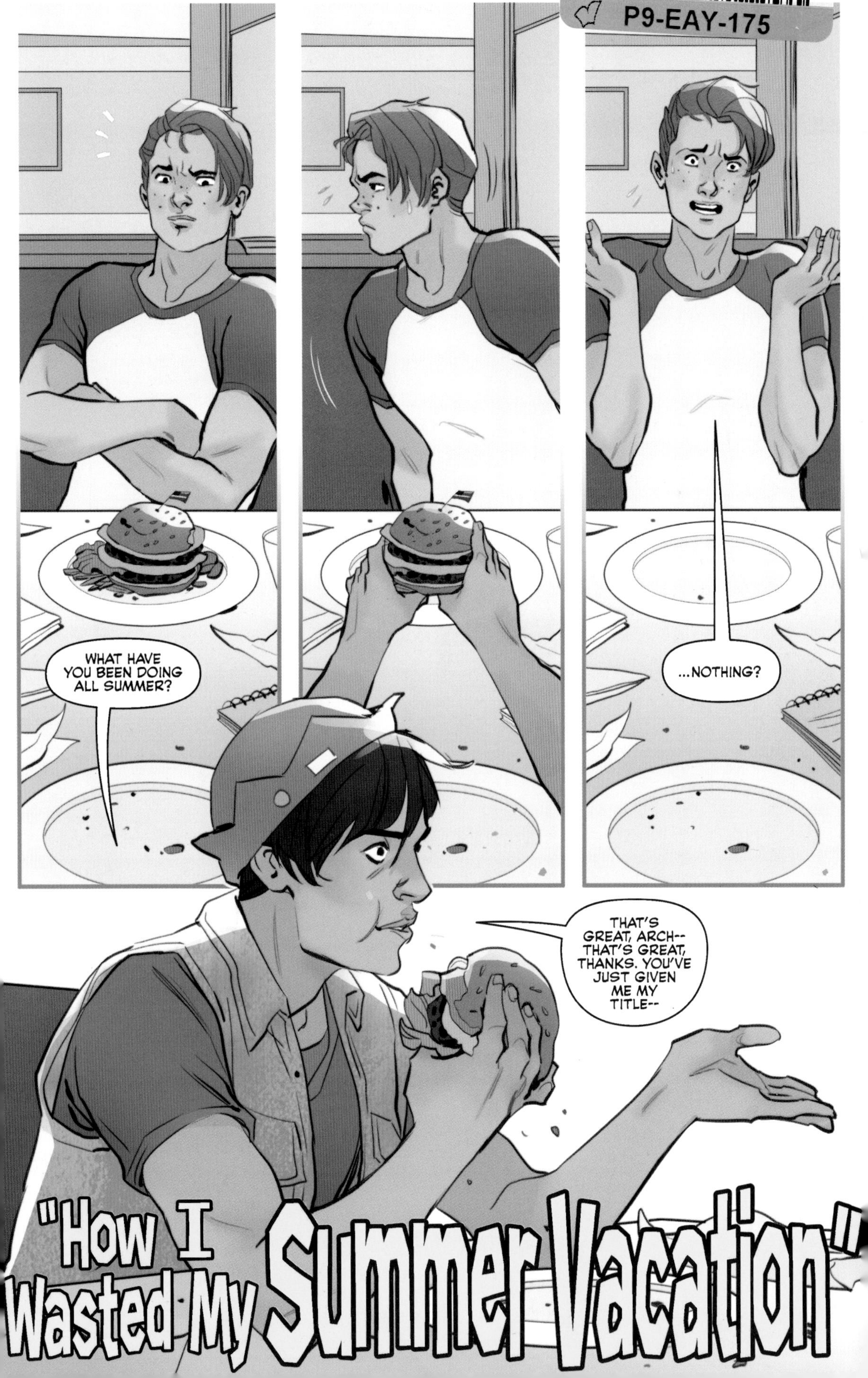
WHAT HAVE YOU BEEN DOING ALL SUMMER?
...NOTHING?
THAT'S GREAT, ARCH-- THAT'S GREAT, THANKS. YOU'VE JUST GIVEN ME MY TITLE--
"How I Wasted My Summer Vacation"

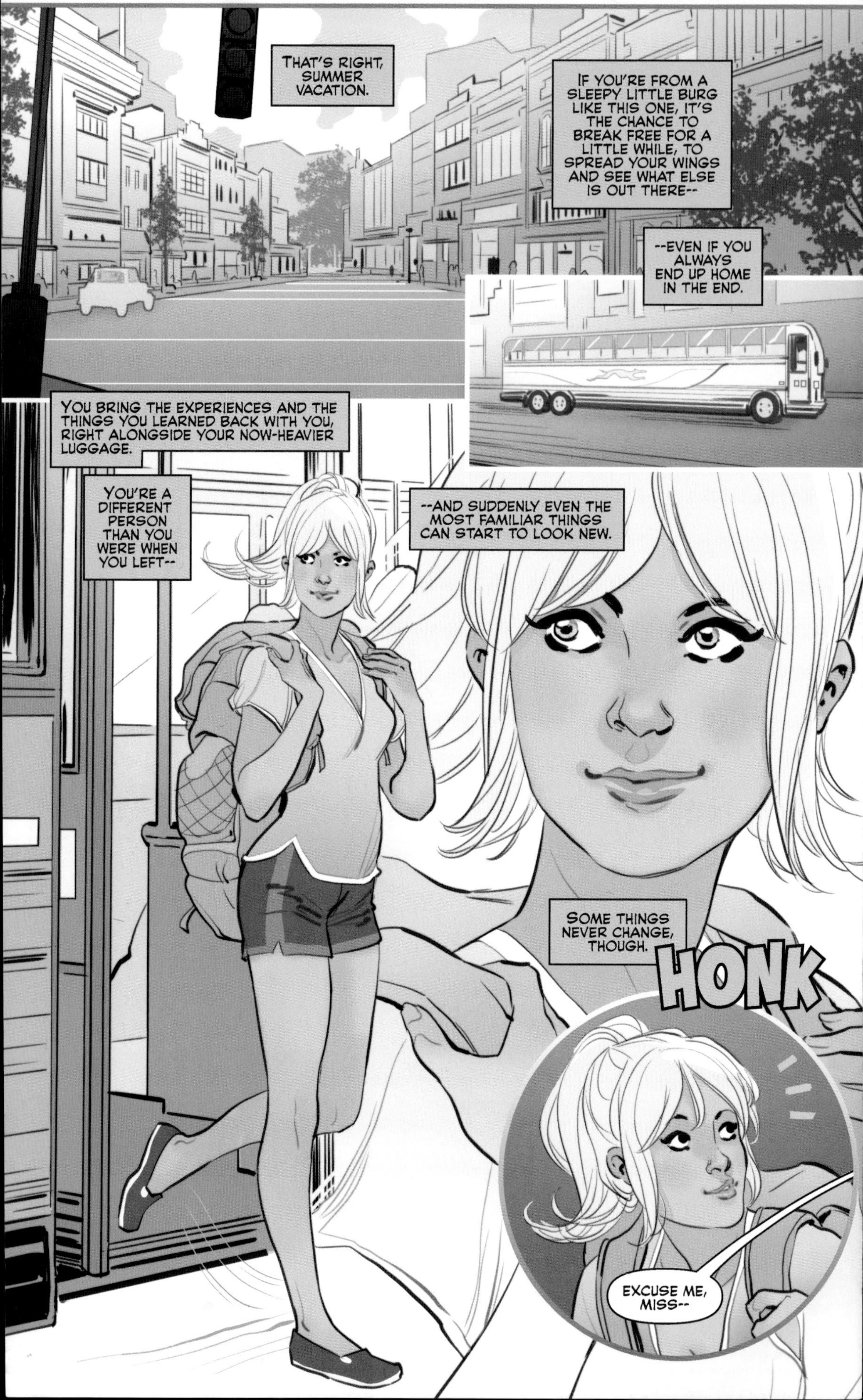
THAT'S RIGHT, SUMMER VACATION.
IF YOU'RE FROM A SLEEPY LITTLE BURG LIKE THIS ONE, IT'S THE CHANCE TO BREAK FREE FOR A LITTLE WHILE, TO SPREAD YOUR WINGS AND SEE WHAT ELSE IS OUT THERE--
--EVEN IF YOU ALWAYS END UP HOME IN THE END.
YOU BRING THE EXPERIENCES AND THE THINGS YOU LEARNED BACK WITH YOU, RIGHT ALONGSIDE YOUR NOW-HEAVIER LUGGAGE.
YOU'RE A DIFFERENT PERSON THAN YOU WERE WHEN YOU LEFT--
--AND SUDDENLY EVEN THE MOST FAMILIAR THINGS CAN START TO LOOK NEW.
SOME THINGS NEVER CHANGE, THOUGH.
HONK
EXCUSE ME, MISS--

How do you follow a character-defining run? A historic story? Well, in short—you don't. You try to honor the past and carve out your own path.

But getting to that realization isn't always easy. When we knew Mark Waid would be winding down his modern *Archie* epic after thirty-odd issues, we faced a unique challenge in a marketplace fraught with reboots, relaunches and ever-shifting creative teams. How do you follow a run that defined a generation for Archie readers?

The answer is you don't, of course. You go back to the source material. Archie is unlike most iconic characters. He doesn't (always) wear a cape, he's not grief-stricken or angry. He's the best of us. A charming everyman who has a great, memorable cast of characters. But the trick with any successful Archie book is finding talent that not only write, draw, ink, color, or letter well—but love these characters. The passion makes the difference.

So, Archie Publisher/CEO Jon Goldwater and I knew we needed to find the perfect mix of Archie fan and superstar talent, which put writer Nick Spencer squarely on my radar. I'd known Nick from my early days at DC, when he wrote a few issues of *Supergirl* and *T.H.U.N.D.E.R. Agents*. He'd gone on to build an impressive career for himself at Marvel and via his indie work at Image, with runs on *Captain America*, the *Amazing Spider-Man*, *The Fix*, and more that I can't rattle off. The guy had the goods. He was also a huge Archie fan.

A few emails and phone calls later, we were locked in. Nick wanted to strike a perfect, challenging balance—to honor Mark's run (we didn't want to erase anything that had come before, with good reason—it's great!), but set out on a new, darker path that still retained Archie's humor and friendships. Not easy, but—spoiler alert, dear reader—Nick nailed it.

His pitch wowed us out of the gate. You could tell there was a passion for Riverdale in how he framed things, and he was playing the long game—something that's always admirable and hard to execute well. Nick wanted to make Archie part of a bigger world, and he wanted to weave a deeper, darker mystery underneath the small town surface of Riverdale.

But we needed an artist.

Luckily, we got two.

Marguerite Sauvage has been one of Archie's top, most beloved cover artists for years. I'd loved her work on *DC's Bombshells* series and we were lucky to get her to lend her pen to almost every title in the Archie library. But would she do interiors? I asked, because it never hurts—and she said yes. But with a caveat—she could probably do the arc, but circumstances outside of all our control might cut it short. We understood, of course. A few issues by Marguerite was better than none. But being the Paranoid Editor is something that comes naturally to me—so I reached out to one of my favorite freelancers, Sandy Jarrell, who'd done a great job on *Reggie & Me* a few years back. He agreed to fill-in where needed and, if it so happened, take the baton from Marguerite.

In the end, we got three über-talented creators to chip in on a bit of history—including the first-ever *Archie* #700—and push forward the story Mark and Fiona Staples started. A tough challenge in any era of comics, but one I'm especially proud of today. I hope you enjoy this first volume of *Archie by Nick Spencer*. It kicks off the next, engaging and unforgettable chapter in our lovable redhead's modern adventures.

Alex Segura
Editor, Archie

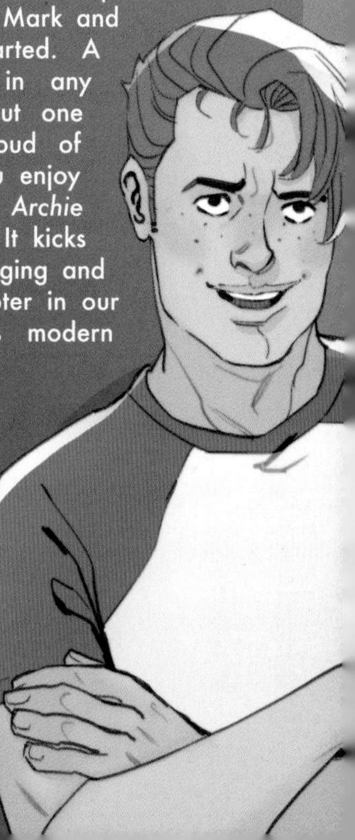

700

STORY BY
NICK SPENCER

ART BY
MARGUERITE SAUVAGE

LETTERING BY
JACK MORELLI

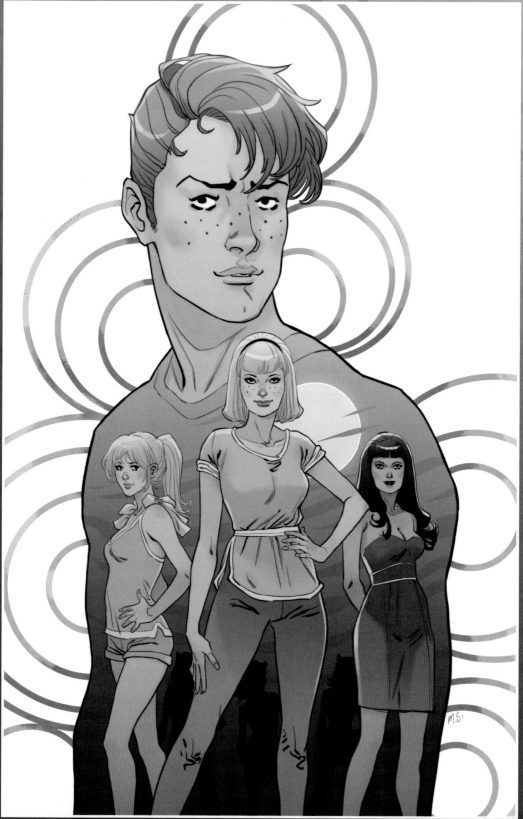

COVER ART: **MARGUERITE SAUVAGE**

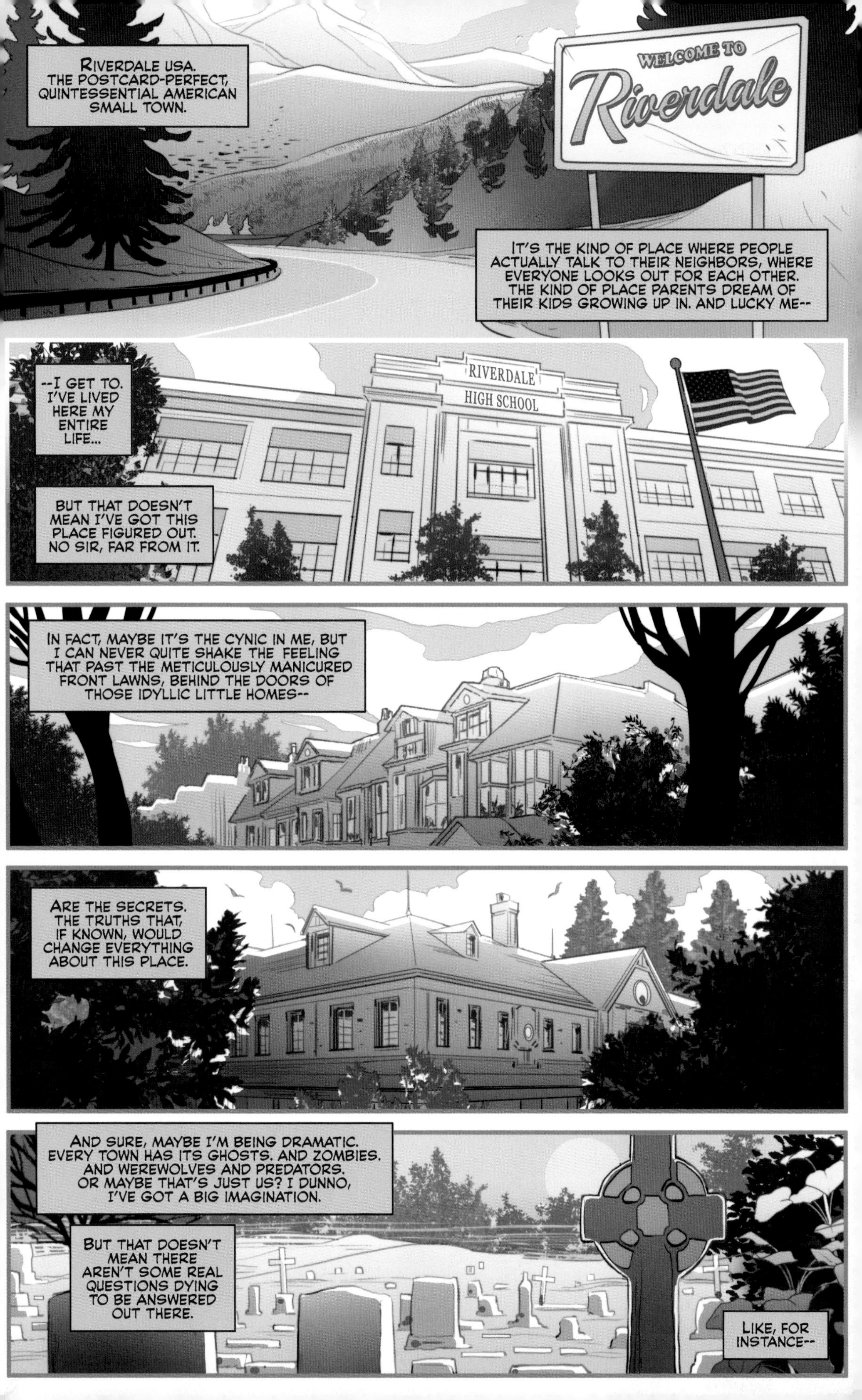
RIVERDALE USA. THE POSTCARD-PERFECT, QUINTESSENTIAL AMERICAN SMALL TOWN.
WELCOME TO Riverdale
IT'S THE KIND OF PLACE WHERE PEOPLE ACTUALLY TALK TO THEIR NEIGHBORS, WHERE EVERYONE LOOKS OUT FOR EACH OTHER. THE KIND OF PLACE PARENTS DREAM OF THEIR KIDS GROWING UP IN. AND LUCKY ME--
--I GET TO. I'VE LIVED HERE MY ENTIRE LIFE...
RIVERDALE HIGH SCHOOL
BUT THAT DOESN'T MEAN I'VE GOT THIS PLACE FIGURED OUT. NO SIR, FAR FROM IT.
IN FACT, MAYBE IT'S THE CYNIC IN ME, BUT I CAN NEVER QUITE SHAKE THE FEELING THAT PAST THE METICULOUSLY MANICURED FRONT LAWNS, BEHIND THE DOORS OF THOSE IDYLLIC LITTLE HOMES--
ARE THE SECRETS. THE TRUTHS THAT, IF KNOWN, WOULD CHANGE EVERYTHING ABOUT THIS PLACE.
AND SURE, MAYBE I'M BEING DRAMATIC. EVERY TOWN HAS ITS GHOSTS. AND ZOMBIES. AND WEREWOLVES AND PREDATORS. OR MAYBE THAT'S JUST US? I DUNNO, I'VE GOT A BIG IMAGINATION.
BUT THAT DOESN'T MEAN THERE AREN'T SOME REAL QUESTIONS DYING TO BE ANSWERED OUT THERE.
LIKE, FOR INSTANCE--

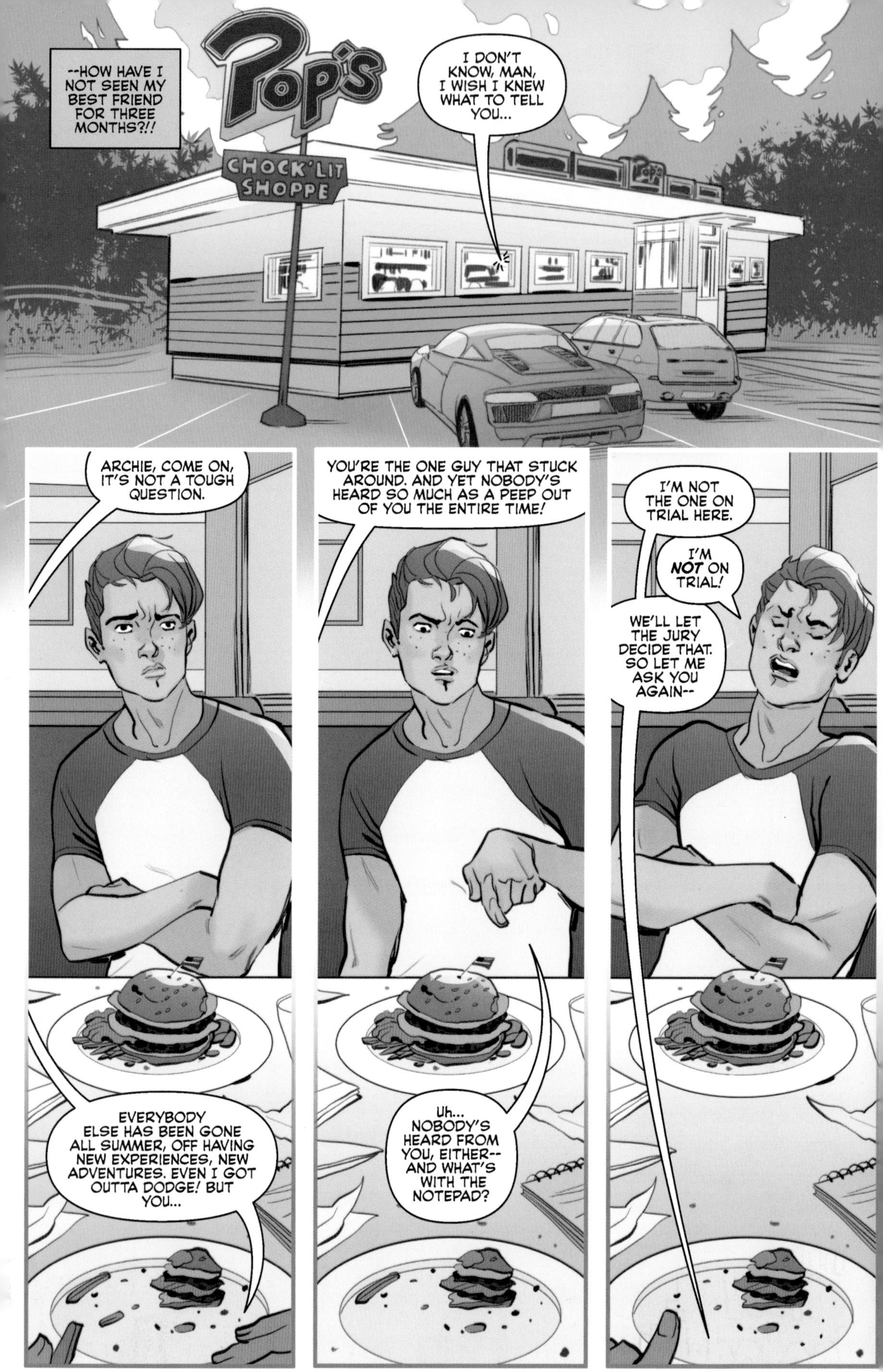
--HOW HAVE I NOT SEEN MY BEST FRIEND FOR THREE MONTHS?!
Pop's
CHOCK'LIT SHOPPE
I DON'T KNOW, MAN, I WISH I KNEW WHAT TO TELL YOU...
ARCHIE, COME ON, IT'S NOT A TOUGH QUESTION.
EVERYBODY ELSE HAS BEEN GONE ALL SUMMER, OFF HAVING NEW EXPERIENCES, NEW ADVENTURES. EVEN I GOT OUTTA DODGE! BUT YOU...
YOU'RE THE ONE GUY THAT STUCK AROUND. AND YET NOBODY'S HEARD SO MUCH AS A PEEP OUT OF YOU THE ENTIRE TIME!
Uh... NOBODY'S HEARD FROM YOU, EITHER-- AND WHAT'S WITH THE NOTEPAD?
I'M NOT THE ONE ON TRIAL HERE.
I'M NOT ON TRIAL!
WE'LL LET THE JURY DECIDE THAT. SO LET ME ASK YOU AGAIN--

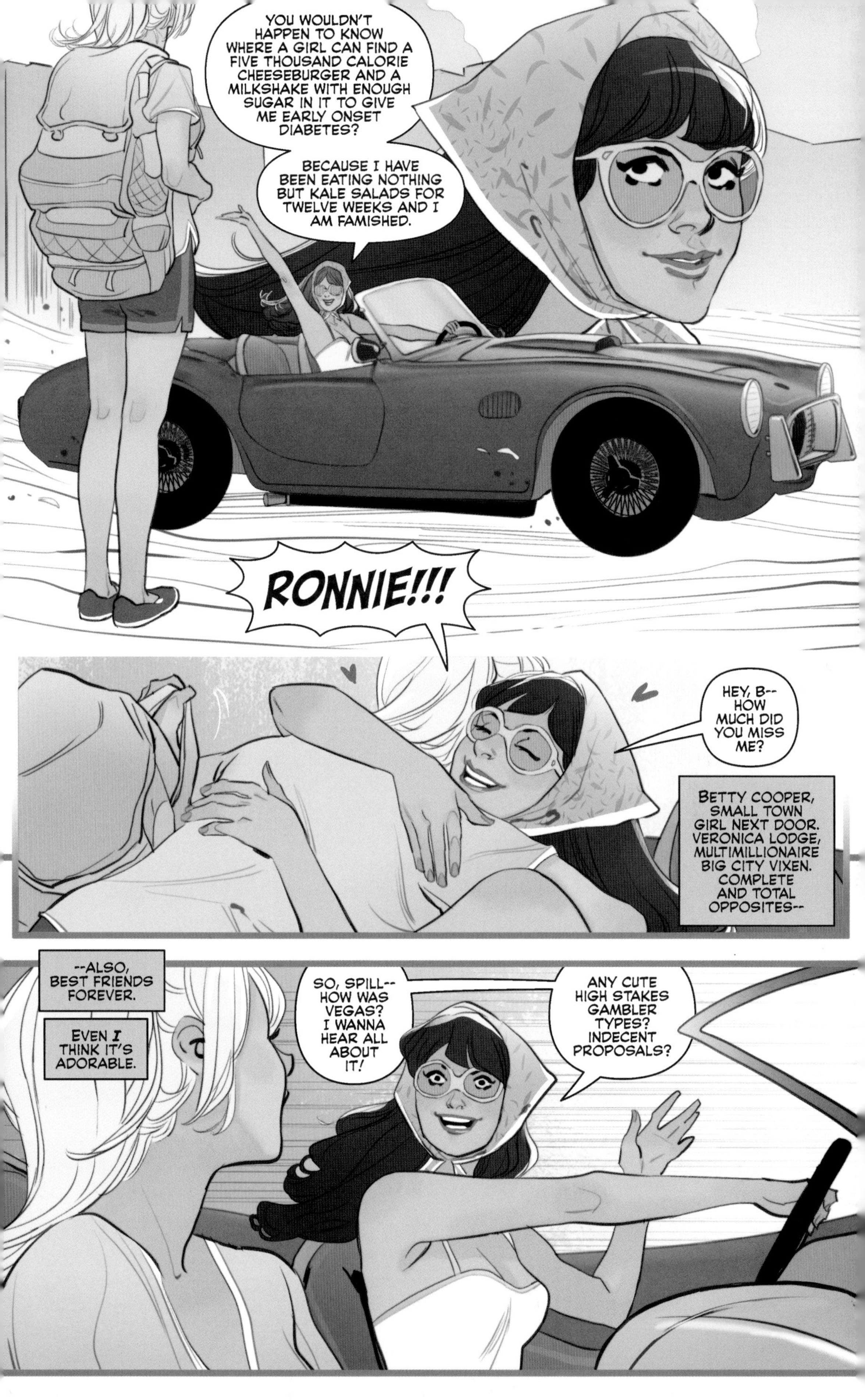
YOU WOULDN'T HAPPEN TO KNOW WHERE A GIRL CAN FIND A FIVE THOUSAND CALORIE CHEESEBURGER AND A MILKSHAKE WITH ENOUGH SUGAR IN IT TO GIVE ME EARLY ONSET DIABETES?
BECAUSE I HAVE BEEN EATING NOTHING BUT KALE SALADS FOR TWELVE WEEKS AND I AM FAMISHED.
RONNIE!!!
HEY, B-- HOW MUCH DID YOU MISS ME?
BETTY COOPER, SMALL TOWN GIRL NEXT DOOR. VERONICA LODGE, MULTIMILLIONAIRE BIG CITY VIXEN. COMPLETE AND TOTAL OPPOSITES--
--ALSO, BEST FRIENDS FOREVER.
EVEN **I** THINK IT'S ADORABLE.
SO, SPILL-- HOW WAS VEGAS? I WANNA HEAR ALL ABOUT IT!
ANY CUTE HIGH STAKES GAMBLER TYPES? INDECENT PROPOSALS?

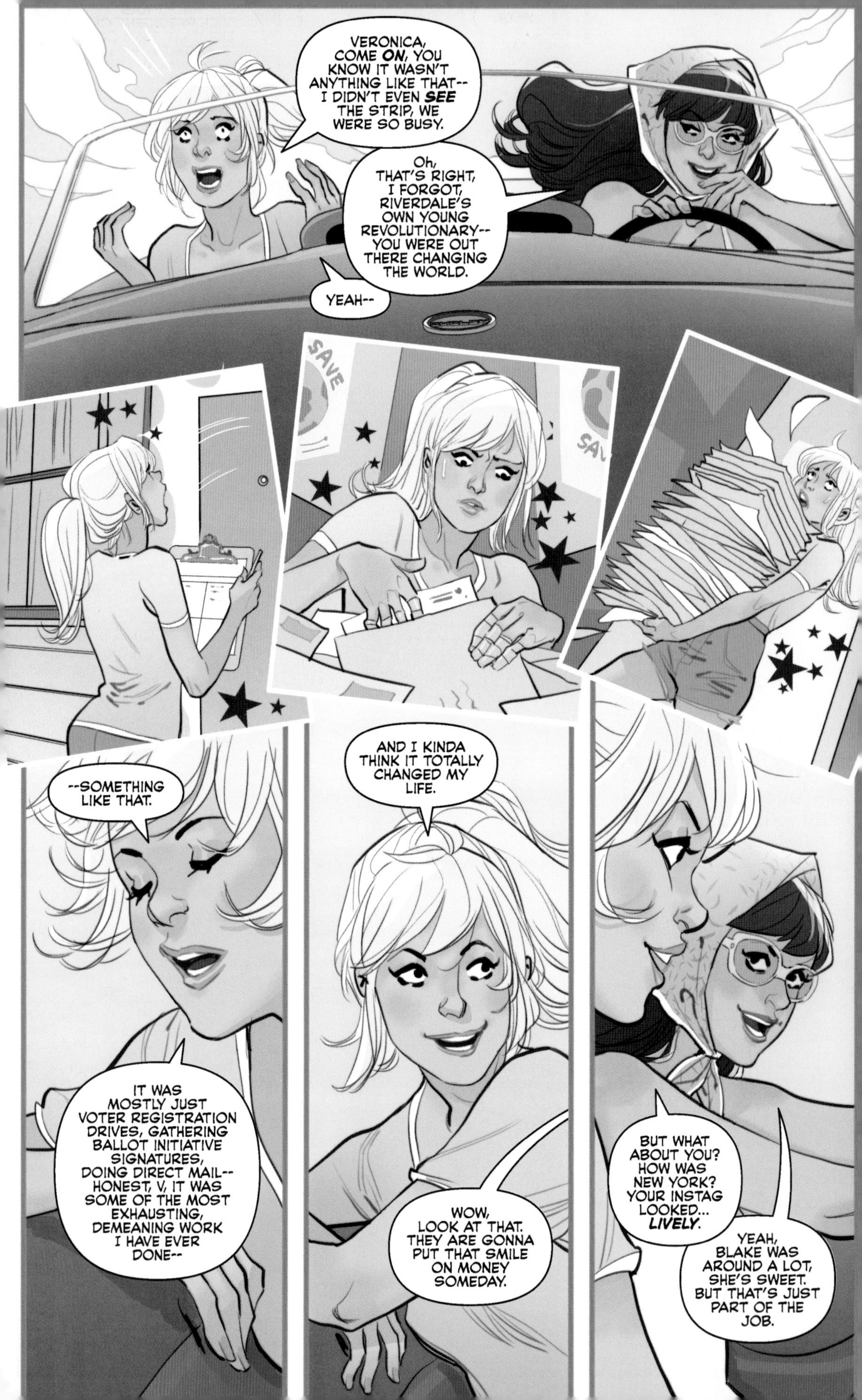

VERONICA, COME ON, YOU KNOW IT WASN'T ANYTHING LIKE THAT-- I DIDN'T EVEN SEE THE STRIP, WE WERE SO BUSY.
Oh, THAT'S RIGHT, I FORGOT, RIVERDALE'S OWN YOUNG REVOLUTIONARY-- YOU WERE OUT THERE CHANGING THE WORLD.
YEAH--
SAVE
SAVE
--SOMETHING LIKE THAT.
IT WAS MOSTLY JUST VOTER REGISTRATION DRIVES, GATHERING BALLOT INITIATIVE SIGNATURES, DOING DIRECT MAIL-- HONEST, V, IT WAS SOME OF THE MOST EXHAUSTING, DEMEANING WORK I HAVE EVER DONE--
AND I KINDA THINK IT TOTALLY CHANGED MY LIFE.
WOW, LOOK AT THAT. THEY ARE GONNA PUT THAT SMILE ON MONEY SOMEDAY.
BUT WHAT ABOUT YOU? HOW WAS NEW YORK? YOUR INSTAG LOOKED... LIVELY.
YEAH, BLAKE WAS AROUND A LOT, SHE'S SWEET. BUT THAT'S JUST PART OF THE JOB.

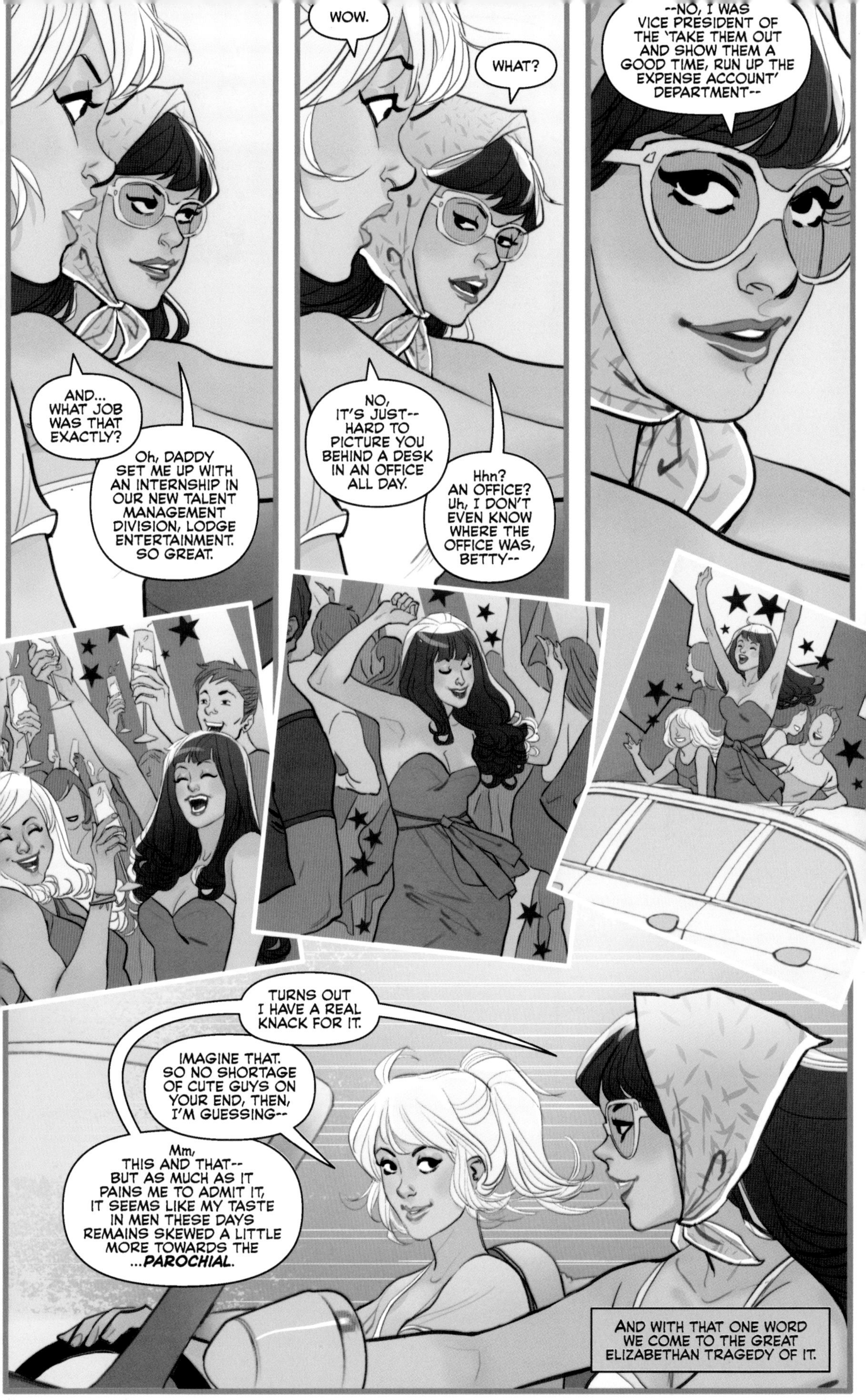
AND... WHAT JOB WAS THAT EXACTLY?
Oh, DADDY SET ME UP WITH AN INTERNSHIP IN OUR NEW TALENT MANAGEMENT DIVISION, LODGE ENTERTAINMENT. SO GREAT.
WOW.
WHAT?
NO, IT'S JUST-- HARD TO PICTURE YOU BEHIND A DESK IN AN OFFICE ALL DAY.
Hhn? AN OFFICE? Uh, I DON'T EVEN KNOW WHERE THE OFFICE WAS, BETTY--
--NO, I WAS VICE PRESIDENT OF THE 'TAKE THEM OUT AND SHOW THEM A GOOD TIME, RUN UP THE EXPENSE ACCOUNT' DEPARTMENT--
TURNS OUT I HAVE A REAL KNACK FOR IT.
IMAGINE THAT. SO NO SHORTAGE OF CUTE GUYS ON YOUR END, THEN, I'M GUESSING--
Mm, THIS AND THAT-- BUT AS MUCH AS IT PAINS ME TO ADMIT IT, IT SEEMS LIKE MY TASTE IN MEN THESE DAYS REMAINS SKEWED A LITTLE MORE TOWARDS THE ...*PAROCHIAL*.
AND WITH THAT ONE WORD WE COME TO THE GREAT ELIZABETHAN TRAGEDY OF IT.

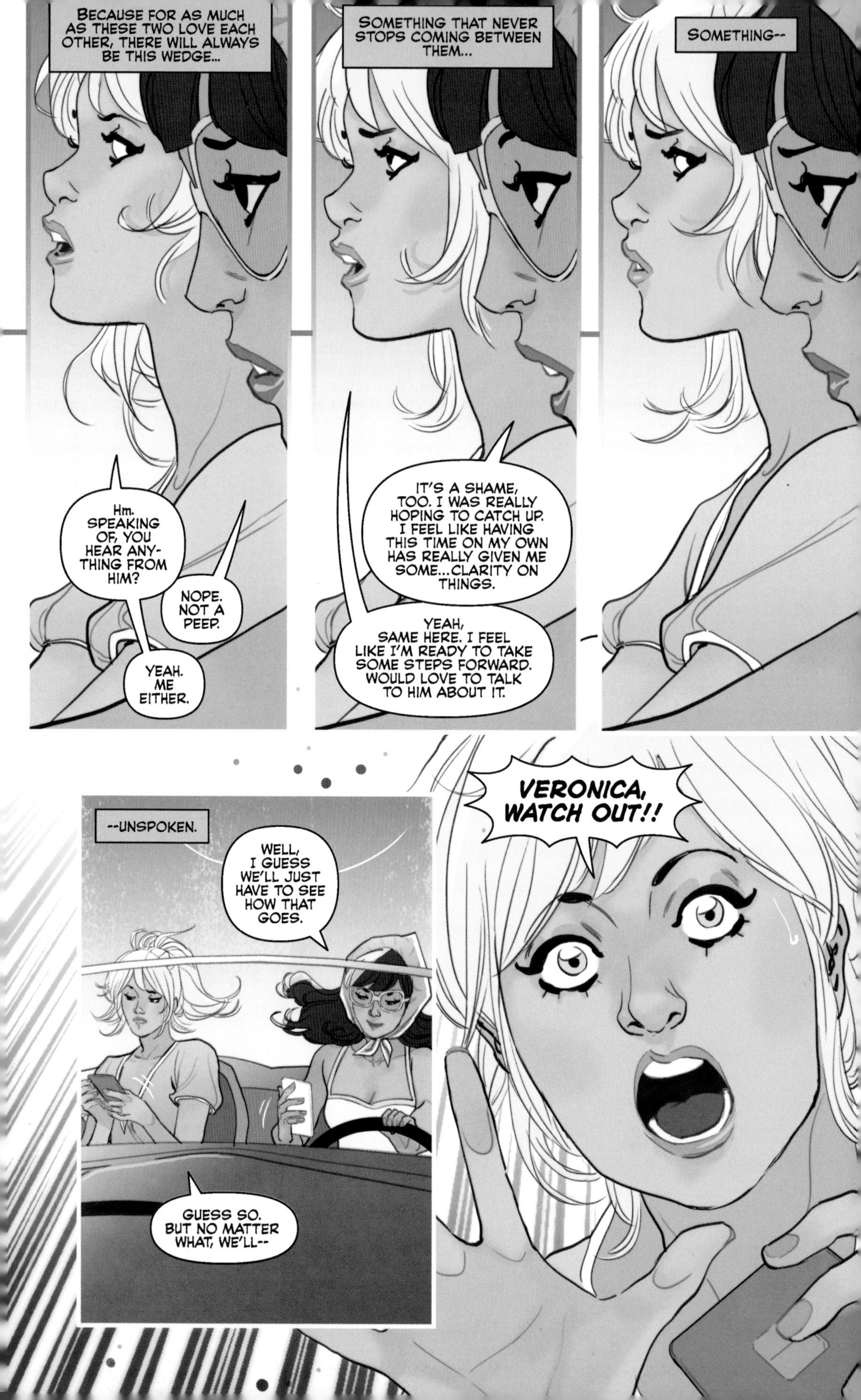
BECAUSE FOR AS MUCH AS THESE TWO LOVE EACH OTHER, THERE WILL ALWAYS BE THIS WEDGE...
Hm. SPEAKING OF, YOU HEAR ANYTHING FROM HIM?
NOPE. NOT A PEEP.
YEAH. ME EITHER.
SOMETHING THAT NEVER STOPS COMING BETWEEN THEM...
IT'S A SHAME, TOO. I WAS REALLY HOPING TO CATCH UP. I FEEL LIKE HAVING THIS TIME ON MY OWN HAS REALLY GIVEN ME SOME...CLARITY ON THINGS.
YEAH, SAME HERE. I FEEL LIKE I'M READY TO TAKE SOME STEPS FORWARD. WOULD LOVE TO TALK TO HIM ABOUT IT.
SOMETHING--
--UNSPOKEN.
WELL, I GUESS WE'LL JUST HAVE TO SEE HOW THAT GOES.
GUESS SO. BUT NO MATTER WHAT, WE'LL--
VERONICA, WATCH OUT!!

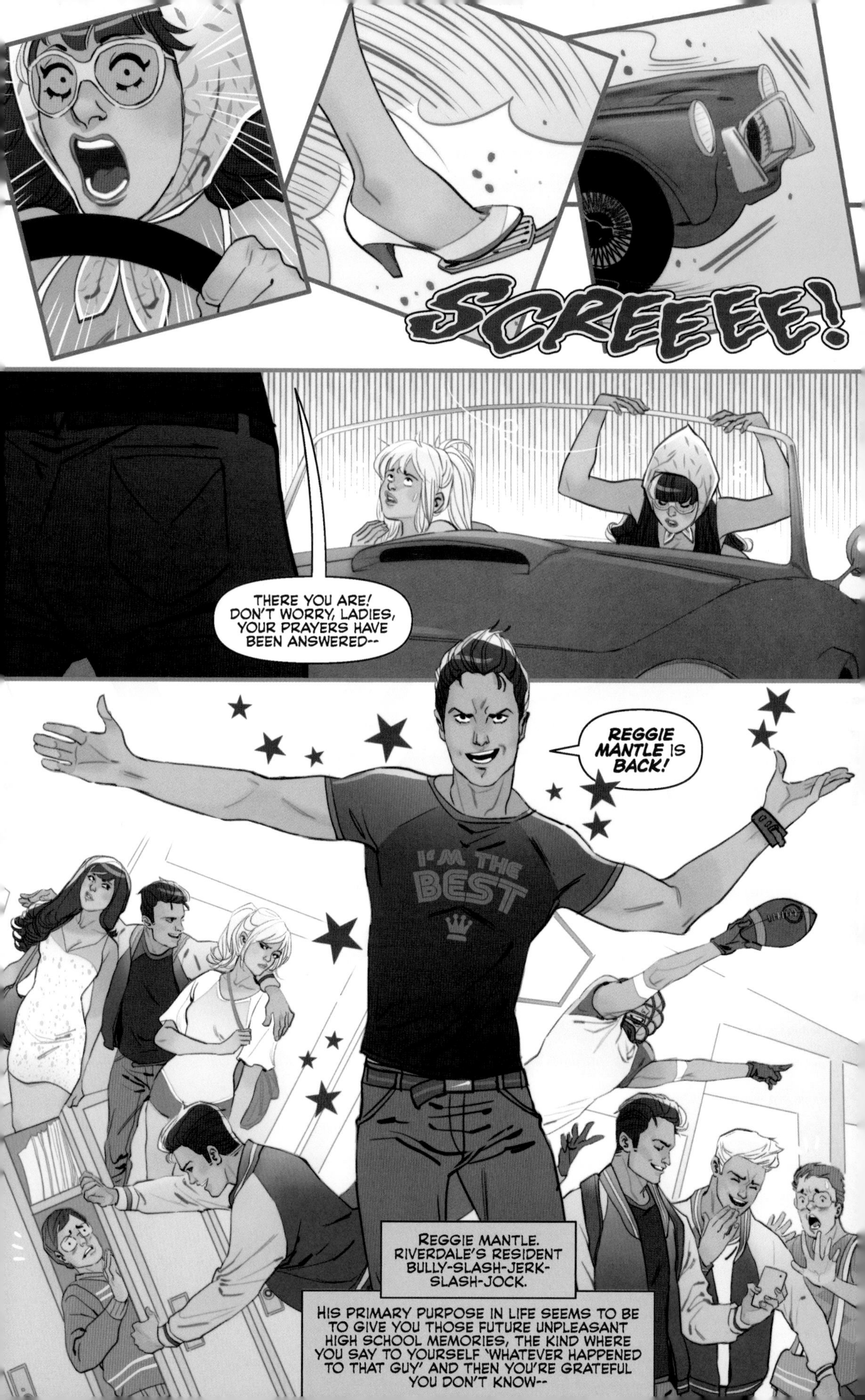
SCREEEE!
THERE YOU ARE! DON'T WORRY, LADIES, YOUR PRAYERS HAVE BEEN ANSWERED--
REGGIE MANTLE IS BACK!
I'M THE BEST
REGGIE MANTLE. RIVERDALE'S RESIDENT BULLY-SLASH-JERK-SLASH-JOCK.
HIS PRIMARY PURPOSE IN LIFE SEEMS TO BE TO GIVE YOU THOSE FUTURE UNPLEASANT HIGH SCHOOL MEMORIES, THE KIND WHERE YOU SAY TO YOURSELF 'WHATEVER HAPPENED TO THAT GUY' AND THEN YOU'RE GRATEFUL YOU DON'T KNOW--

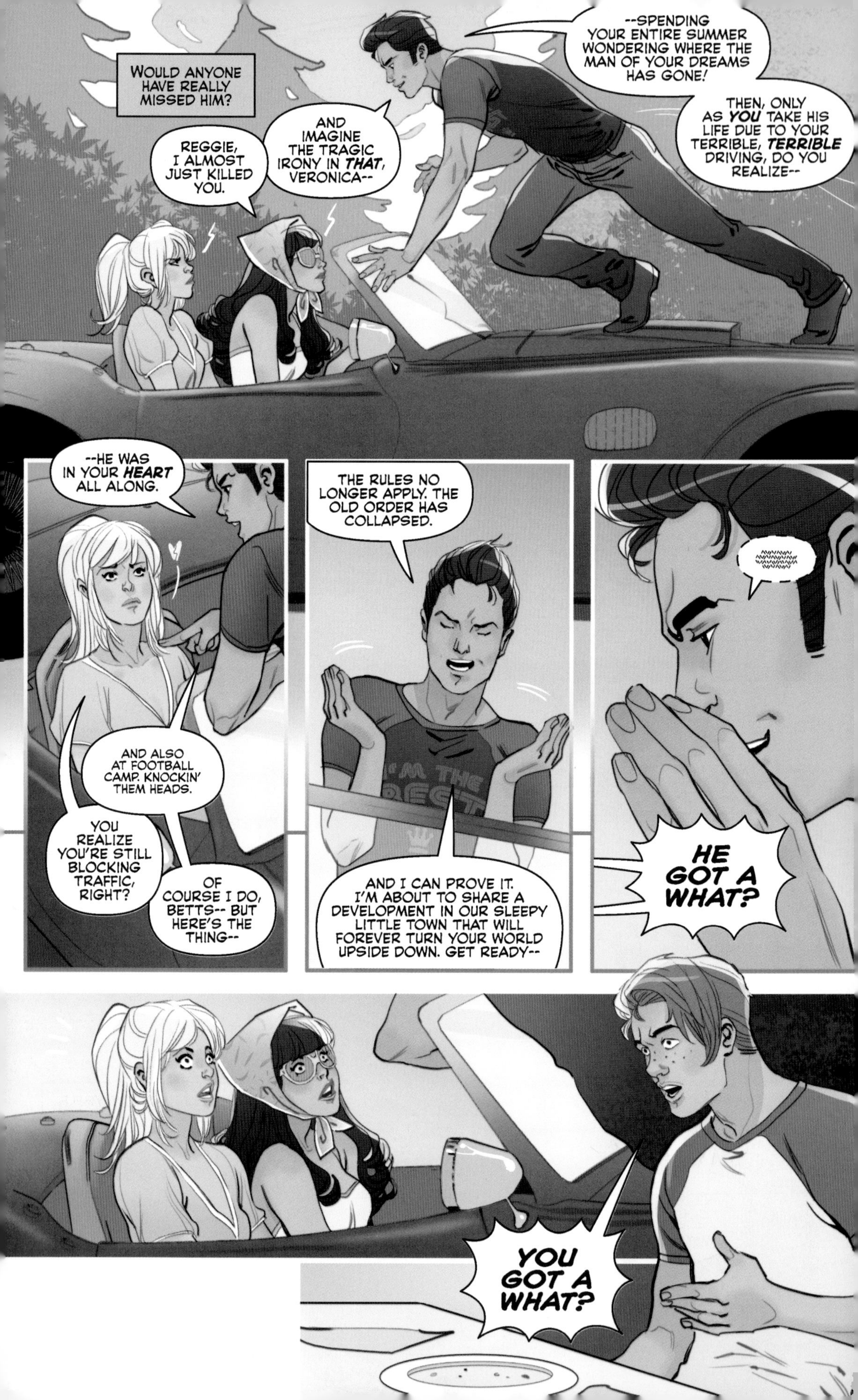

WOULD ANYONE HAVE REALLY MISSED HIM?
REGGIE, I ALMOST JUST KILLED YOU.
AND IMAGINE THE TRAGIC IRONY IN *THAT*, VERONICA--
--SPENDING YOUR ENTIRE SUMMER WONDERING WHERE THE MAN OF YOUR DREAMS HAS GONE!
THEN, ONLY AS *YOU* TAKE HIS LIFE DUE TO YOUR TERRIBLE, *TERRIBLE* DRIVING, DO YOU REALIZE--
--HE WAS IN YOUR *HEART* ALL ALONG.
AND ALSO AT FOOTBALL CAMP. KNOCKIN' THEM HEADS.
YOU REALIZE YOU'RE STILL BLOCKING TRAFFIC, RIGHT?
OF COURSE I DO, BETTS-- BUT HERE'S THE THING--
THE RULES NO LONGER APPLY. THE OLD ORDER HAS COLLAPSED.
AND I CAN PROVE IT. I'M ABOUT TO SHARE A DEVELOPMENT IN OUR SLEEPY LITTLE TOWN THAT WILL FOREVER TURN YOUR WORLD UPSIDE DOWN. GET READY--
HE GOT A WHAT?
YOU GOT A WHAT?

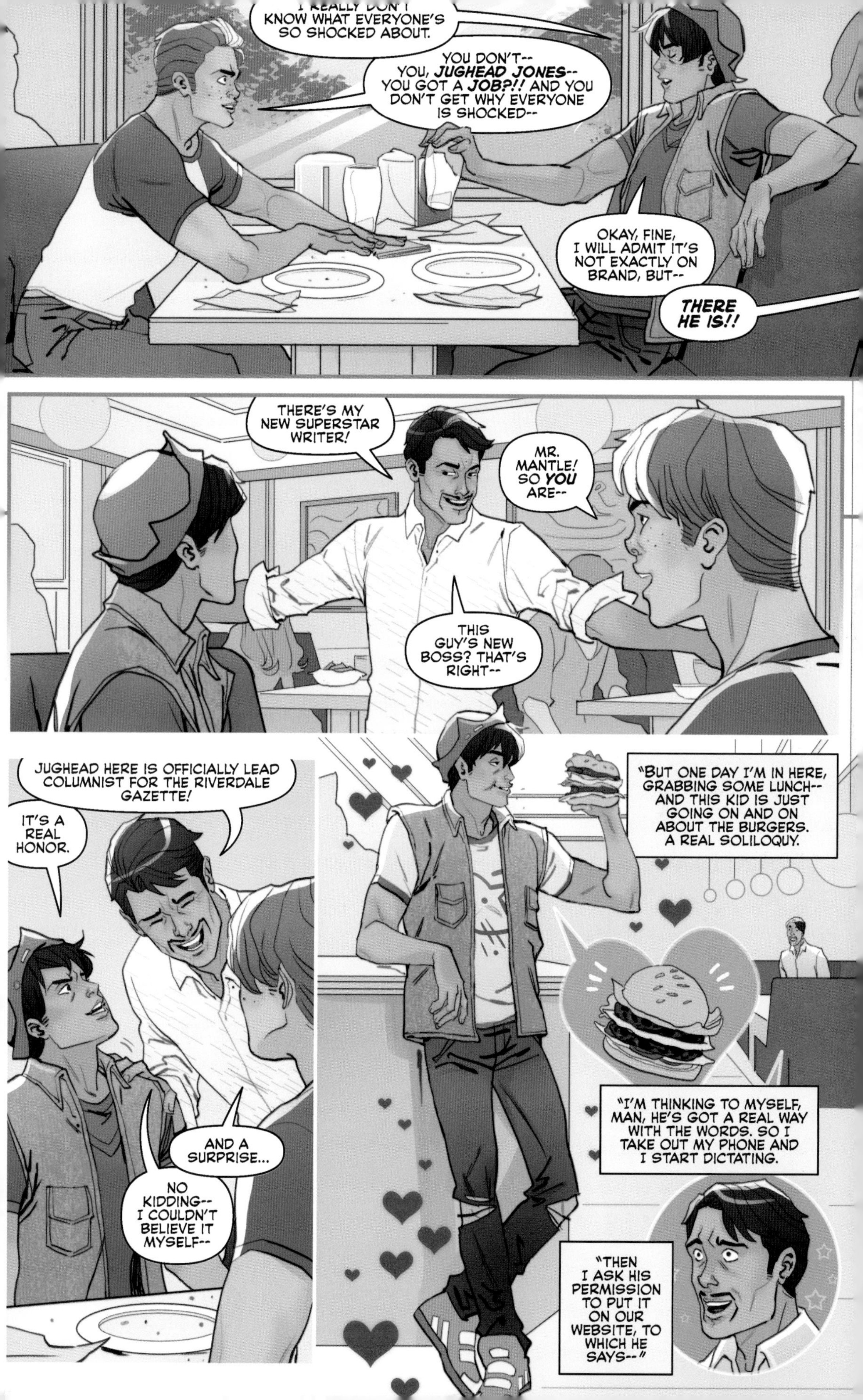
I REALLY DON'T KNOW WHAT EVERYONE'S SO SHOCKED ABOUT.
YOU DON'T-- YOU, JUGHEAD JONES-- YOU GOT A JOB?!! AND YOU DON'T GET WHY EVERYONE IS SHOCKED--
OKAY, FINE, I WILL ADMIT IT'S NOT EXACTLY ON BRAND, BUT--
THERE HE IS!!
THERE'S MY NEW SUPERSTAR WRITER!
MR. MANTLE! SO YOU ARE--
THIS GUY'S NEW BOSS? THAT'S RIGHT--
JUGHEAD HERE IS OFFICIALLY LEAD COLUMNIST FOR THE RIVERDALE GAZETTE!
IT'S A REAL HONOR.
AND A SURPRISE...
NO KIDDING-- I COULDN'T BELIEVE IT MYSELF--
"BUT ONE DAY I'M IN HERE, GRABBING SOME LUNCH-- AND THIS KID IS JUST GOING ON AND ON ABOUT THE BURGERS. A REAL SOLILOQUY.
"I'M THINKING TO MYSELF, MAN, HE'S GOT A REAL WAY WITH THE WORDS. SO I TAKE OUT MY PHONE AND I START DICTATING.
"THEN I ASK HIS PERMISSION TO PUT IT ON OUR WEBSITE, TO WHICH HE SAYS--"

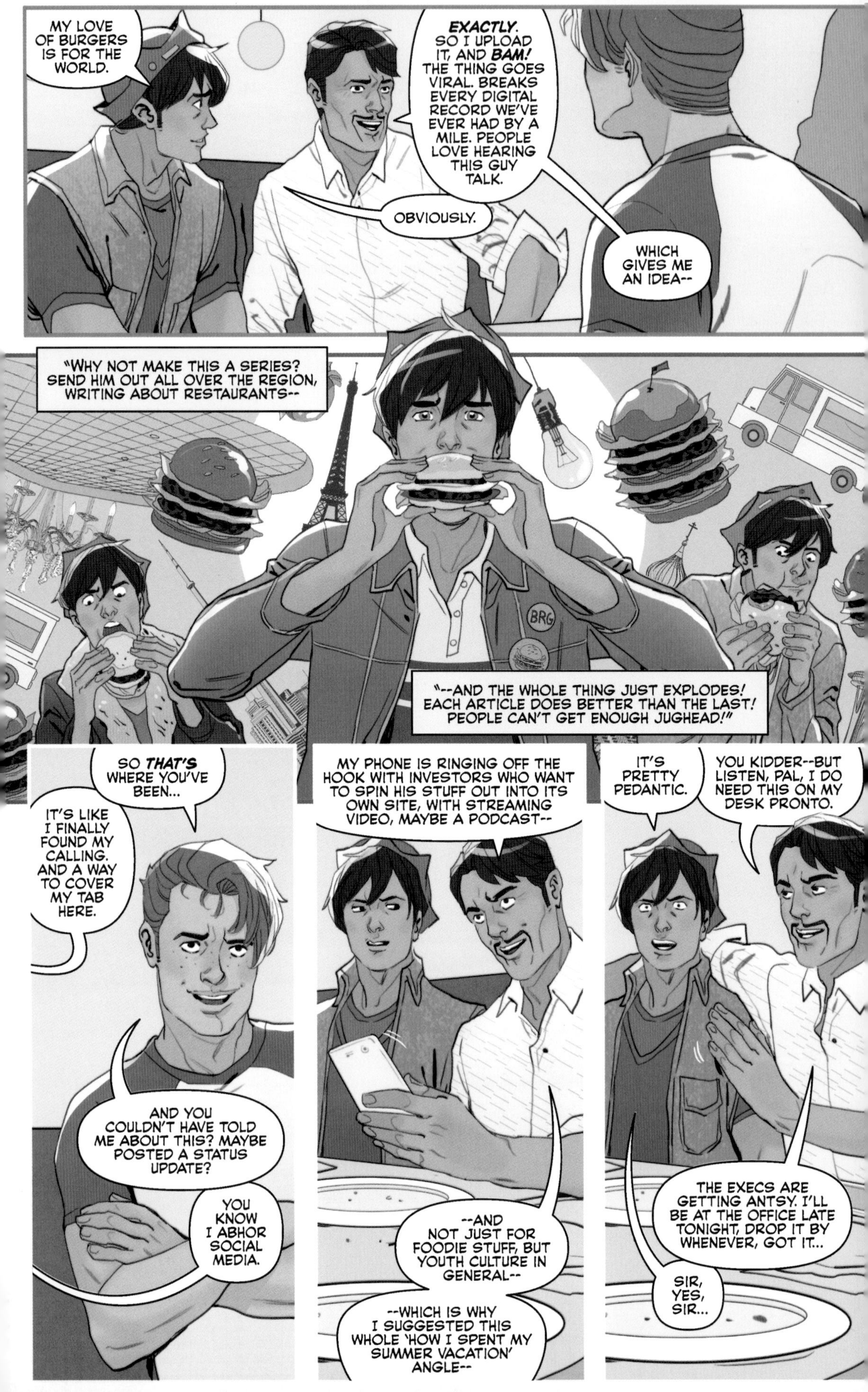

MY LOVE OF BURGERS IS FOR THE WORLD.
EXACTLY. SO I UPLOAD IT, AND *BAM!* THE THING GOES VIRAL. BREAKS EVERY DIGITAL RECORD WE'VE EVER HAD BY A MILE. PEOPLE LOVE HEARING THIS GUY TALK.
OBVIOUSLY.
WHICH GIVES ME AN IDEA--
"WHY NOT MAKE THIS A SERIES? SEND HIM OUT ALL OVER THE REGION, WRITING ABOUT RESTAURANTS--
BRG
"--AND THE WHOLE THING JUST EXPLODES! EACH ARTICLE DOES BETTER THAN THE LAST! PEOPLE CAN'T GET ENOUGH JUGHEAD!"
SO *THAT'S* WHERE YOU'VE BEEN...
IT'S LIKE I FINALLY FOUND MY CALLING. AND A WAY TO COVER MY TAB HERE.
AND YOU COULDN'T HAVE TOLD ME ABOUT THIS? MAYBE POSTED A STATUS UPDATE?
YOU KNOW I ABHOR SOCIAL MEDIA.
MY PHONE IS RINGING OFF THE HOOK WITH INVESTORS WHO WANT TO SPIN HIS STUFF OUT INTO ITS OWN SITE, WITH STREAMING VIDEO, MAYBE A PODCAST--
--AND NOT JUST FOR FOODIE STUFF, BUT YOUTH CULTURE IN GENERAL--
--WHICH IS WHY I SUGGESTED THIS WHOLE 'HOW I SPENT MY SUMMER VACATION' ANGLE--
IT'S PRETTY PEDANTIC.
YOU KIDDER--BUT LISTEN, PAL, I DO NEED THIS ON MY DESK PRONTO.
THE EXECS ARE GETTING ANTSY. I'LL BE AT THE OFFICE LATE TONIGHT, DROP IT BY WHENEVER, GOT IT...
SIR, YES, SIR...

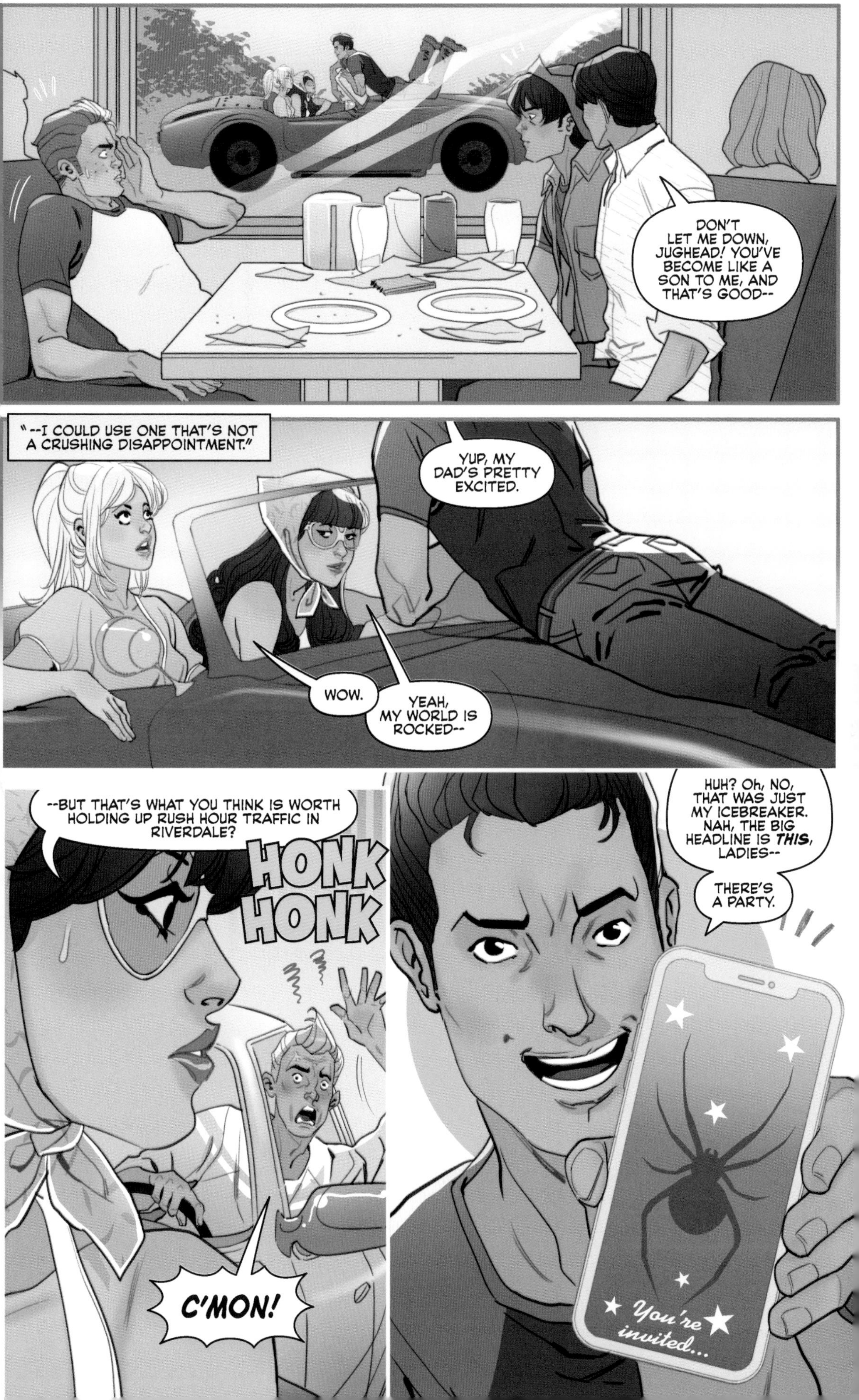
DON'T LET ME DOWN, JUGHEAD! YOU'VE BECOME LIKE A SON TO ME, AND THAT'S GOOD--
"--I COULD USE ONE THAT'S NOT A CRUSHING DISAPPOINTMENT."
YUP, MY DAD'S PRETTY EXCITED.
WOW.
YEAH, MY WORLD IS ROCKED--
--BUT THAT'S WHAT YOU THINK IS WORTH HOLDING UP RUSH HOUR TRAFFIC IN RIVERDALE?
HONK HONK
C'MON!
HUH? Oh, NO, THAT WAS JUST MY ICEBREAKER. NAH, THE BIG HEADLINE IS *THIS*, LADIES--
THERE'S A PARTY.
You're invited...

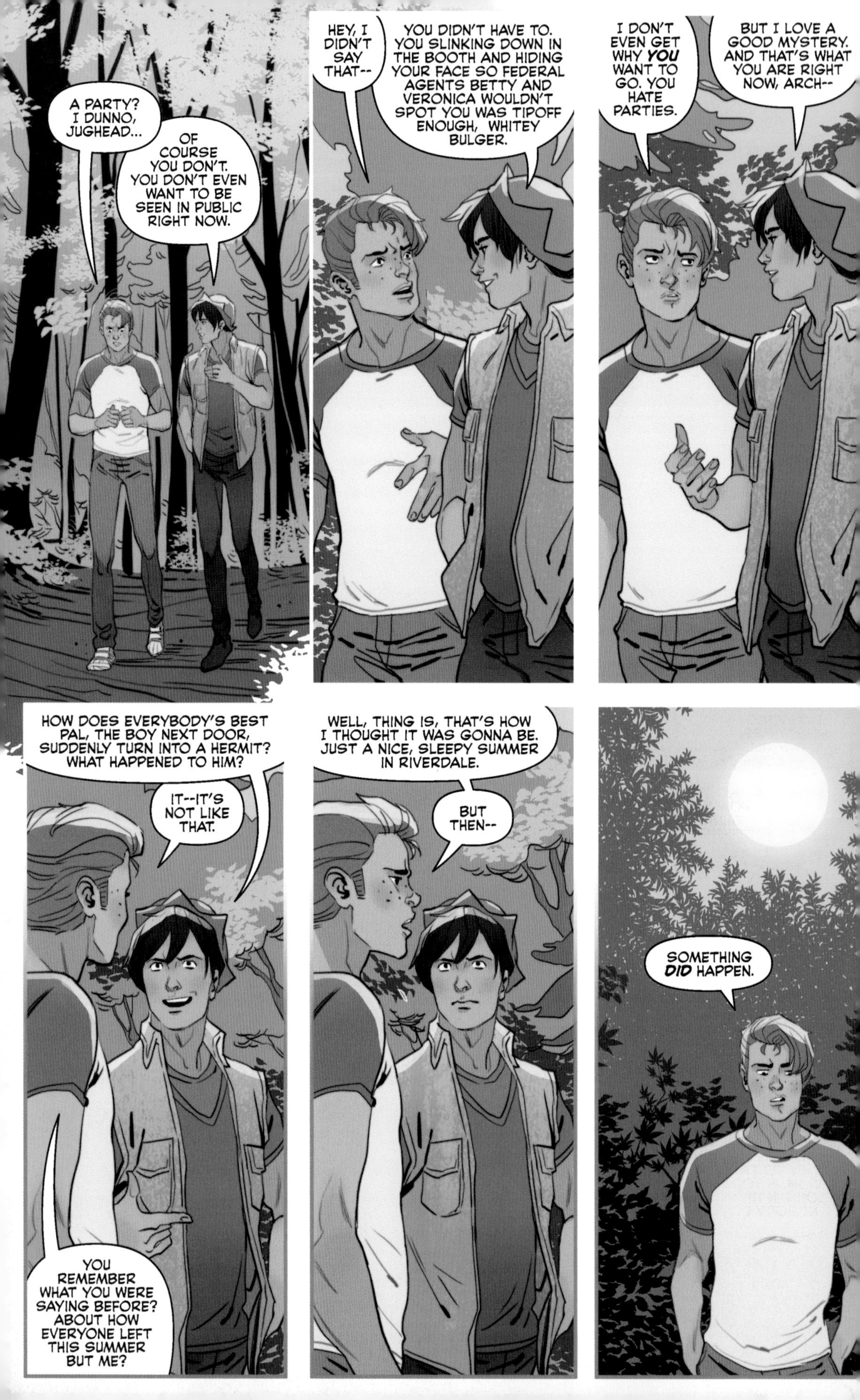

A PARTY? I DUNNO, JUGHEAD...
OF COURSE YOU DON'T. YOU DON'T EVEN WANT TO BE SEEN IN PUBLIC RIGHT NOW.
HEY, I DIDN'T SAY THAT--
YOU DIDN'T HAVE TO. YOU SLINKING DOWN IN THE BOOTH AND HIDING YOUR FACE SO FEDERAL AGENTS BETTY AND VERONICA WOULDN'T SPOT YOU WAS TIPOFF ENOUGH, WHITEY BULGER.
I DON'T EVEN GET WHY YOU WANT TO GO. YOU HATE PARTIES.
BUT I LOVE A GOOD MYSTERY. AND THAT'S WHAT YOU ARE RIGHT NOW, ARCH--
HOW DOES EVERYBODY'S BEST PAL, THE BOY NEXT DOOR, SUDDENLY TURN INTO A HERMIT? WHAT HAPPENED TO HIM?
IT--IT'S NOT LIKE THAT.
YOU REMEMBER WHAT YOU WERE SAYING BEFORE? ABOUT HOW EVERYONE LEFT THIS SUMMER BUT ME?
WELL, THING IS, THAT'S HOW I THOUGHT IT WAS GONNA BE. JUST A NICE, SLEEPY SUMMER IN RIVERDALE.
BUT THEN--
SOMETHING DID HAPPEN.

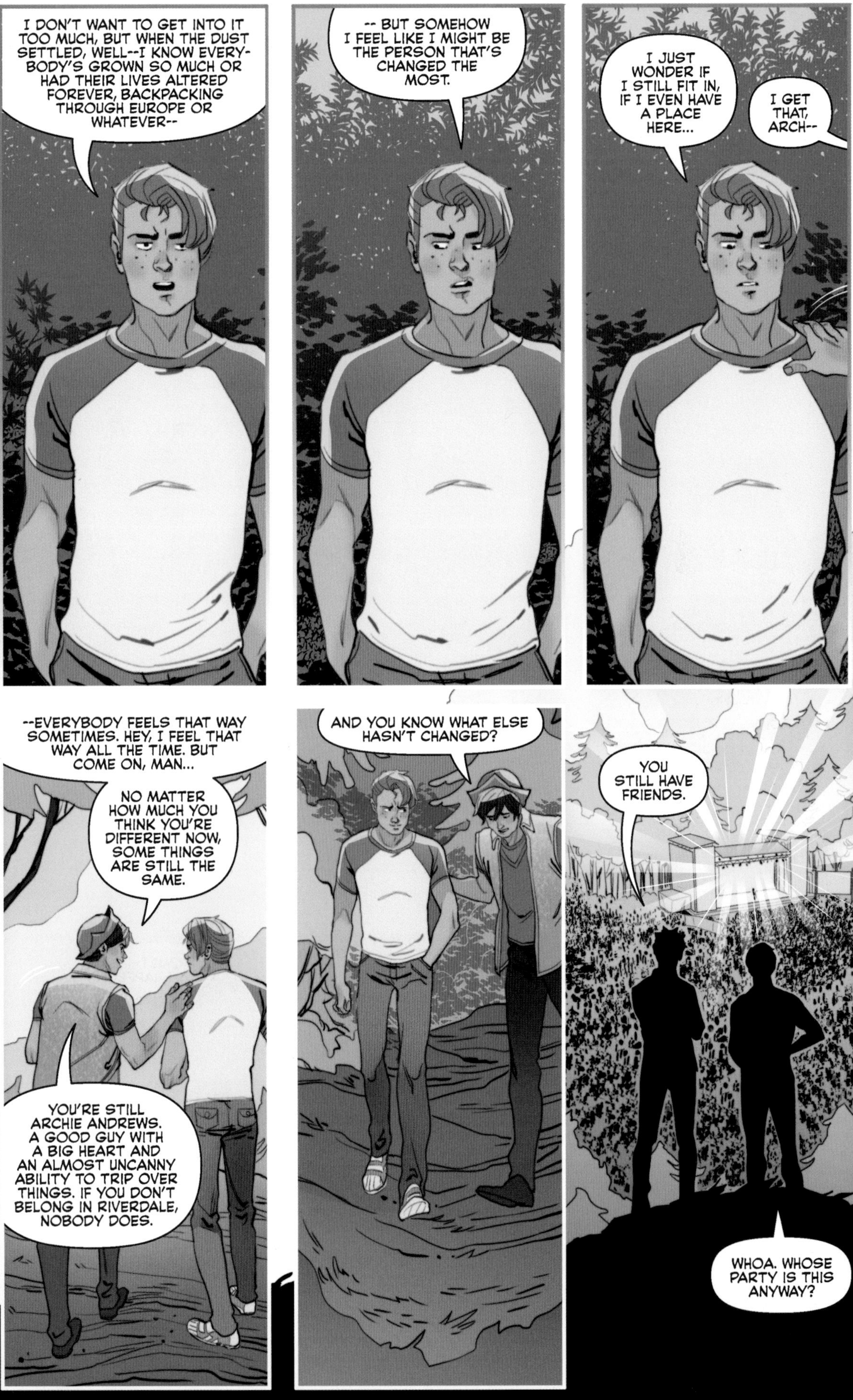
I DON'T WANT TO GET INTO IT TOO MUCH, BUT WHEN THE DUST SETTLED, WELL--I KNOW EVERY-BODY'S GROWN SO MUCH OR HAD THEIR LIVES ALTERED FOREVER, BACKPACKING THROUGH EUROPE OR WHATEVER--
-- BUT SOMEHOW I FEEL LIKE I MIGHT BE THE PERSON THAT'S CHANGED THE MOST.
I JUST WONDER IF I STILL FIT IN, IF I EVEN HAVE A PLACE HERE...
I GET THAT, ARCH--
--EVERYBODY FEELS THAT WAY SOMETIMES. HEY, I FEEL THAT WAY ALL THE TIME. BUT COME ON, MAN...
NO MATTER HOW MUCH YOU THINK YOU'RE DIFFERENT NOW, SOME THINGS ARE STILL THE SAME.
YOU'RE STILL ARCHIE ANDREWS. A GOOD GUY WITH A BIG HEART AND AN ALMOST UNCANNY ABILITY TO TRIP OVER THINGS. IF YOU DON'T BELONG IN RIVERDALE, NOBODY DOES.
AND YOU KNOW WHAT ELSE HASN'T CHANGED?
YOU STILL HAVE FRIENDS.
WHOA. WHOSE PARTY IS THIS ANYWAY?

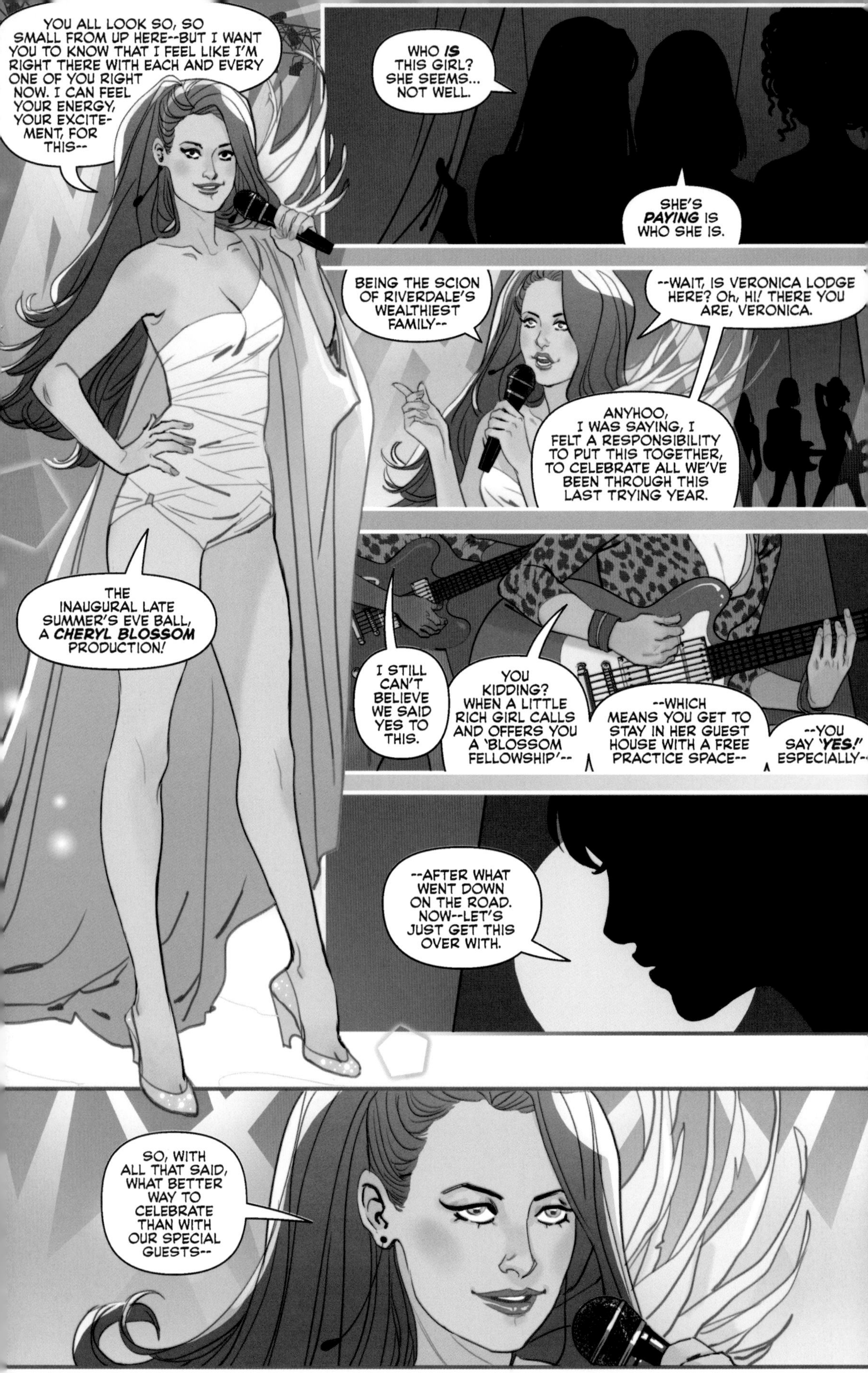
YOU ALL LOOK SO, SO SMALL FROM UP HERE--BUT I WANT YOU TO KNOW THAT I FEEL LIKE I'M RIGHT THERE WITH EACH AND EVERY ONE OF YOU RIGHT NOW. I CAN FEEL YOUR ENERGY, YOUR EXCITE-MENT, FOR THIS--
THE INAUGURAL LATE SUMMER'S EVE BALL, A CHERYL BLOSSOM PRODUCTION!
WHO IS THIS GIRL? SHE SEEMS... NOT WELL.
SHE'S PAYING IS WHO SHE IS.
BEING THE SCION OF RIVERDALE'S WEALTHIEST FAMILY--
--WAIT, IS VERONICA LODGE HERE? Oh, HI! THERE YOU ARE, VERONICA.
ANYHOO, I WAS SAYING, I FELT A RESPONSIBILITY TO PUT THIS TOGETHER, TO CELEBRATE ALL WE'VE BEEN THROUGH THIS LAST TRYING YEAR.
I STILL CAN'T BELIEVE WE SAID YES TO THIS.
YOU KIDDING? WHEN A LITTLE RICH GIRL CALLS AND OFFERS YOU A 'BLOSSOM FELLOWSHIP'--
--WHICH MEANS YOU GET TO STAY IN HER GUEST HOUSE WITH A FREE PRACTICE SPACE--
--YOU SAY 'YES!' ESPECIALLY--
--AFTER WHAT WENT DOWN ON THE ROAD. NOW--LET'S JUST GET THIS OVER WITH.
SO, WITH ALL THAT SAID, WHAT BETTER WAY TO CELEBRATE THAN WITH OUR SPECIAL GUESTS--

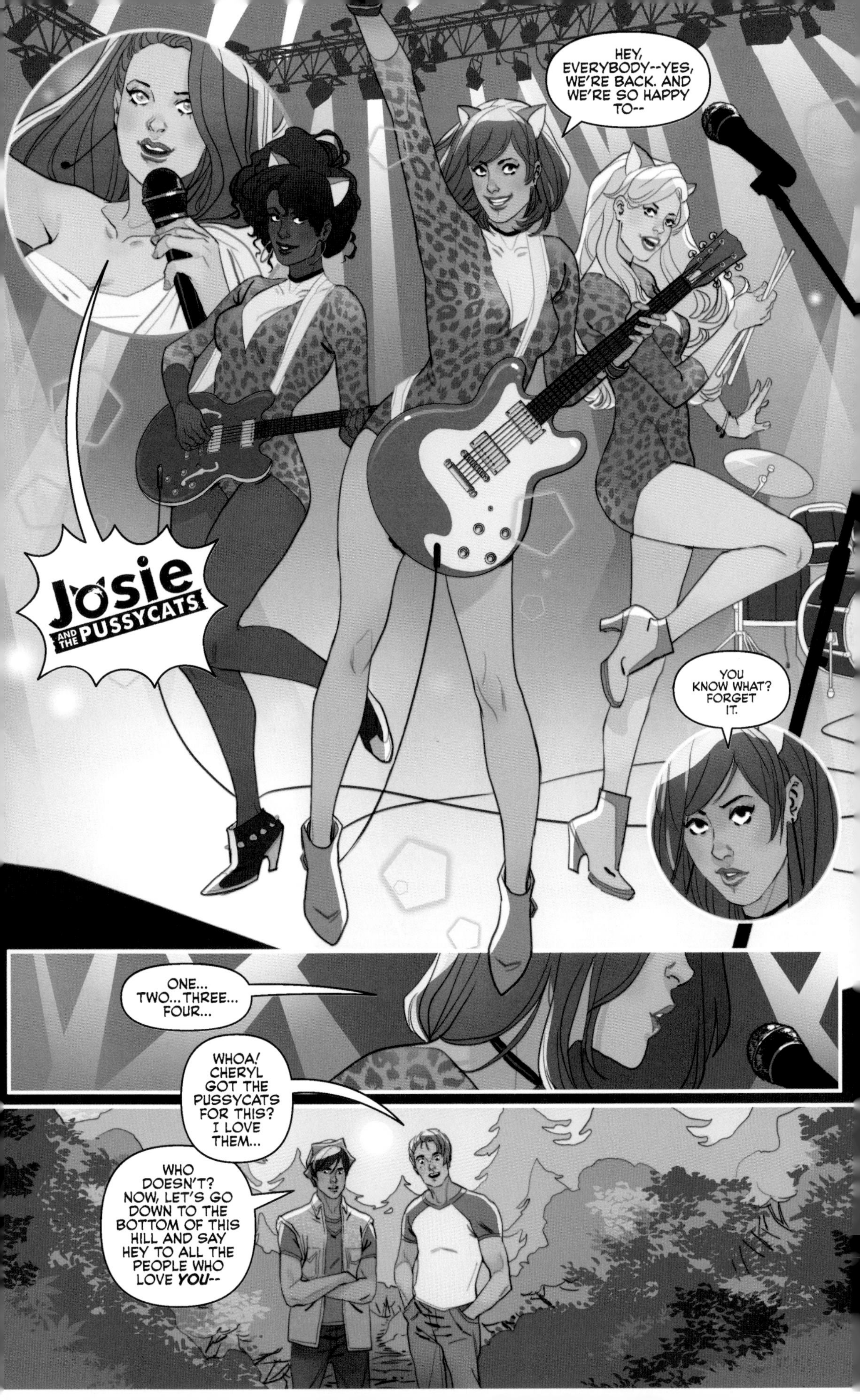

HEY, EVERYBODY--YES, WE'RE BACK. AND WE'RE SO HAPPY TO--
JOSIE AND THE PUSSYCATS
YOU KNOW WHAT? FORGET IT.
ONE... TWO...THREE... FOUR...
WHOA! CHERYL GOT THE PUSSYCATS FOR THIS? I LOVE THEM...
WHO DOESN'T? NOW, LET'S GO DOWN TO THE BOTTOM OF THIS HILL AND SAY HEY TO ALL THE PEOPLE WHO LOVE *YOU*--

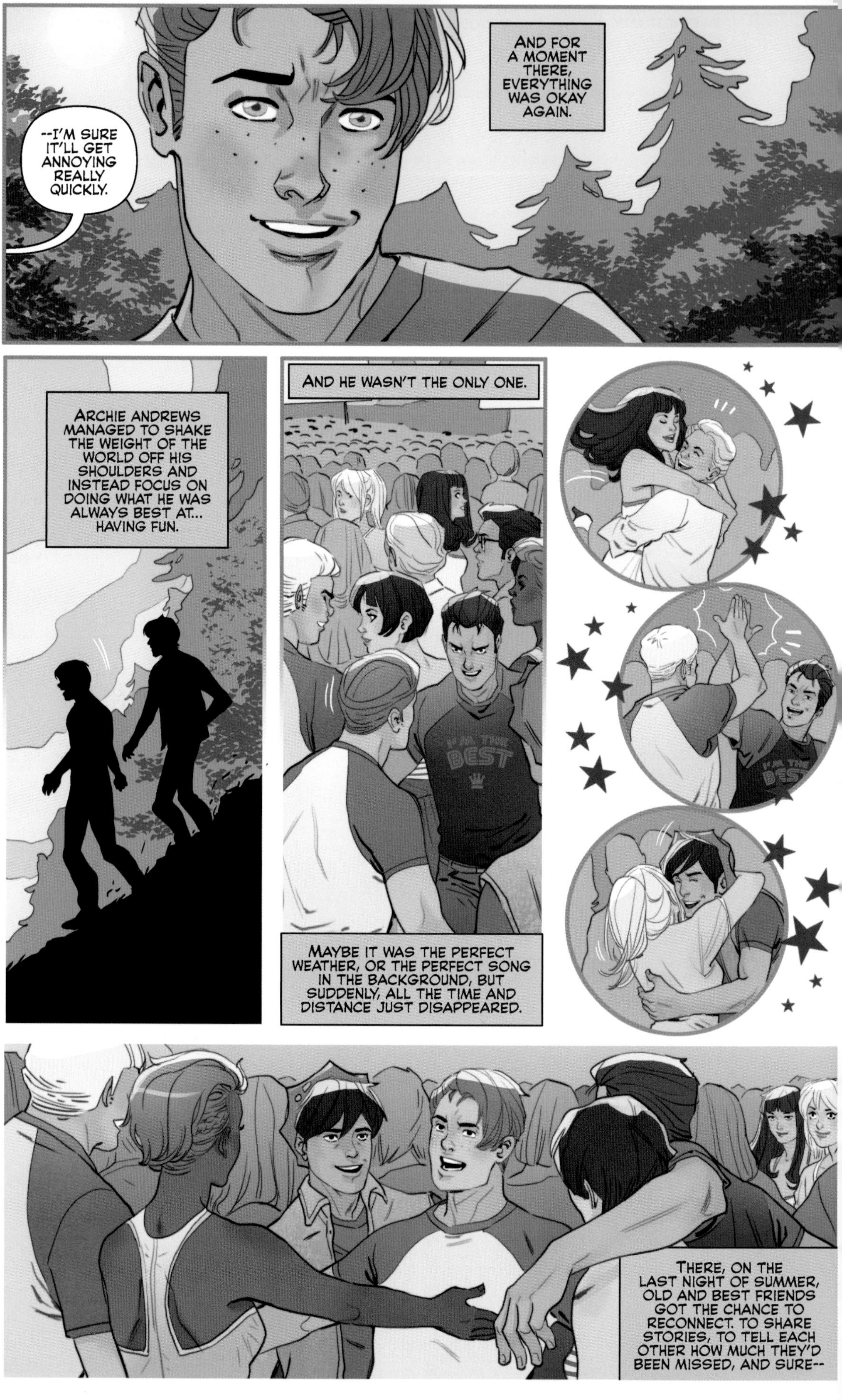
--I'M SURE IT'LL GET ANNOYING REALLY QUICKLY.
AND FOR A MOMENT THERE, EVERYTHING WAS OKAY AGAIN.
ARCHIE ANDREWS MANAGED TO SHAKE THE WEIGHT OF THE WORLD OFF HIS SHOULDERS AND INSTEAD FOCUS ON DOING WHAT HE WAS ALWAYS BEST AT... HAVING FUN.
AND HE WASN'T THE ONLY ONE.
I'M THE BEST
MAYBE IT WAS THE PERFECT WEATHER, OR THE PERFECT SONG IN THE BACKGROUND, BUT SUDDENLY, ALL THE TIME AND DISTANCE JUST DISAPPEARED.
THERE, ON THE LAST NIGHT OF SUMMER, OLD AND BEST FRIENDS GOT THE CHANCE TO RECONNECT. TO SHARE STORIES, TO TELL EACH OTHER HOW MUCH THEY'D BEEN MISSED, AND SURE--

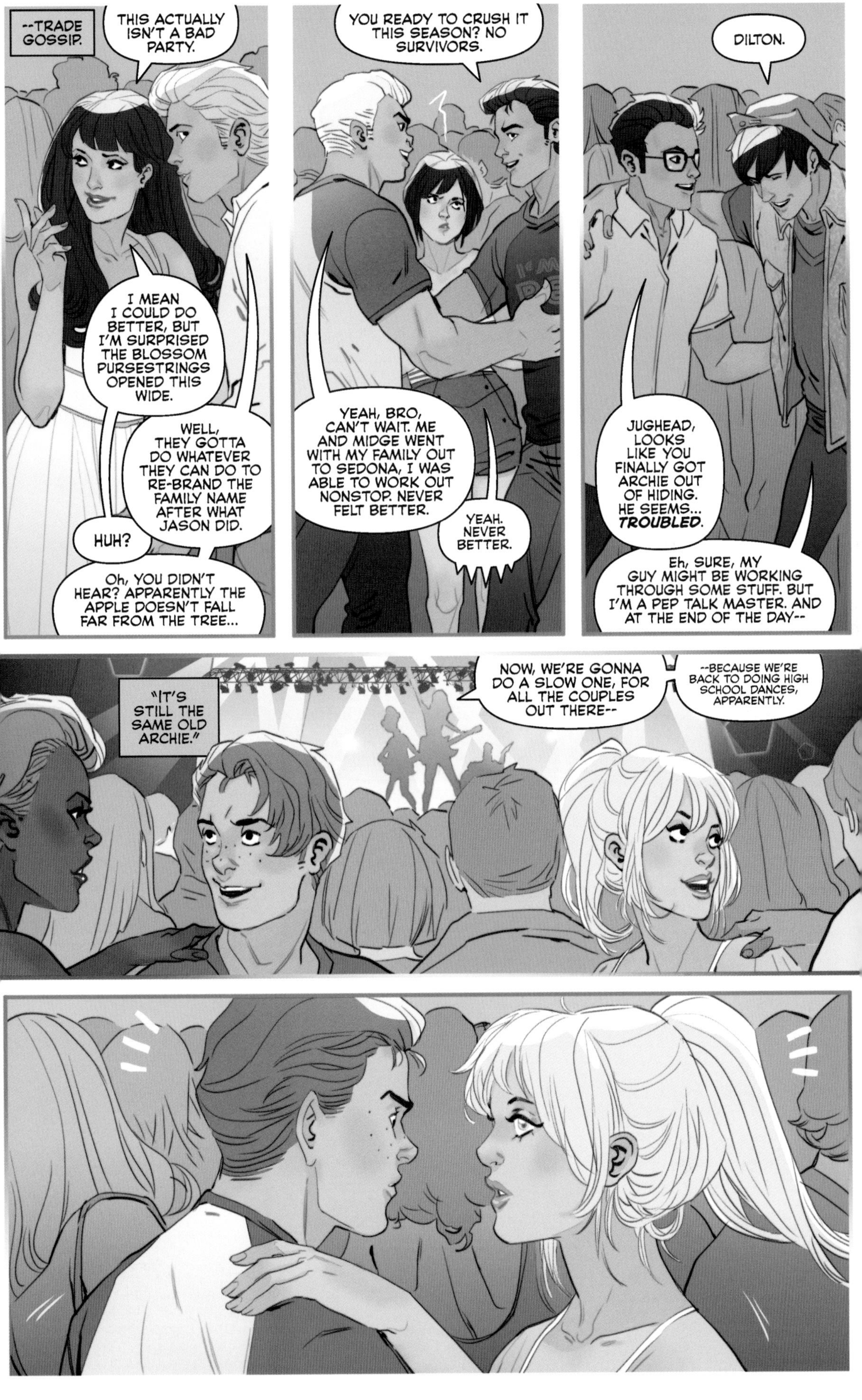
--TRADE GOSSIP.
THIS ACTUALLY ISN'T A BAD PARTY.
I MEAN I COULD DO BETTER, BUT I'M SURPRISED THE BLOSSOM PURSESTRINGS OPENED THIS WIDE.
WELL, THEY GOTTA DO WHATEVER THEY CAN DO TO RE-BRAND THE FAMILY NAME AFTER WHAT JASON DID.
HUH?
Oh, YOU DIDN'T HEAR? APPARENTLY THE APPLE DOESN'T FALL FAR FROM THE TREE...
YOU READY TO CRUSH IT THIS SEASON? NO SURVIVORS.
YEAH, BRO, CAN'T WAIT. ME AND MIDGE WENT WITH MY FAMILY OUT TO SEDONA, I WAS ABLE TO WORK OUT NONSTOP. NEVER FELT BETTER.
YEAH. NEVER BETTER.
DILTON.
JUGHEAD, LOOKS LIKE YOU FINALLY GOT ARCHIE OUT OF HIDING. HE SEEMS... ***TROUBLED***.
Eh, SURE, MY GUY MIGHT BE WORKING THROUGH SOME STUFF. BUT I'M A PEP TALK MASTER. AND AT THE END OF THE DAY--
"IT'S STILL THE SAME OLD ARCHIE."
NOW, WE'RE GONNA DO A SLOW ONE, FOR ALL THE COUPLES OUT THERE--
--BECAUSE WE'RE BACK TO DOING HIGH SCHOOL DANCES, APPARENTLY.

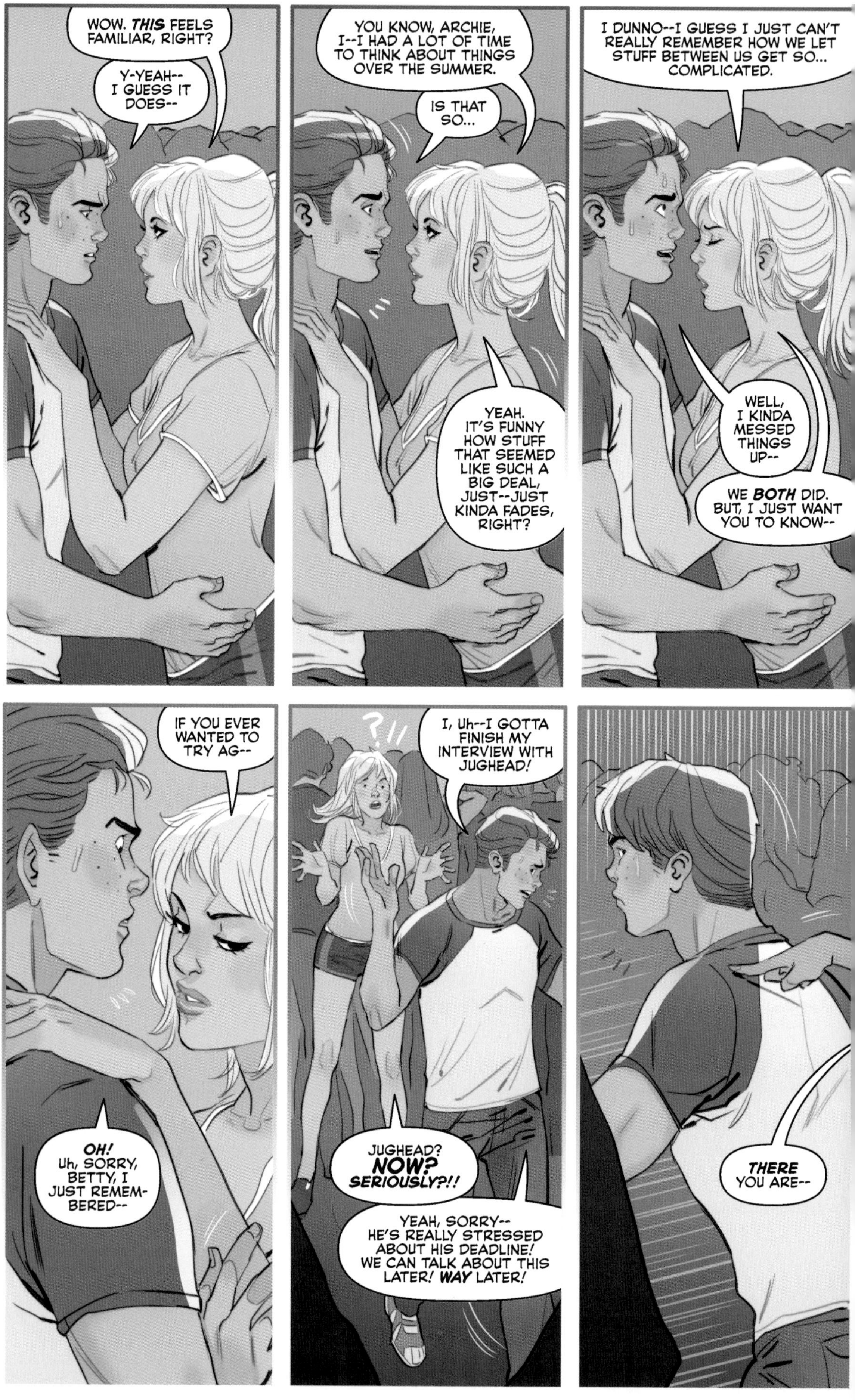
WOW. THIS FEELS FAMILIAR, RIGHT?
Y-YEAH-- I GUESS IT DOES--
YOU KNOW, ARCHIE, I--I HAD A LOT OF TIME TO THINK ABOUT THINGS OVER THE SUMMER.
IS THAT SO...
YEAH. IT'S FUNNY HOW STUFF THAT SEEMED LIKE SUCH A BIG DEAL, JUST--JUST KINDA FADES, RIGHT?
I DUNNO--I GUESS I JUST CAN'T REALLY REMEMBER HOW WE LET STUFF BETWEEN US GET SO... COMPLICATED.
WELL, I KINDA MESSED THINGS UP--
WE BOTH DID. BUT, I JUST WANT YOU TO KNOW--
IF YOU EVER WANTED TO TRY AG--
OH! Uh, SORRY, BETTY, I JUST REMEMBERED--
I, Uh--I GOTTA FINISH MY INTERVIEW WITH JUGHEAD!
JUGHEAD? NOW? SERIOUSLY?!!
YEAH, SORRY-- HE'S REALLY STRESSED ABOUT HIS DEADLINE! WE CAN TALK ABOUT THIS LATER! WAY LATER!
THERE YOU ARE--

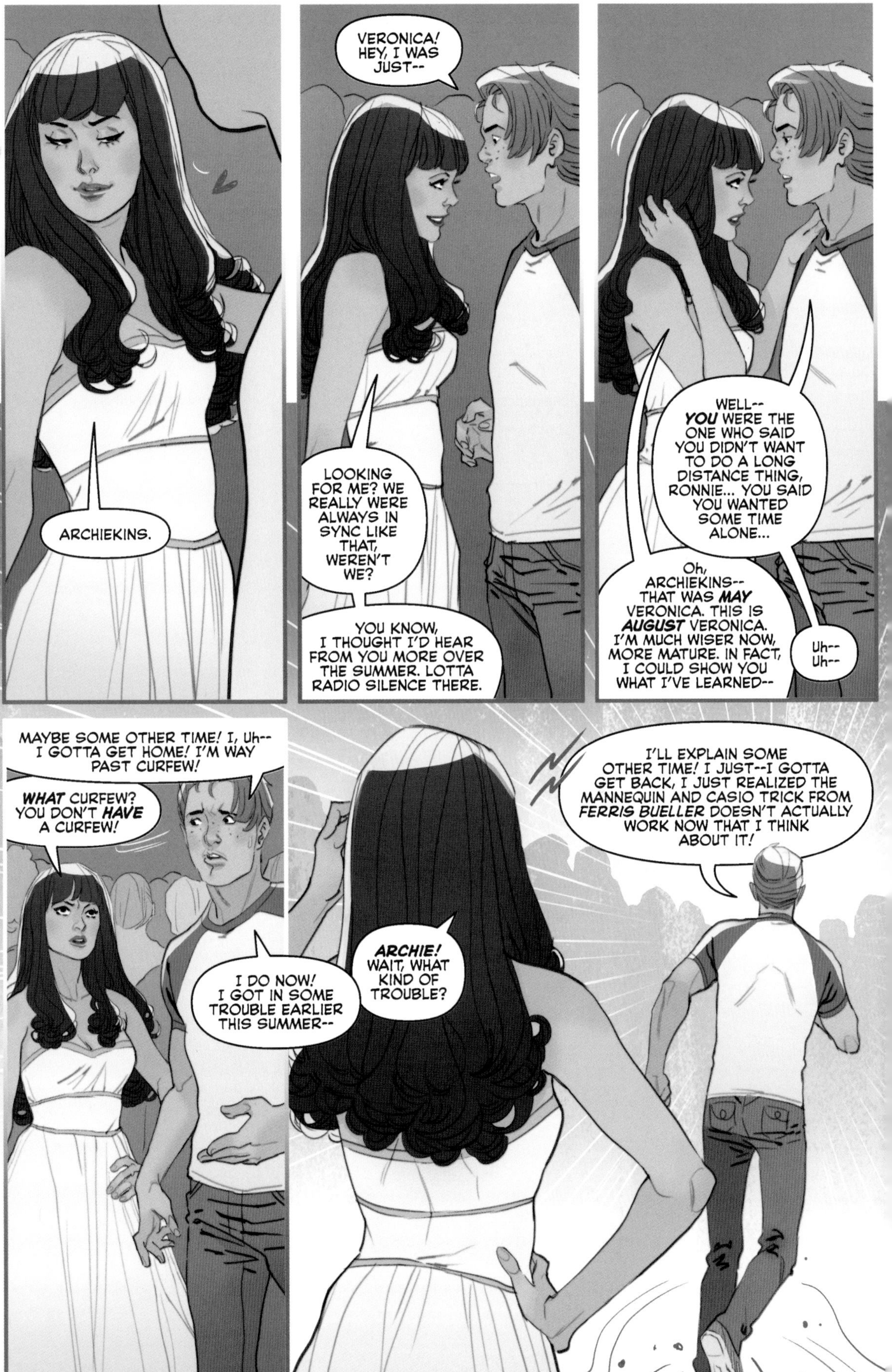
ARCHIEKINS.
VERONICA! HEY, I WAS JUST--
LOOKING FOR ME? WE REALLY WERE ALWAYS IN SYNC LIKE THAT, WEREN'T WE?
YOU KNOW, I THOUGHT I'D HEAR FROM YOU MORE OVER THE SUMMER. LOTTA RADIO SILENCE THERE.
WELL-- ***YOU*** WERE THE ONE WHO SAID YOU DIDN'T WANT TO DO A LONG DISTANCE THING, RONNIE... YOU SAID YOU WANTED SOME TIME ALONE...
Oh, ARCHIEKINS-- THAT WAS ***MAY*** VERONICA. THIS IS ***AUGUST*** VERONICA. I'M MUCH WISER NOW, MORE MATURE. IN FACT, I COULD SHOW YOU WHAT I'VE LEARNED--
Uh-- Uh--
MAYBE SOME OTHER TIME! I, Uh-- I GOTTA GET HOME! I'M WAY PAST CURFEW!
WHAT CURFEW? YOU DON'T ***HAVE*** A CURFEW!
I DO NOW! I GOT IN SOME TROUBLE EARLIER THIS SUMMER--
ARCHIE! WAIT, WHAT KIND OF TROUBLE?
I'LL EXPLAIN SOME OTHER TIME! I JUST--I GOTTA GET BACK, I JUST REALIZED THE MANNEQUIN AND CASIO TRICK FROM ***FERRIS BUELLER*** DOESN'T ACTUALLY WORK NOW THAT I THINK ABOUT IT!

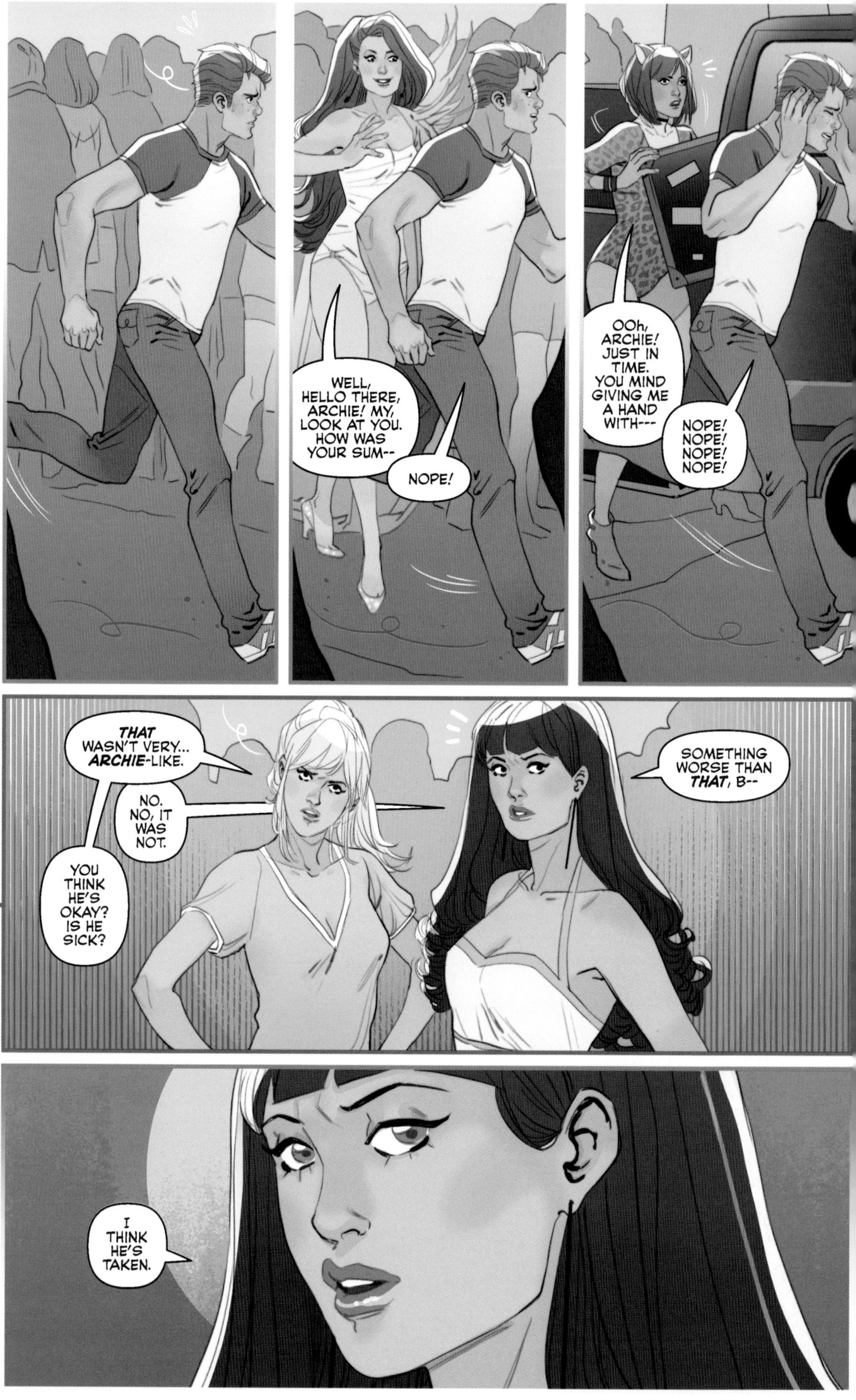
WELL, HELLO THERE, ARCHIE! MY, LOOK AT YOU. HOW WAS YOUR SUM--
NOPE!
OOh, ARCHIE! JUST IN TIME. YOU MIND GIVING ME A HAND WITH---
NOPE! NOPE! NOPE! NOPE!
THAT WASN'T VERY... *ARCHIE*-LIKE.
NO. NO, IT WAS NOT.
YOU THINK HE'S OKAY? IS HE SICK?
SOMETHING WORSE THAN *THAT*, B--
I THINK HE'S TAKEN.

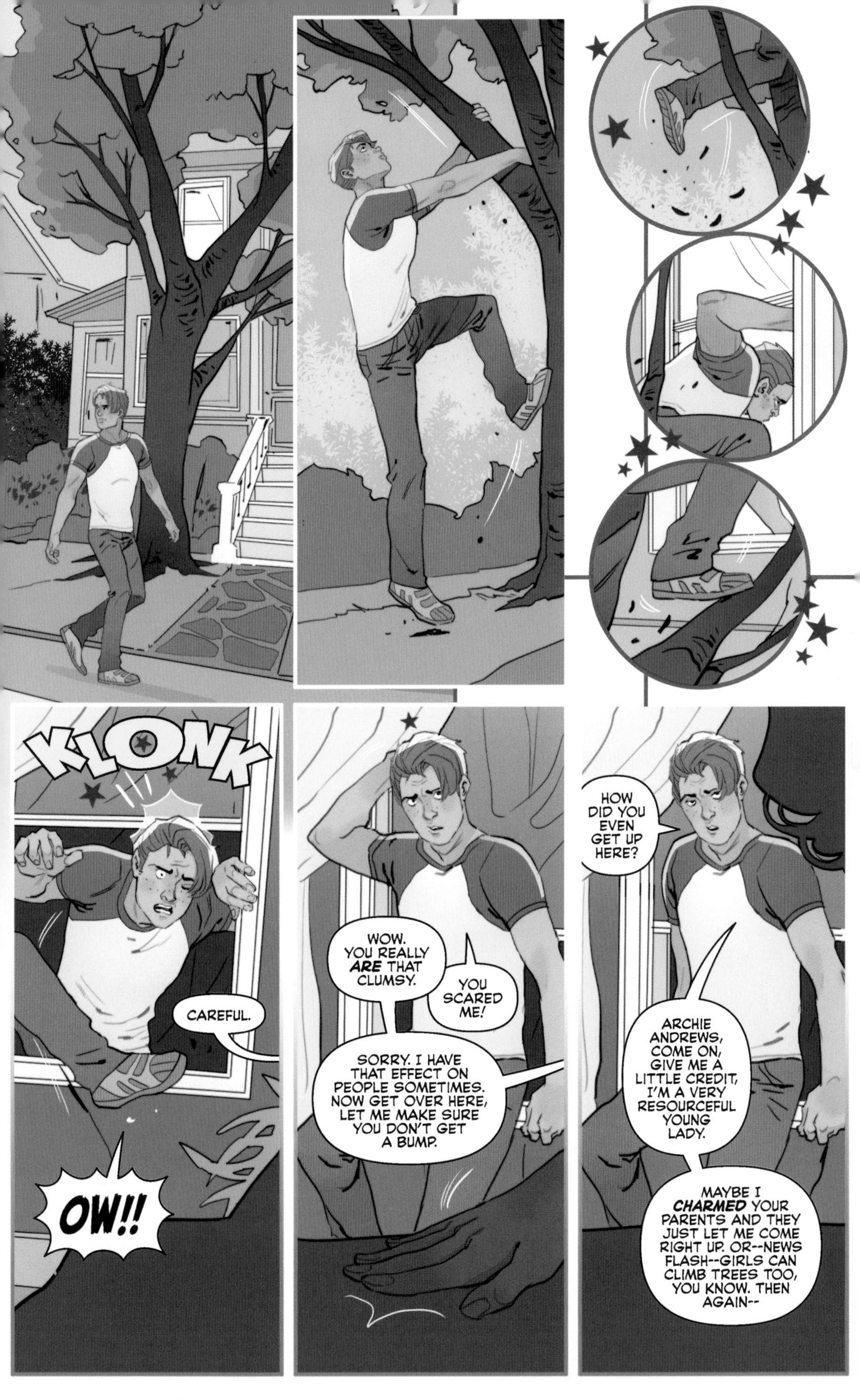
KLONK
OW!!
CAREFUL.
WOW. YOU REALLY ARE THAT CLUMSY.
YOU SCARED ME!
SORRY. I HAVE THAT EFFECT ON PEOPLE SOMETIMES. NOW GET OVER HERE, LET ME MAKE SURE YOU DON'T GET A BUMP.
HOW DID YOU EVEN GET UP HERE?
ARCHIE ANDREWS, COME ON, GIVE ME A LITTLE CREDIT, I'M A VERY RESOURCEFUL YOUNG LADY.
MAYBE I CHARMED YOUR PARENTS AND THEY JUST LET ME COME RIGHT UP. OR--NEWS FLASH--GIRLS CAN CLIMB TREES TOO, YOU KNOW. THEN AGAIN--

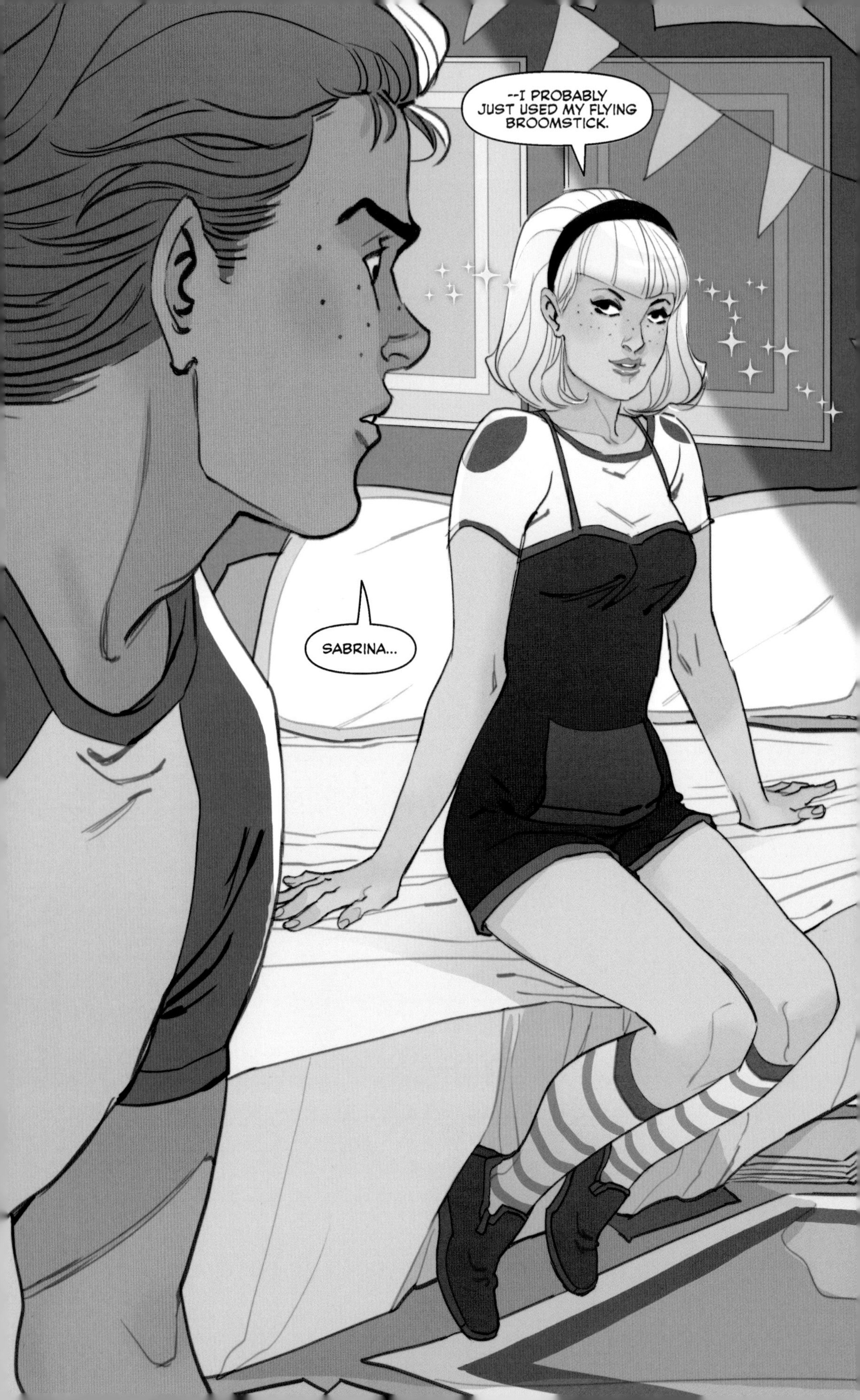
--I PROBABLY JUST USED MY FLYING BROOMSTICK.
SABRINA...

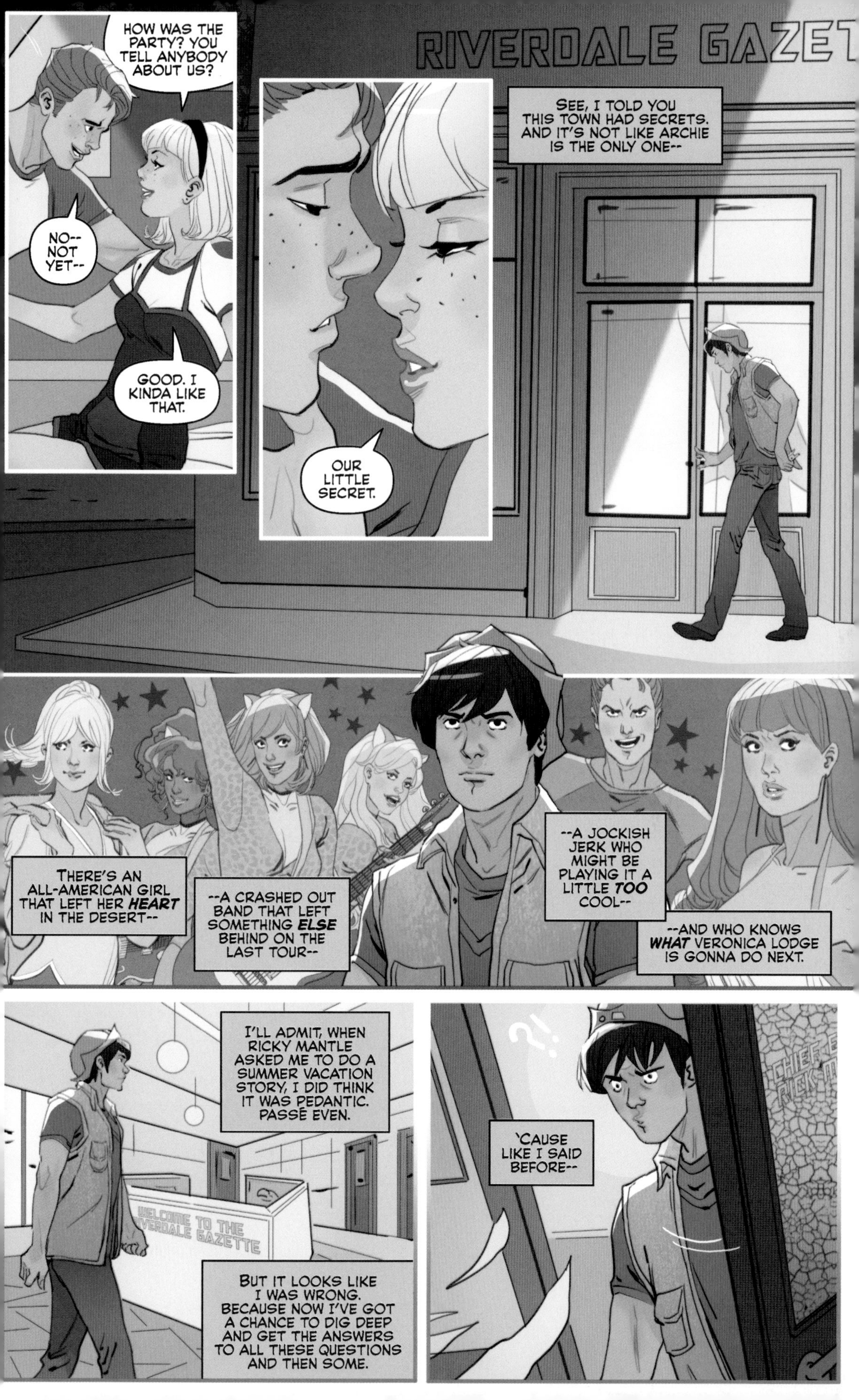
RIVERDALE GAZET
HOW WAS THE PARTY? YOU TELL ANYBODY ABOUT US?
NO-- NOT YET--
GOOD. I KINDA LIKE THAT.
OUR LITTLE SECRET.
SEE, I TOLD YOU THIS TOWN HAD SECRETS. AND IT'S NOT LIKE ARCHIE IS THE ONLY ONE--
THERE'S AN ALL-AMERICAN GIRL THAT LEFT HER HEART IN THE DESERT--
--A CRASHED OUT BAND THAT LEFT SOMETHING ELSE BEHIND ON THE LAST TOUR--
--A JOCKISH JERK WHO MIGHT BE PLAYING IT A LITTLE TOO COOL--
--AND WHO KNOWS WHAT VERONICA LODGE IS GONNA DO NEXT.
I'LL ADMIT, WHEN RICKY MANTLE ASKED ME TO DO A SUMMER VACATION STORY, I DID THINK IT WAS PEDANTIC. PASSÉ EVEN.
WELCOME TO THE RIVERDALE GAZETTE
BUT IT LOOKS LIKE I WAS WRONG. BECAUSE NOW I'VE GOT A CHANCE TO DIG DEEP AND GET THE ANSWERS TO ALL THESE QUESTIONS AND THEN SOME.
?!
'CAUSE LIKE I SAID BEFORE--

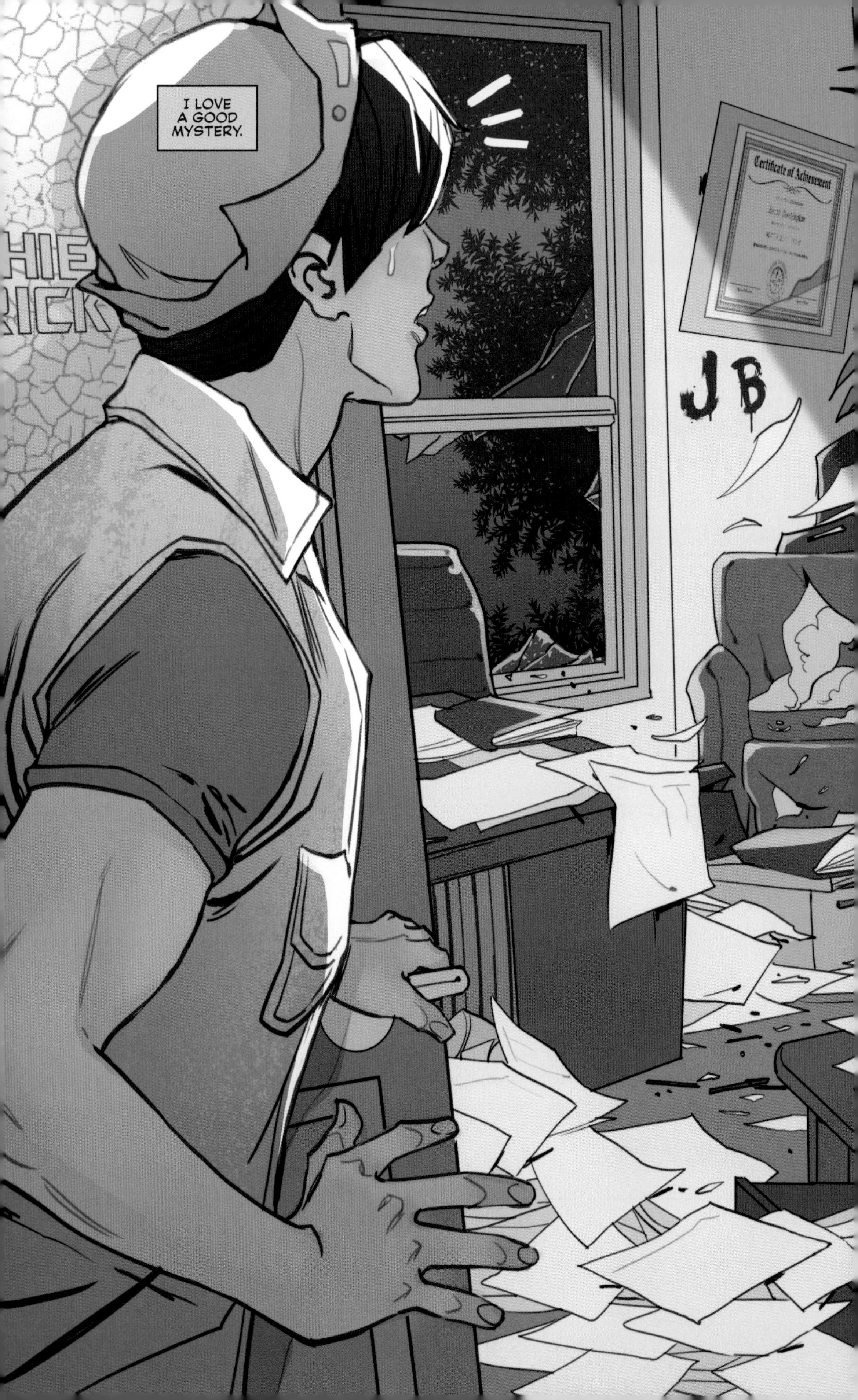
I LOVE A GOOD MYSTERY.
Certificate of Achievement
JB

TO BE CONTINUED...

701

STORY BY
NICK SPENCER

ART BY
MARGUERITE SAUVAGE

LETTERING BY
JACK MORELLI

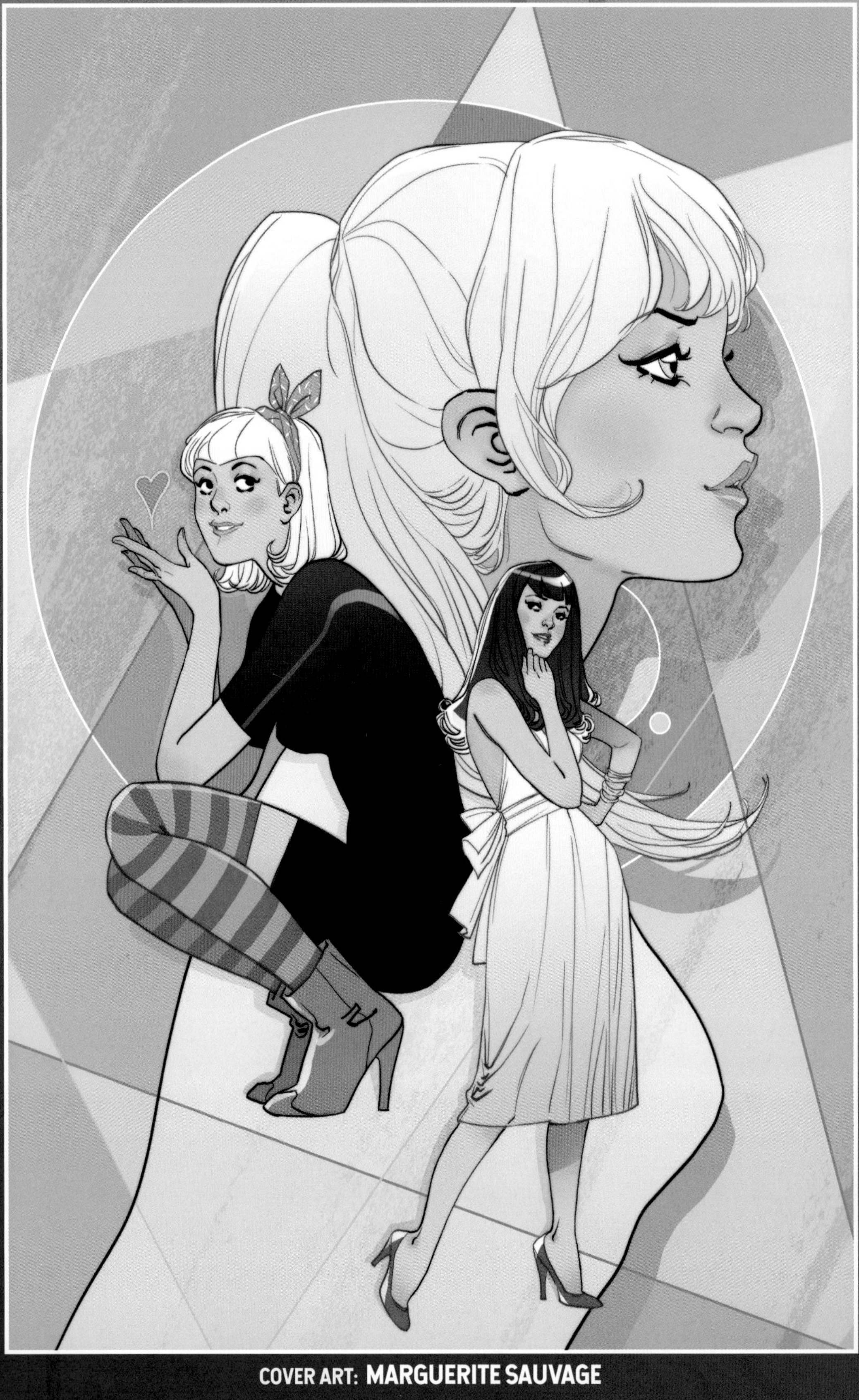

COVER ART: MARGUERITE SAUVAGE

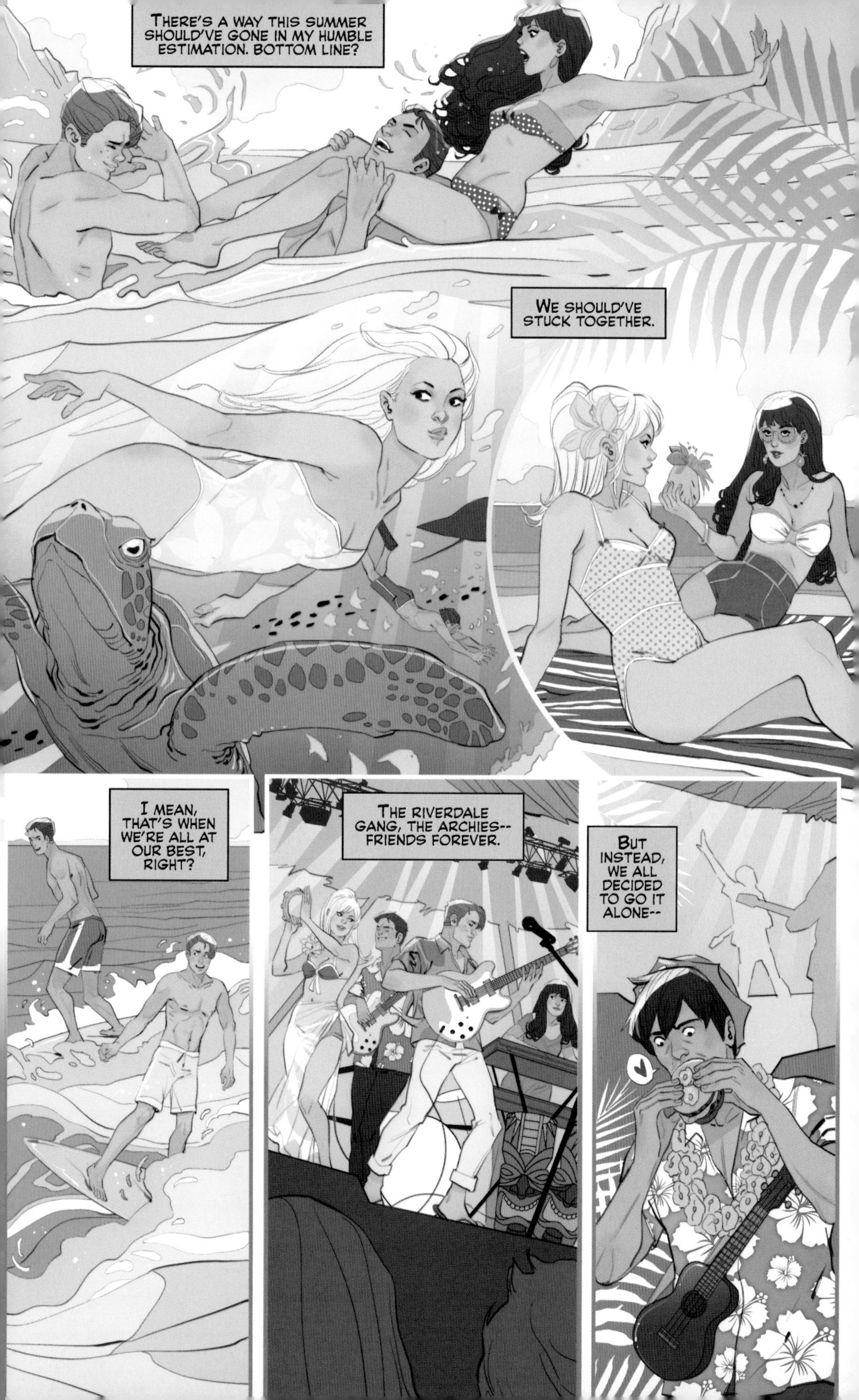
THERE'S A WAY THIS SUMMER SHOULD'VE GONE IN MY HUMBLE ESTIMATION. BOTTOM LINE?
WE SHOULD'VE STUCK TOGETHER.
I MEAN, THAT'S WHEN WE'RE ALL AT OUR BEST, RIGHT?
THE RIVERDALE GANG, THE ARCHIES-- FRIENDS FOREVER.
BUT INSTEAD, WE ALL DECIDED TO GO IT ALONE--

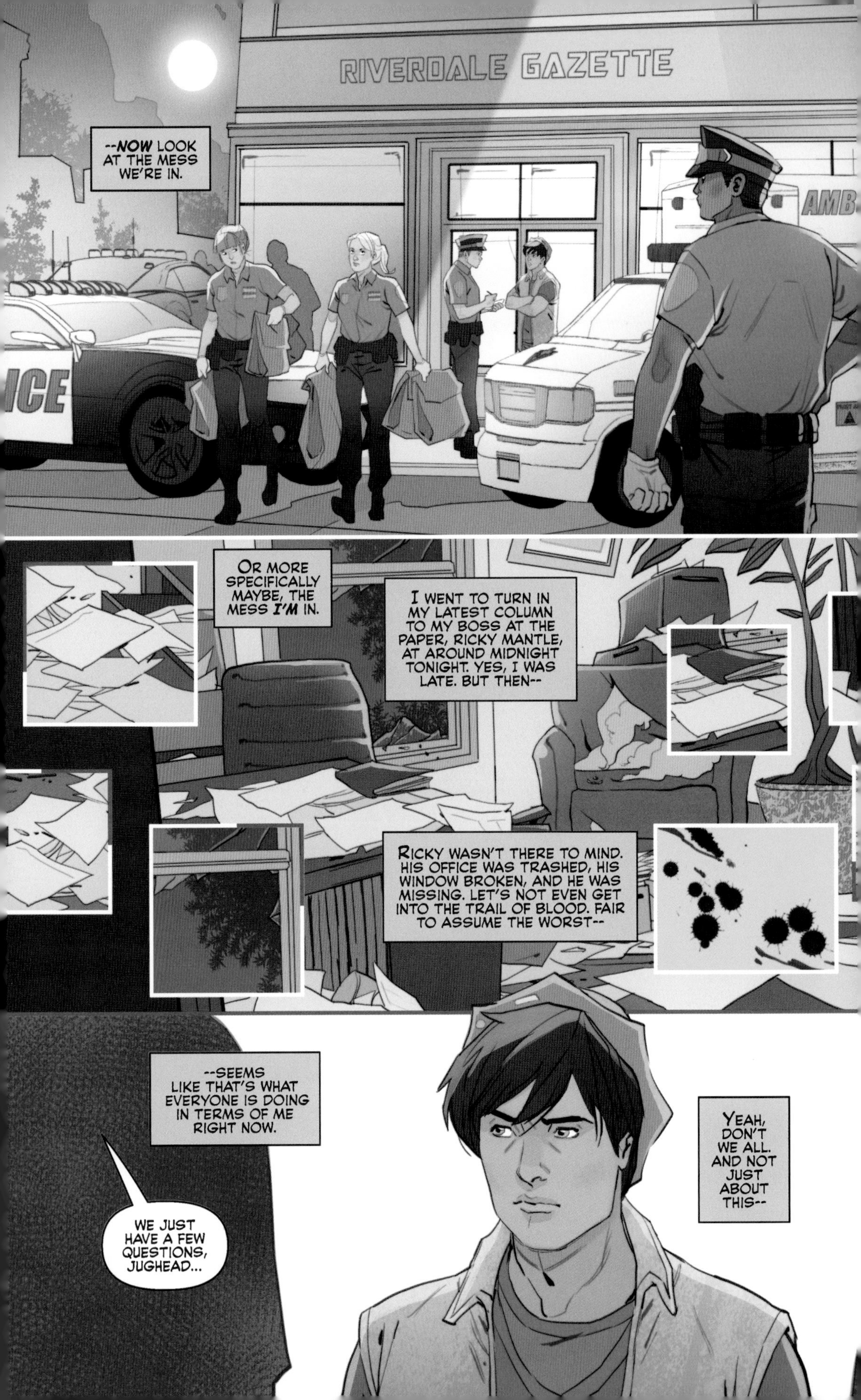
RIVERDALE GAZETTE
--NOW LOOK AT THE MESS WE'RE IN.
AMB
ICE
OR MORE SPECIFICALLY MAYBE, THE MESS I'M IN.
I WENT TO TURN IN MY LATEST COLUMN TO MY BOSS AT THE PAPER, RICKY MANTLE, AT AROUND MIDNIGHT TONIGHT. YES, I WAS LATE. BUT THEN--
RICKY WASN'T THERE TO MIND. HIS OFFICE WAS TRASHED, HIS WINDOW BROKEN, AND HE WAS MISSING. LET'S NOT EVEN GET INTO THE TRAIL OF BLOOD. FAIR TO ASSUME THE WORST--
--SEEMS LIKE THAT'S WHAT EVERYONE IS DOING IN TERMS OF ME RIGHT NOW.
WE JUST HAVE A FEW QUESTIONS, JUGHEAD...
YEAH, DON'T WE ALL. AND NOT JUST ABOUT THIS--

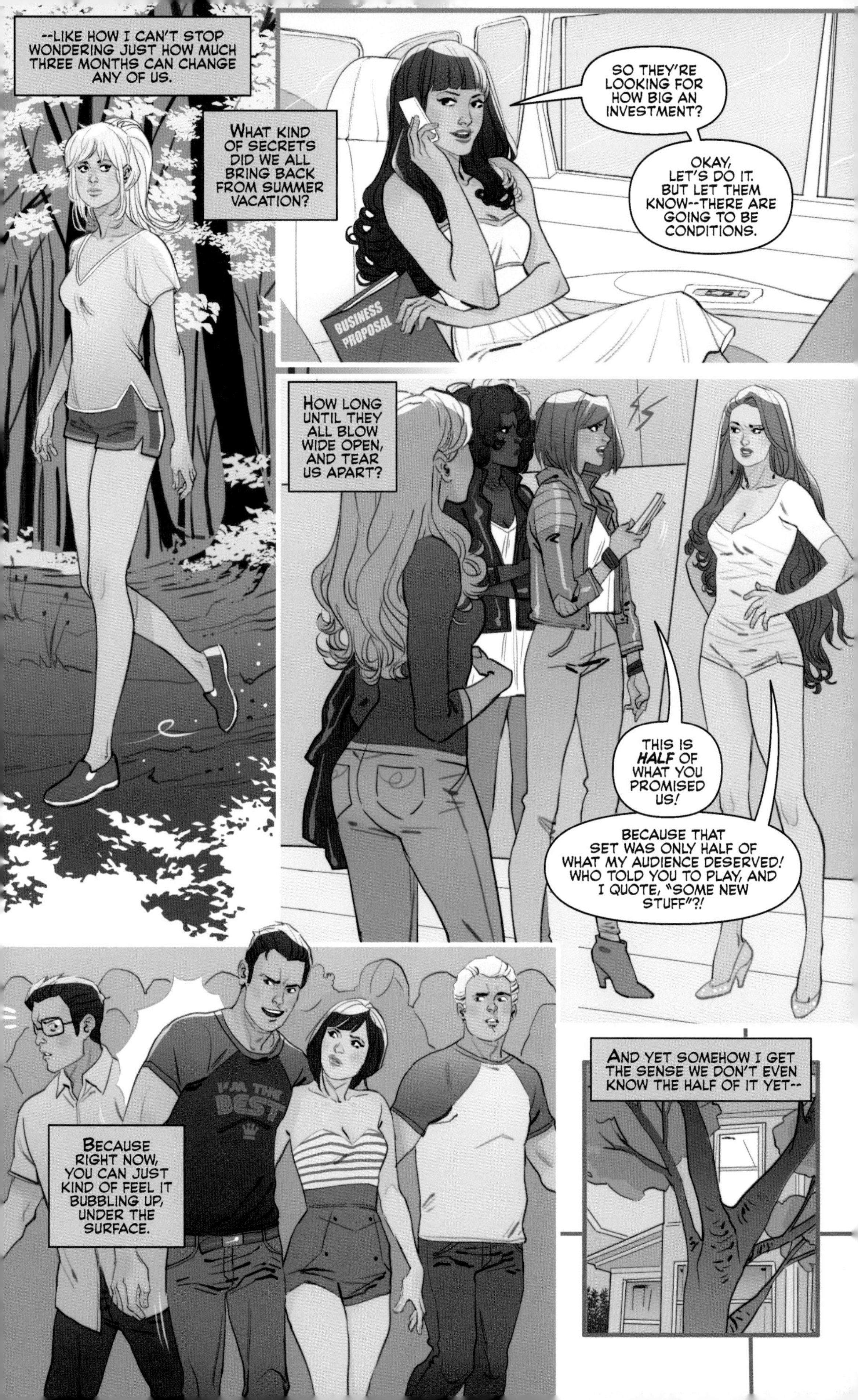
--LIKE HOW I CAN'T STOP WONDERING JUST HOW MUCH THREE MONTHS CAN CHANGE ANY OF US.
WHAT KIND OF SECRETS DID WE ALL BRING BACK FROM SUMMER VACATION?
SO THEY'RE LOOKING FOR HOW BIG AN INVESTMENT?
OKAY, LET'S DO IT. BUT LET THEM KNOW--THERE ARE GOING TO BE CONDITIONS.
BUSINESS PROPOSAL
HOW LONG UNTIL THEY ALL BLOW WIDE OPEN, AND TEAR US APART?
THIS IS ***HALF*** OF WHAT YOU PROMISED US!
BECAUSE THAT SET WAS ONLY HALF OF WHAT MY AUDIENCE DESERVED! WHO TOLD YOU TO PLAY, AND I QUOTE, "SOME NEW STUFF"?!
I'M THE BEST
BECAUSE RIGHT NOW, YOU CAN JUST KIND OF FEEL IT BUBBLING UP, UNDER THE SURFACE.
AND YET SOMEHOW I GET THE SENSE WE DON'T EVEN KNOW THE HALF OF IT YET--

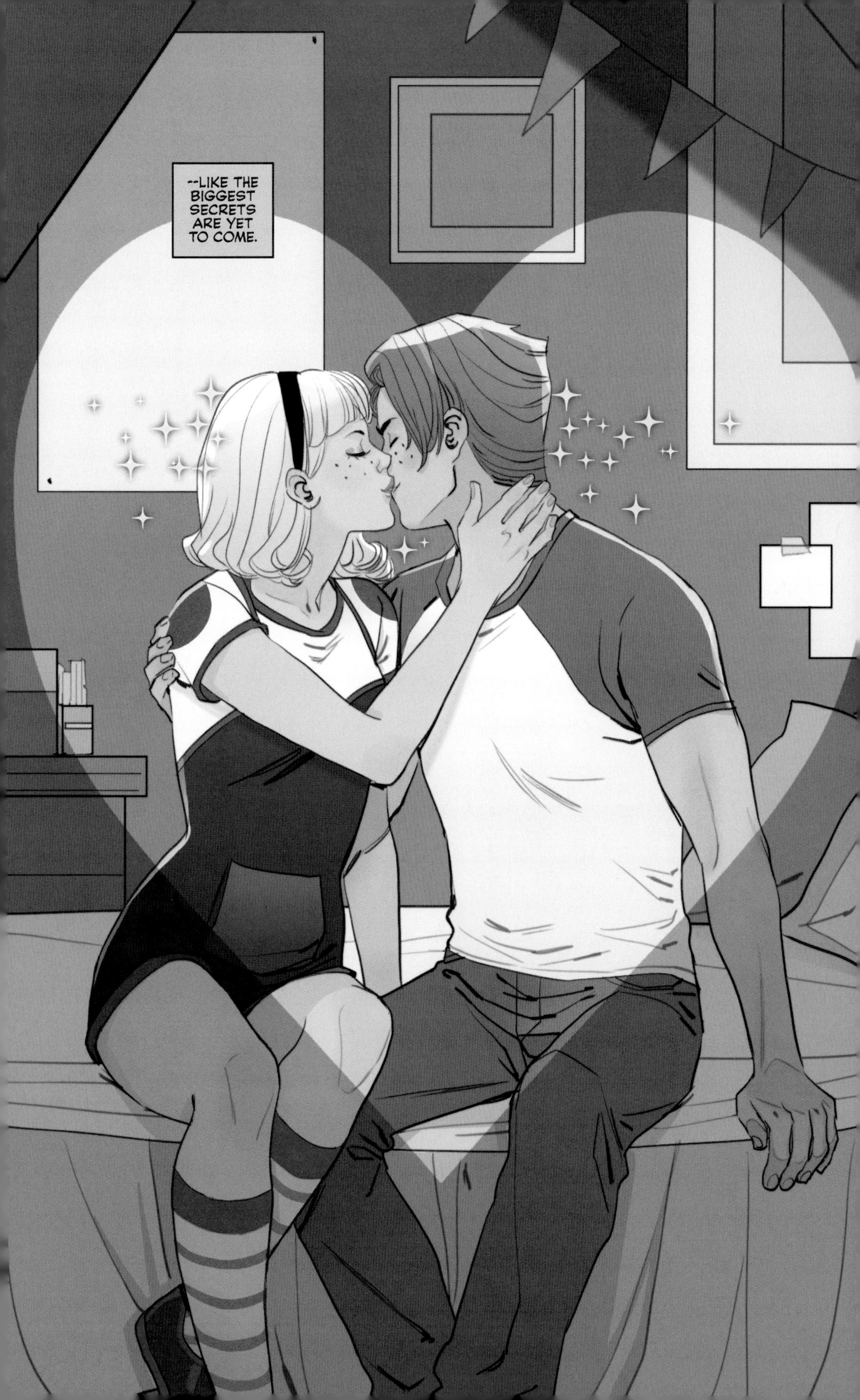
--LIKE THE BIGGEST SECRETS ARE YET TO COME.

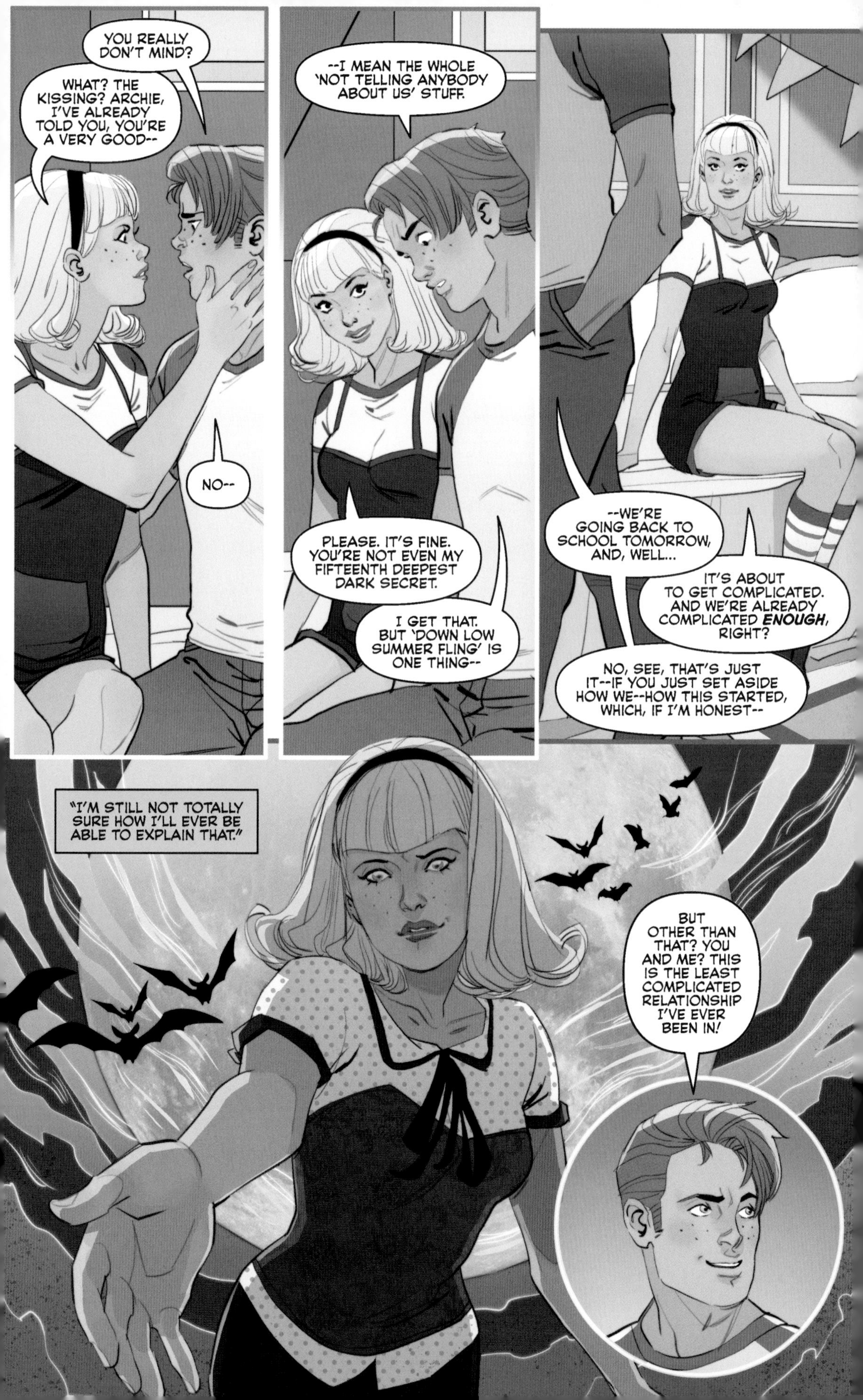
YOU REALLY DON'T MIND?
WHAT? THE KISSING? ARCHIE, I'VE ALREADY TOLD YOU, YOU'RE A VERY GOOD--
NO--
--I MEAN THE WHOLE 'NOT TELLING ANYBODY ABOUT US' STUFF.
PLEASE. IT'S FINE. YOU'RE NOT EVEN MY FIFTEENTH DEEPEST DARK SECRET.
I GET THAT. BUT 'DOWN LOW SUMMER FLING' IS ONE THING--
--WE'RE GOING BACK TO SCHOOL TOMORROW, AND, WELL...
IT'S ABOUT TO GET COMPLICATED. AND WE'RE ALREADY COMPLICATED ENOUGH, RIGHT?
NO, SEE, THAT'S JUST IT--IF YOU JUST SET ASIDE HOW WE--HOW THIS STARTED, WHICH, IF I'M HONEST--
"I'M STILL NOT TOTALLY SURE HOW I'LL EVER BE ABLE TO EXPLAIN THAT."
BUT OTHER THAN THAT? YOU AND ME? THIS IS THE LEAST COMPLICATED RELATIONSHIP I'VE EVER BEEN IN!

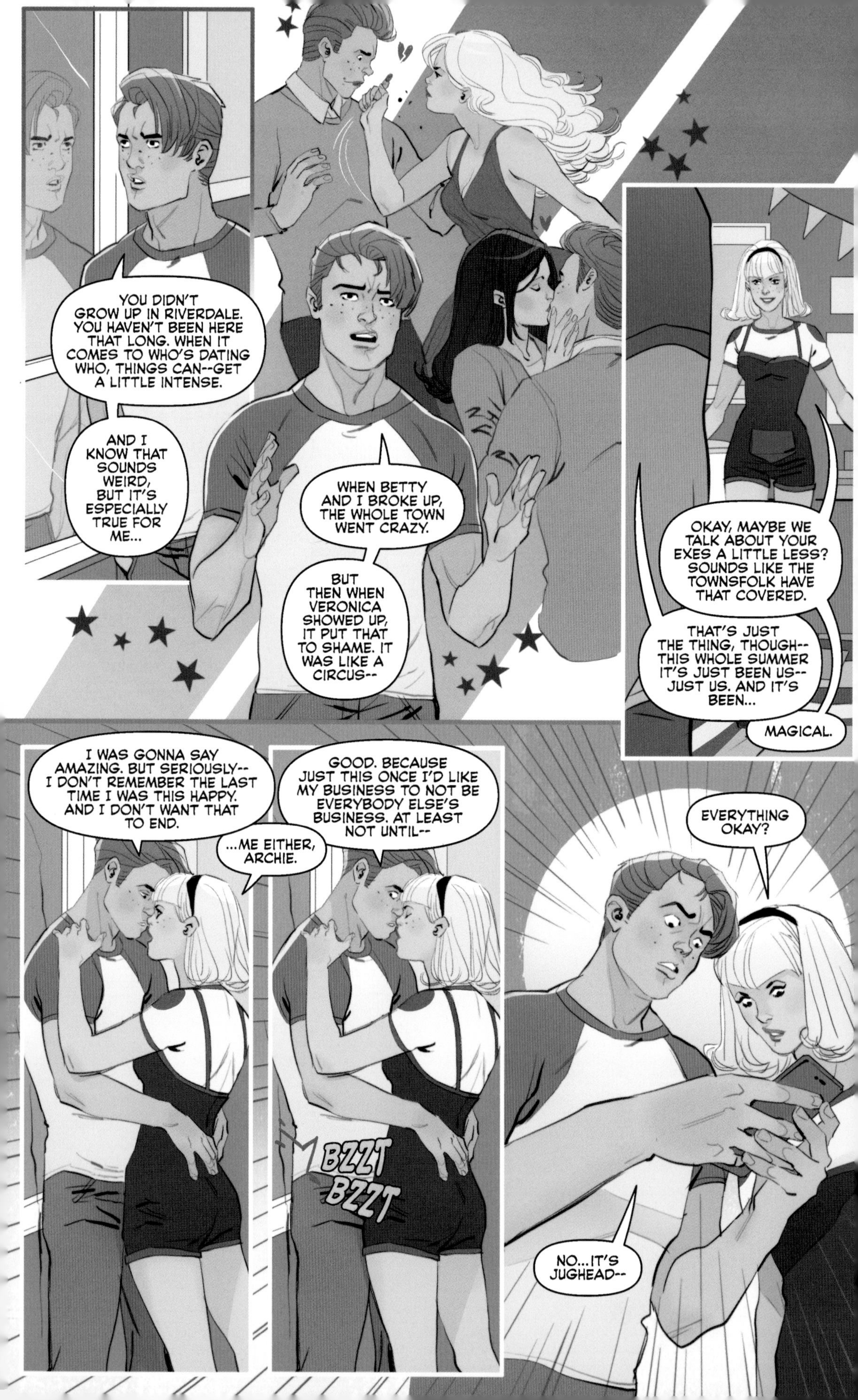
YOU DIDN'T GROW UP IN RIVERDALE. YOU HAVEN'T BEEN HERE THAT LONG. WHEN IT COMES TO WHO'S DATING WHO, THINGS CAN--GET A LITTLE INTENSE.
AND I KNOW THAT SOUNDS WEIRD, BUT IT'S ESPECIALLY TRUE FOR ME...
WHEN BETTY AND I BROKE UP, THE WHOLE TOWN WENT CRAZY.
BUT THEN WHEN VERONICA SHOWED UP, IT PUT THAT TO SHAME. IT WAS LIKE A CIRCUS--
OKAY, MAYBE WE TALK ABOUT YOUR EXES A LITTLE LESS? SOUNDS LIKE THE TOWNSFOLK HAVE THAT COVERED.
THAT'S JUST THE THING, THOUGH-- THIS WHOLE SUMMER IT'S JUST BEEN US-- JUST US. AND IT'S BEEN...
MAGICAL.
I WAS GONNA SAY AMAZING. BUT SERIOUSLY-- I DON'T REMEMBER THE LAST TIME I WAS THIS HAPPY. AND I DON'T WANT THAT TO END.
...ME EITHER, ARCHIE.
GOOD. BECAUSE JUST THIS ONCE I'D LIKE MY BUSINESS TO NOT BE EVERYBODY ELSE'S BUSINESS. AT LEAST NOT UNTIL--
BZZT
BZZT
EVERYTHING OKAY?
NO...IT'S JUGHEAD--

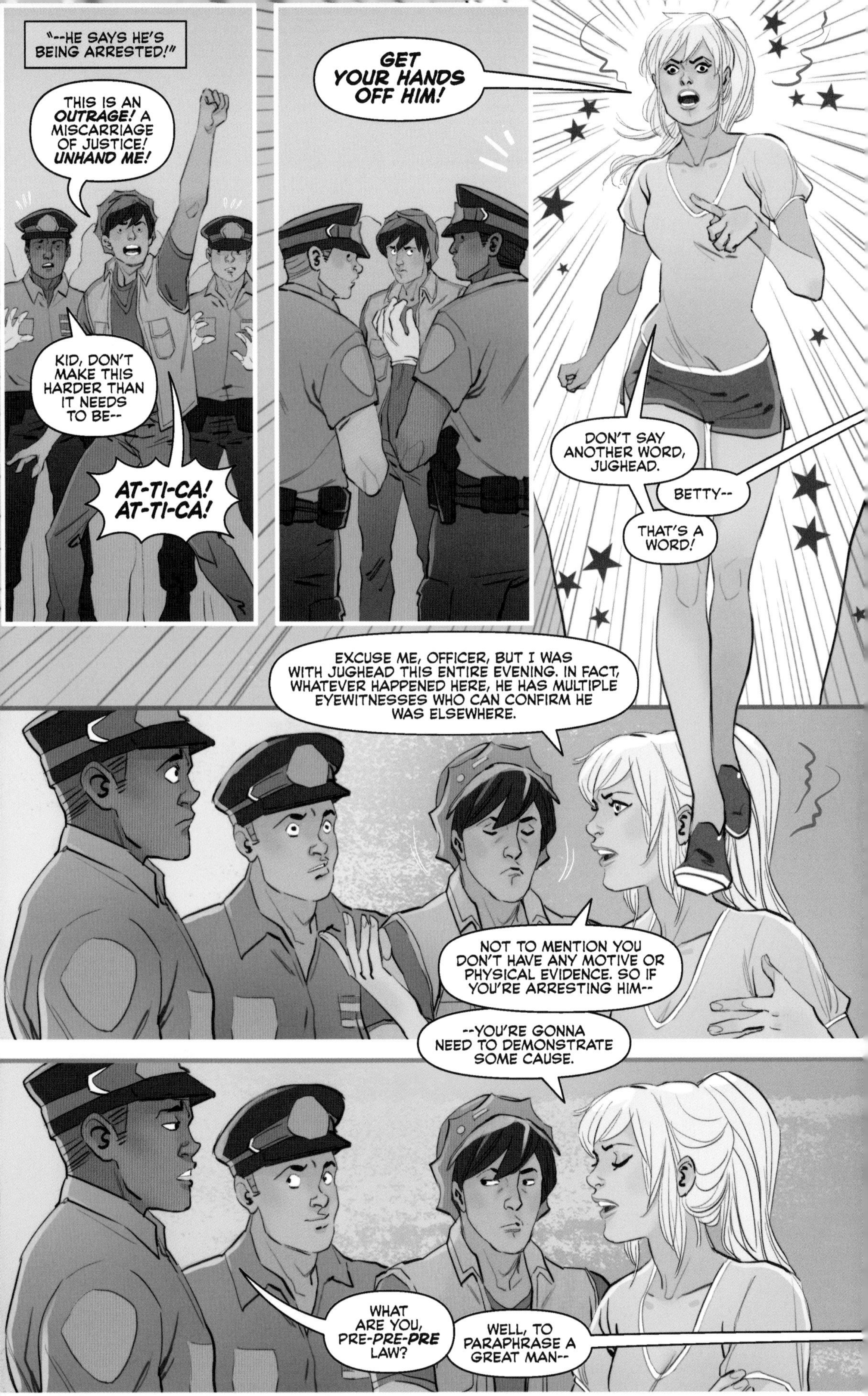
"--HE SAYS HE'S BEING ARRESTED!"
THIS IS AN OUTRAGE! A MISCARRIAGE OF JUSTICE! UNHAND ME!
KID, DON'T MAKE THIS HARDER THAN IT NEEDS TO BE--
AT-TI-CA! AT-TI-CA!
GET YOUR HANDS OFF HIM!
DON'T SAY ANOTHER WORD, JUGHEAD.
BETTY--
THAT'S A WORD!
EXCUSE ME, OFFICER, BUT I WAS WITH JUGHEAD THIS ENTIRE EVENING. IN FACT, WHATEVER HAPPENED HERE, HE HAS MULTIPLE EYEWITNESSES WHO CAN CONFIRM HE WAS ELSEWHERE.
NOT TO MENTION YOU DON'T HAVE ANY MOTIVE OR PHYSICAL EVIDENCE. SO IF YOU'RE ARRESTING HIM--
--YOU'RE GONNA NEED TO DEMONSTRATE SOME CAUSE.
WHAT ARE YOU, PRE-PRE-PRE LAW?
WELL, TO PARAPHRASE A GREAT MAN--

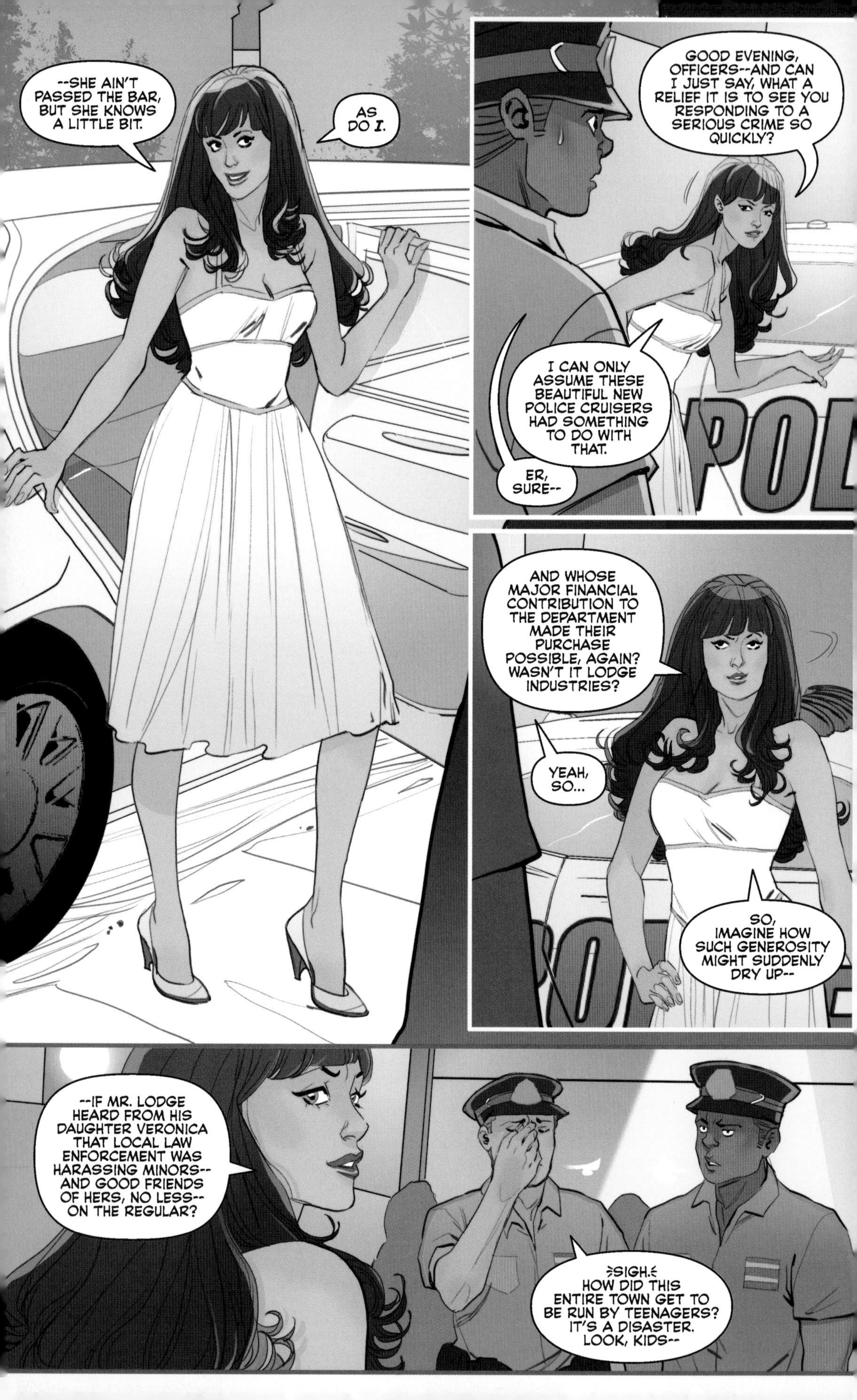

--SHE AIN'T PASSED THE BAR, BUT SHE KNOWS A LITTLE BIT.
AS DO I.
GOOD EVENING, OFFICERS--AND CAN I JUST SAY, WHAT A RELIEF IT IS TO SEE YOU RESPONDING TO A SERIOUS CRIME SO QUICKLY?
I CAN ONLY ASSUME THESE BEAUTIFUL NEW POLICE CRUISERS HAD SOMETHING TO DO WITH THAT.
ER, SURE--
POL
AND WHOSE MAJOR FINANCIAL CONTRIBUTION TO THE DEPARTMENT MADE THEIR PURCHASE POSSIBLE, AGAIN? WASN'T IT LODGE INDUSTRIES?
YEAH, SO...
SO, IMAGINE HOW SUCH GENEROSITY MIGHT SUDDENLY DRY UP--
--IF MR. LODGE HEARD FROM HIS DAUGHTER VERONICA THAT LOCAL LAW ENFORCEMENT WAS HARASSING MINORS--AND GOOD FRIENDS OF HERS, NO LESS--ON THE REGULAR?
SIGH.
HOW DID THIS ENTIRE TOWN GET TO BE RUN BY TEENAGERS? IT'S A DISASTER. LOOK, KIDS--

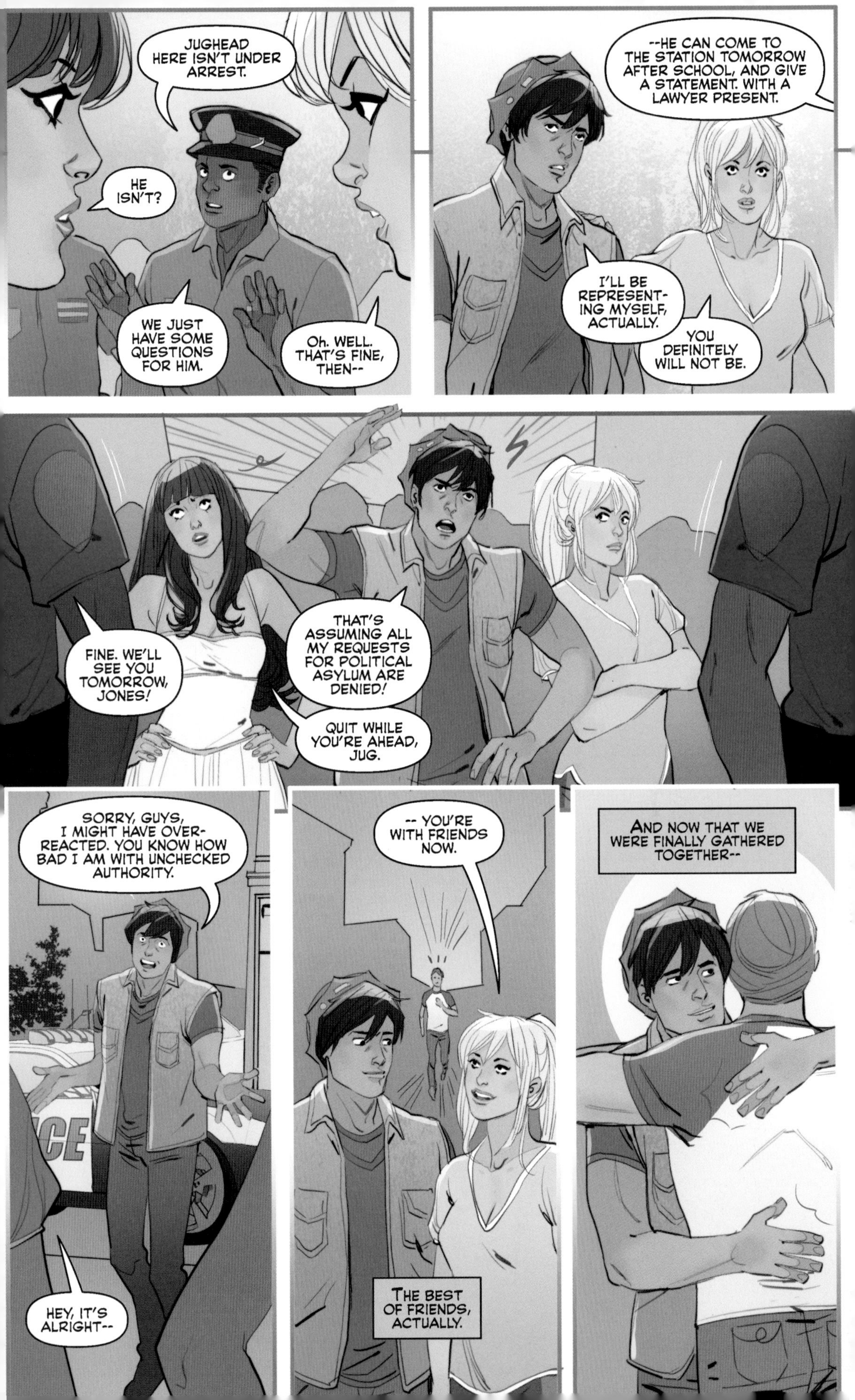
JUGHEAD HERE ISN'T UNDER ARREST.
HE ISN'T?
WE JUST HAVE SOME QUESTIONS FOR HIM.
Oh. WELL. THAT'S FINE, THEN--
--HE CAN COME TO THE STATION TOMORROW AFTER SCHOOL, AND GIVE A STATEMENT. WITH A LAWYER PRESENT.
I'LL BE REPRESENT-ING MYSELF, ACTUALLY.
YOU DEFINITELY WILL NOT BE.
FINE. WE'LL SEE YOU TOMORROW, JONES!
THAT'S ASSUMING ALL MY REQUESTS FOR POLITICAL ASYLUM ARE DENIED!
QUIT WHILE YOU'RE AHEAD, JUG.
SORRY, GUYS, I MIGHT HAVE OVER-REACTED. YOU KNOW HOW BAD I AM WITH UNCHECKED AUTHORITY.
HEY, IT'S ALRIGHT--
-- YOU'RE WITH FRIENDS NOW.
THE BEST OF FRIENDS, ACTUALLY.
AND NOW THAT WE WERE FINALLY GATHERED TOGETHER--

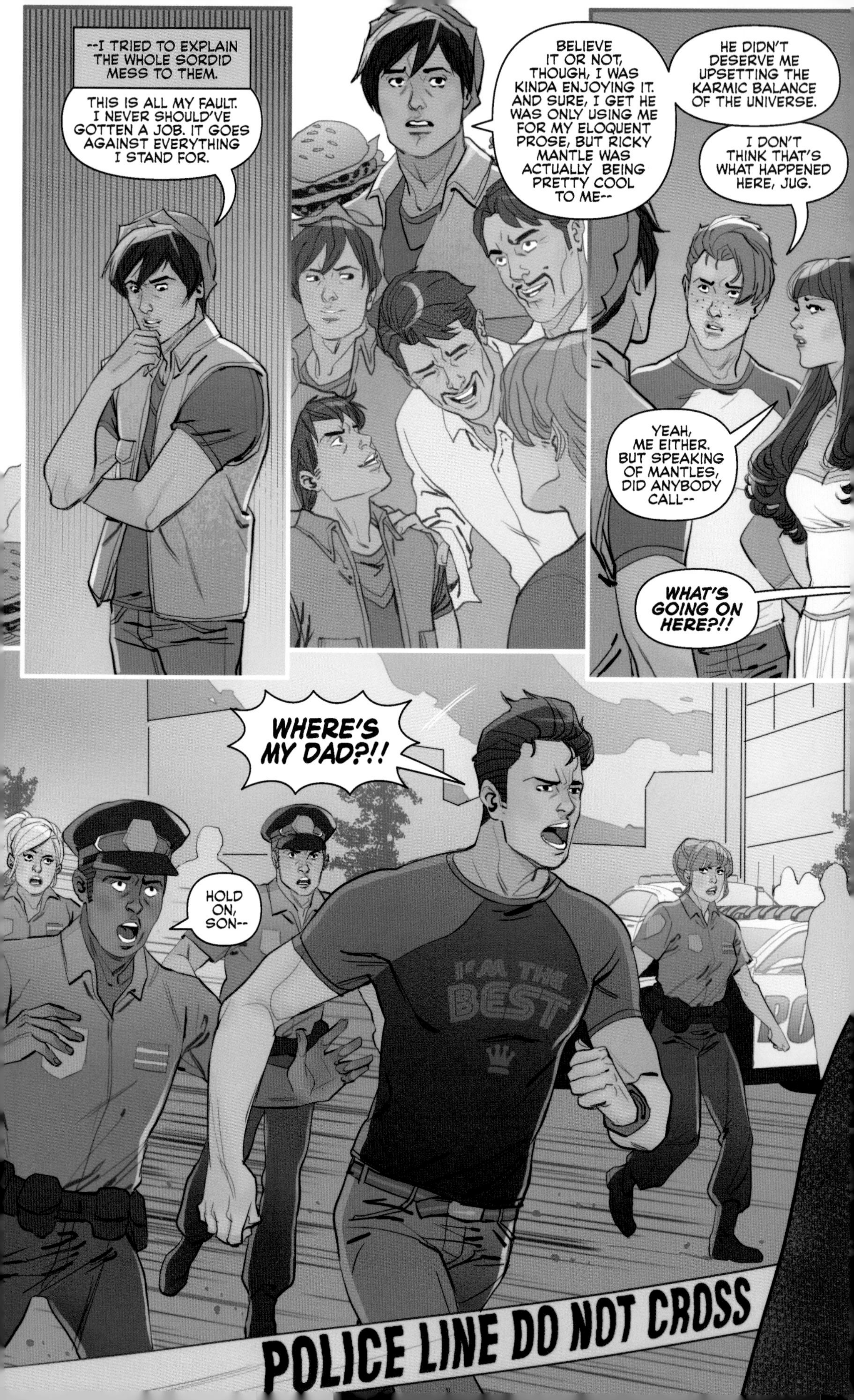
--I TRIED TO EXPLAIN THE WHOLE SORDID MESS TO THEM.
THIS IS ALL MY FAULT. I NEVER SHOULD'VE GOTTEN A JOB. IT GOES AGAINST EVERYTHING I STAND FOR.
BELIEVE IT OR NOT, THOUGH, I WAS KINDA ENJOYING IT. AND SURE, I GET HE WAS ONLY USING ME FOR MY ELOQUENT PROSE, BUT RICKY MANTLE WAS ACTUALLY BEING PRETTY COOL TO ME--
HE DIDN'T DESERVE ME UPSETTING THE KARMIC BALANCE OF THE UNIVERSE.
I DON'T THINK THAT'S WHAT HAPPENED HERE, JUG.
YEAH, ME EITHER. BUT SPEAKING OF MANTLES, DID ANYBODY CALL--
WHAT'S GOING ON HERE?!!
WHERE'S MY DAD?!!
HOLD ON, SON--
I'M THE BEST
POLICE LINE DO NOT CROSS

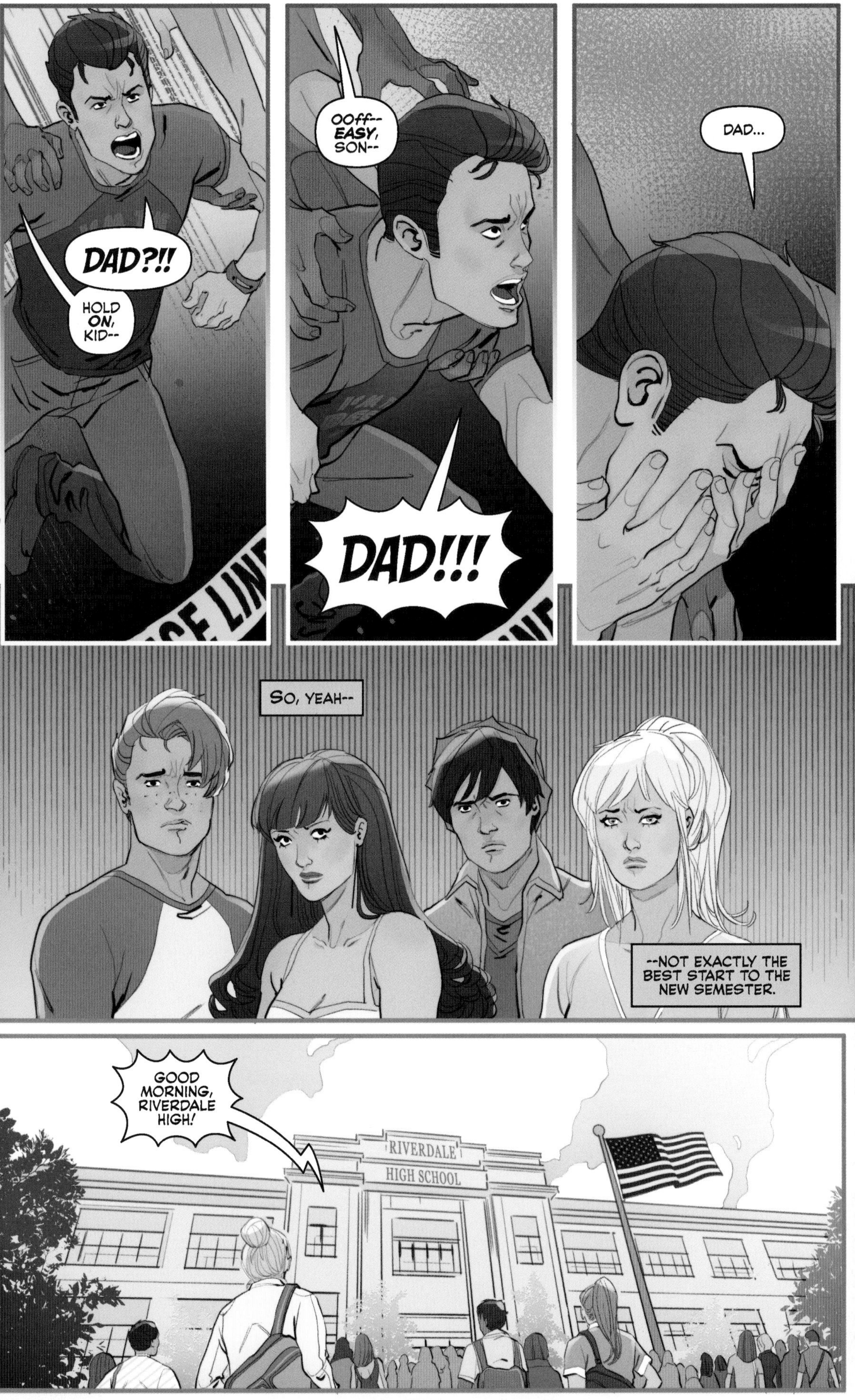
DAD?!!
HOLD ON, KID--
OOff-- EASY, SON--
DAD!!!
DAD...
SO, YEAH--
--NOT EXACTLY THE BEST START TO THE NEW SEMESTER.
GOOD MORNING, RIVERDALE HIGH!
RIVERDALE HIGH SCHOOL

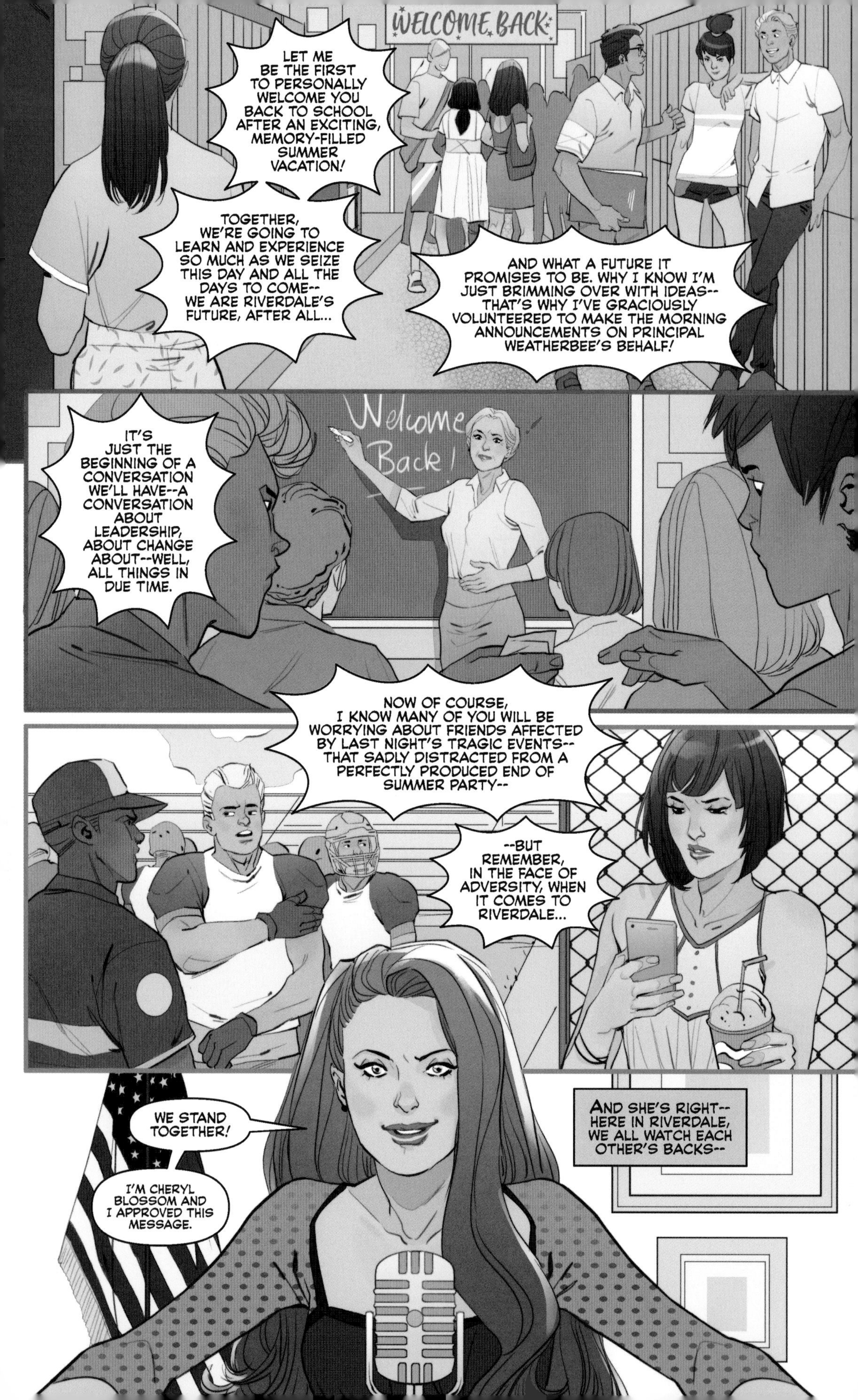
WELCOME BACK
LET ME BE THE FIRST TO PERSONALLY WELCOME YOU BACK TO SCHOOL AFTER AN EXCITING, MEMORY-FILLED SUMMER VACATION!
TOGETHER, WE'RE GOING TO LEARN AND EXPERIENCE SO MUCH AS WE SEIZE THIS DAY AND ALL THE DAYS TO COME--WE ARE RIVERDALE'S FUTURE, AFTER ALL...
AND WHAT A FUTURE IT PROMISES TO BE. WHY I KNOW I'M JUST BRIMMING OVER WITH IDEAS--THAT'S WHY I'VE GRACIOUSLY VOLUNTEERED TO MAKE THE MORNING ANNOUNCEMENTS ON PRINCIPAL WEATHERBEE'S BEHALF!
Welcome Back!
IT'S JUST THE BEGINNING OF A CONVERSATION WE'LL HAVE--A CONVERSATION ABOUT LEADERSHIP, ABOUT CHANGE ABOUT--WELL, ALL THINGS IN DUE TIME.
NOW OF COURSE, I KNOW MANY OF YOU WILL BE WORRYING ABOUT FRIENDS AFFECTED BY LAST NIGHT'S TRAGIC EVENTS--THAT SADLY DISTRACTED FROM A PERFECTLY PRODUCED END OF SUMMER PARTY--
--BUT REMEMBER, IN THE FACE OF ADVERSITY, WHEN IT COMES TO RIVERDALE...
WE STAND TOGETHER!
I'M CHERYL BLOSSOM AND I APPROVED THIS MESSAGE.
AND SHE'S RIGHT--HERE IN RIVERDALE, WE ALL WATCH EACH OTHER'S BACKS--

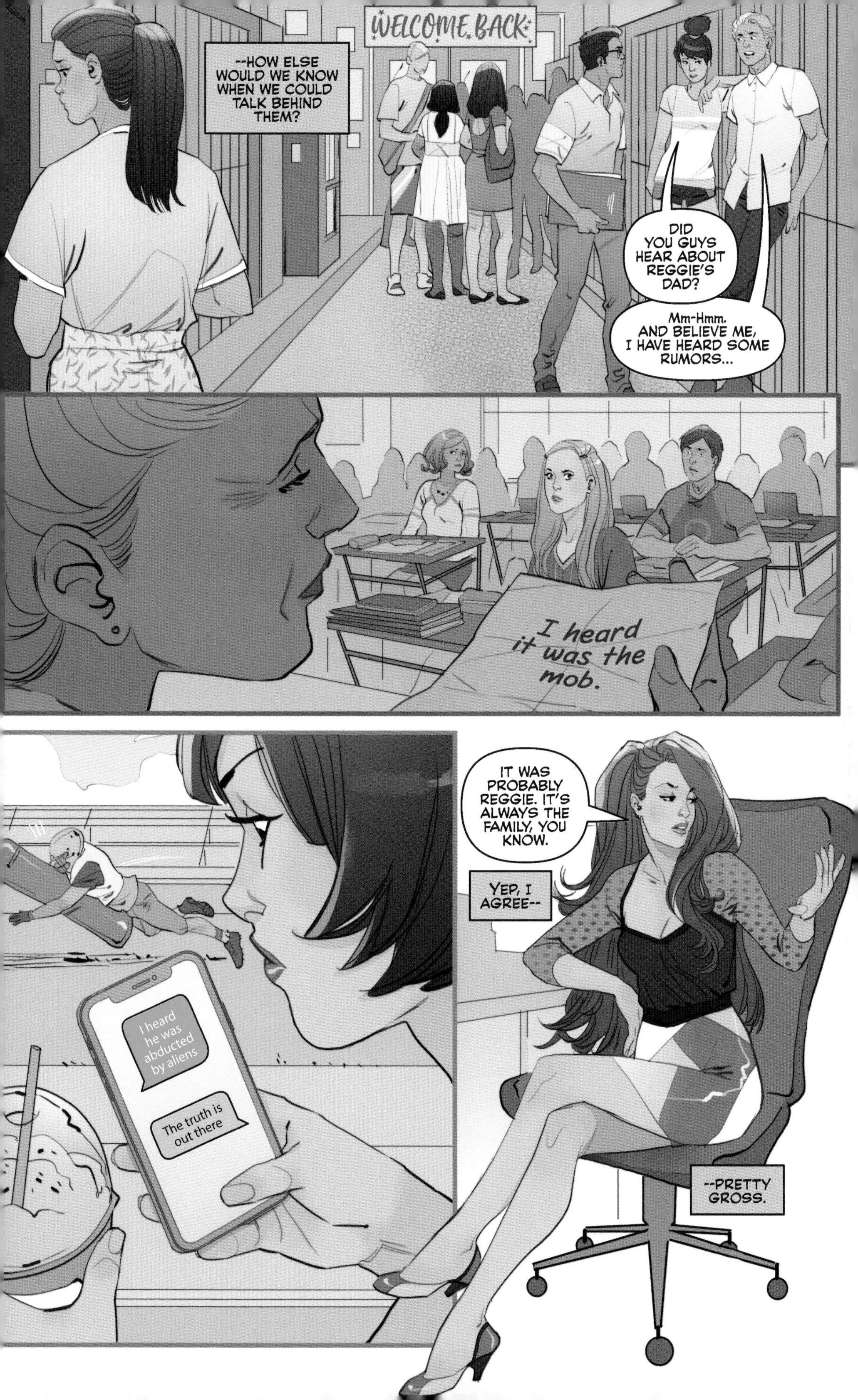
WELCOME BACK
--HOW ELSE WOULD WE KNOW WHEN WE COULD TALK BEHIND THEM?
DID YOU GUYS HEAR ABOUT REGGIE'S DAD?
Mm-Hmm. AND BELIEVE ME, I HAVE HEARD SOME RUMORS...
I heard it was the mob.
I heard he was abducted by aliens
The truth is out there
IT WAS PROBABLY REGGIE. IT'S ALWAYS THE FAMILY, YOU KNOW.
YEP, I AGREE--
--PRETTY GROSS.

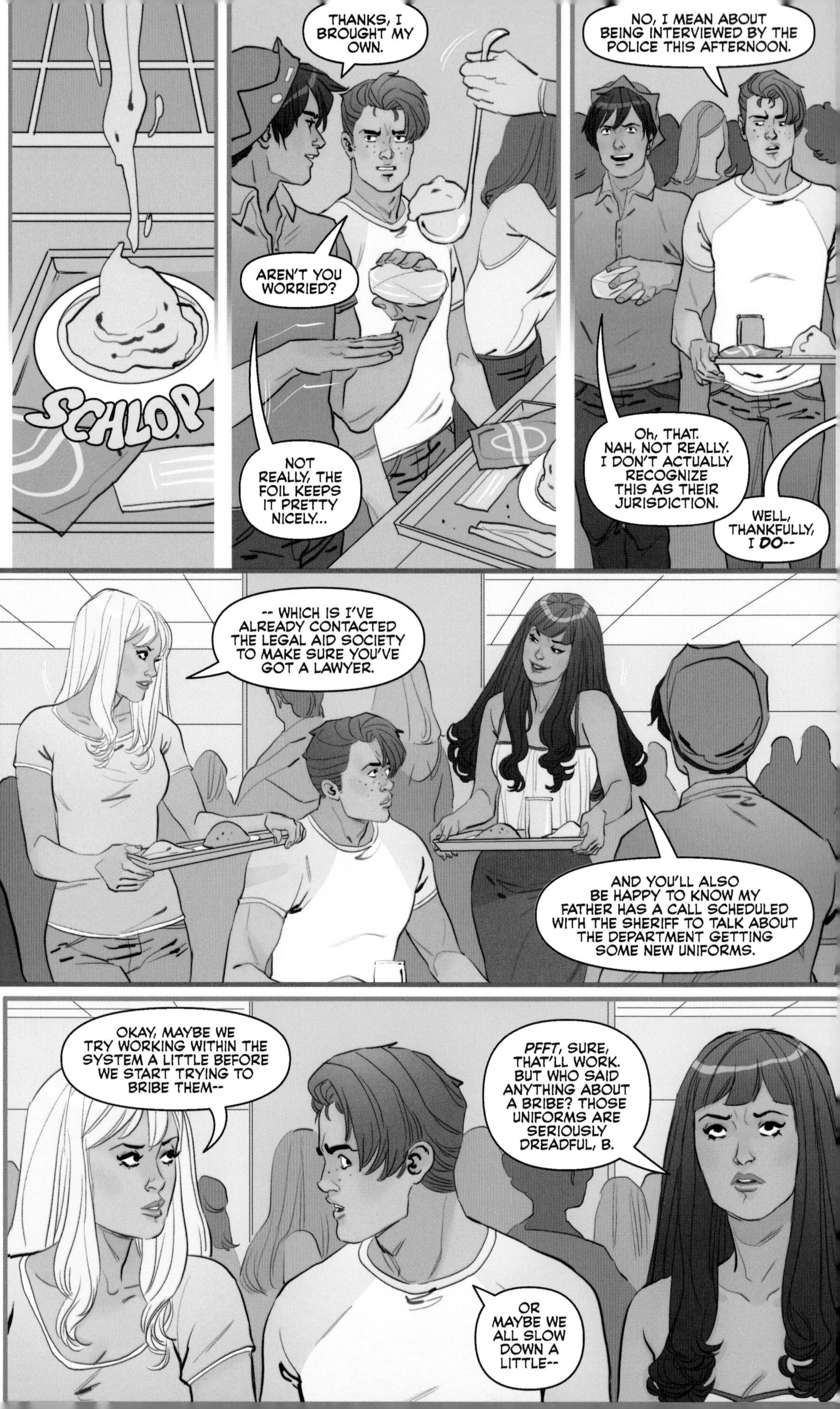
SCHLOP
THANKS, I BROUGHT MY OWN.
AREN'T YOU WORRIED?
NOT REALLY, THE FOIL KEEPS IT PRETTY NICELY...
NO, I MEAN ABOUT BEING INTERVIEWED BY THE POLICE THIS AFTERNOON.
Oh, THAT. NAH, NOT REALLY. I DON'T ACTUALLY RECOGNIZE THIS AS THEIR JURISDICTION.
WELL, THANKFULLY, I DO--
-- WHICH IS I'VE ALREADY CONTACTED THE LEGAL AID SOCIETY TO MAKE SURE YOU'VE GOT A LAWYER.
AND YOU'LL ALSO BE HAPPY TO KNOW MY FATHER HAS A CALL SCHEDULED WITH THE SHERIFF TO TALK ABOUT THE DEPARTMENT GETTING SOME NEW UNIFORMS.
OKAY, MAYBE WE TRY WORKING WITHIN THE SYSTEM A LITTLE BEFORE WE START TRYING TO BRIBE THEM--
PFFT, SURE, THAT'LL WORK. BUT WHO SAID ANYTHING ABOUT A BRIBE? THOSE UNIFORMS ARE SERIOUSLY DREADFUL, B.
OR MAYBE WE ALL SLOW DOWN A LITTLE--

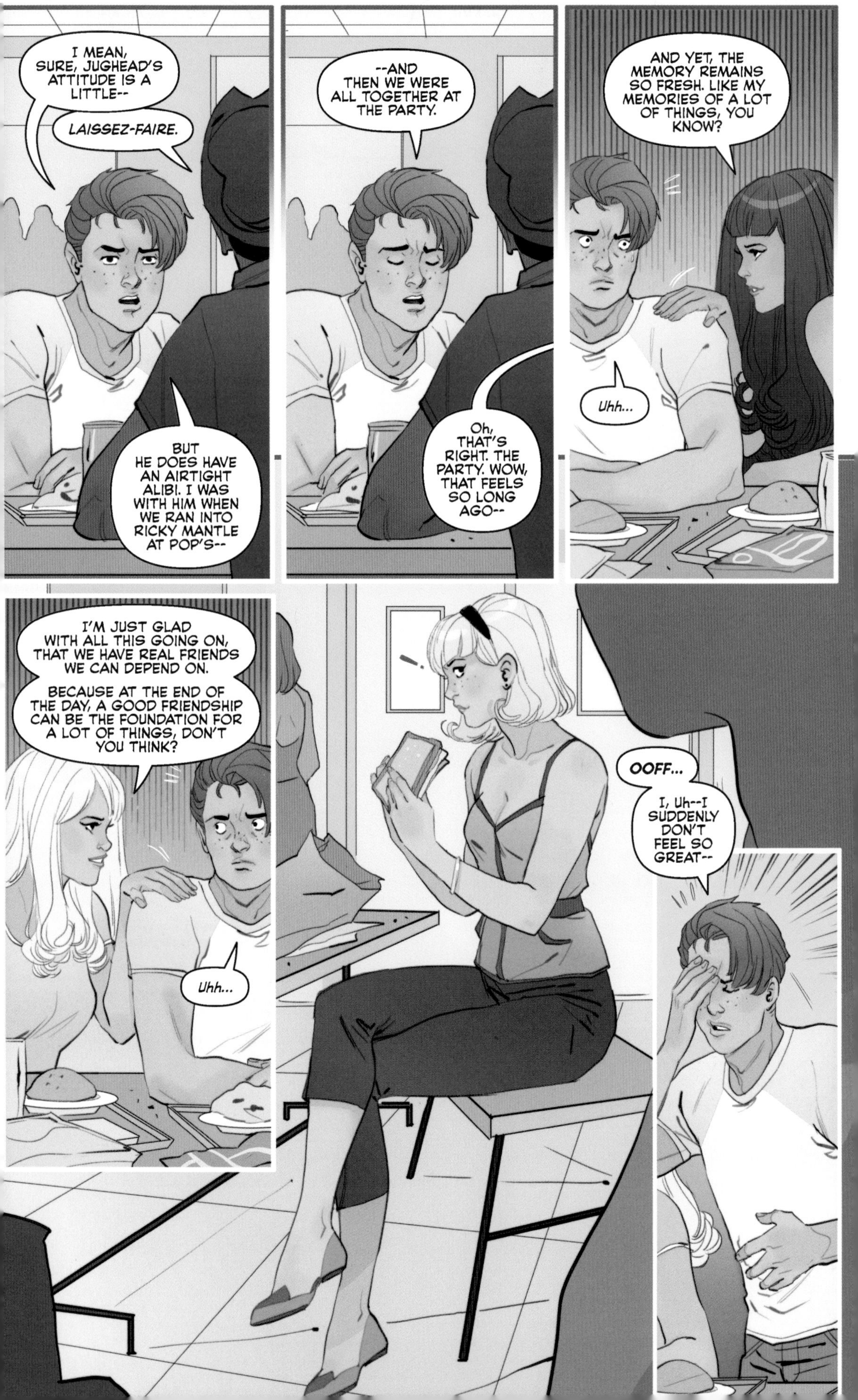
I MEAN, SURE, JUGHEAD'S ATTITUDE IS A LITTLE--
LAISSEZ-FAIRE.
BUT HE DOES HAVE AN AIRTIGHT ALIBI. I WAS WITH HIM WHEN WE RAN INTO RICKY MANTLE AT POP'S--
--AND THEN WE WERE ALL TOGETHER AT THE PARTY.
Oh, THAT'S RIGHT. THE PARTY. WOW, THAT FEELS SO LONG AGO--
AND YET, THE MEMORY REMAINS SO FRESH. LIKE MY MEMORIES OF A LOT OF THINGS, YOU KNOW?
Uhh...
I'M JUST GLAD WITH ALL THIS GOING ON, THAT WE HAVE REAL FRIENDS WE CAN DEPEND ON.
BECAUSE AT THE END OF THE DAY, A GOOD FRIENDSHIP CAN BE THE FOUNDATION FOR A LOT OF THINGS, DON'T YOU THINK?
Uhh...
OOFF...
I, Uh--I SUDDENLY DON'T FEEL SO GREAT--

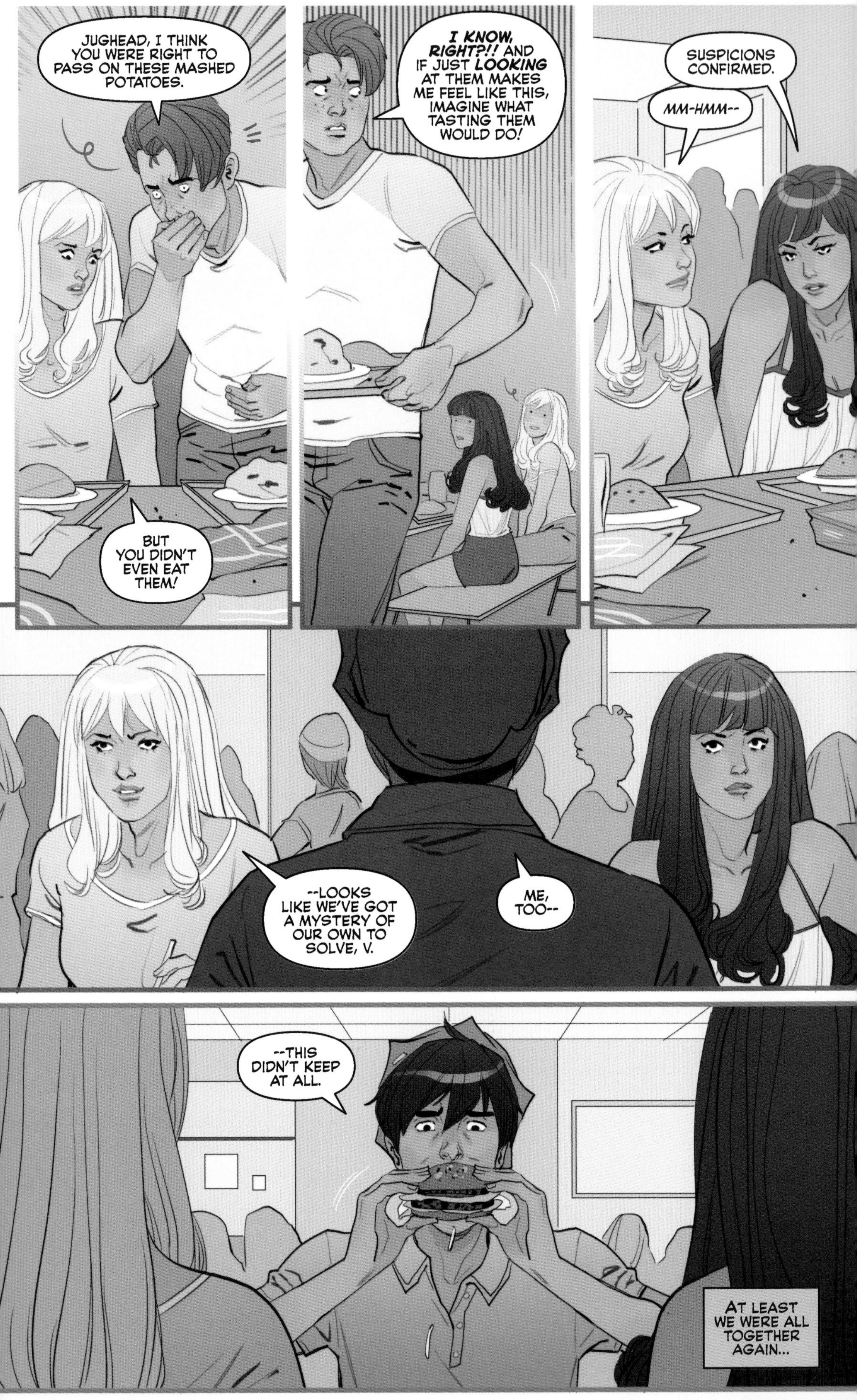
JUGHEAD, I THINK YOU WERE RIGHT TO PASS ON THESE MASHED POTATOES.
BUT YOU DIDN'T EVEN EAT THEM!
I KNOW, RIGHT?!! AND IF JUST LOOKING AT THEM MAKES ME FEEL LIKE THIS, IMAGINE WHAT TASTING THEM WOULD DO!
SUSPICIONS CONFIRMED.
MM-HMM--
--LOOKS LIKE WE'VE GOT A MYSTERY OF OUR OWN TO SOLVE, V.
ME, TOO--
--THIS DIDN'T KEEP AT ALL.
AT LEAST WE WERE ALL TOGETHER AGAIN...

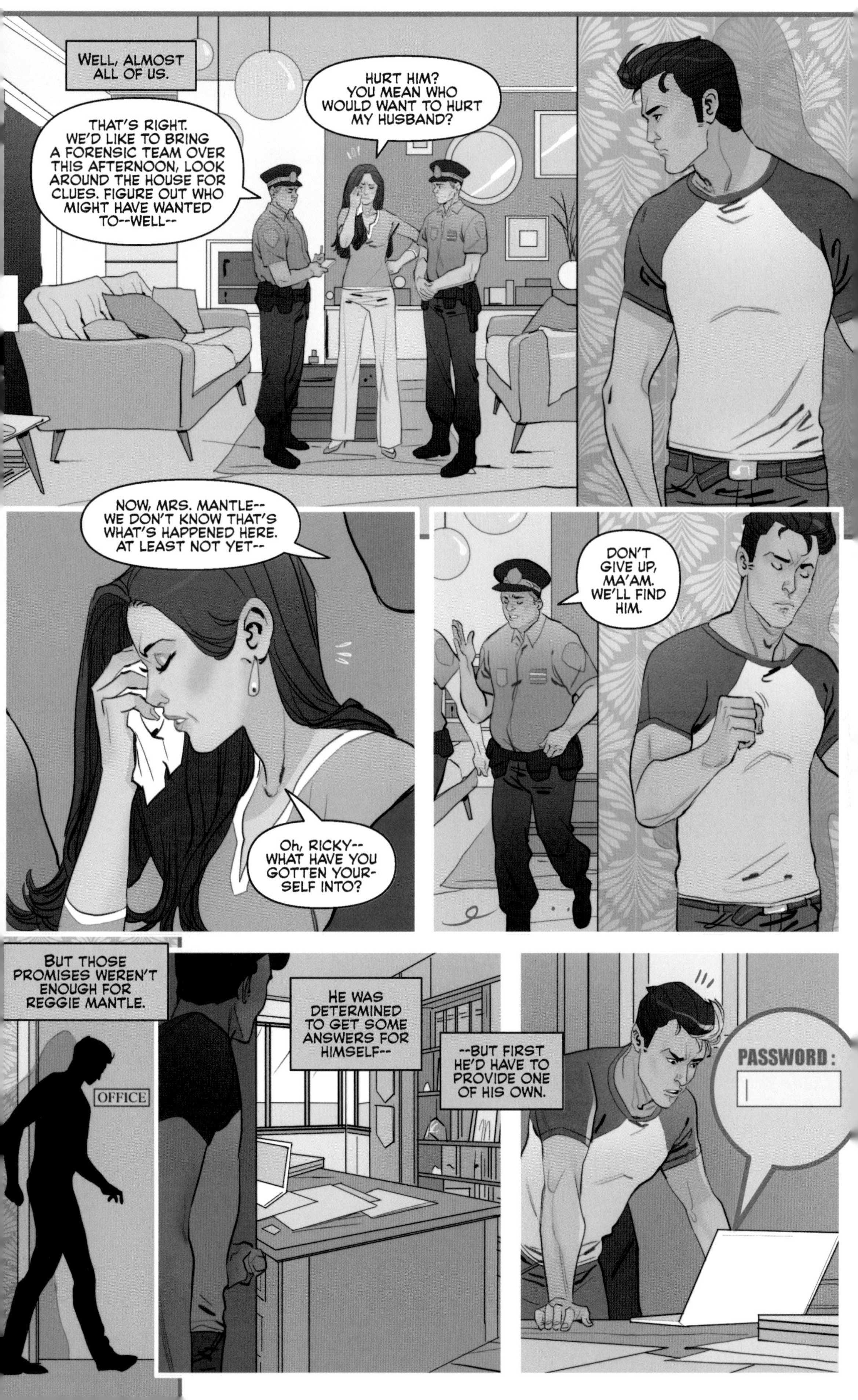
WELL, ALMOST ALL OF US.
THAT'S RIGHT. WE'D LIKE TO BRING A FORENSIC TEAM OVER THIS AFTERNOON, LOOK AROUND THE HOUSE FOR CLUES. FIGURE OUT WHO MIGHT HAVE WANTED TO--WELL--
HURT HIM? YOU MEAN WHO WOULD WANT TO HURT MY HUSBAND?
NOW, MRS. MANTLE-- WE DON'T KNOW THAT'S WHAT'S HAPPENED HERE. AT LEAST NOT YET--
Oh, RICKY-- WHAT HAVE YOU GOTTEN YOUR-SELF INTO?
DON'T GIVE UP, MA'AM. WE'LL FIND HIM.
BUT THOSE PROMISES WEREN'T ENOUGH FOR REGGIE MANTLE.
OFFICE
HE WAS DETERMINED TO GET SOME ANSWERS FOR HIMSELF--
--BUT FIRST HE'D HAVE TO PROVIDE ONE OF HIS OWN.
PASSWORD :

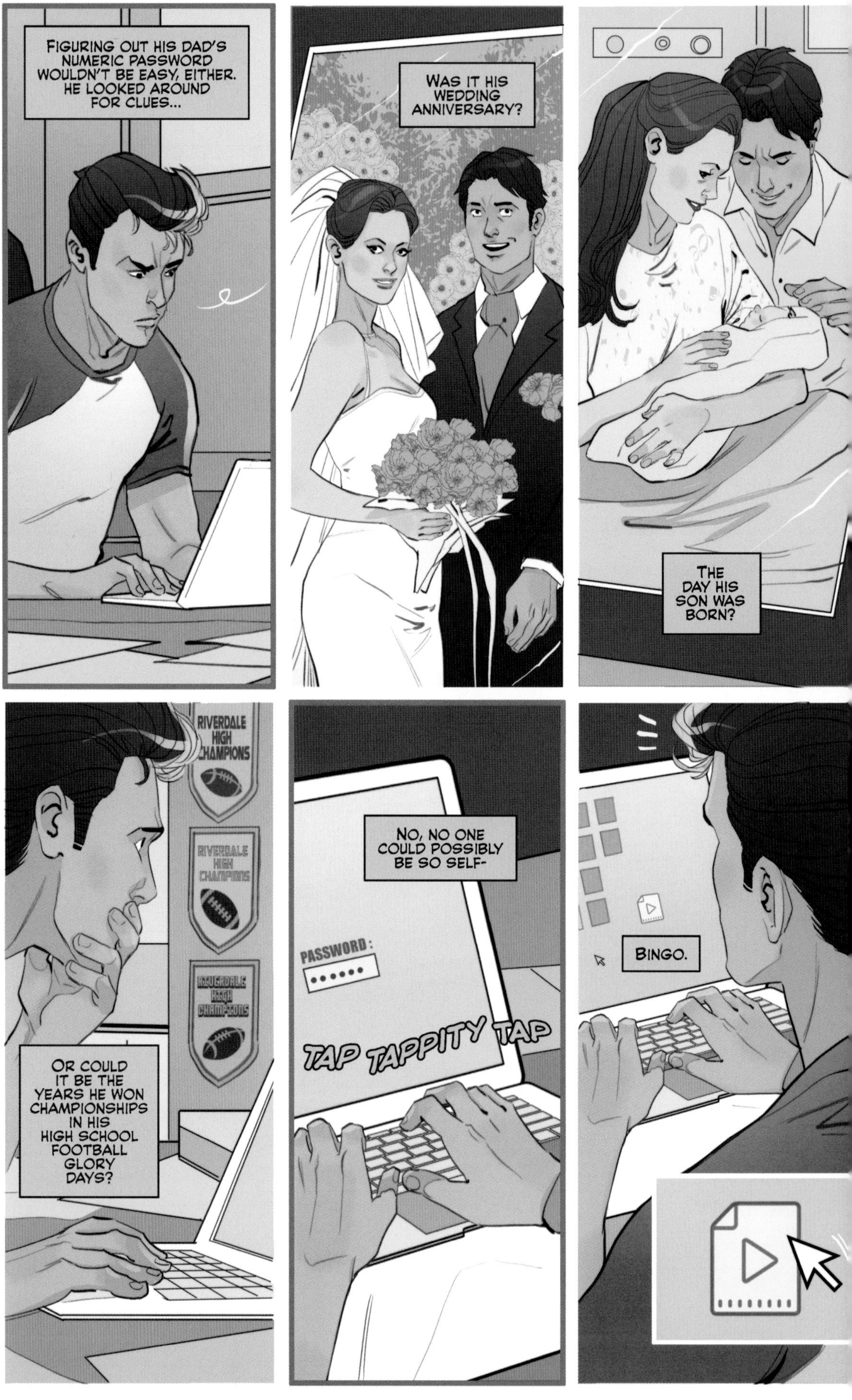
FIGURING OUT HIS DAD'S NUMERIC PASSWORD WOULDN'T BE EASY, EITHER. HE LOOKED AROUND FOR CLUES...
WAS IT HIS WEDDING ANNIVERSARY?
THE DAY HIS SON WAS BORN?
RIVERDALE HIGH CHAMPIONS
RIVERDALE HIGH CHAMPIONS
RIVERDALE HIGH CHAMPIONS
OR COULD IT BE THE YEARS HE WON CHAMPIONSHIPS IN HIS HIGH SCHOOL FOOTBALL GLORY DAYS?
NO, NO ONE COULD POSSIBLY BE SO SELF-
PASSWORD:
TAP TAPPITY TAP
BINGO.

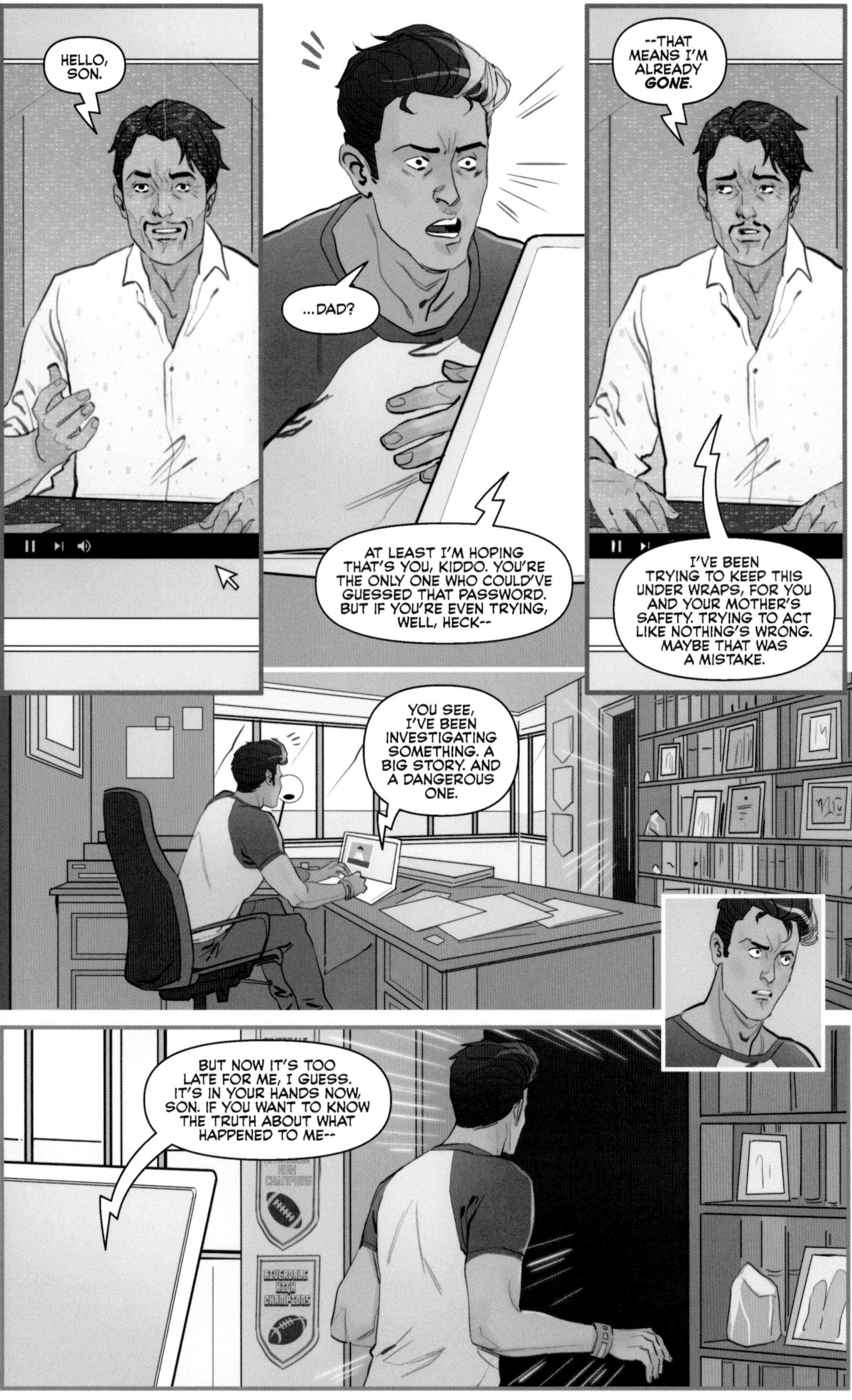
HELLO, SON.
...DAD?
AT LEAST I'M HOPING THAT'S YOU, KIDDO. YOU'RE THE ONLY ONE WHO COULD'VE GUESSED THAT PASSWORD. BUT IF YOU'RE EVEN TRYING, WELL, HECK--
--THAT MEANS I'M ALREADY GONE.
I'VE BEEN TRYING TO KEEP THIS UNDER WRAPS, FOR YOU AND YOUR MOTHER'S SAFETY. TRYING TO ACT LIKE NOTHING'S WRONG. MAYBE THAT WAS A MISTAKE.
YOU SEE, I'VE BEEN INVESTIGATING SOMETHING. A BIG STORY. AND A DANGEROUS ONE.
BUT NOW IT'S TOO LATE FOR ME, I GUESS. IT'S IN YOUR HANDS NOW, SON. IF YOU WANT TO KNOW THE TRUTH ABOUT WHAT HAPPENED TO ME--
RIVERDALE HIGH CHAMPIONS

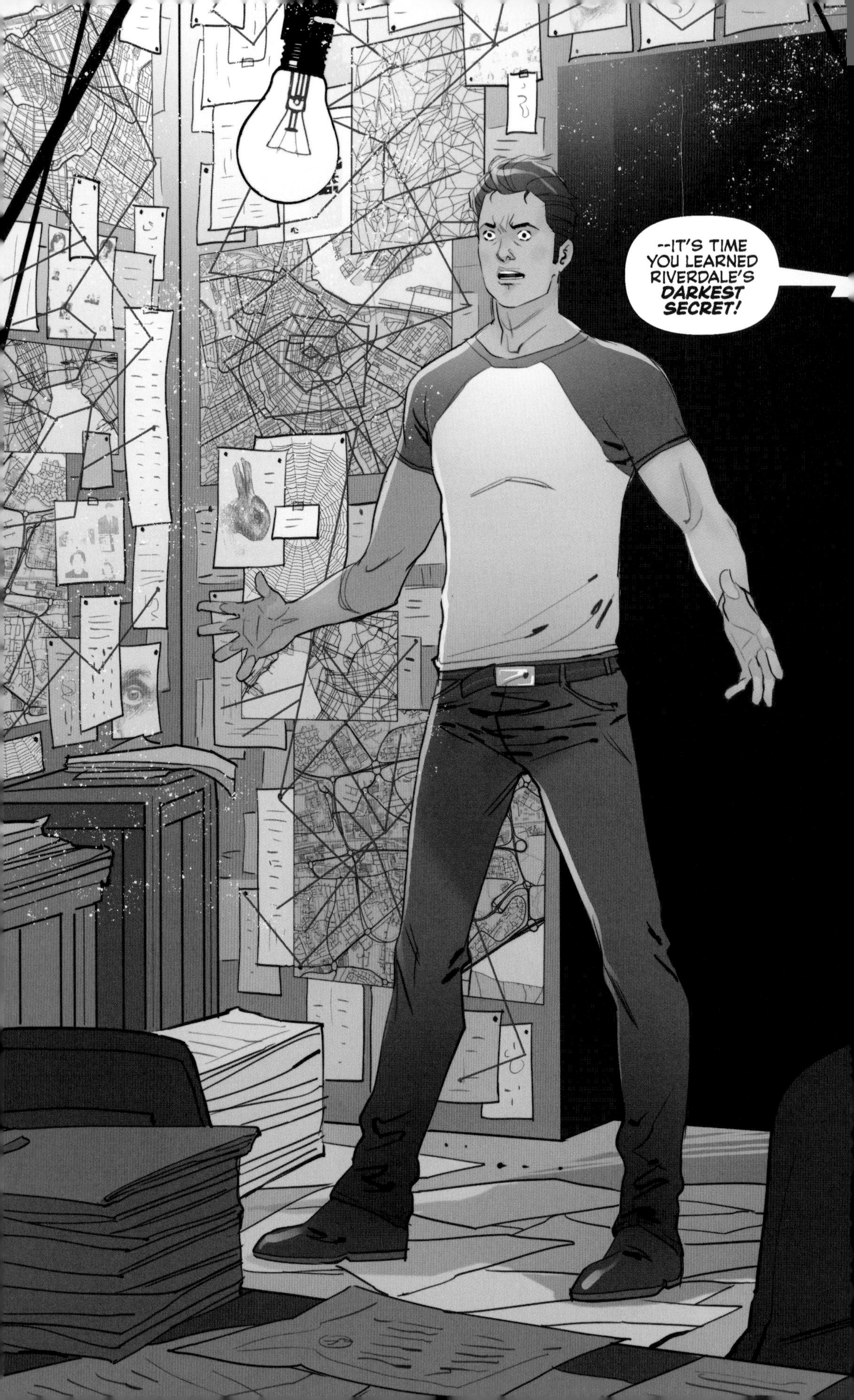
--IT'S TIME YOU LEARNED RIVERDALE'S ***DARKEST SECRET!***

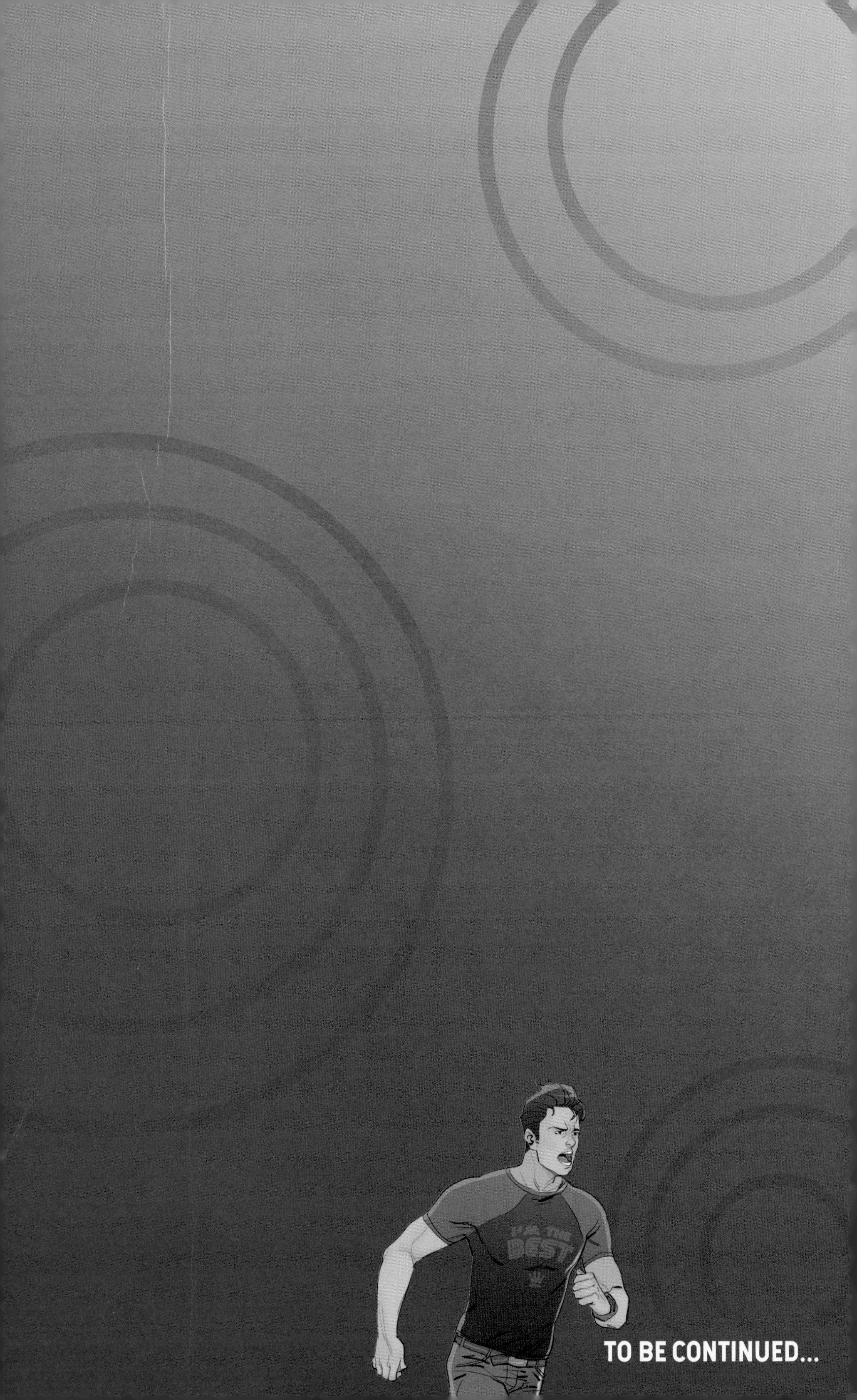
I'M THE BEST
TO BE CONTINUED...

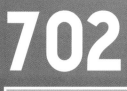

702

STORY BY
NICK SPENCER

ART BY
MARGUERITE SAUVAGE (1-4)

LETTERING BY
JACK MORELLI

ART BY
SANDY JARRELL (5-20)

COLORS BY
MATT HERMS (5-20)

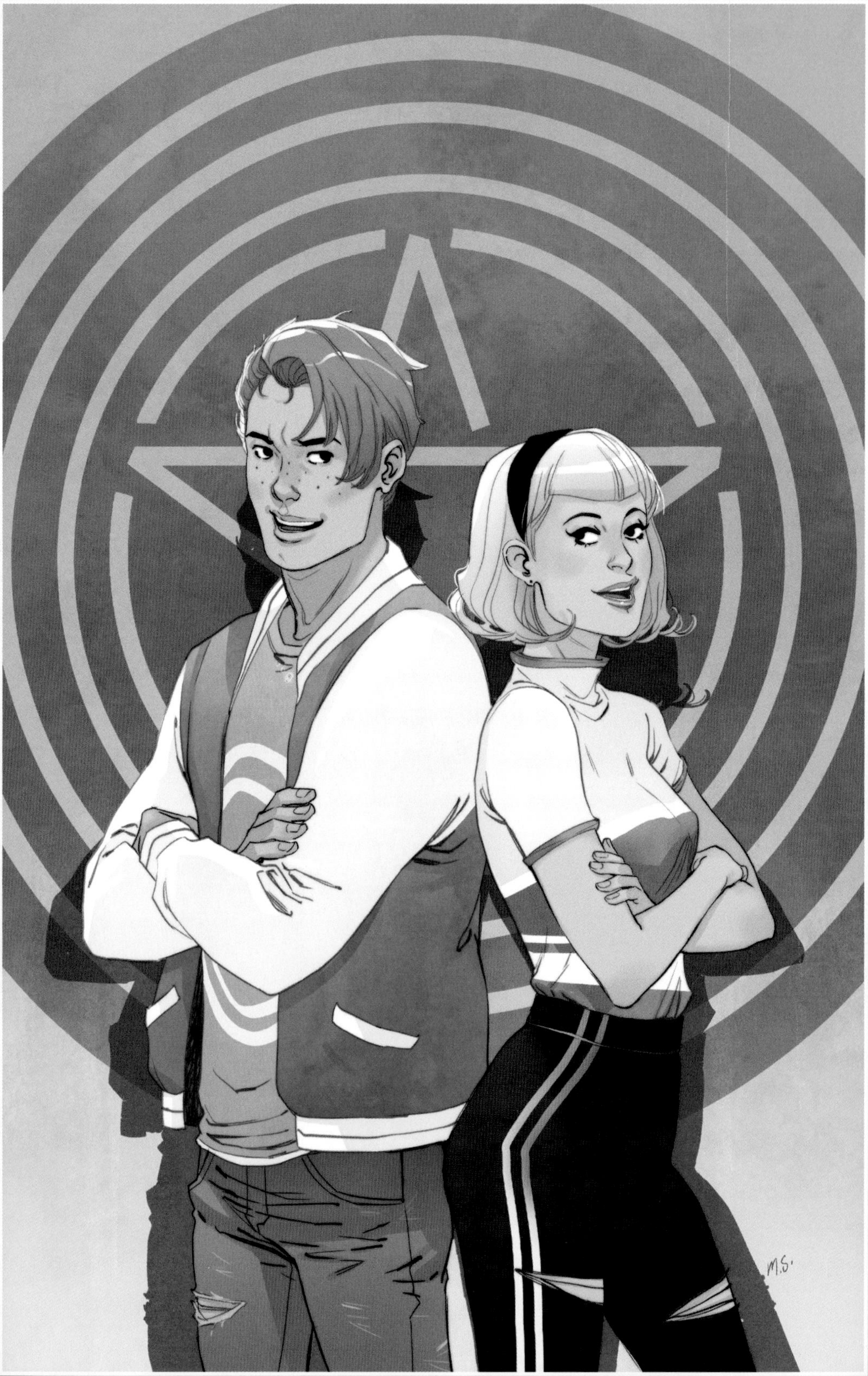
M.S.

COVER ART: MARGUERITE SAUVAGE

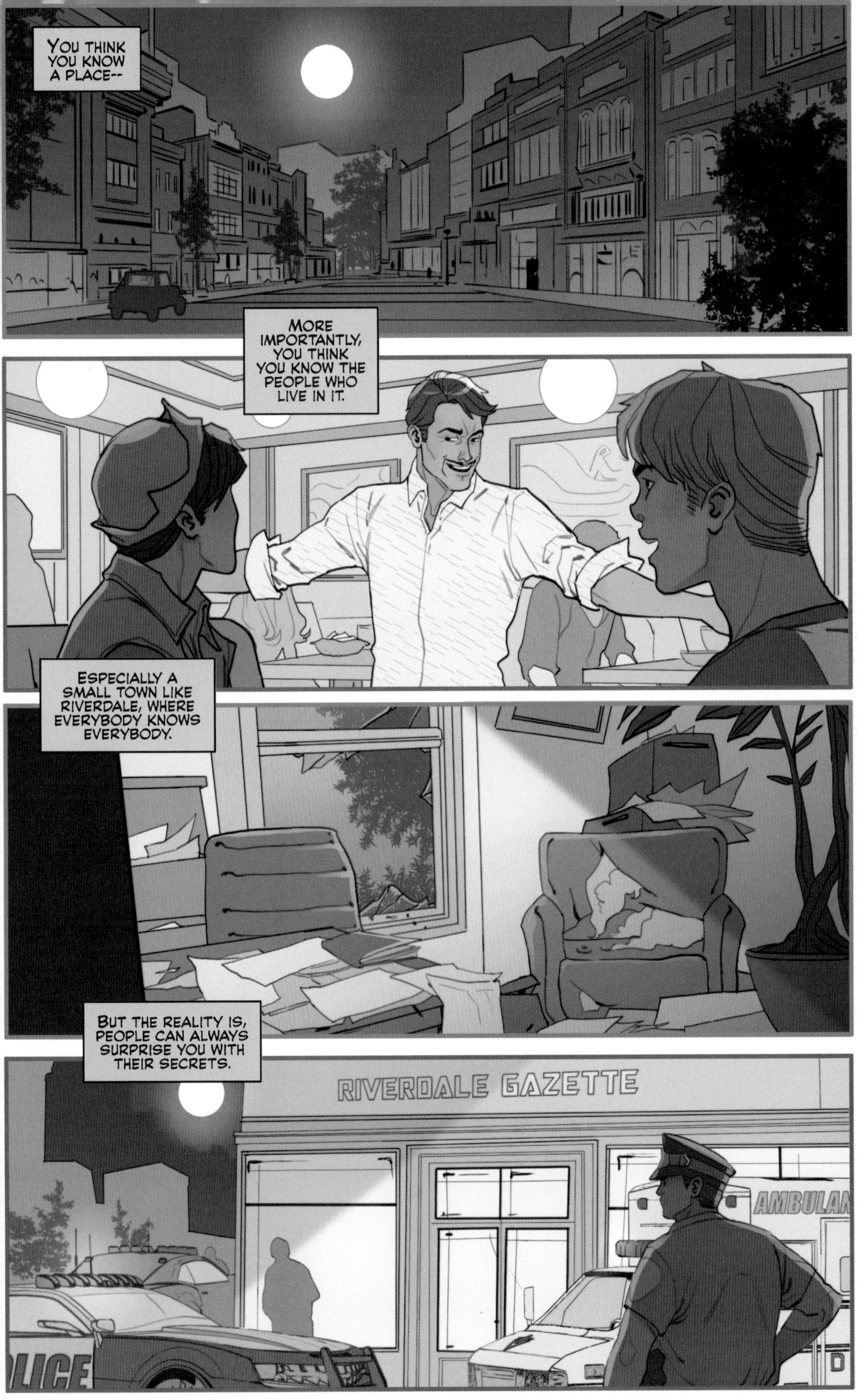
YOU THINK YOU KNOW A PLACE--
MORE IMPORTANTLY, YOU THINK YOU KNOW THE PEOPLE WHO LIVE IN IT.
ESPECIALLY A SMALL TOWN LIKE RIVERDALE, WHERE EVERYBODY KNOWS EVERYBODY.
BUT THE REALITY IS, PEOPLE CAN ALWAYS SURPRISE YOU WITH THEIR SECRETS.
RIVERDALE GAZETTE
AMBULAN
LICE

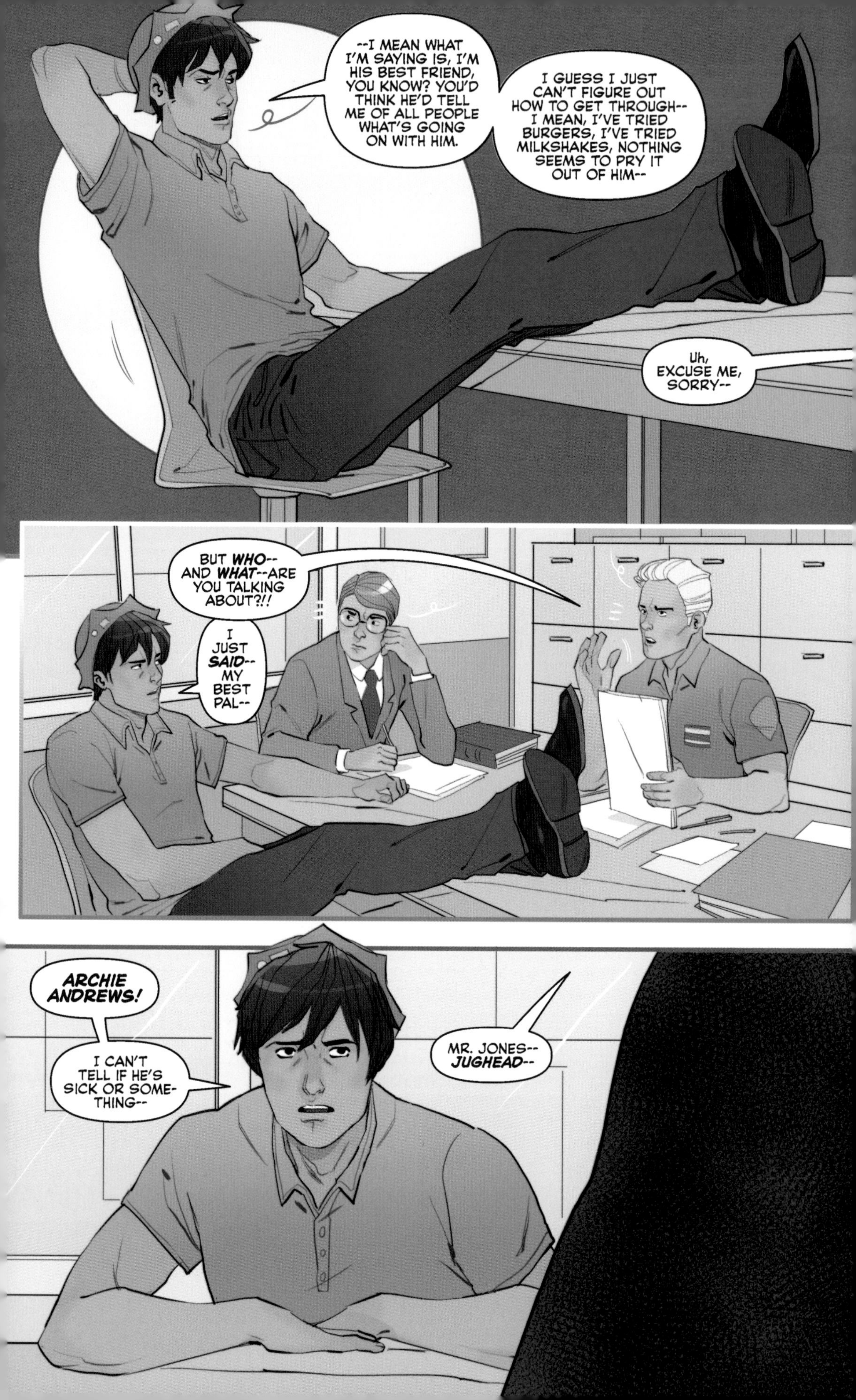
--I MEAN WHAT I'M SAYING IS, I'M HIS BEST FRIEND, YOU KNOW? YOU'D THINK HE'D TELL ME OF ALL PEOPLE WHAT'S GOING ON WITH HIM.
I GUESS I JUST CAN'T FIGURE OUT HOW TO GET THROUGH-- I MEAN, I'VE TRIED BURGERS, I'VE TRIED MILKSHAKES, NOTHING SEEMS TO PRY IT OUT OF HIM--
Uh, EXCUSE ME, SORRY--
BUT WHO-- AND WHAT--ARE YOU TALKING ABOUT?!!
I JUST SAID-- MY BEST PAL--
ARCHIE ANDREWS!
I CAN'T TELL IF HE'S SICK OR SOME-THING--
MR. JONES-- JUGHEAD--

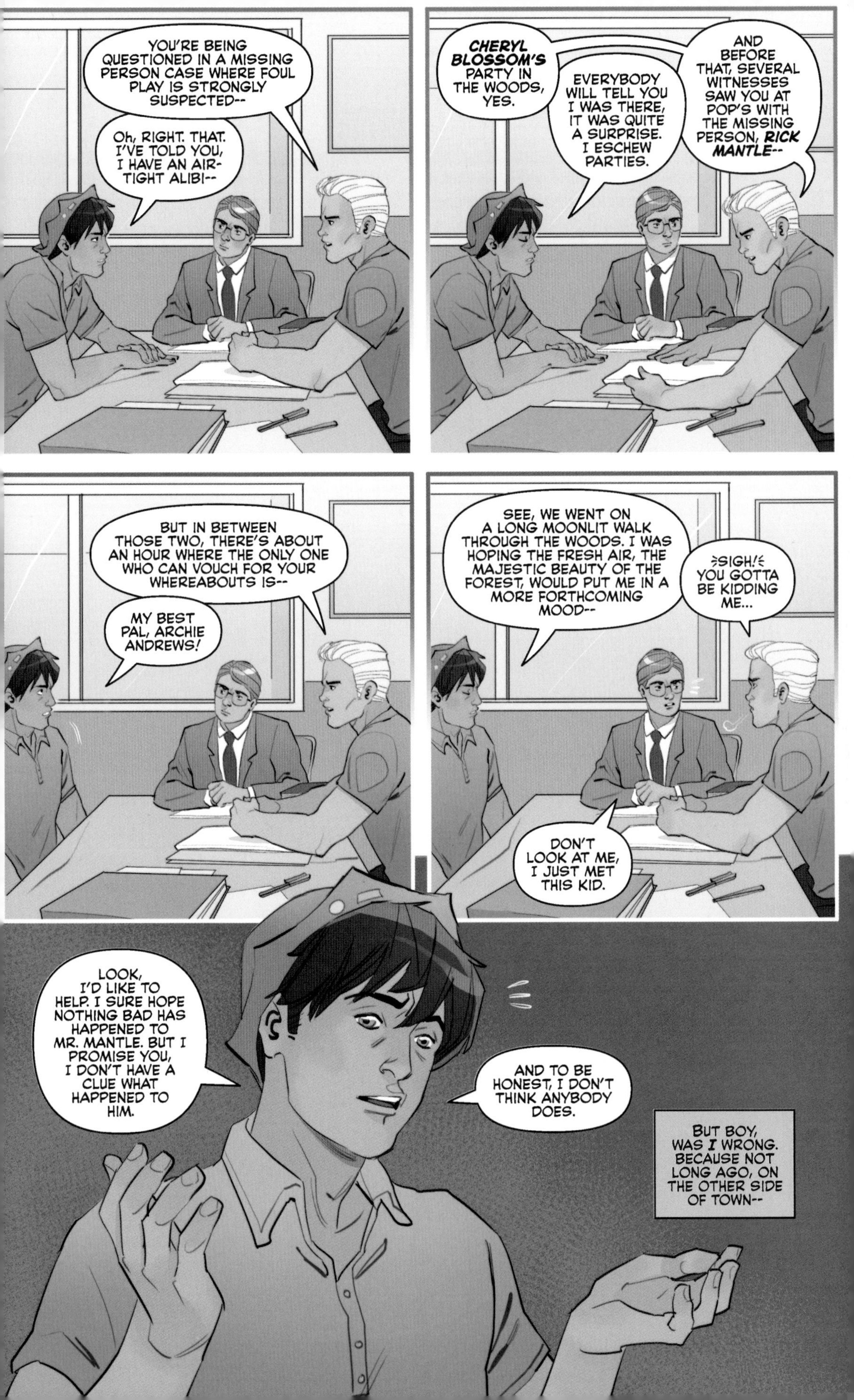
YOU'RE BEING QUESTIONED IN A MISSING PERSON CASE WHERE FOUL PLAY IS STRONGLY SUSPECTED--
Oh, RIGHT. THAT. I'VE TOLD YOU, I HAVE AN AIR-TIGHT ALIBI--
CHERYL BLOSSOM'S PARTY IN THE WOODS, YES.
EVERYBODY WILL TELL YOU I WAS THERE, IT WAS QUITE A SURPRISE. I ESCHEW PARTIES.
AND BEFORE THAT, SEVERAL WITNESSES SAW YOU AT POP'S WITH THE MISSING PERSON, RICK MANTLE--
BUT IN BETWEEN THOSE TWO, THERE'S ABOUT AN HOUR WHERE THE ONLY ONE WHO CAN VOUCH FOR YOUR WHEREABOUTS IS--
MY BEST PAL, ARCHIE ANDREWS!
SEE, WE WENT ON A LONG MOONLIT WALK THROUGH THE WOODS. I WAS HOPING THE FRESH AIR, THE MAJESTIC BEAUTY OF THE FOREST, WOULD PUT ME IN A MORE FORTHCOMING MOOD--
SIGH! YOU GOTTA BE KIDDING ME...
DON'T LOOK AT ME, I JUST MET THIS KID.
LOOK, I'D LIKE TO HELP. I SURE HOPE NOTHING BAD HAS HAPPENED TO MR. MANTLE. BUT I PROMISE YOU, I DON'T HAVE A CLUE WHAT HAPPENED TO HIM.
AND TO BE HONEST, I DON'T THINK ANYBODY DOES.
BUT BOY, WAS I WRONG. BECAUSE NOT LONG AGO, ON THE OTHER SIDE OF TOWN--

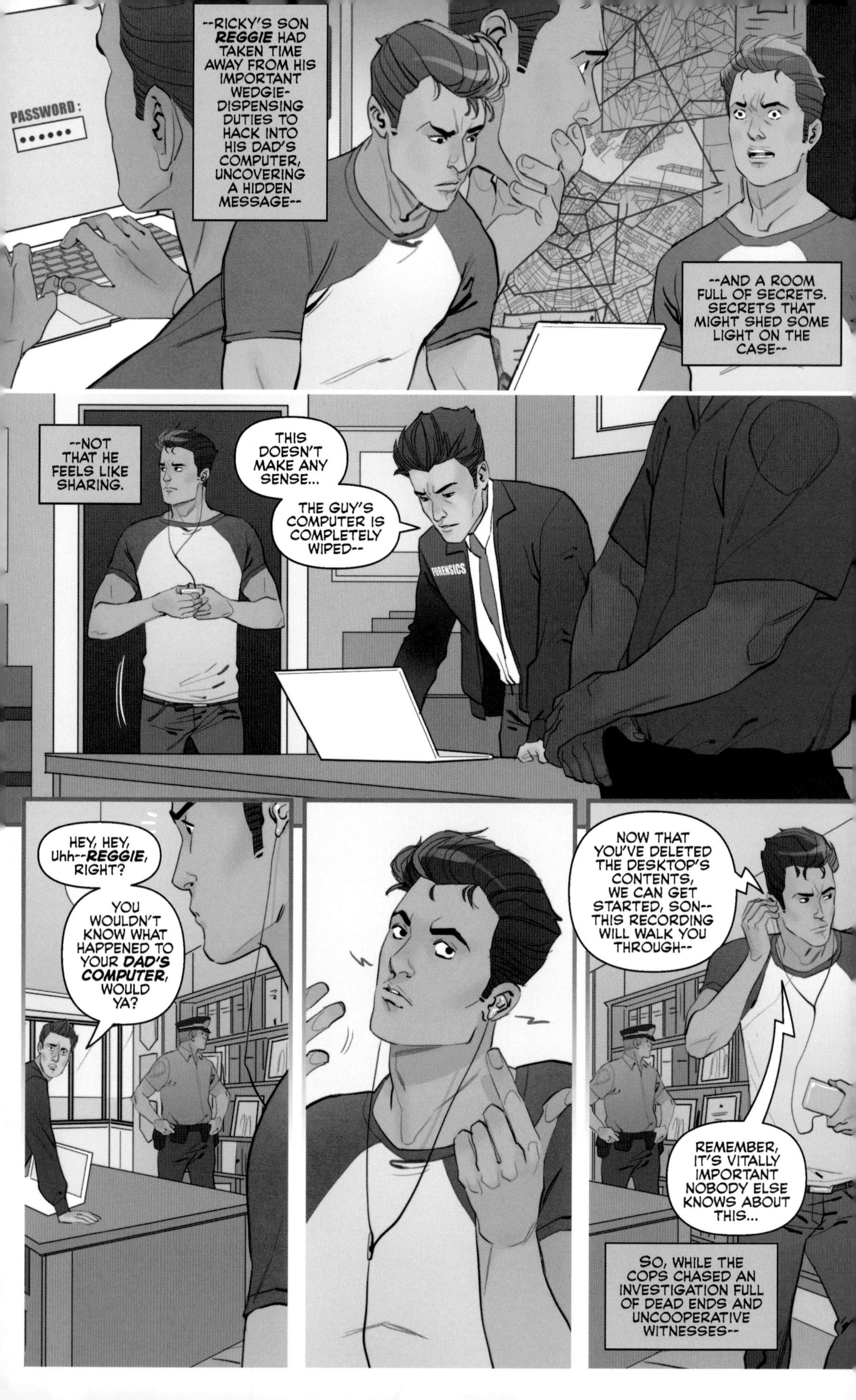

PASSWORD :
--RICKY'S SON REGGIE HAD TAKEN TIME AWAY FROM HIS IMPORTANT WEDGIE-DISPENSING DUTIES TO HACK INTO HIS DAD'S COMPUTER, UNCOVERING A HIDDEN MESSAGE--
--AND A ROOM FULL OF SECRETS. SECRETS THAT MIGHT SHED SOME LIGHT ON THE CASE--
--NOT THAT HE FEELS LIKE SHARING.
THIS DOESN'T MAKE ANY SENSE...
THE GUY'S COMPUTER IS COMPLETELY WIPED--
FORENSICS
HEY, HEY, Uhh--REGGIE, RIGHT?
YOU WOULDN'T KNOW WHAT HAPPENED TO YOUR DAD'S COMPUTER, WOULD YA?
NOW THAT YOU'VE DELETED THE DESKTOP'S CONTENTS, WE CAN GET STARTED, SON-- THIS RECORDING WILL WALK YOU THROUGH--
REMEMBER, IT'S VITALLY IMPORTANT NOBODY ELSE KNOWS ABOUT THIS...
SO, WHILE THE COPS CHASED AN INVESTIGATION FULL OF DEAD ENDS AND UNCOOPERATIVE WITNESSES--

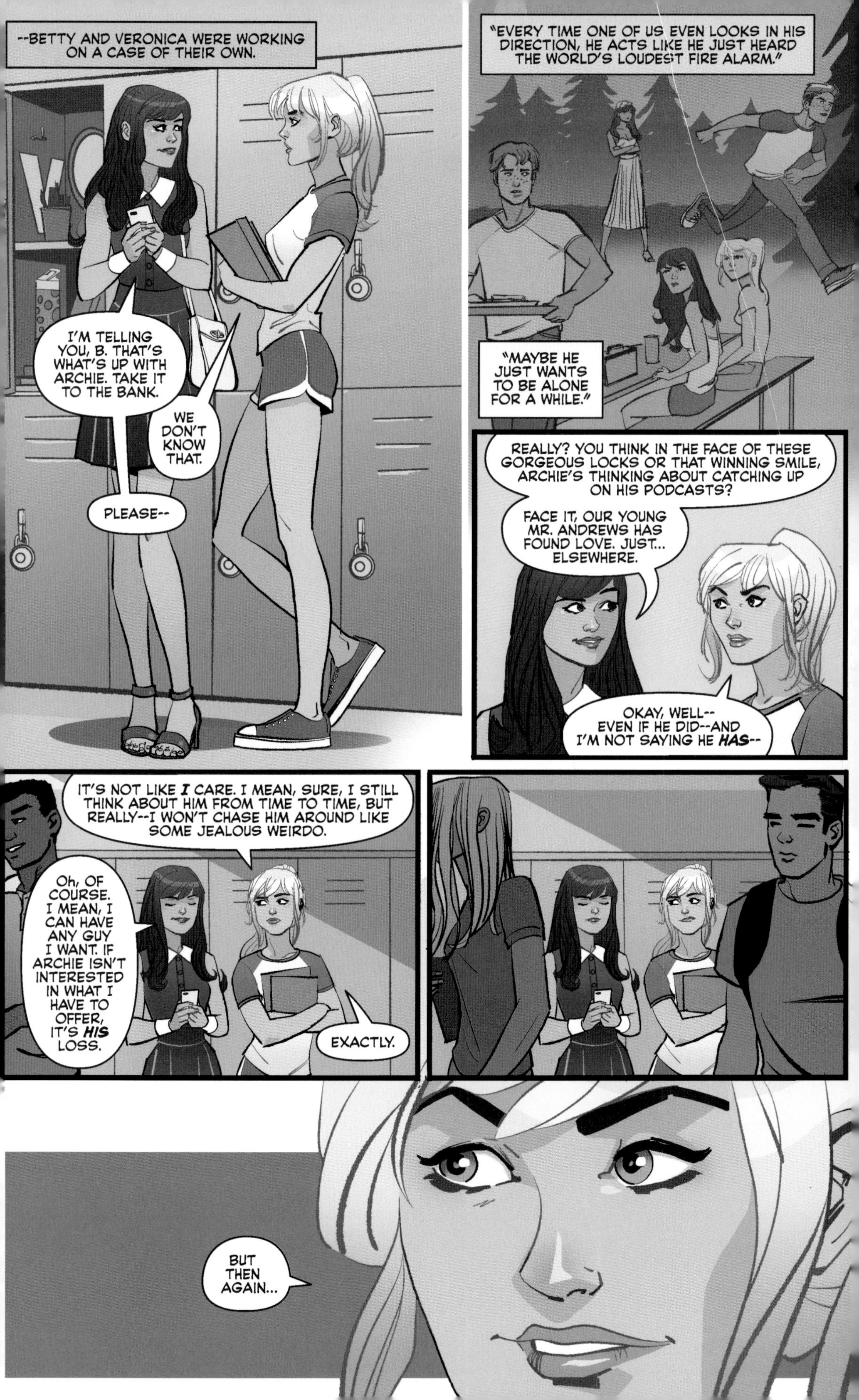
--BETTY AND VERONICA WERE WORKING ON A CASE OF THEIR OWN.
I'M TELLING YOU, B. THAT'S WHAT'S UP WITH ARCHIE. TAKE IT TO THE BANK.
WE DON'T KNOW THAT.
PLEASE--
"EVERY TIME ONE OF US EVEN LOOKS IN HIS DIRECTION, HE ACTS LIKE HE JUST HEARD THE WORLD'S LOUDEST FIRE ALARM."
"MAYBE HE JUST WANTS TO BE ALONE FOR A WHILE."
REALLY? YOU THINK IN THE FACE OF THESE GORGEOUS LOCKS OR THAT WINNING SMILE, ARCHIE'S THINKING ABOUT CATCHING UP ON HIS PODCASTS?
FACE IT, OUR YOUNG MR. ANDREWS HAS FOUND LOVE. JUST... ELSEWHERE.
OKAY, WELL-- EVEN IF HE DID--AND I'M NOT SAYING HE ***HAS***--
IT'S NOT LIKE ***I*** CARE. I MEAN, SURE, I STILL THINK ABOUT HIM FROM TIME TO TIME, BUT REALLY--I WON'T CHASE HIM AROUND LIKE SOME JEALOUS WEIRDO.
Oh, OF COURSE. I MEAN, I CAN HAVE ANY GUY I WANT. IF ARCHIE ISN'T INTERESTED IN WHAT I HAVE TO OFFER, IT'S ***HIS*** LOSS.
EXACTLY.
BUT THEN AGAIN...

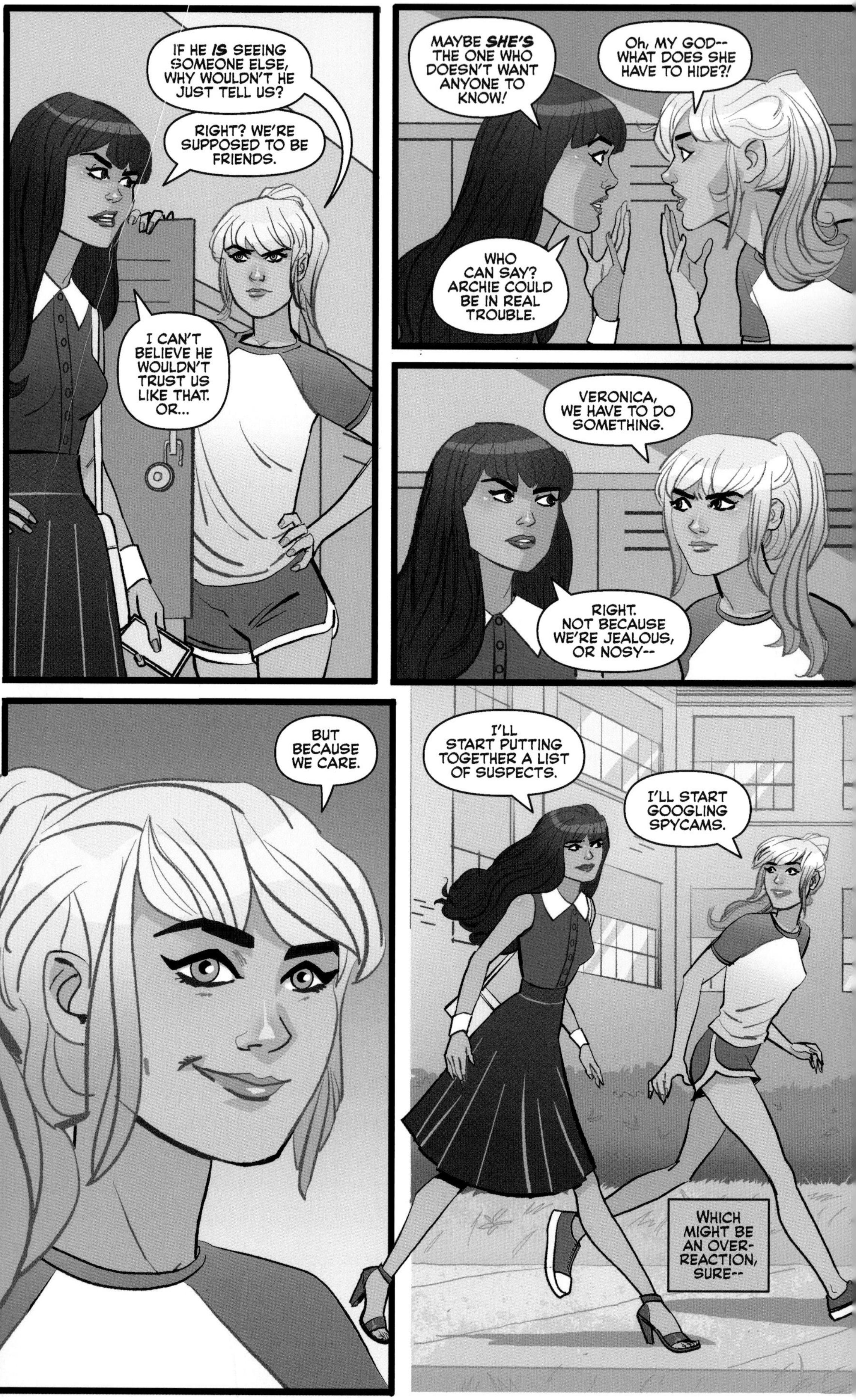
IF HE *IS* SEEING SOMEONE ELSE, WHY WOULDN'T HE JUST TELL US?
RIGHT? WE'RE SUPPOSED TO BE FRIENDS.
I CAN'T BELIEVE HE WOULDN'T TRUST US LIKE THAT. OR...
MAYBE *SHE'S* THE ONE WHO DOESN'T WANT ANYONE TO KNOW!
Oh, MY GOD-- WHAT DOES SHE HAVE TO HIDE?!
WHO CAN SAY? ARCHIE COULD BE IN REAL TROUBLE.
VERONICA, WE HAVE TO DO SOMETHING.
RIGHT. NOT BECAUSE WE'RE JEALOUS, OR NOSY--
BUT BECAUSE WE CARE.
I'LL START PUTTING TOGETHER A LIST OF SUSPECTS.
I'LL START GOOGLING SPYCAMS.
WHICH MIGHT BE AN OVER-REACTION, SURE--

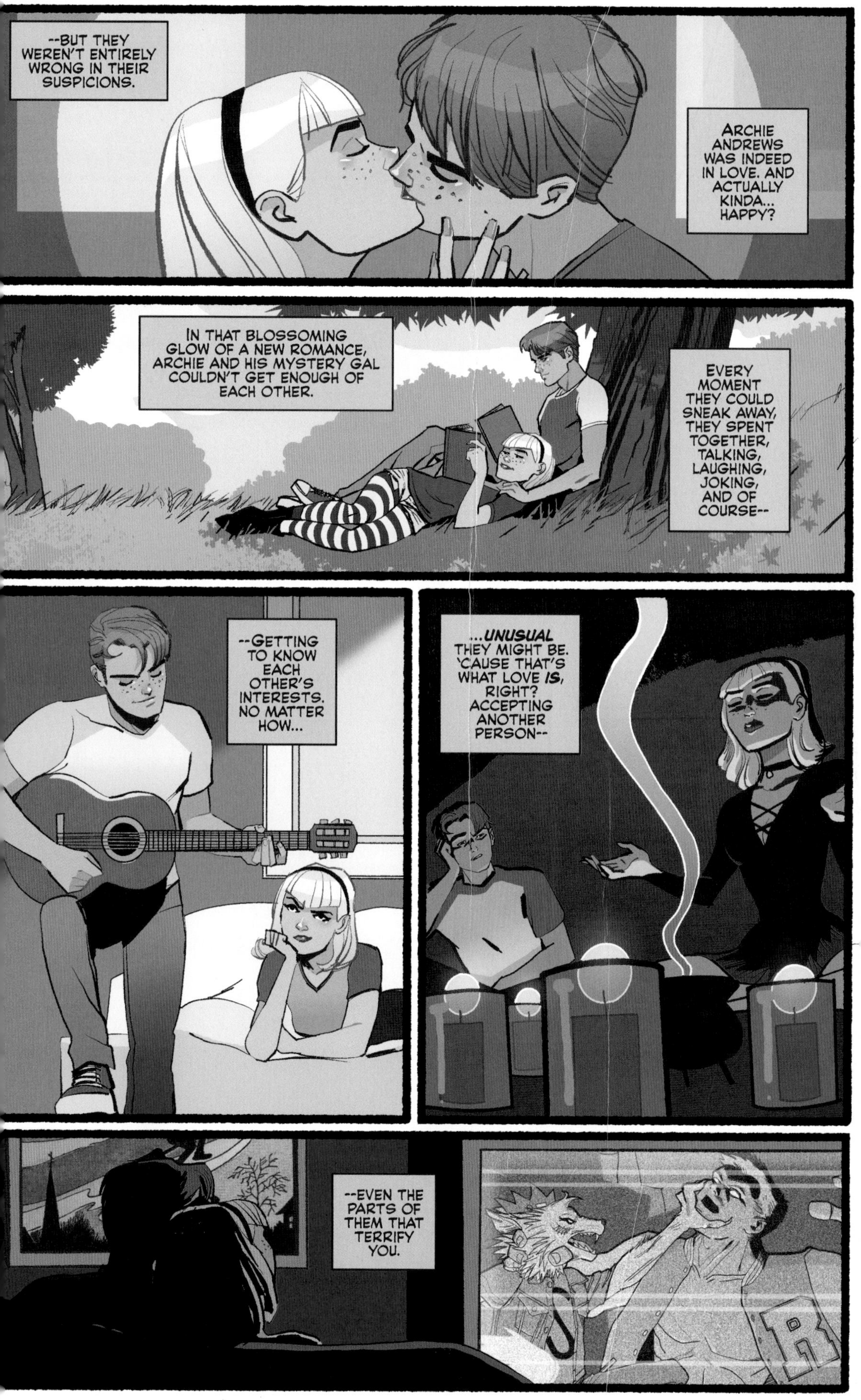
--BUT THEY WEREN'T ENTIRELY WRONG IN THEIR SUSPICIONS.
ARCHIE ANDREWS WAS INDEED IN LOVE. AND ACTUALLY KINDA... HAPPY?
IN THAT BLOSSOMING GLOW OF A NEW ROMANCE, ARCHIE AND HIS MYSTERY GAL COULDN'T GET ENOUGH OF EACH OTHER.
EVERY MOMENT THEY COULD SNEAK AWAY, THEY SPENT TOGETHER, TALKING, LAUGHING, JOKING, AND OF COURSE--
--GETTING TO KNOW EACH OTHER'S INTERESTS. NO MATTER HOW...
...UNUSUAL THEY MIGHT BE. 'CAUSE THAT'S WHAT LOVE IS, RIGHT? ACCEPTING ANOTHER PERSON--
--EVEN THE PARTS OF THEM THAT TERRIFY YOU.

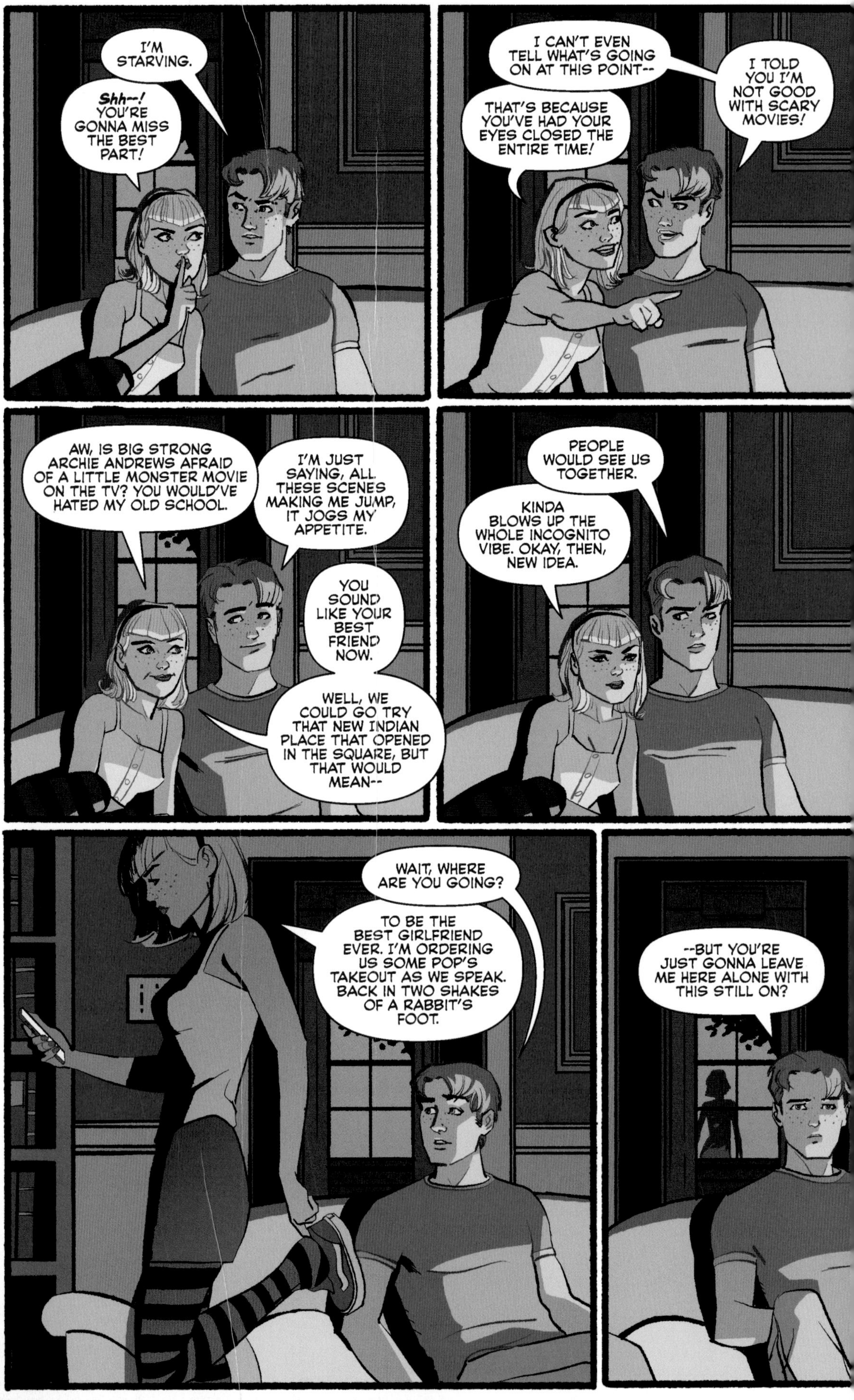
I'M STARVING.
Shh--! YOU'RE GONNA MISS THE BEST PART!
I CAN'T EVEN TELL WHAT'S GOING ON AT THIS POINT--
THAT'S BECAUSE YOU'VE HAD YOUR EYES CLOSED THE ENTIRE TIME!
I TOLD YOU I'M NOT GOOD WITH SCARY MOVIES!
AW, IS BIG STRONG ARCHIE ANDREWS AFRAID OF A LITTLE MONSTER MOVIE ON THE TV? YOU WOULD'VE HATED MY OLD SCHOOL.
I'M JUST SAYING, ALL THESE SCENES MAKING ME JUMP, IT JOGS MY APPETITE.
YOU SOUND LIKE YOUR BEST FRIEND NOW.
WELL, WE COULD GO TRY THAT NEW INDIAN PLACE THAT OPENED IN THE SQUARE, BUT THAT WOULD MEAN--
PEOPLE WOULD SEE US TOGETHER.
KINDA BLOWS UP THE WHOLE INCOGNITO VIBE. OKAY, THEN, NEW IDEA.
WAIT, WHERE ARE YOU GOING?
TO BE THE BEST GIRLFRIEND EVER. I'M ORDERING US SOME POP'S TAKEOUT AS WE SPEAK. BACK IN TWO SHAKES OF A RABBIT'S FOOT.
--BUT YOU'RE JUST GONNA LEAVE ME HERE ALONE WITH THIS STILL ON?

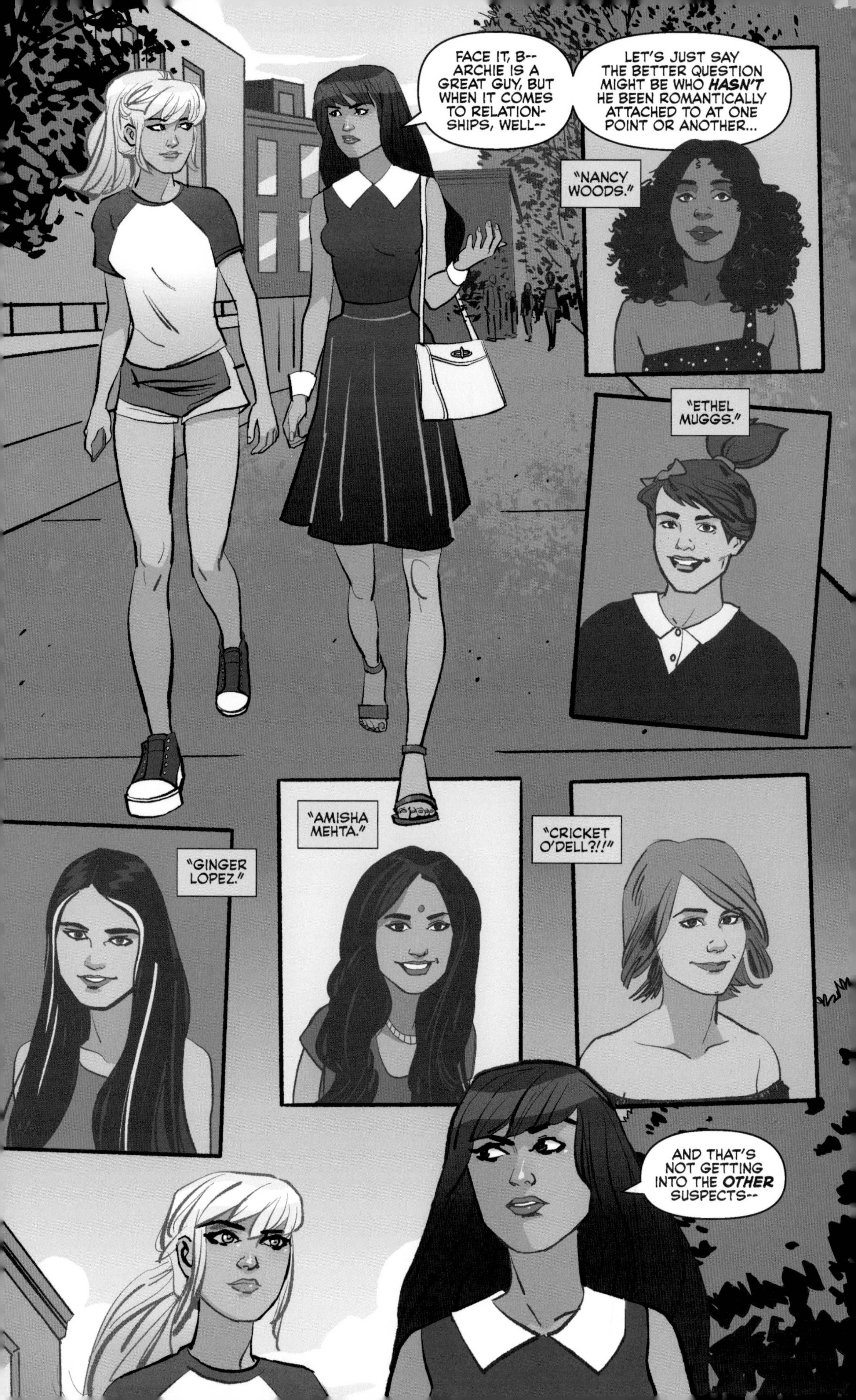

FACE IT, B-- ARCHIE IS A GREAT GUY, BUT WHEN IT COMES TO RELATION-SHIPS, WELL--
LET'S JUST SAY THE BETTER QUESTION MIGHT BE WHO HASN'T HE BEEN ROMANTICALLY ATTACHED TO AT ONE POINT OR ANOTHER...
"NANCY WOODS."
"ETHEL MUGGS."
"GINGER LOPEZ."
"AMISHA MEHTA."
"CRICKET O'DELL?!"
AND THAT'S NOT GETTING INTO THE OTHER SUSPECTS--

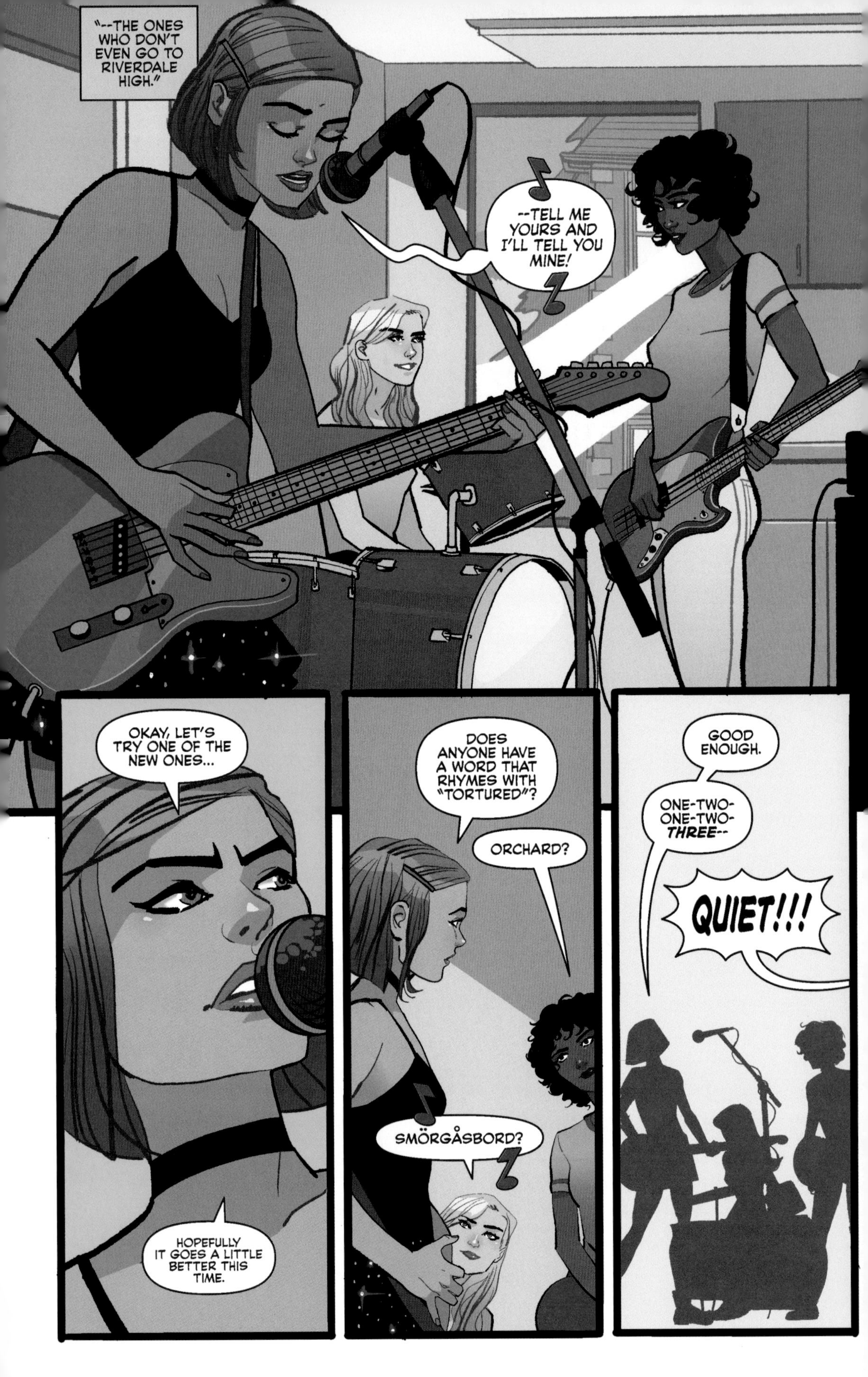
"--THE ONES WHO DON'T EVEN GO TO RIVERDALE HIGH."
--TELL ME YOURS AND I'LL TELL YOU MINE!
OKAY, LET'S TRY ONE OF THE NEW ONES...
HOPEFULLY IT GOES A LITTLE BETTER THIS TIME.
DOES ANYONE HAVE A WORD THAT RHYMES WITH "TORTURED"?
ORCHARD?
SMÖRGÅSBORD?
GOOD ENOUGH.
ONE-TWO-ONE-TWO-*THREE*--
QUIET!!!

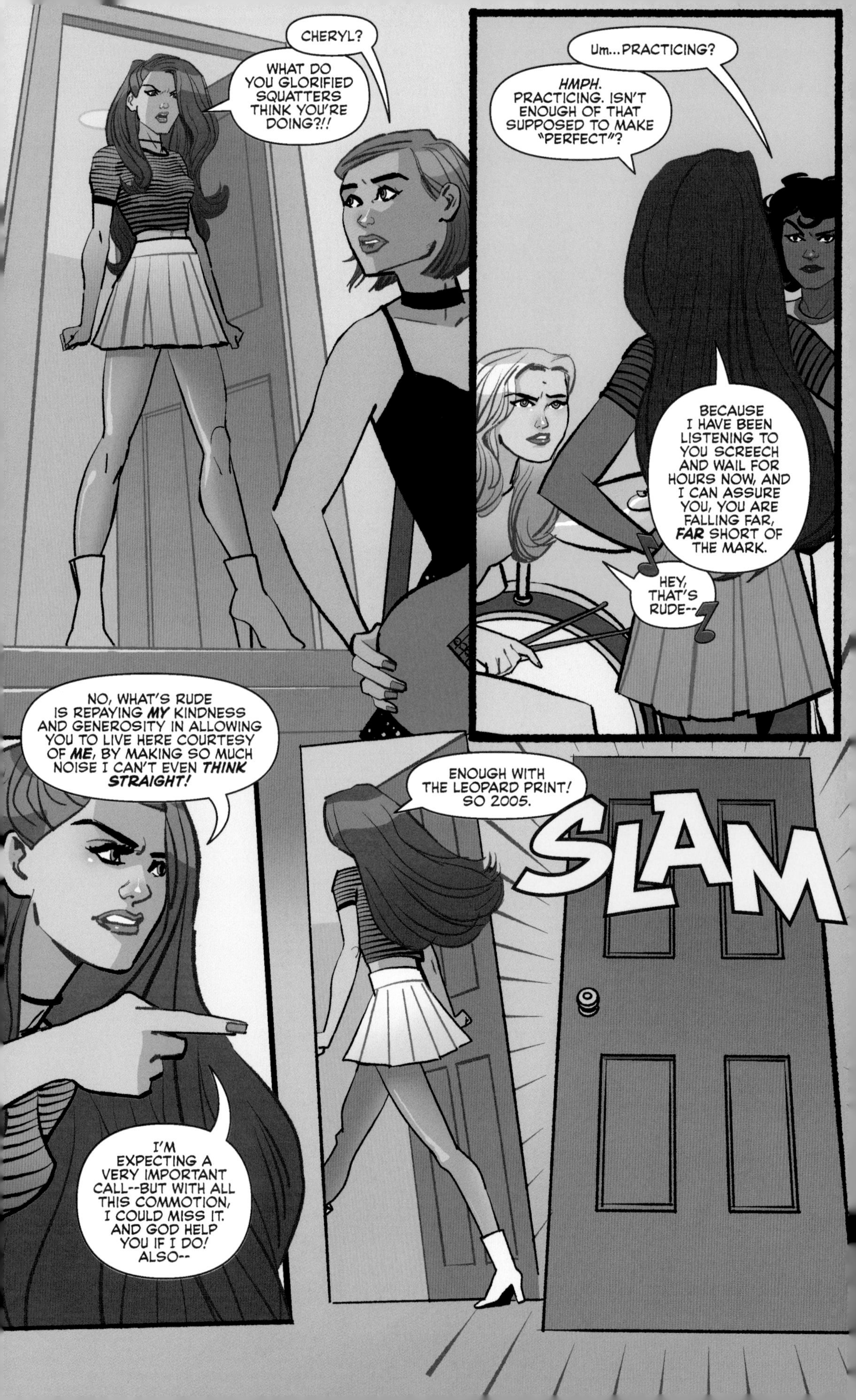
CHERYL?
WHAT DO YOU GLORIFIED SQUATTERS THINK YOU'RE DOING?!!
Um...PRACTICING?
HMPH. PRACTICING. ISN'T ENOUGH OF THAT SUPPOSED TO MAKE "PERFECT"?
BECAUSE I HAVE BEEN LISTENING TO YOU SCREECH AND WAIL FOR HOURS NOW, AND I CAN ASSURE YOU, YOU ARE FALLING FAR, **FAR** SHORT OF THE MARK.
HEY, THAT'S RUDE--
NO, WHAT'S RUDE IS REPAYING **MY** KINDNESS AND GENEROSITY IN ALLOWING YOU TO LIVE HERE COURTESY OF **ME**, BY MAKING SO MUCH NOISE I CAN'T EVEN **THINK STRAIGHT!**
I'M EXPECTING A VERY IMPORTANT CALL--BUT WITH ALL THIS COMMOTION, I COULD MISS IT. AND GOD HELP YOU IF I DO! ALSO--
ENOUGH WITH THE LEOPARD PRINT! SO 2005.
SLAM

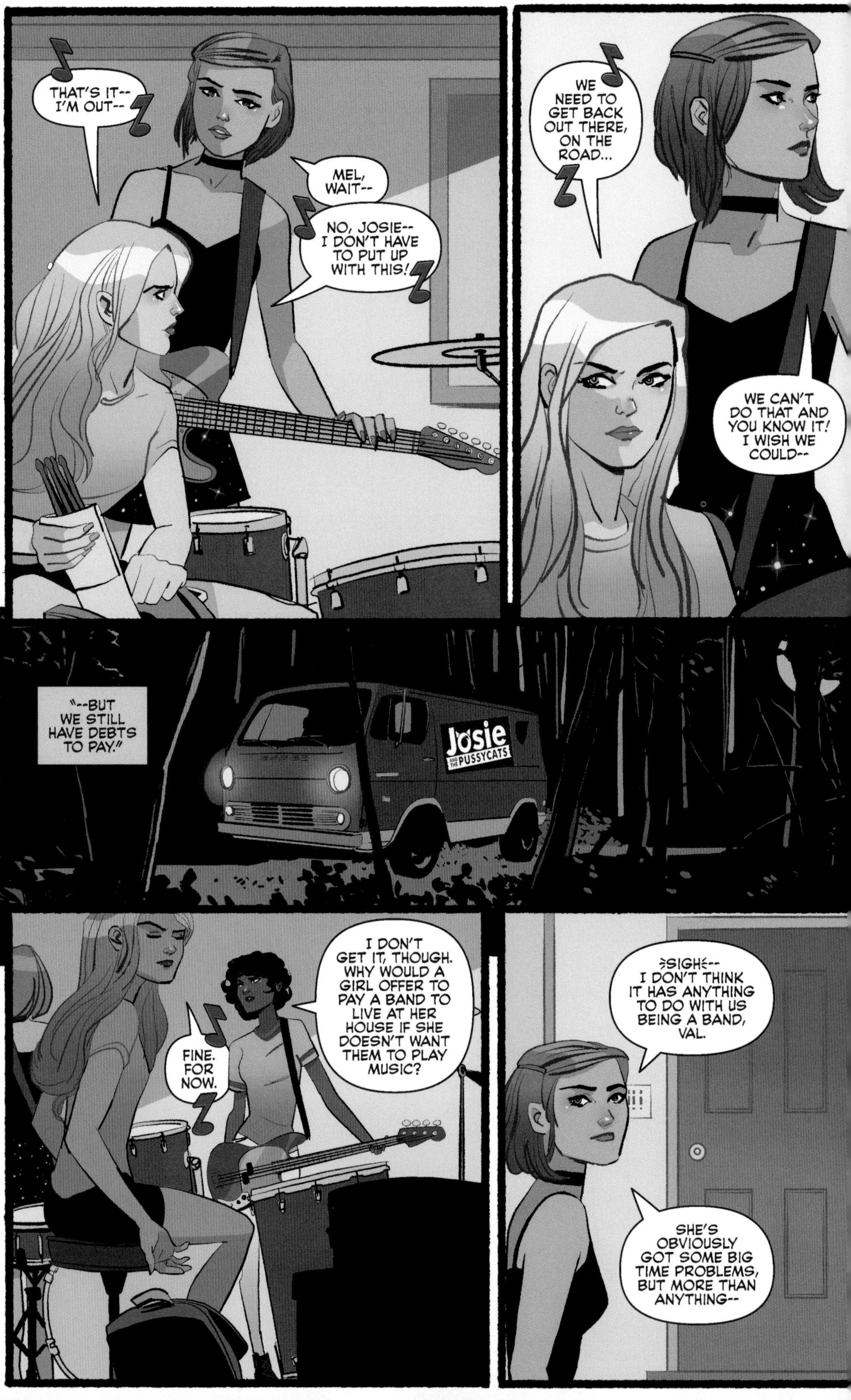
THAT'S IT-- I'M OUT--
MEL, WAIT--
NO, JOSIE-- I DON'T HAVE TO PUT UP WITH THIS!
WE NEED TO GET BACK OUT THERE, ON THE ROAD...
WE CAN'T DO THAT AND YOU KNOW IT! I WISH WE COULD--
"--BUT WE STILL HAVE DEBTS TO PAY."
JOSIE AND THE PUSSYCATS
FINE. FOR NOW.
I DON'T GET IT, THOUGH. WHY WOULD A GIRL OFFER TO PAY A BAND TO LIVE AT HER HOUSE IF SHE DOESN'T WANT THEM TO PLAY MUSIC?
SIGH-- I DON'T THINK IT HAS ANYTHING TO DO WITH US BEING A BAND, VAL.
SHE'S OBVIOUSLY GOT SOME BIG TIME PROBLEMS, BUT MORE THAN ANYTHING--

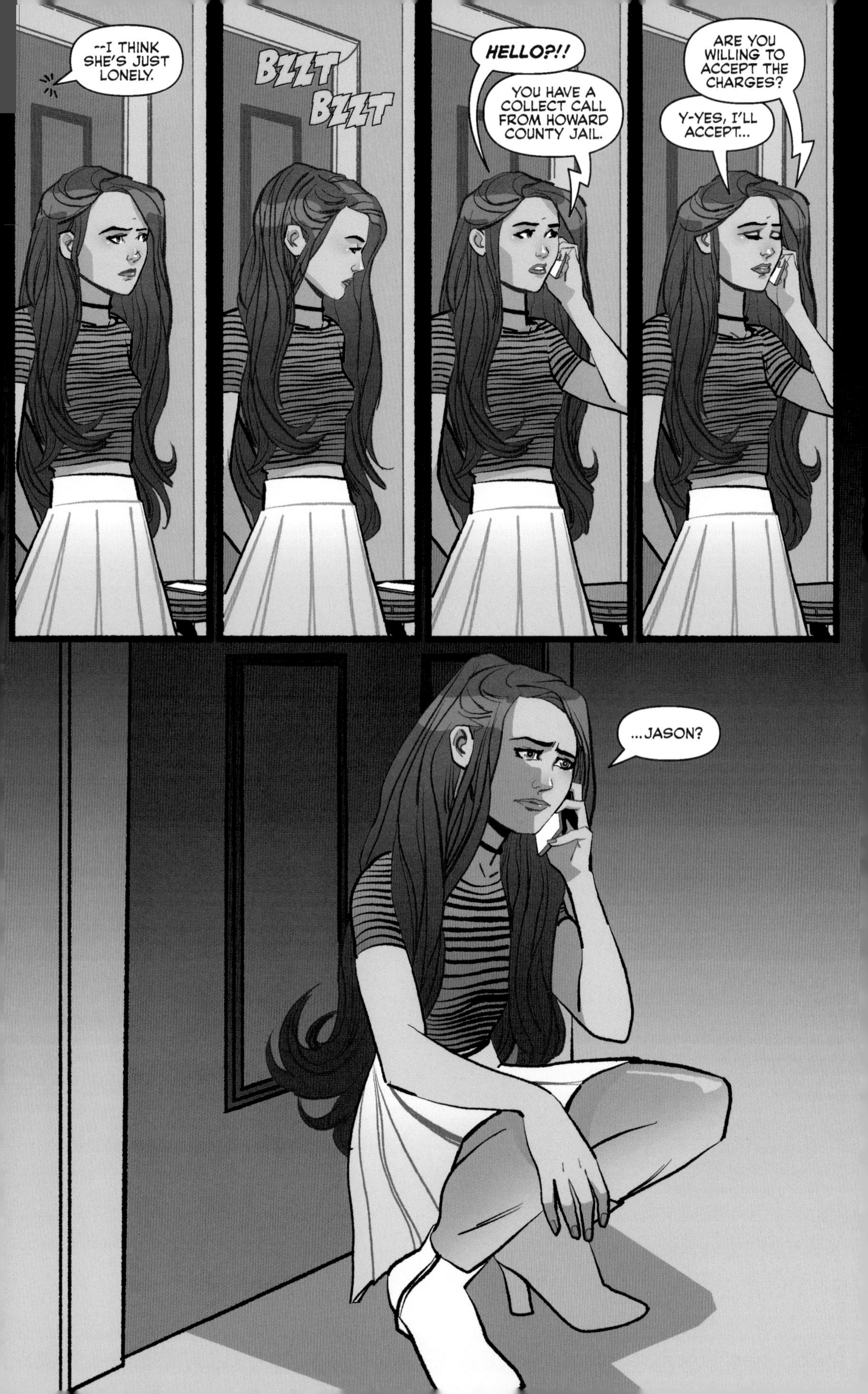
--I THINK SHE'S JUST LONELY.
BZZT BZZT
HELLO?!!
YOU HAVE A COLLECT CALL FROM HOWARD COUNTY JAIL.
ARE YOU WILLING TO ACCEPT THE CHARGES?
Y-YES, I'LL ACCEPT...
...JASON?

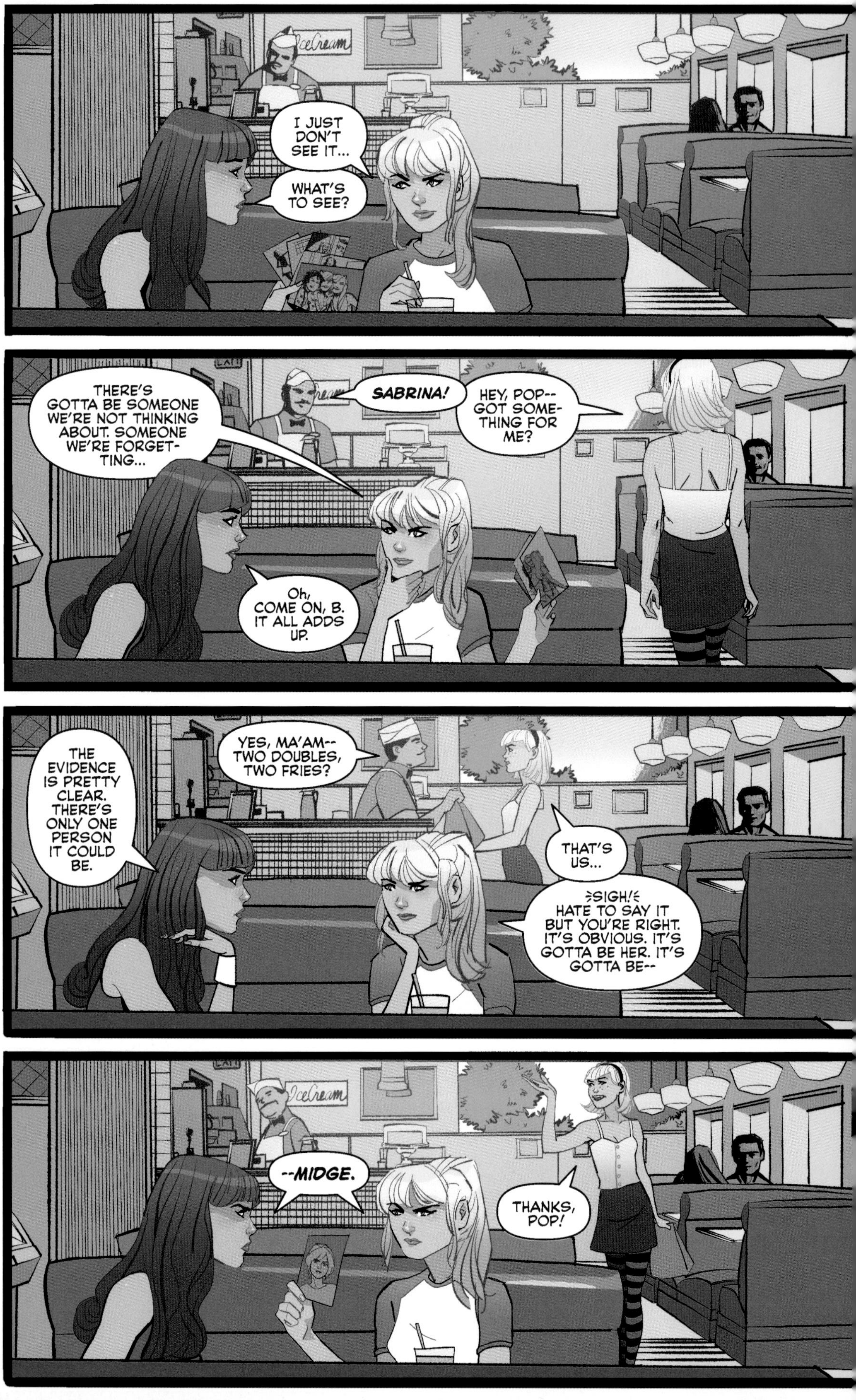
I JUST DON'T SEE IT...
WHAT'S TO SEE?
IceCream
THERE'S GOTTA BE SOMEONE WE'RE NOT THINKING ABOUT. SOMEONE WE'RE FORGET-TING...
SABRINA!
HEY, POP-- GOT SOME-THING FOR ME?
Oh, COME ON, B. IT ALL ADDS UP.
THE EVIDENCE IS PRETTY CLEAR. THERE'S ONLY ONE PERSON IT COULD BE.
YES, MA'AM-- TWO DOUBLES, TWO FRIES?
THAT'S US...
SIGH! HATE TO SAY IT BUT YOU'RE RIGHT. IT'S OBVIOUS. IT'S GOTTA BE HER. IT'S GOTTA BE--
IceCream
--MIDGE.
THANKS, POP!

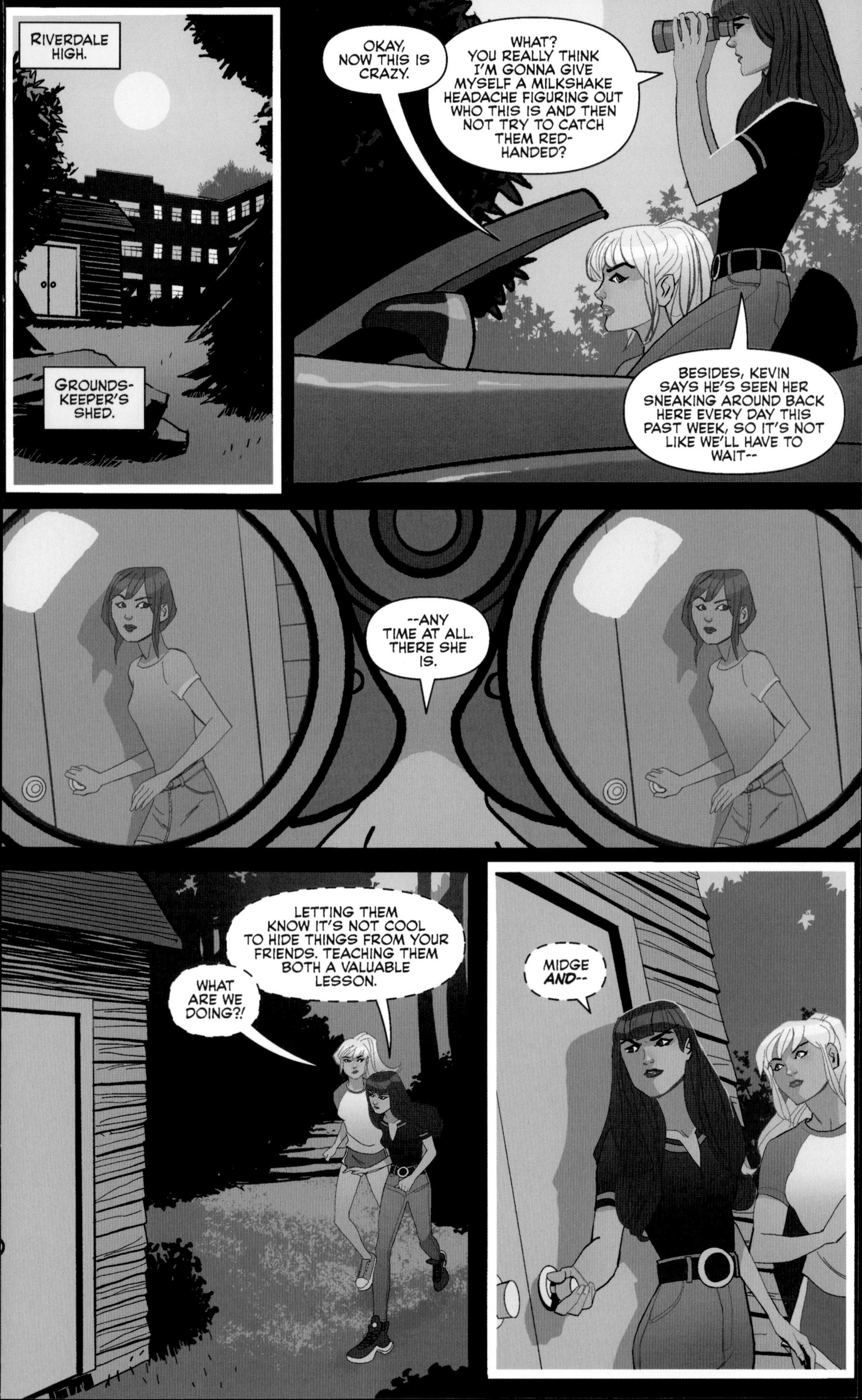
RIVERDALE HIGH.
GROUNDS-KEEPER'S SHED.
OKAY, NOW THIS IS CRAZY.
WHAT? YOU REALLY THINK I'M GONNA GIVE MYSELF A MILKSHAKE HEADACHE FIGURING OUT WHO THIS IS AND THEN NOT TRY TO CATCH THEM RED-HANDED?
BESIDES, KEVIN SAYS HE'S SEEN HER SNEAKING AROUND BACK HERE EVERY DAY THIS PAST WEEK, SO IT'S NOT LIKE WE'LL HAVE TO WAIT--
--ANY TIME AT ALL. THERE SHE IS.
WHAT ARE WE DOING?!
LETTING THEM KNOW IT'S NOT COOL TO HIDE THINGS FROM YOUR FRIENDS. TEACHING THEM BOTH A VALUABLE LESSON.
MIDGE *AND*--

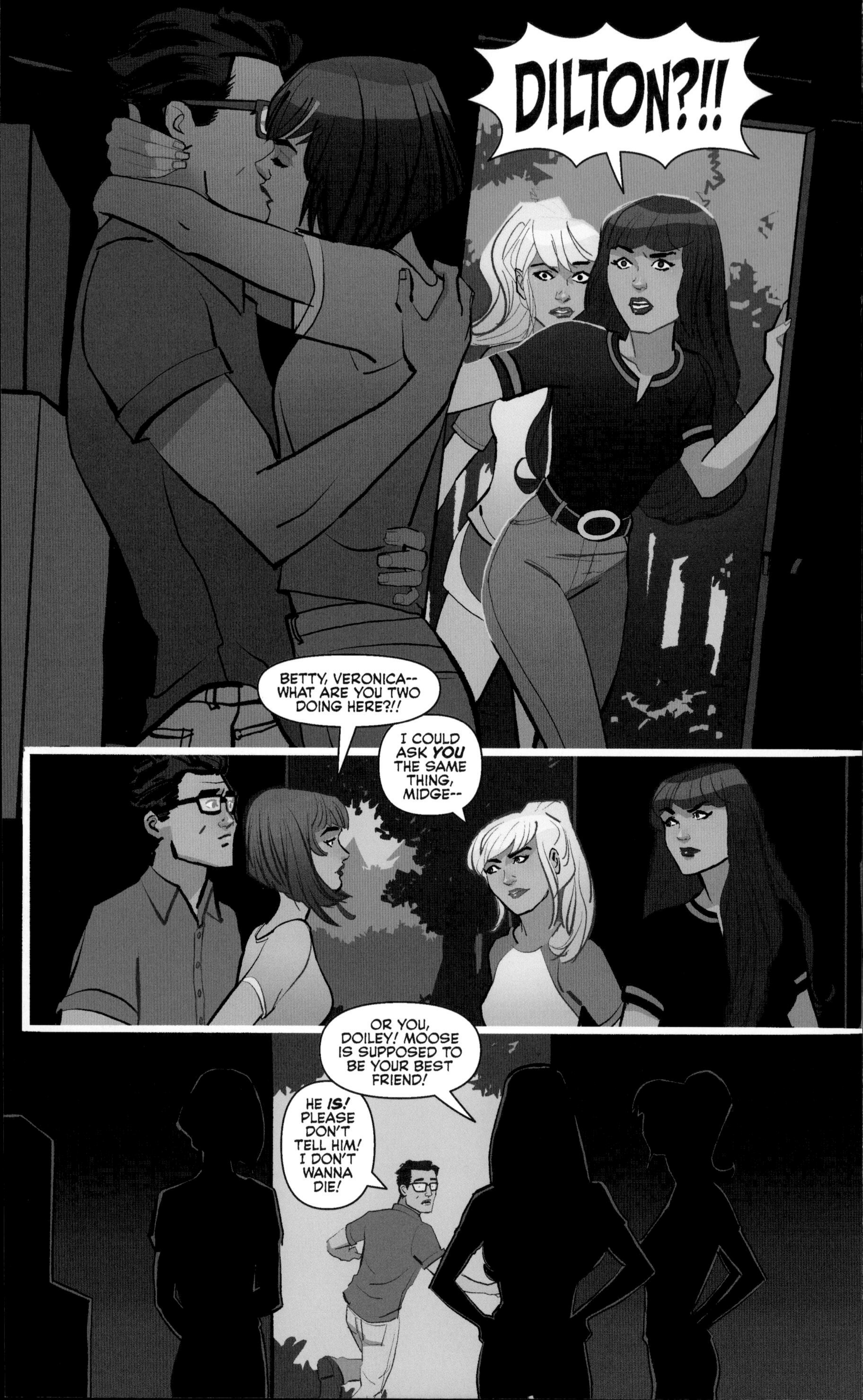
DILTON?!!
BETTY, VERONICA-- WHAT ARE YOU TWO DOING HERE?!!
I COULD ASK YOU THE SAME THING, MIDGE--
OR YOU, DOILEY! MOOSE IS SUPPOSED TO BE YOUR BEST FRIEND!
HE IS! PLEASE DON'T TELL HIM! I DON'T WANNA DIE!

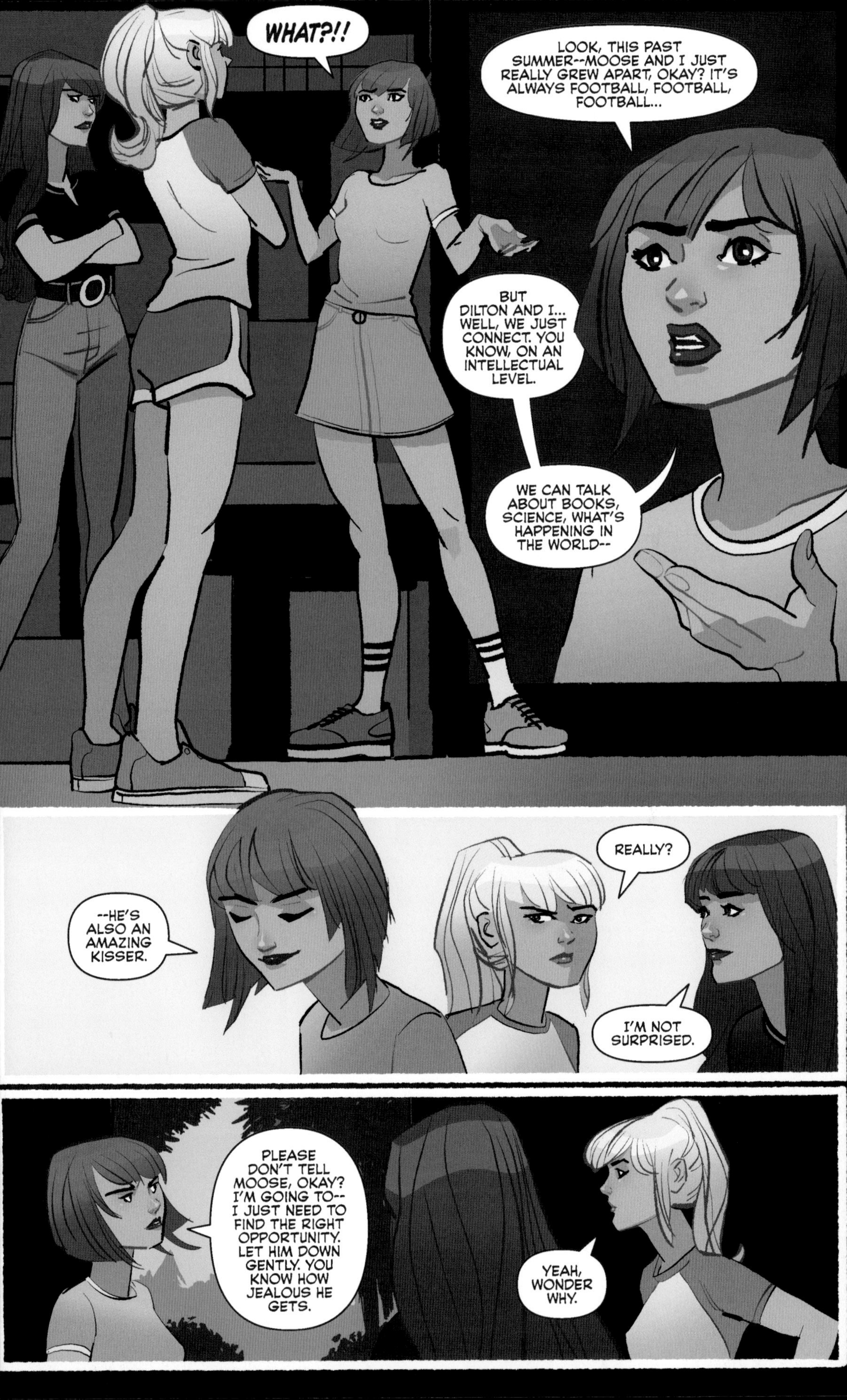
WHAT?!!
LOOK, THIS PAST SUMMER--MOOSE AND I JUST REALLY GREW APART, OKAY? IT'S ALWAYS FOOTBALL, FOOTBALL, FOOTBALL...
BUT DILTON AND I... WELL, WE JUST CONNECT. YOU KNOW, ON AN INTELLECTUAL LEVEL.
WE CAN TALK ABOUT BOOKS, SCIENCE, WHAT'S HAPPENING IN THE WORLD--
--HE'S ALSO AN AMAZING KISSER.
REALLY?
I'M NOT SURPRISED.
PLEASE DON'T TELL MOOSE, OKAY? I'M GOING TO-- I JUST NEED TO FIND THE RIGHT OPPORTUNITY. LET HIM DOWN GENTLY. YOU KNOW HOW JEALOUS HE GETS.
YEAH, WONDER WHY.

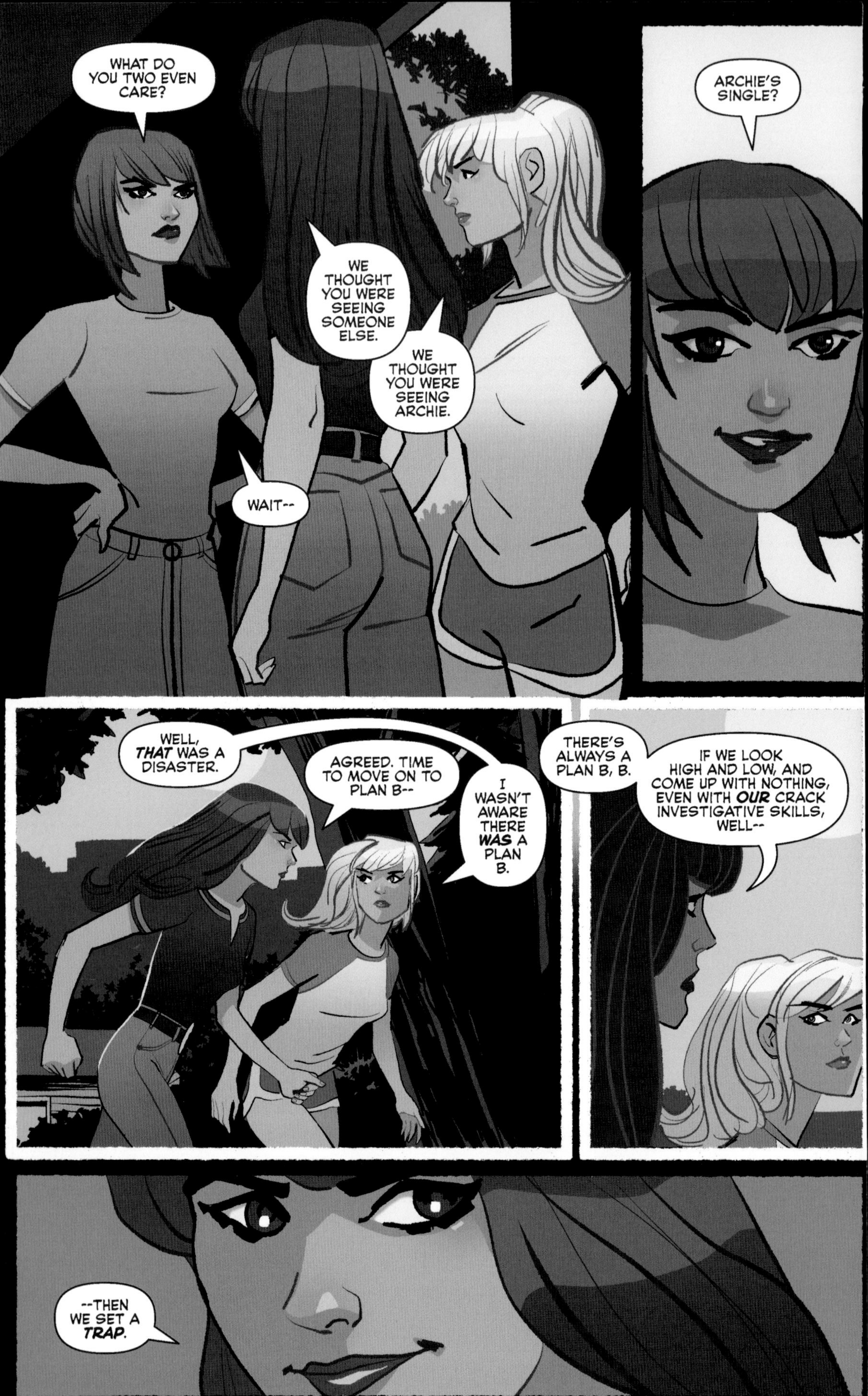
WHAT DO YOU TWO EVEN CARE?
WE THOUGHT YOU WERE SEEING SOMEONE ELSE.
WE THOUGHT YOU WERE SEEING ARCHIE.
WAIT--
ARCHIE'S SINGLE?
WELL, *THAT* WAS A DISASTER.
AGREED. TIME TO MOVE ON TO PLAN B--
I WASN'T AWARE THERE *WAS* A PLAN B.
THERE'S ALWAYS A PLAN B, B.
IF WE LOOK HIGH AND LOW, AND COME UP WITH NOTHING, EVEN WITH *OUR* CRACK INVESTIGATIVE SKILLS, WELL--
--THEN WE SET A *TRAP*.

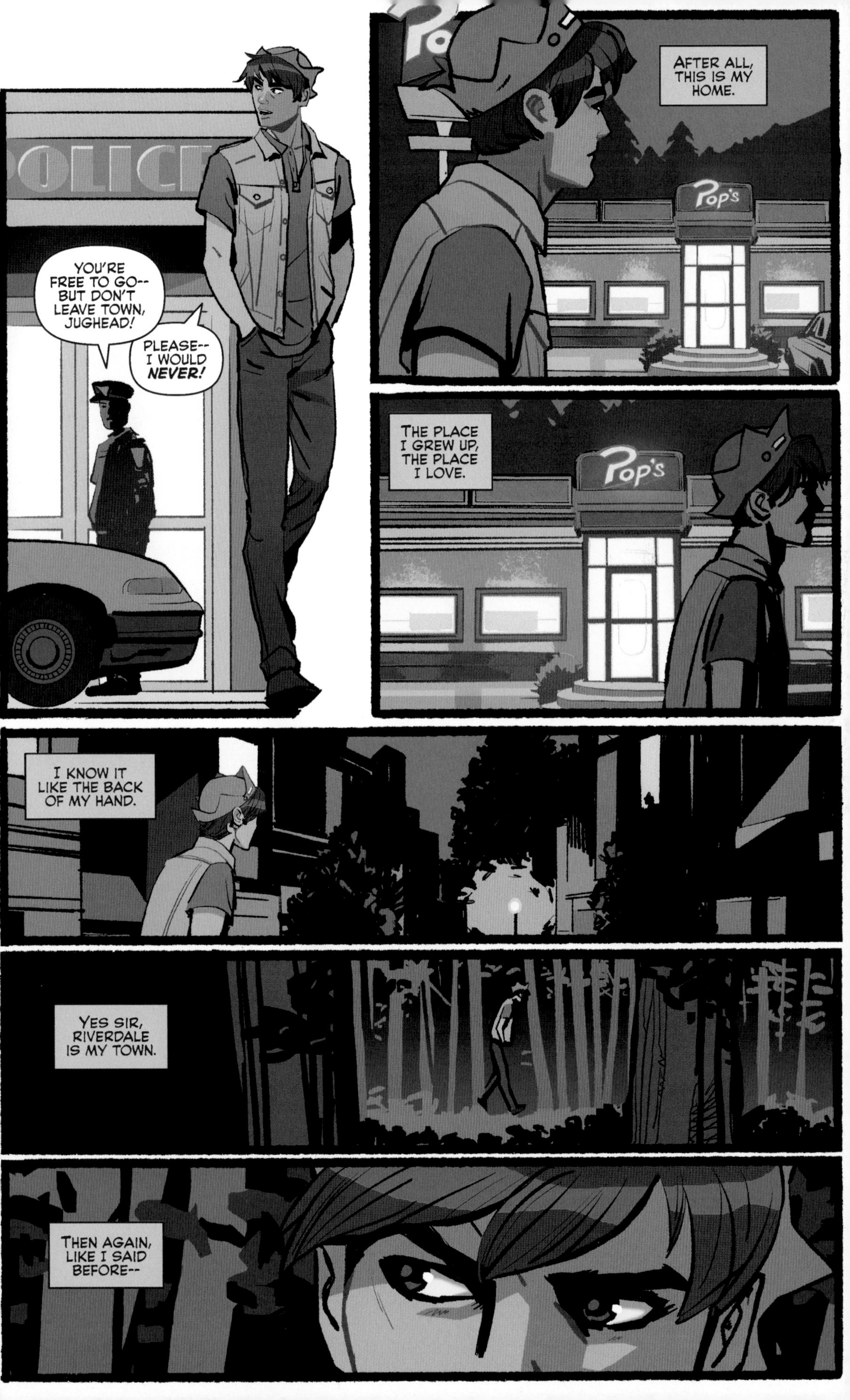

YOU'RE FREE TO GO-- BUT DON'T LEAVE TOWN, JUGHEAD!
PLEASE-- I WOULD NEVER!
POLICE
AFTER ALL, THIS IS MY HOME.
Pop's
THE PLACE I GREW UP, THE PLACE I LOVE.
Pop's
I KNOW IT LIKE THE BACK OF MY HAND.
YES SIR, RIVERDALE IS MY TOWN.
THEN AGAIN, LIKE I SAID BEFORE--

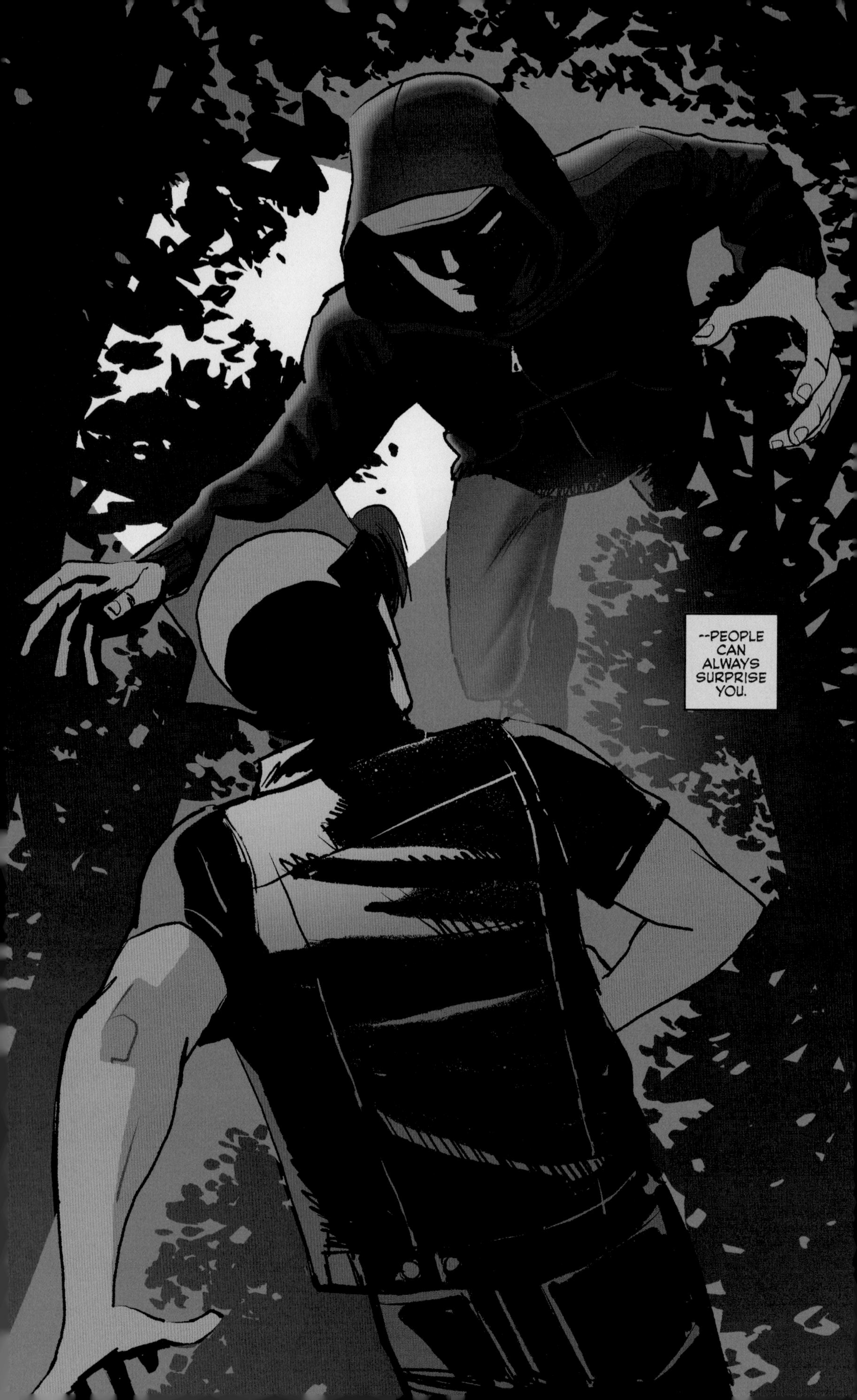
--PEOPLE CAN ALWAYS SURPRISE YOU.

TO BE CONTINUED...

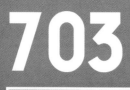

703

STORY BY
NICK SPENCER

ART BY
SANDY JARRELL

LETTERING BY
JACK MORELLI

COLORS BY
MATT HERMS

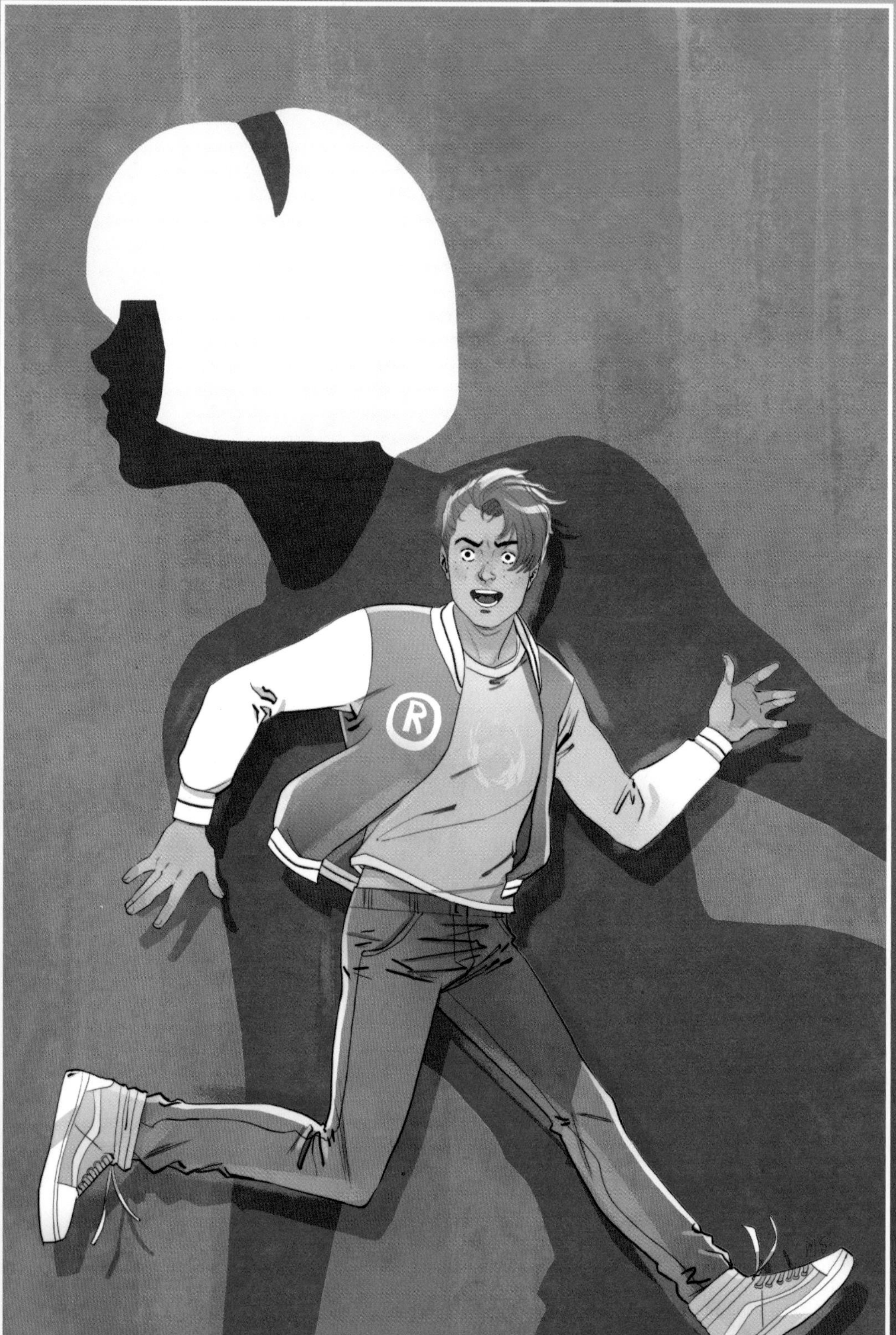

COVER ART: **MARGUERITE SAUVAGE**

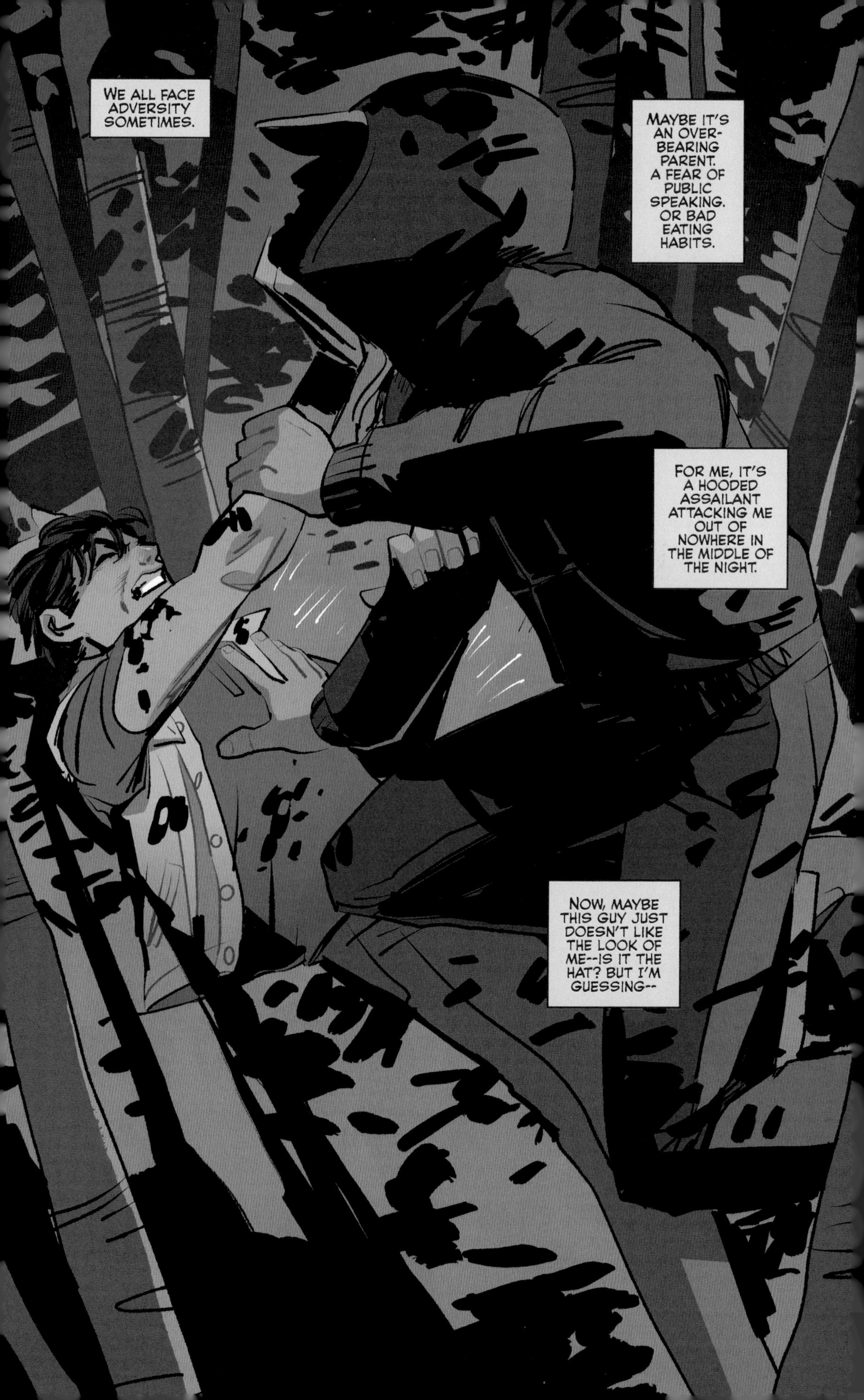
WE ALL FACE ADVERSITY SOMETIMES.
MAYBE IT'S AN OVER-BEARING PARENT. A FEAR OF PUBLIC SPEAKING. OR BAD EATING HABITS.
FOR ME, IT'S A HOODED ASSAILANT ATTACKING ME OUT OF NOWHERE IN THE MIDDLE OF THE NIGHT.
NOW, MAYBE THIS GUY JUST DOESN'T LIKE THE LOOK OF ME--IS IT THE HAT? BUT I'M GUESSING--

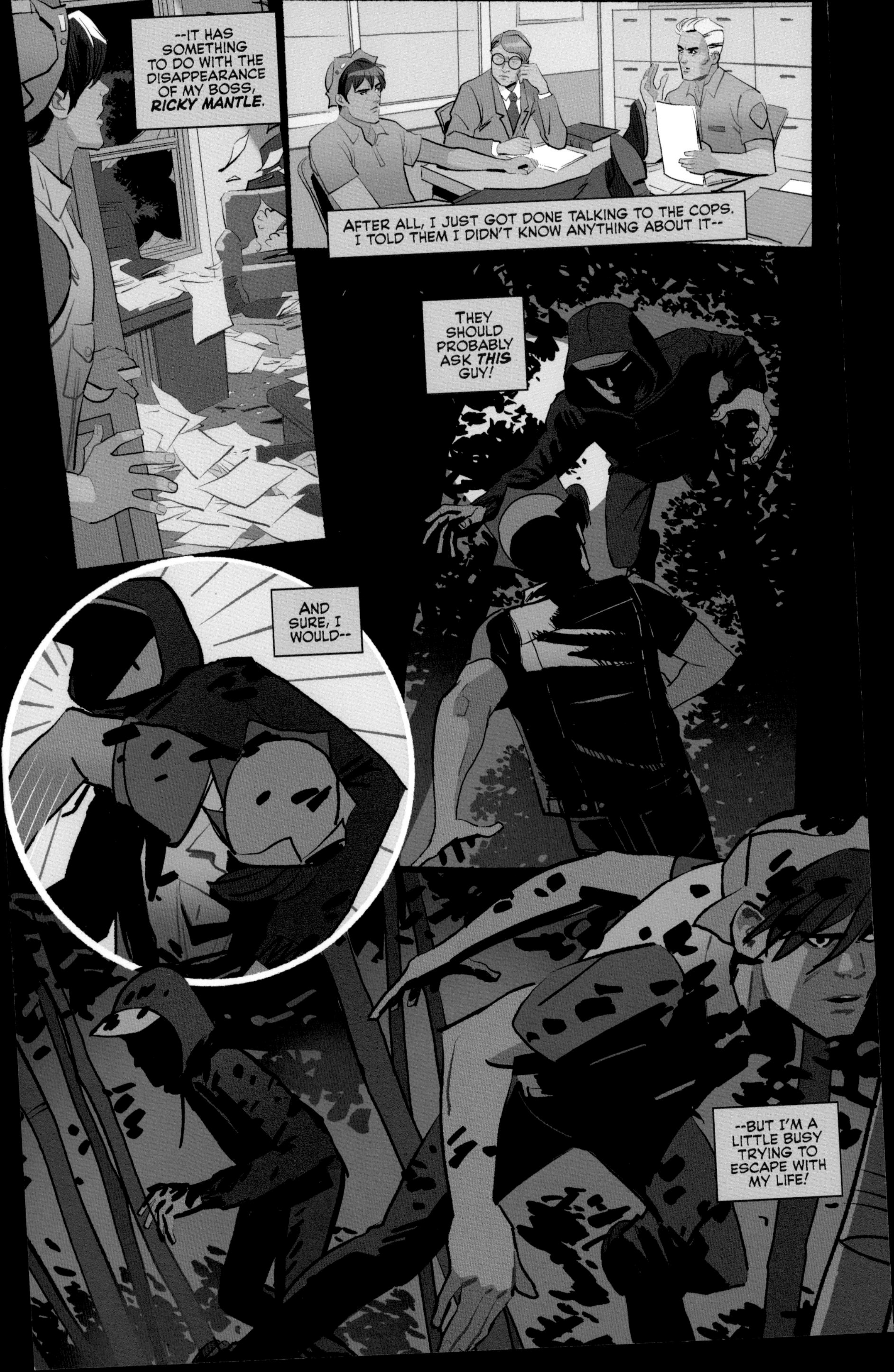
--IT HAS SOMETHING TO DO WITH THE DISAPPEARANCE OF MY BOSS, RICKY MANTLE.
AFTER ALL, I JUST GOT DONE TALKING TO THE COPS. I TOLD THEM I DIDN'T KNOW ANYTHING ABOUT IT--
THEY SHOULD PROBABLY ASK THIS GUY!
AND SURE, I WOULD--
--BUT I'M A LITTLE BUSY TRYING TO ESCAPE WITH MY LIFE!

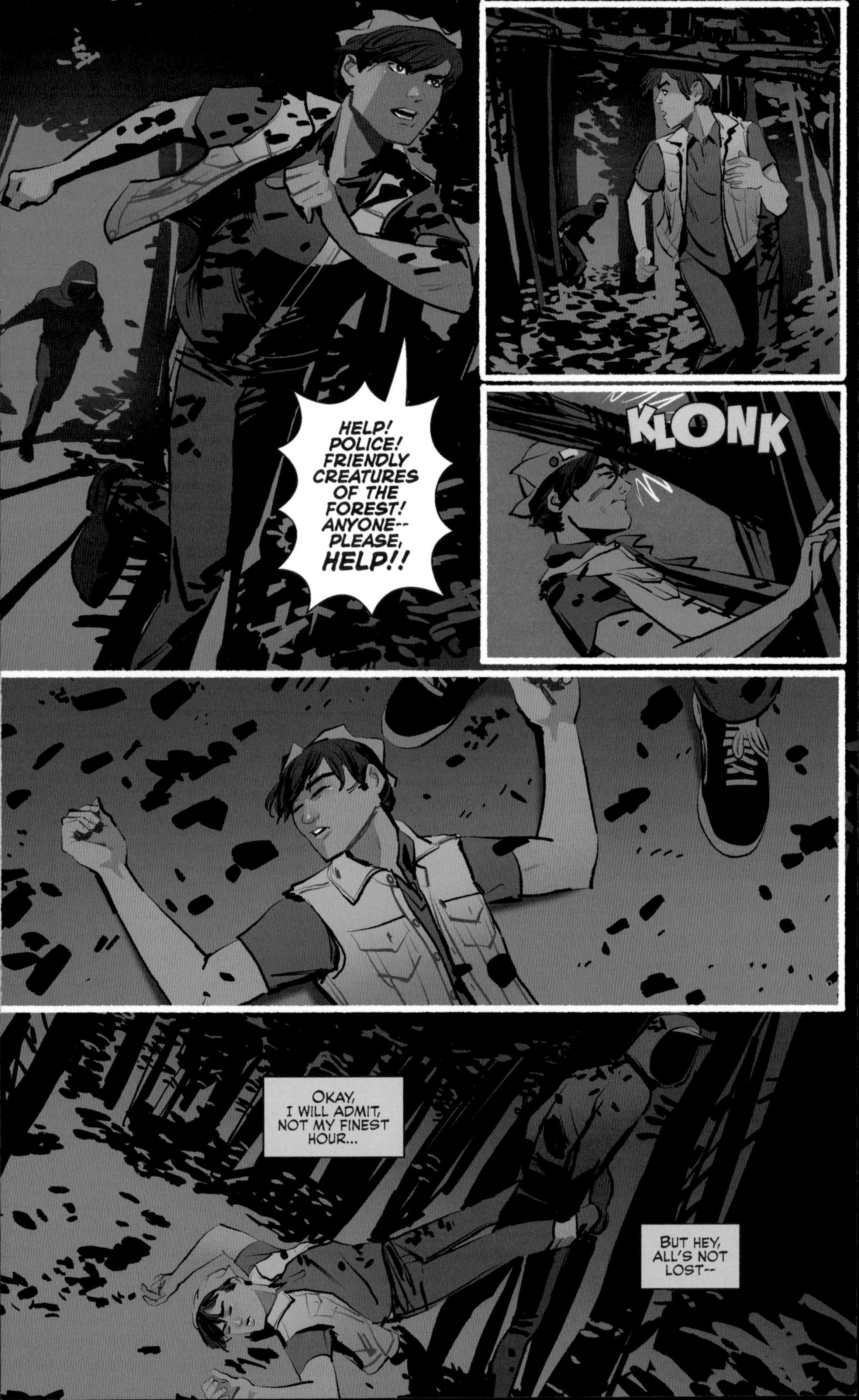
HELP! POLICE! FRIENDLY CREATURES OF THE FOREST! ANYONE-- PLEASE, HELP!!
KLONK
OKAY, I WILL ADMIT, NOT MY FINEST HOUR...
BUT HEY, ALL'S NOT LOST--

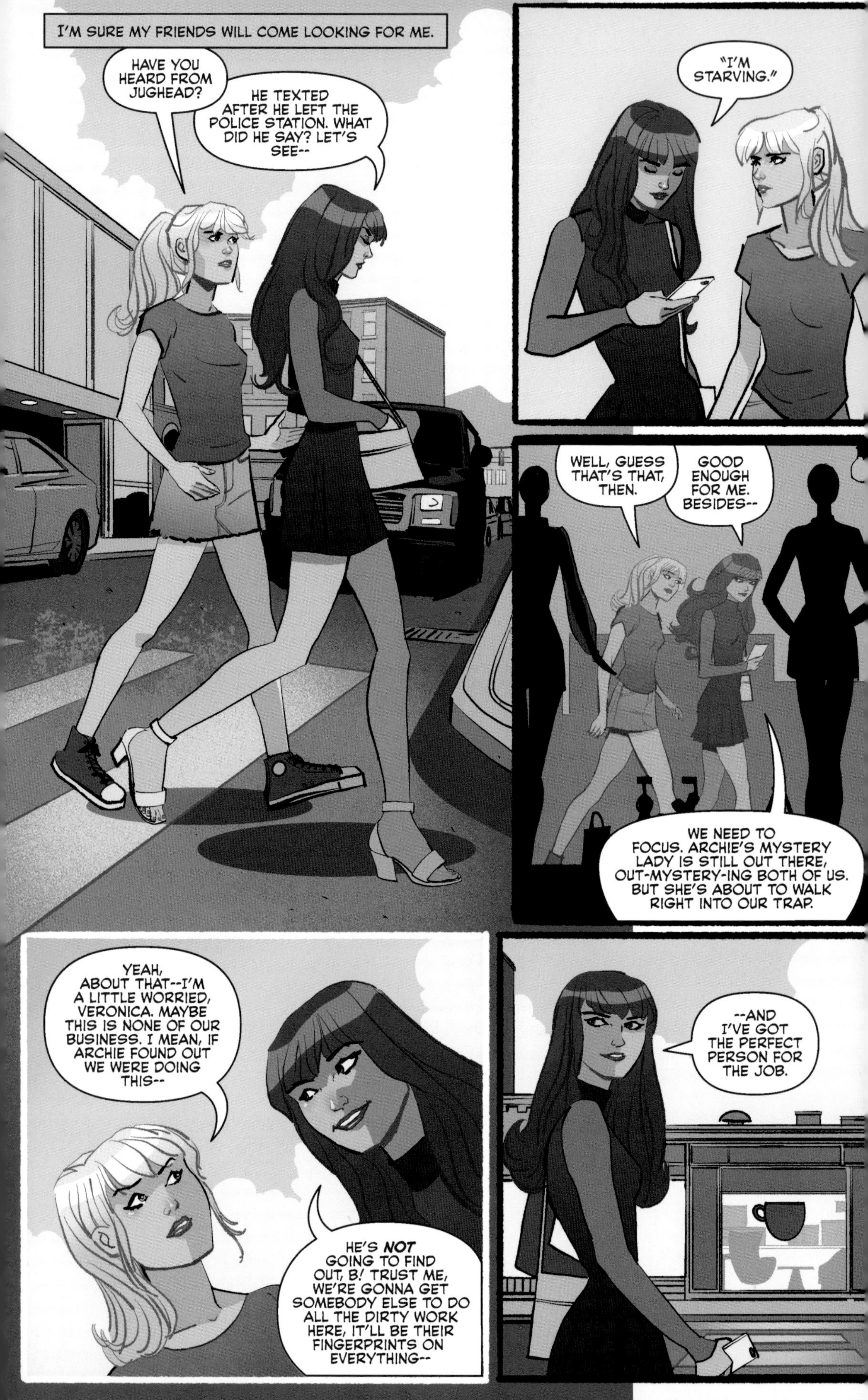
I'M SURE MY FRIENDS WILL COME LOOKING FOR ME.
HAVE YOU HEARD FROM JUGHEAD?
HE TEXTED AFTER HE LEFT THE POLICE STATION. WHAT DID HE SAY? LET'S SEE--
"I'M STARVING."
WELL, GUESS THAT'S THAT, THEN.
GOOD ENOUGH FOR ME. BESIDES--
WE NEED TO FOCUS. ARCHIE'S MYSTERY LADY IS STILL OUT THERE, OUT-MYSTERY-ING BOTH OF US. BUT SHE'S ABOUT TO WALK RIGHT INTO OUR TRAP.
YEAH, ABOUT THAT--I'M A LITTLE WORRIED, VERONICA. MAYBE THIS IS NONE OF OUR BUSINESS. I MEAN, IF ARCHIE FOUND OUT WE WERE DOING THIS--
HE'S ***NOT*** GOING TO FIND OUT, B! TRUST ME, WE'RE GONNA GET SOMEBODY ELSE TO DO ALL THE DIRTY WORK HERE, IT'LL BE THEIR FINGERPRINTS ON EVERYTHING--
--AND I'VE GOT THE PERFECT PERSON FOR THE JOB.

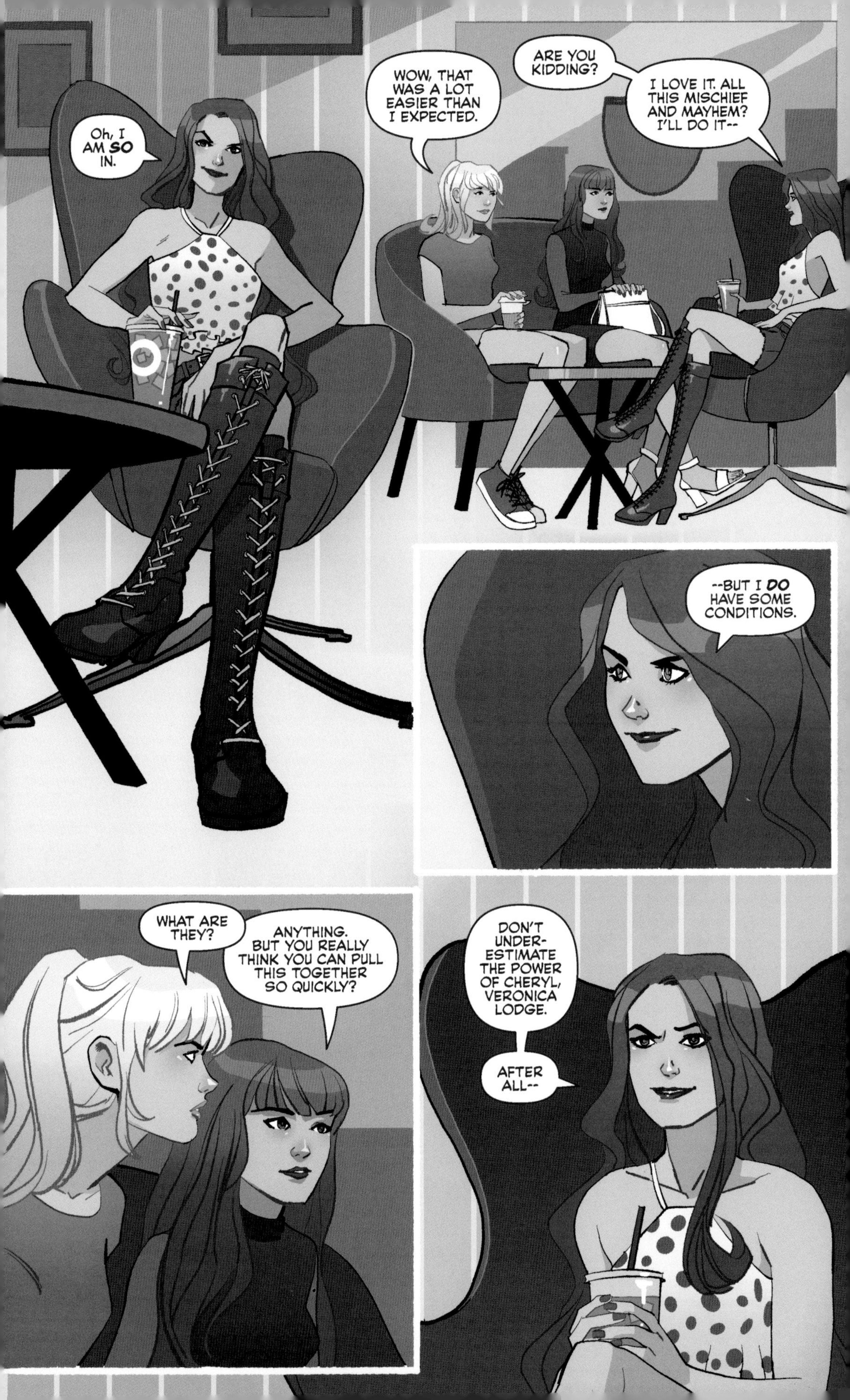

Oh, I AM **SO** IN.
WOW, THAT WAS A LOT EASIER THAN I EXPECTED.
ARE YOU KIDDING?
I LOVE IT. ALL THIS MISCHIEF AND MAYHEM? I'LL DO IT--
--BUT I **DO** HAVE SOME CONDITIONS.
WHAT ARE THEY?
ANYTHING. BUT YOU REALLY THINK YOU CAN PULL THIS TOGETHER SO QUICKLY?
DON'T UNDER-ESTIMATE THE POWER OF CHERYL, VERONICA LODGE.
AFTER ALL--

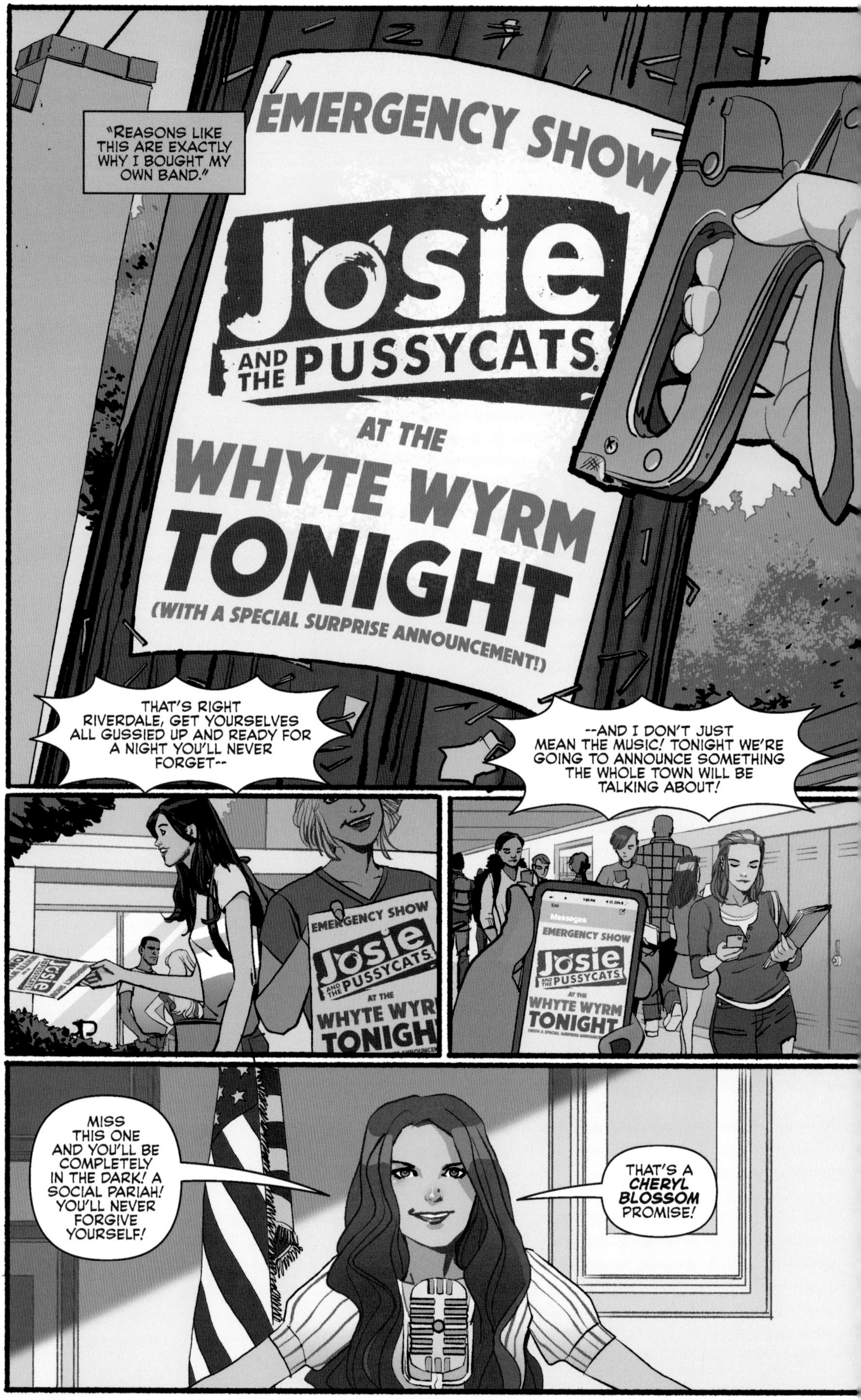
"REASONS LIKE THIS ARE EXACTLY WHY I BOUGHT MY OWN BAND."
EMERGENCY SHOW
JOSIE AND THE PUSSYCATS
AT THE
WHYTE WYRM
TONIGHT
(WITH A SPECIAL SURPRISE ANNOUNCEMENT!)
THAT'S RIGHT RIVERDALE, GET YOURSELVES ALL GUSSIED UP AND READY FOR A NIGHT YOU'LL NEVER FORGET--
--AND I DON'T JUST MEAN THE MUSIC! TONIGHT WE'RE GOING TO ANNOUNCE SOMETHING THE WHOLE TOWN WILL BE TALKING ABOUT!
EMERGENCY SHOW
JOSIE AND THE PUSSYCATS
AT THE
WHYTE WYR
TONIGH
Messages
EMERGENCY SHOW
JOSIE AND THE PUSSYCATS
AT THE
WHYTE WYRM
TONIGHT
MISS THIS ONE AND YOU'LL BE COMPLETELY IN THE DARK! A SOCIAL PARIAH! YOU'LL NEVER FORGIVE YOURSELF!
THAT'S A *CHERYL BLOSSOM* PROMISE!

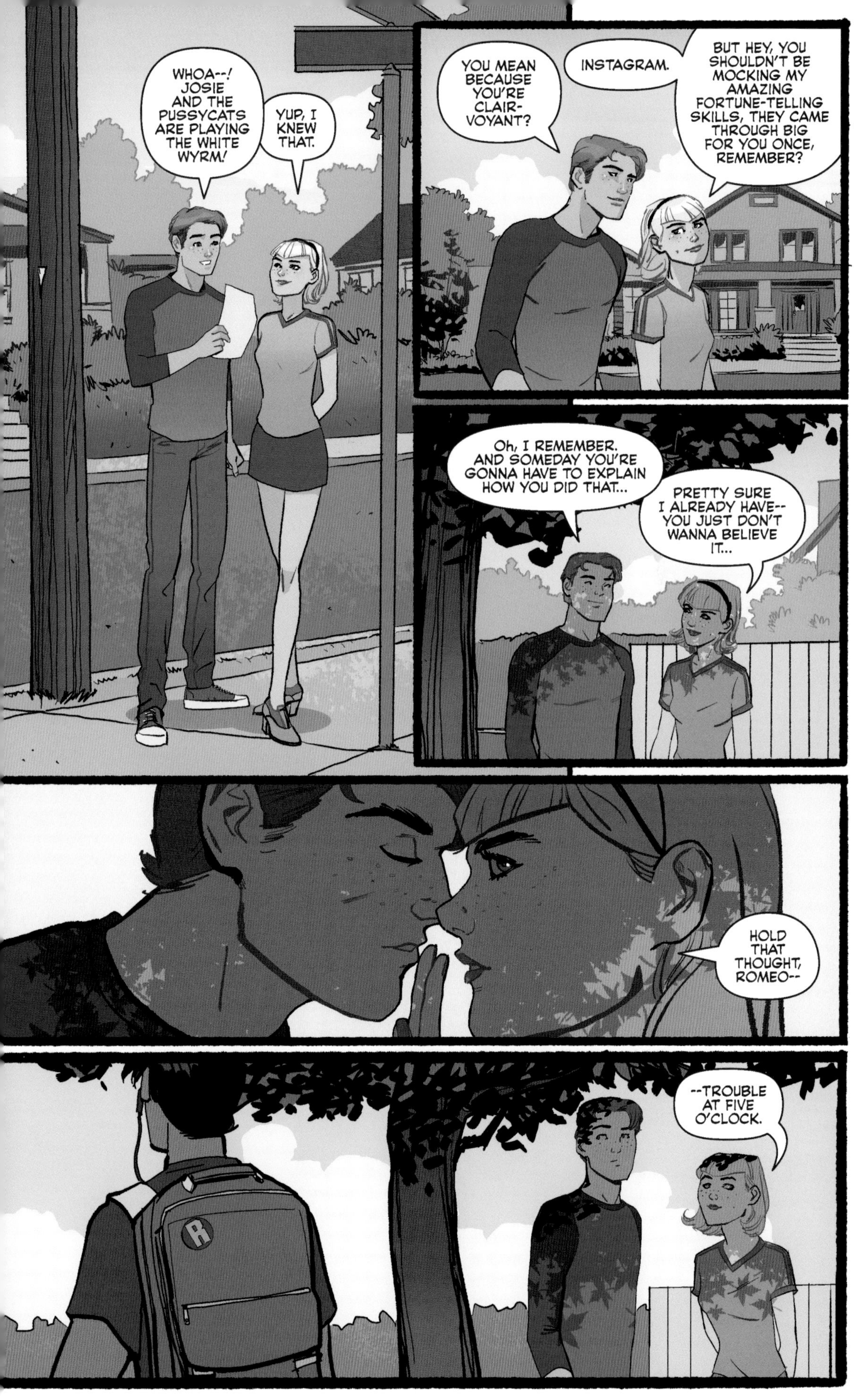
WHOA--! JOSIE AND THE PUSSYCATS ARE PLAYING THE WHITE WYRM!
YUP, I KNEW THAT.
YOU MEAN BECAUSE YOU'RE CLAIR-VOYANT?
INSTAGRAM.
BUT HEY, YOU SHOULDN'T BE MOCKING MY AMAZING FORTUNE-TELLING SKILLS, THEY CAME THROUGH BIG FOR YOU ONCE, REMEMBER?
Oh, I REMEMBER. AND SOMEDAY YOU'RE GONNA HAVE TO EXPLAIN HOW YOU DID THAT...
PRETTY SURE I ALREADY HAVE-- YOU JUST DON'T WANNA BELIEVE IT...
HOLD THAT THOUGHT, ROMEO--
--TROUBLE AT FIVE O'CLOCK.

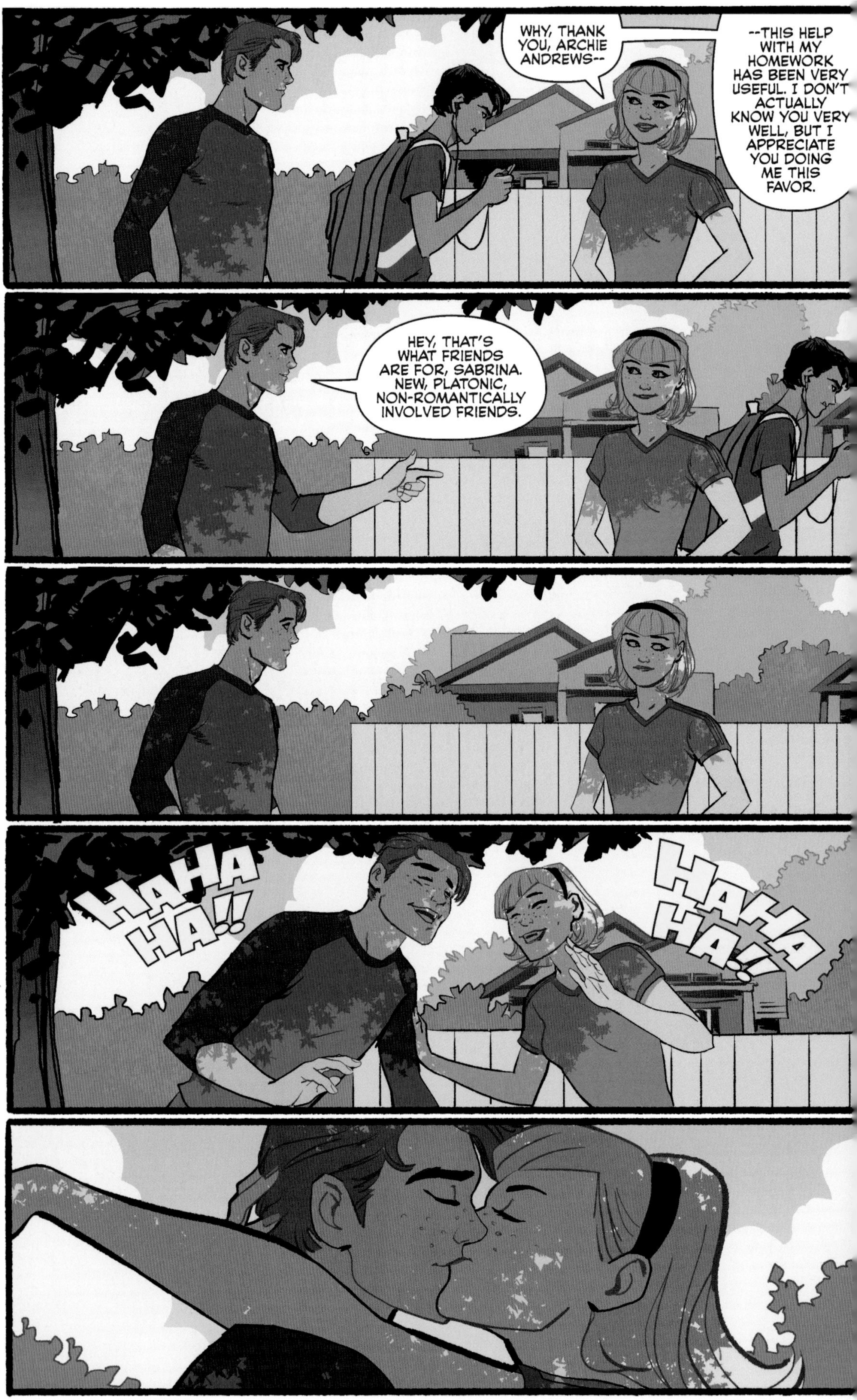
WHY, THANK YOU, ARCHIE ANDREWS--
--THIS HELP WITH MY HOMEWORK HAS BEEN VERY USEFUL. I DON'T ACTUALLY KNOW YOU VERY WELL, BUT I APPRECIATE YOU DOING ME THIS FAVOR.
HEY, THAT'S WHAT FRIENDS ARE FOR, SABRINA. NEW, PLATONIC, NON-ROMANTICALLY INVOLVED FRIENDS.
HAHA HA!!
HAHA HA!!

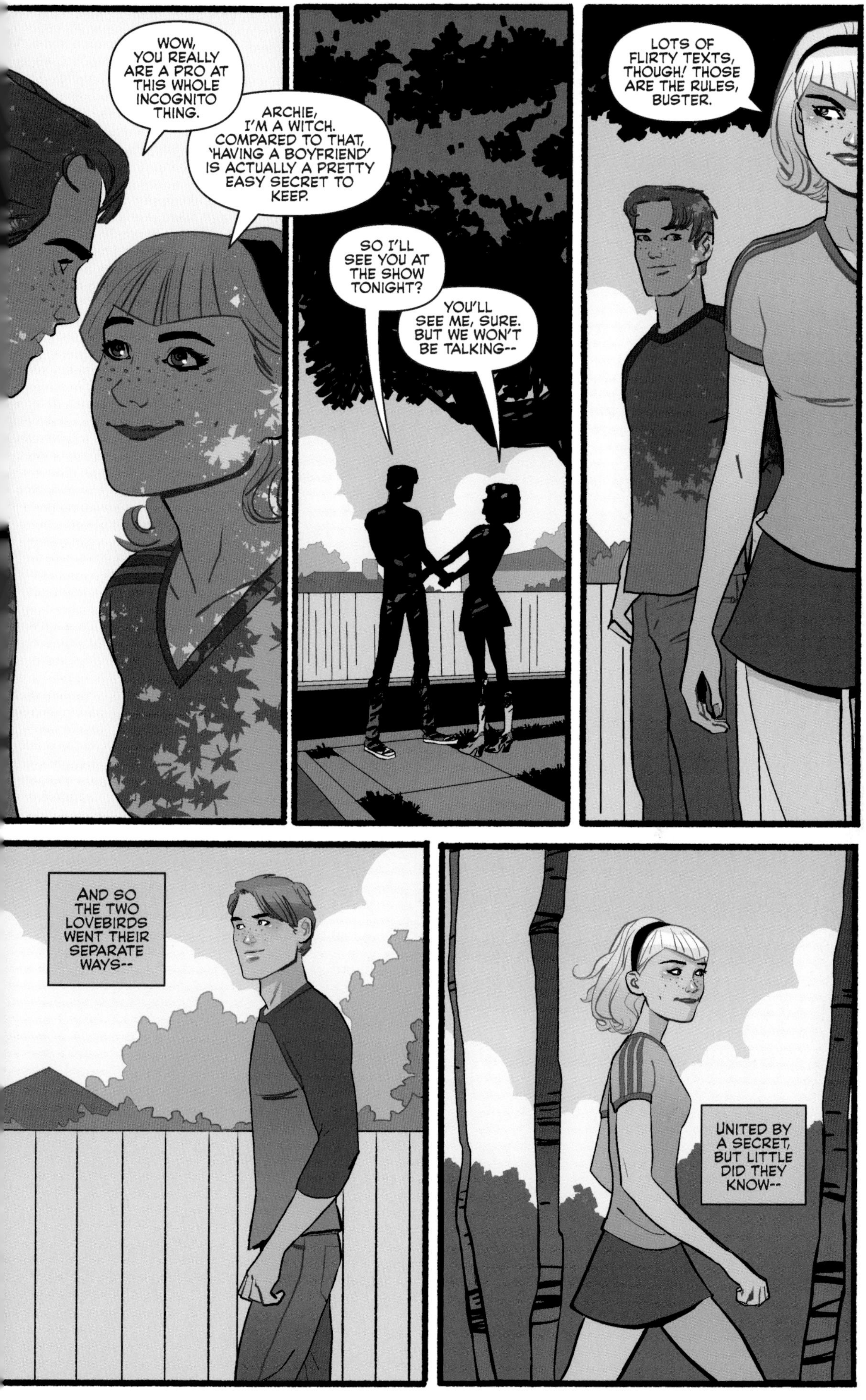
WOW, YOU REALLY ARE A PRO AT THIS WHOLE INCOGNITO THING.
ARCHIE, I'M A WITCH. COMPARED TO THAT, 'HAVING A BOYFRIEND' IS ACTUALLY A PRETTY EASY SECRET TO KEEP.
SO I'LL SEE YOU AT THE SHOW TONIGHT?
YOU'LL SEE ME, SURE. BUT WE WON'T BE TALKING--
LOTS OF FLIRTY TEXTS, THOUGH! THOSE ARE THE RULES, BUSTER.
AND SO THE TWO LOVEBIRDS WENT THEIR SEPARATE WAYS--
UNITED BY A SECRET, BUT LITTLE DID THEY KNOW--

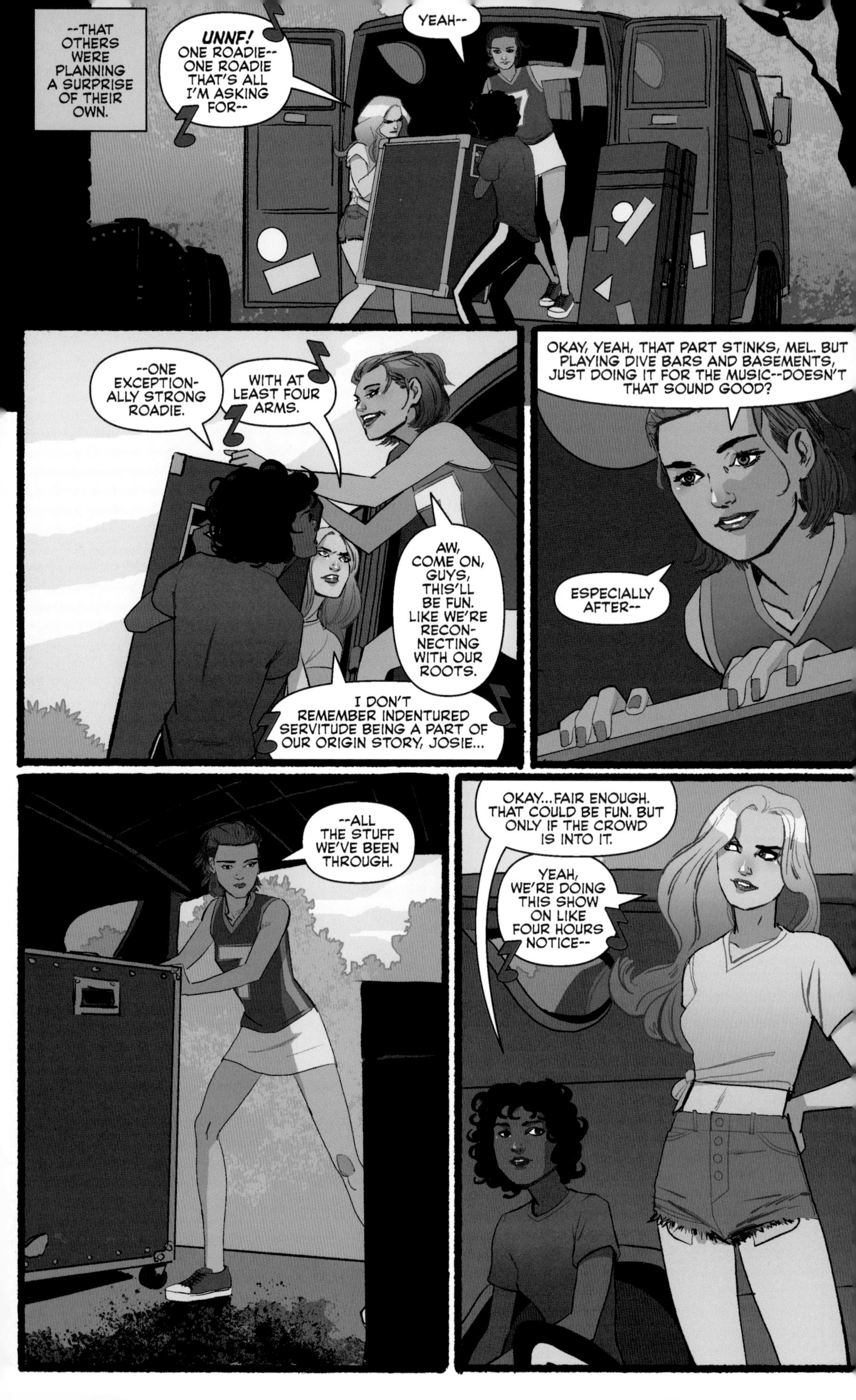
--THAT OTHERS WERE PLANNING A SURPRISE OF THEIR OWN.
UNNF! ONE ROADIE-- ONE ROADIE THAT'S ALL I'M ASKING FOR--
YEAH--
--ONE EXCEPTION-ALLY STRONG ROADIE.
WITH AT LEAST FOUR ARMS.
AW, COME ON, GUYS, THIS'LL BE FUN. LIKE WE'RE RECON-NECTING WITH OUR ROOTS.
I DON'T REMEMBER INDENTURED SERVITUDE BEING A PART OF OUR ORIGIN STORY, JOSIE...
OKAY, YEAH, THAT PART STINKS, MEL. BUT PLAYING DIVE BARS AND BASEMENTS, JUST DOING IT FOR THE MUSIC--DOESN'T THAT SOUND GOOD?
ESPECIALLY AFTER--
--ALL THE STUFF WE'VE BEEN THROUGH.
OKAY...FAIR ENOUGH. THAT COULD BE FUN. BUT ONLY IF THE CROWD IS INTO IT.
YEAH, WE'RE DOING THIS SHOW ON LIKE FOUR HOURS NOTICE--

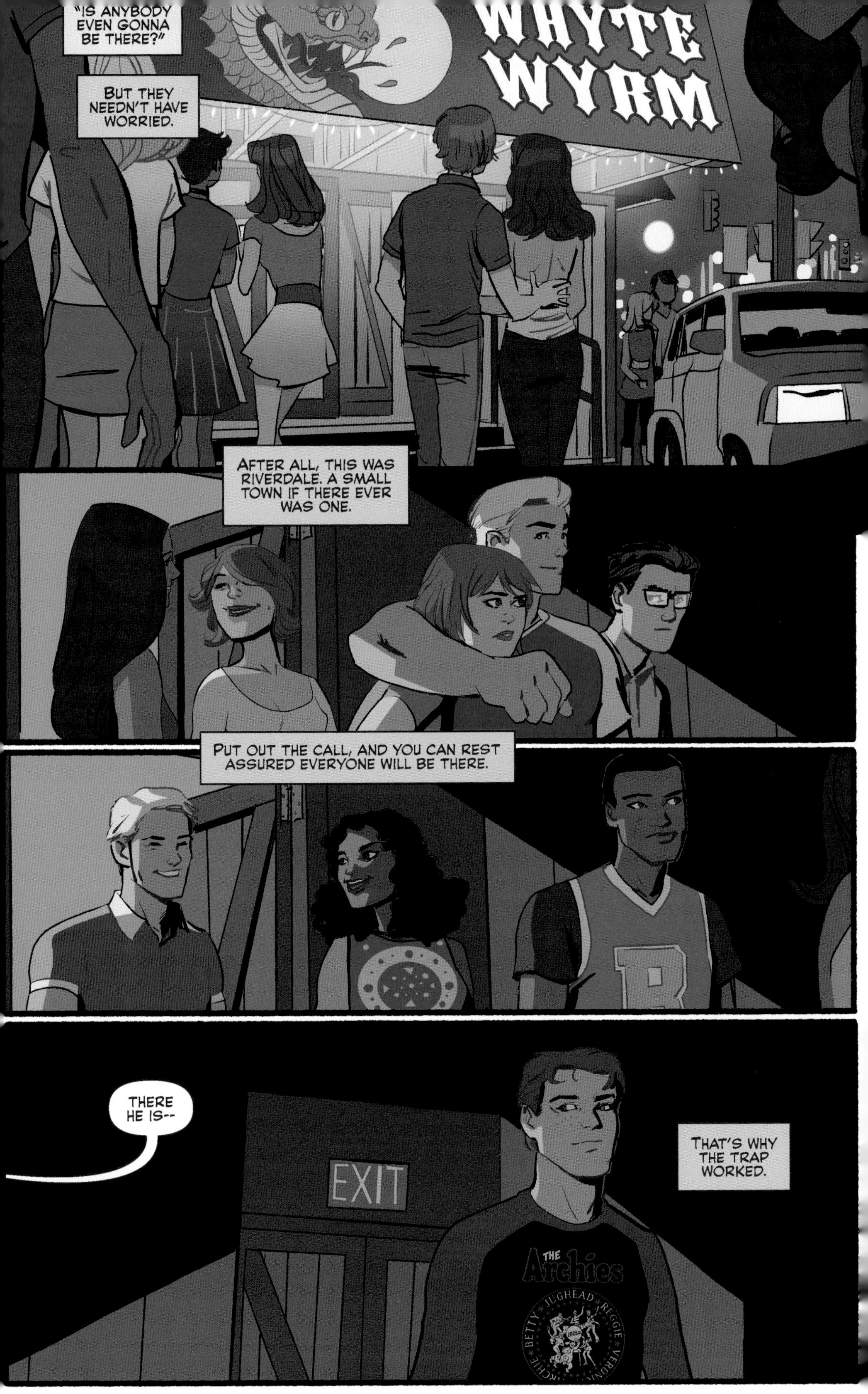
"IS ANYBODY EVEN GONNA BE THERE?"
BUT THEY NEEDN'T HAVE WORRIED.
WHYTE WYRM
AFTER ALL, THIS WAS RIVERDALE. A SMALL TOWN IF THERE EVER WAS ONE.
PUT OUT THE CALL, AND YOU CAN REST ASSURED EVERYONE WILL BE THERE.
THERE HE IS--
EXIT
THAT'S WHY THE TRAP WORKED.
THE Archies
BETTY JUGHEAD REGGIE VERONICA ARCHIE

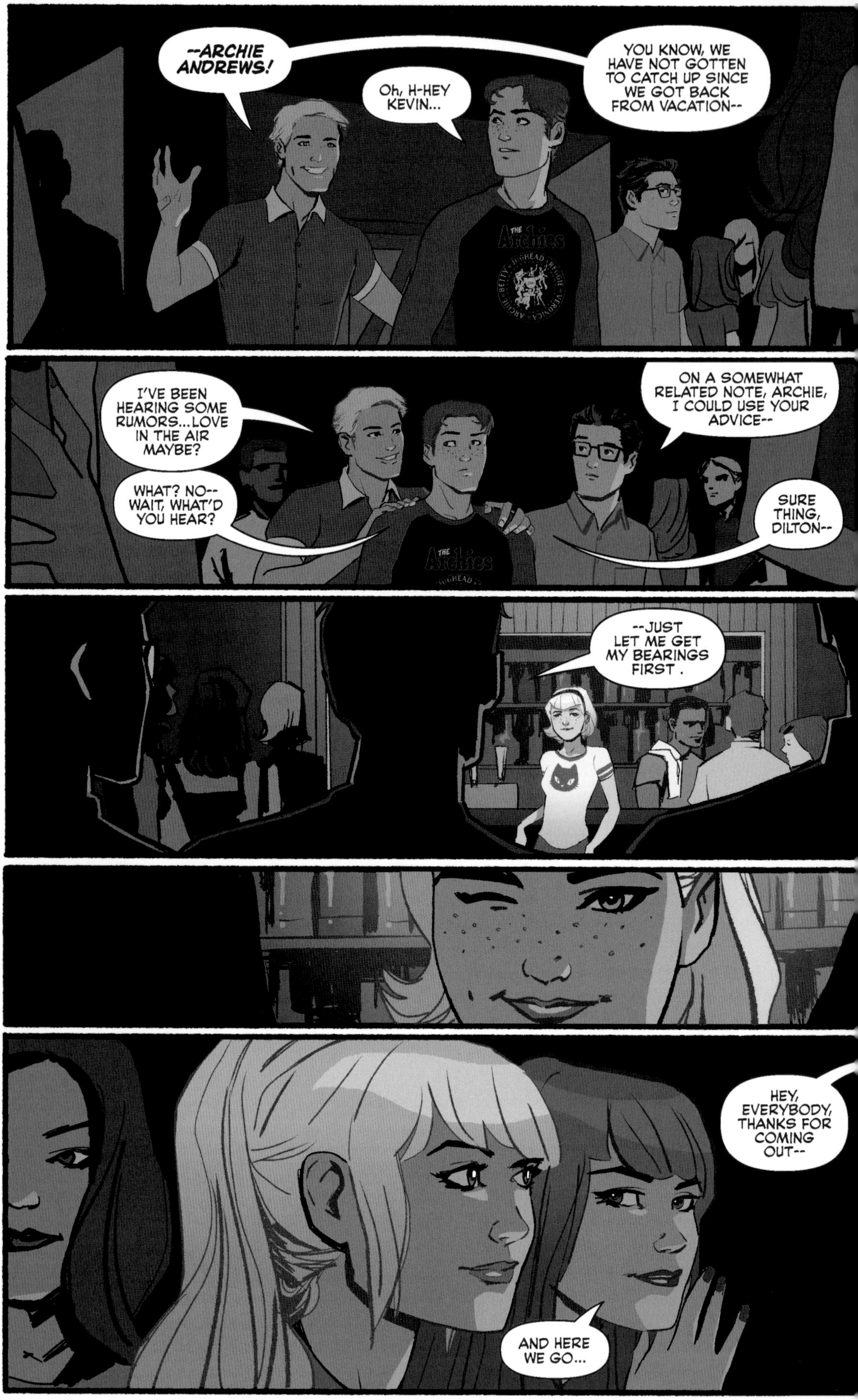
--ARCHIE ANDREWS!
Oh, H-HEY KEVIN...
YOU KNOW, WE HAVE NOT GOTTEN TO CATCH UP SINCE WE GOT BACK FROM VACATION--
THE Archies
I'VE BEEN HEARING SOME RUMORS...LOVE IN THE AIR MAYBE?
WHAT? NO--WAIT, WHAT'D YOU HEAR?
ON A SOMEWHAT RELATED NOTE, ARCHIE, I COULD USE YOUR ADVICE--
SURE THING, DILTON--
--JUST LET ME GET MY BEARINGS FIRST .
HEY, EVERYBODY, THANKS FOR COMING OUT--
AND HERE WE GO...

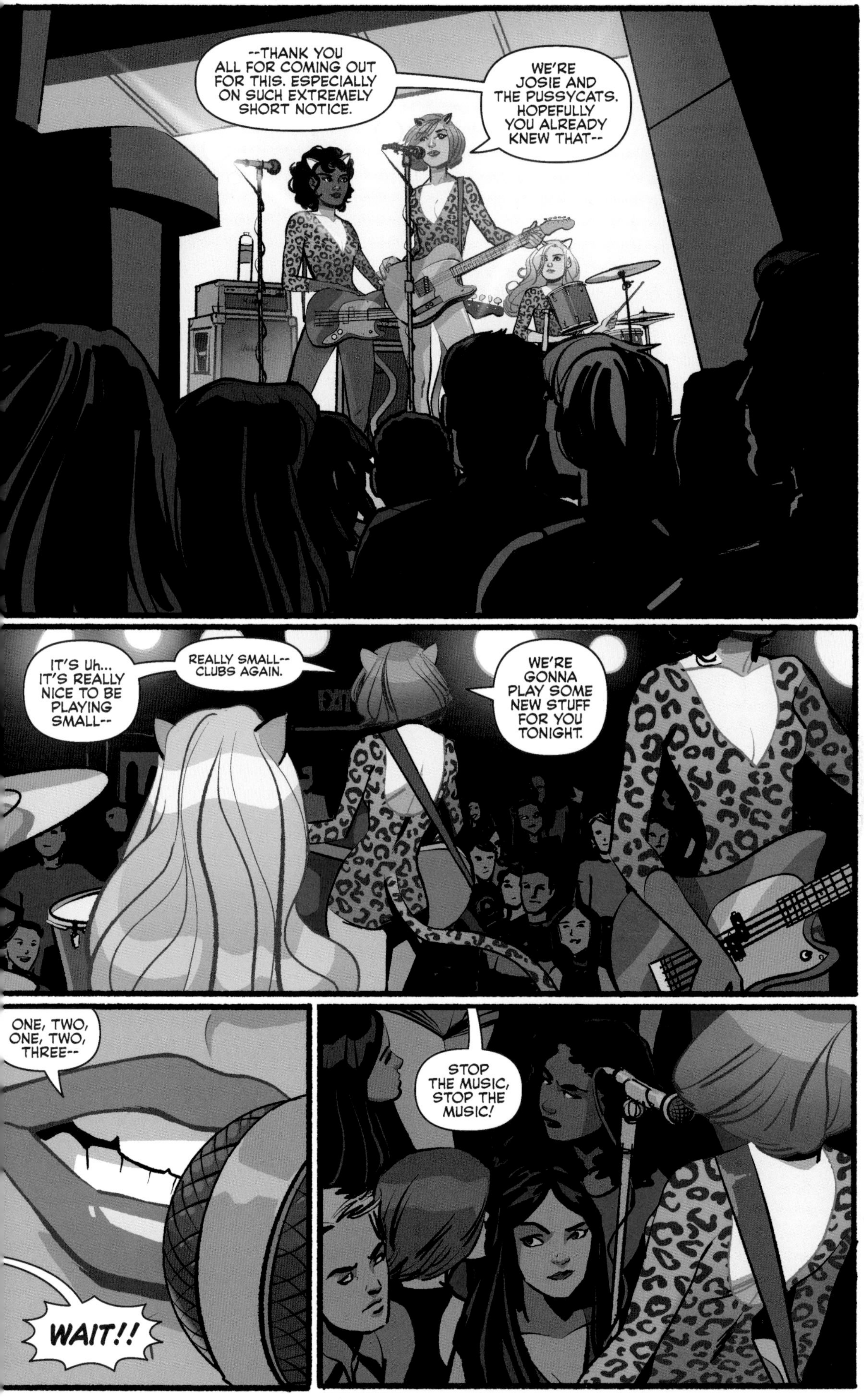
--THANK YOU ALL FOR COMING OUT FOR THIS. ESPECIALLY ON SUCH EXTREMELY SHORT NOTICE.
WE'RE JOSIE AND THE PUSSYCATS. HOPEFULLY YOU ALREADY KNEW THAT--
IT'S UH... IT'S REALLY NICE TO BE PLAYING SMALL--
REALLY SMALL--CLUBS AGAIN.
WE'RE GONNA PLAY SOME NEW STUFF FOR YOU TONIGHT.
ONE, TWO, ONE, TWO, THREE--
WAIT!!
STOP THE MUSIC, STOP THE MUSIC!

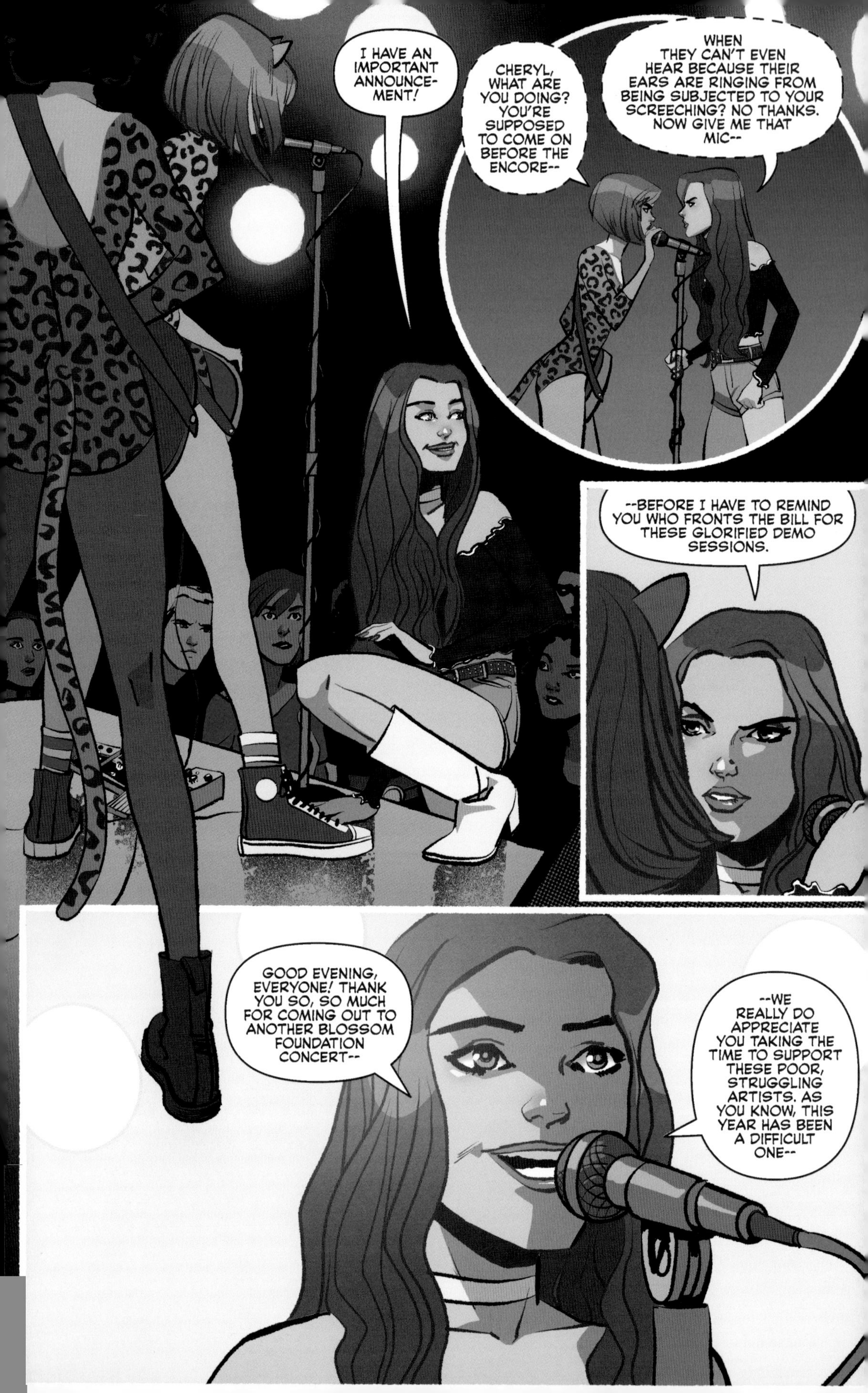
I HAVE AN IMPORTANT ANNOUNCE- MENT!
CHERYL, WHAT ARE YOU DOING? YOU'RE SUPPOSED TO COME ON BEFORE THE ENCORE--
WHEN THEY CAN'T EVEN HEAR BECAUSE THEIR EARS ARE RINGING FROM BEING SUBJECTED TO YOUR SCREECHING? NO THANKS. NOW GIVE ME THAT MIC--
--BEFORE I HAVE TO REMIND YOU WHO FRONTS THE BILL FOR THESE GLORIFIED DEMO SESSIONS.
GOOD EVENING, EVERYONE! THANK YOU SO, SO MUCH FOR COMING OUT TO ANOTHER BLOSSOM FOUNDATION CONCERT--
--WE REALLY DO APPRECIATE YOU TAKING THE TIME TO SUPPORT THESE POOR, STRUGGLING ARTISTS. AS YOU KNOW, THIS YEAR HAS BEEN A DIFFICULT ONE--

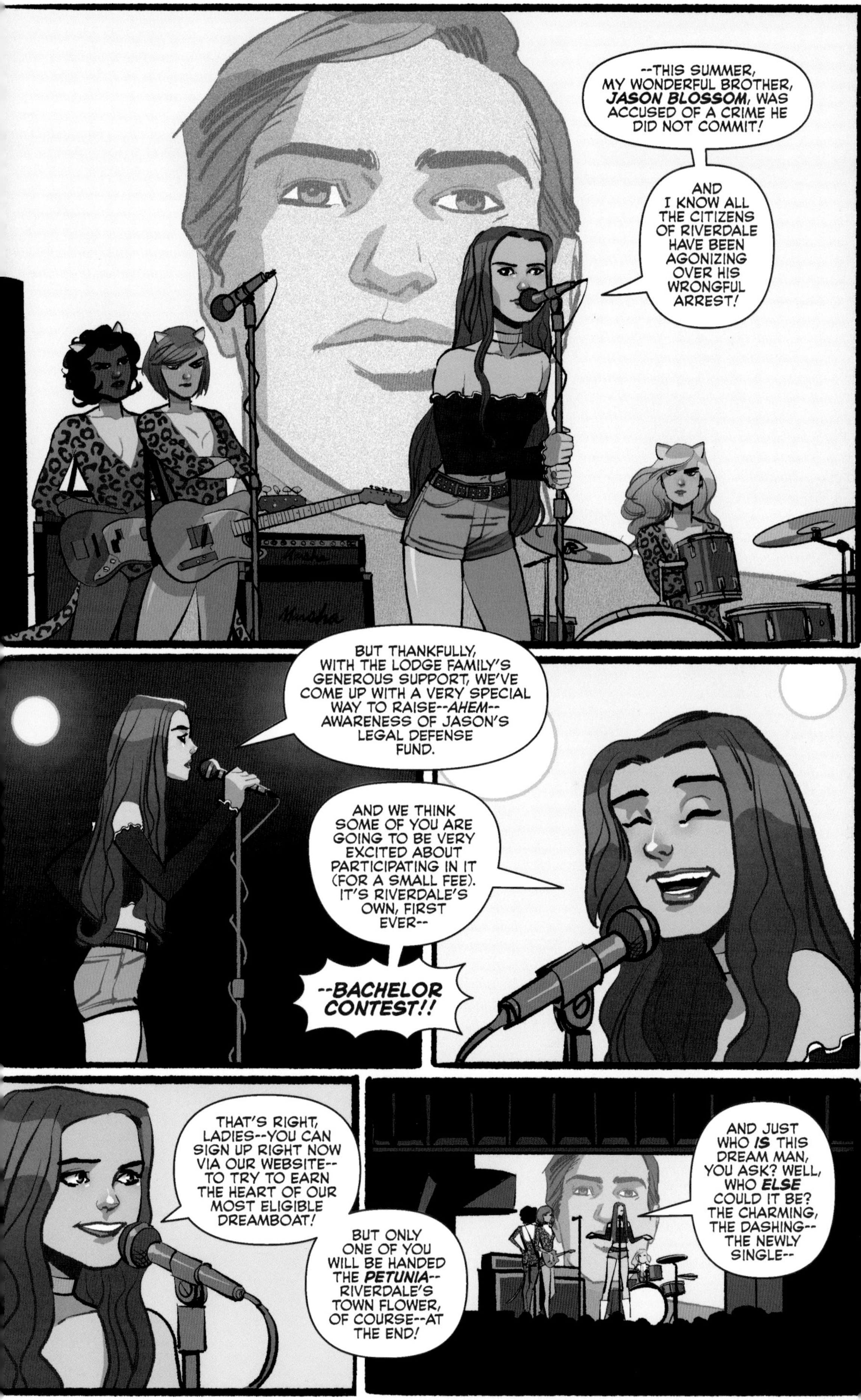
--THIS SUMMER, MY WONDERFUL BROTHER, *JASON BLOSSOM*, WAS ACCUSED OF A CRIME HE DID NOT COMMIT!
AND I KNOW ALL THE CITIZENS OF RIVERDALE HAVE BEEN AGONIZING OVER HIS WRONGFUL ARREST!
BUT THANKFULLY, WITH THE LODGE FAMILY'S GENEROUS SUPPORT, WE'VE COME UP WITH A VERY SPECIAL WAY TO RAISE--*AHEM*--AWARENESS OF JASON'S LEGAL DEFENSE FUND.
AND WE THINK SOME OF YOU ARE GOING TO BE VERY EXCITED ABOUT PARTICIPATING IN IT (FOR A SMALL FEE). IT'S RIVERDALE'S OWN, FIRST EVER--
--BACHELOR CONTEST!!
THAT'S RIGHT, LADIES--YOU CAN SIGN UP RIGHT NOW VIA OUR WEBSITE--TO TRY TO EARN THE HEART OF OUR MOST ELIGIBLE DREAMBOAT!
BUT ONLY ONE OF YOU WILL BE HANDED THE *PETUNIA*--RIVERDALE'S TOWN FLOWER, OF COURSE--AT THE END!
AND JUST WHO *IS* THIS DREAM MAN, YOU ASK? WELL, WHO *ELSE* COULD IT BE? THE CHARMING, THE DASHING--THE NEWLY SINGLE--

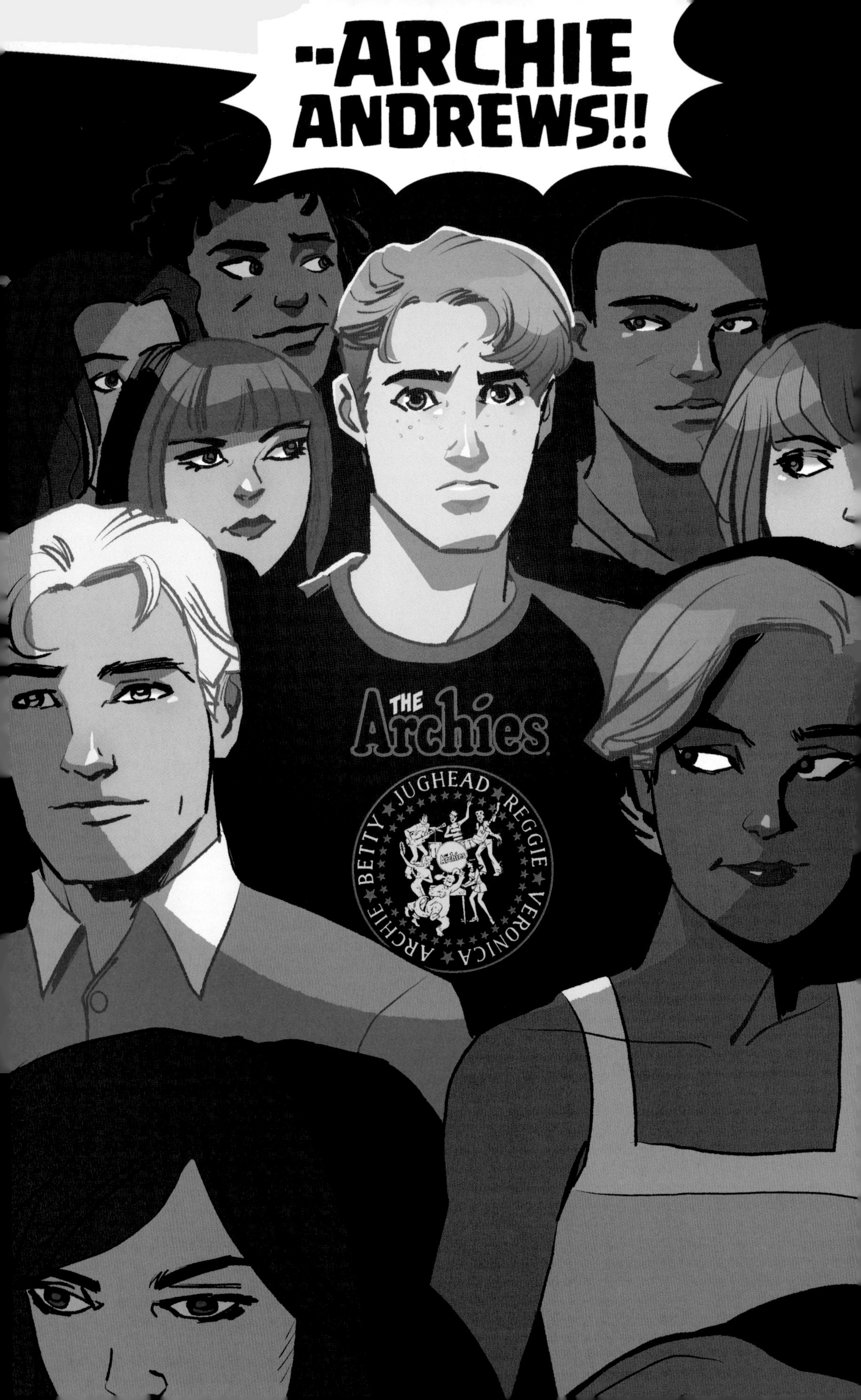
--ARCHIE ANDREWS!!
THE Archies
JUGHEAD REGGIE VERONICA ARCHIE BETTY
Archies

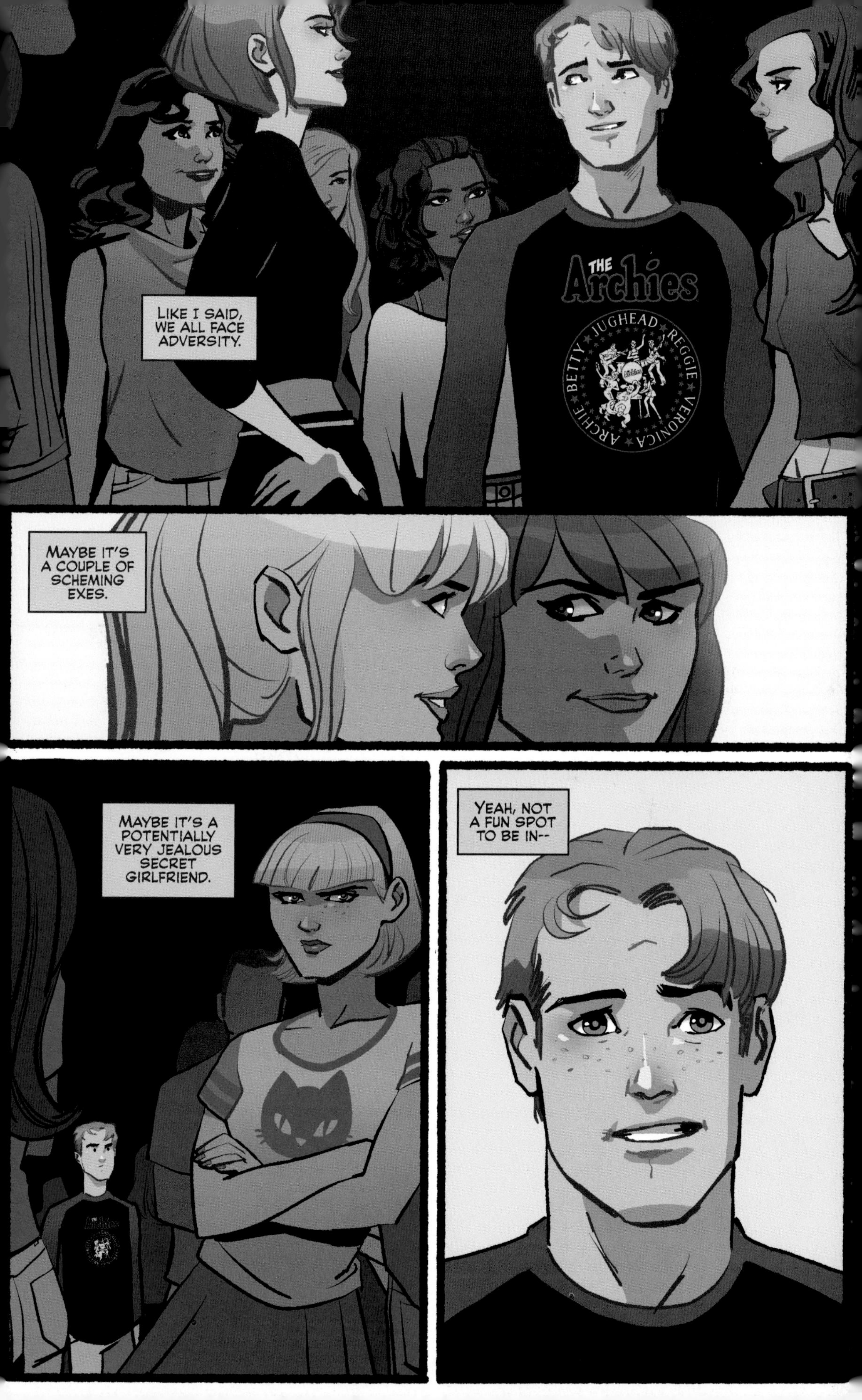
LIKE I SAID, WE ALL FACE ADVERSITY.
THE Archies
JUGHEAD REGGIE VERONICA ARCHIE BETTY
MAYBE IT'S A COUPLE OF SCHEMING EXES.
MAYBE IT'S A POTENTIALLY VERY JEALOUS SECRET GIRLFRIEND.
YEAH, NOT A FUN SPOT TO BE IN--

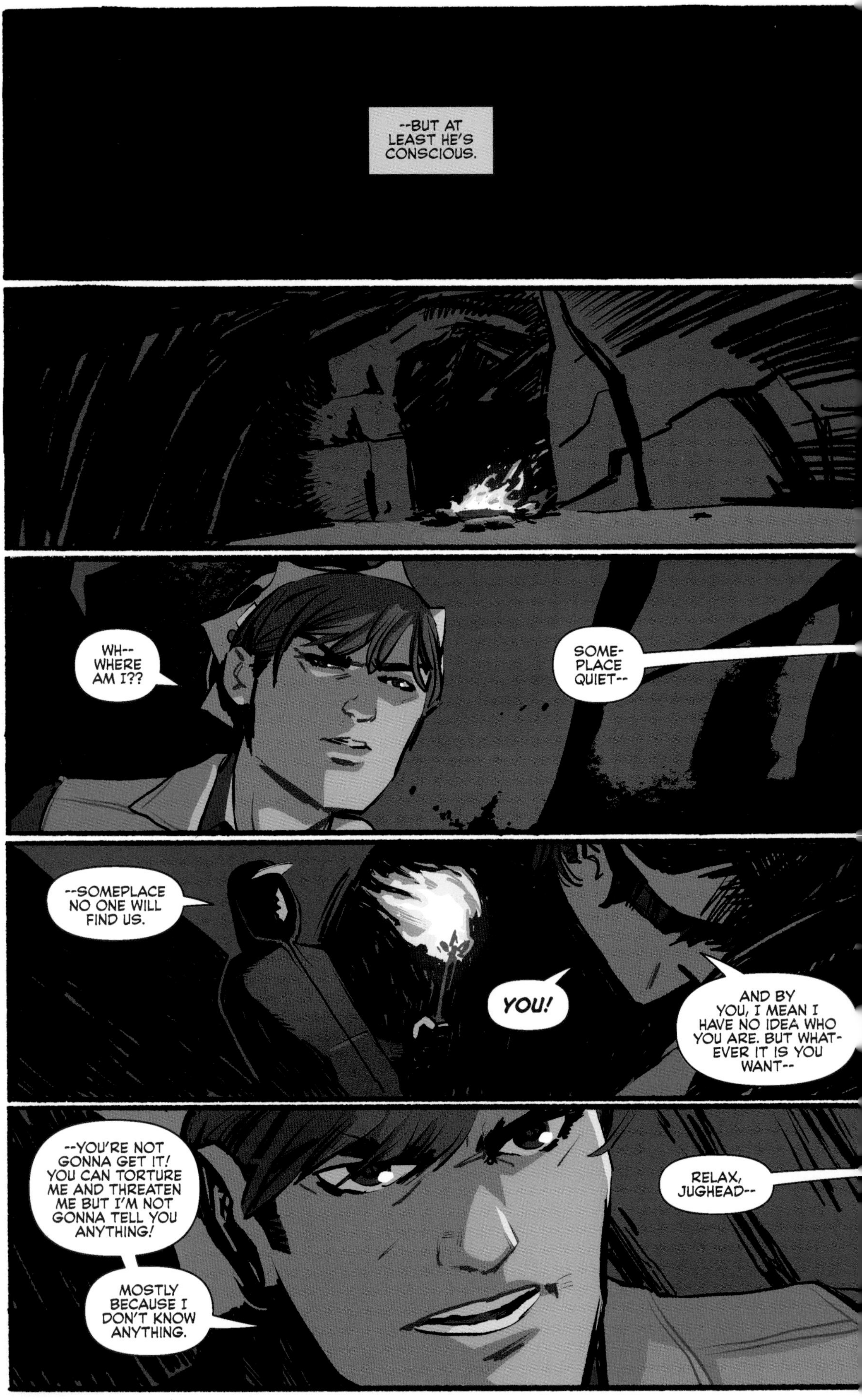
--BUT AT LEAST HE'S CONSCIOUS.
WH-- WHERE AM I??
SOME-PLACE QUIET--
--SOMEPLACE NO ONE WILL FIND US.
YOU!
AND BY YOU, I MEAN I HAVE NO IDEA WHO YOU ARE. BUT WHAT-EVER IT IS YOU WANT--
--YOU'RE NOT GONNA GET IT! YOU CAN TORTURE ME AND THREATEN ME BUT I'M NOT GONNA TELL YOU ANYTHING!
MOSTLY BECAUSE I DON'T KNOW ANYTHING.
RELAX, JUGHEAD--

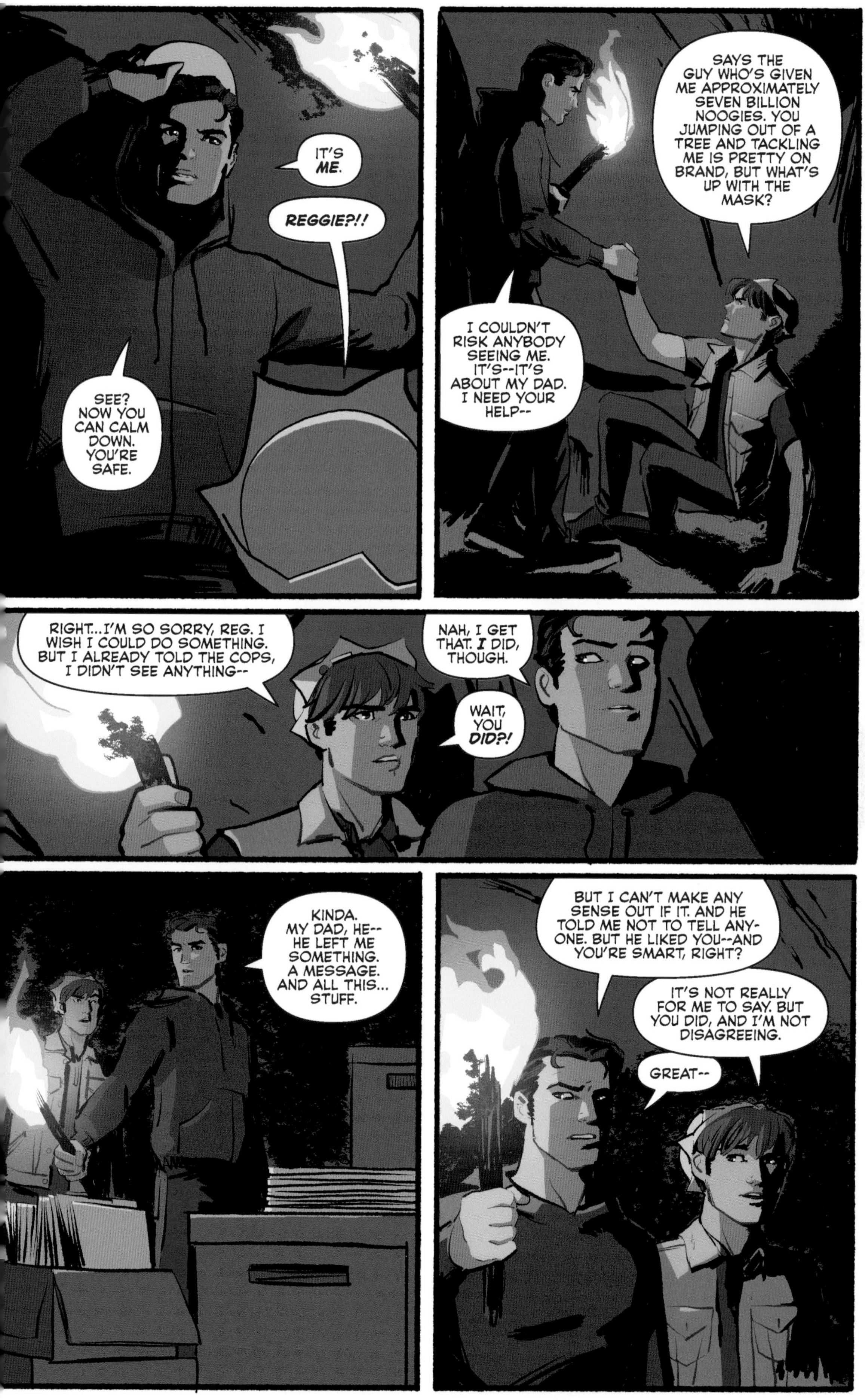
IT'S ME.
REGGIE?!!
SEE? NOW YOU CAN CALM DOWN. YOU'RE SAFE.
SAYS THE GUY WHO'S GIVEN ME APPROXIMATELY SEVEN BILLION NOOGIES. YOU JUMPING OUT OF A TREE AND TACKLING ME IS PRETTY ON BRAND, BUT WHAT'S UP WITH THE MASK?
I COULDN'T RISK ANYBODY SEEING ME. IT'S--IT'S ABOUT MY DAD. I NEED YOUR HELP--
RIGHT...I'M SO SORRY, REG. I WISH I COULD DO SOMETHING. BUT I ALREADY TOLD THE COPS, I DIDN'T SEE ANYTHING--
NAH, I GET THAT. I DID, THOUGH.
WAIT, YOU DID?!
KINDA. MY DAD, HE--HE LEFT ME SOMETHING. A MESSAGE. AND ALL THIS... STUFF.
BUT I CAN'T MAKE ANY SENSE OUT IF IT. AND HE TOLD ME NOT TO TELL ANYONE. BUT HE LIKED YOU--AND YOU'RE SMART, RIGHT?
IT'S NOT REALLY FOR ME TO SAY. BUT YOU DID, AND I'M NOT DISAGREEING.
GREAT--

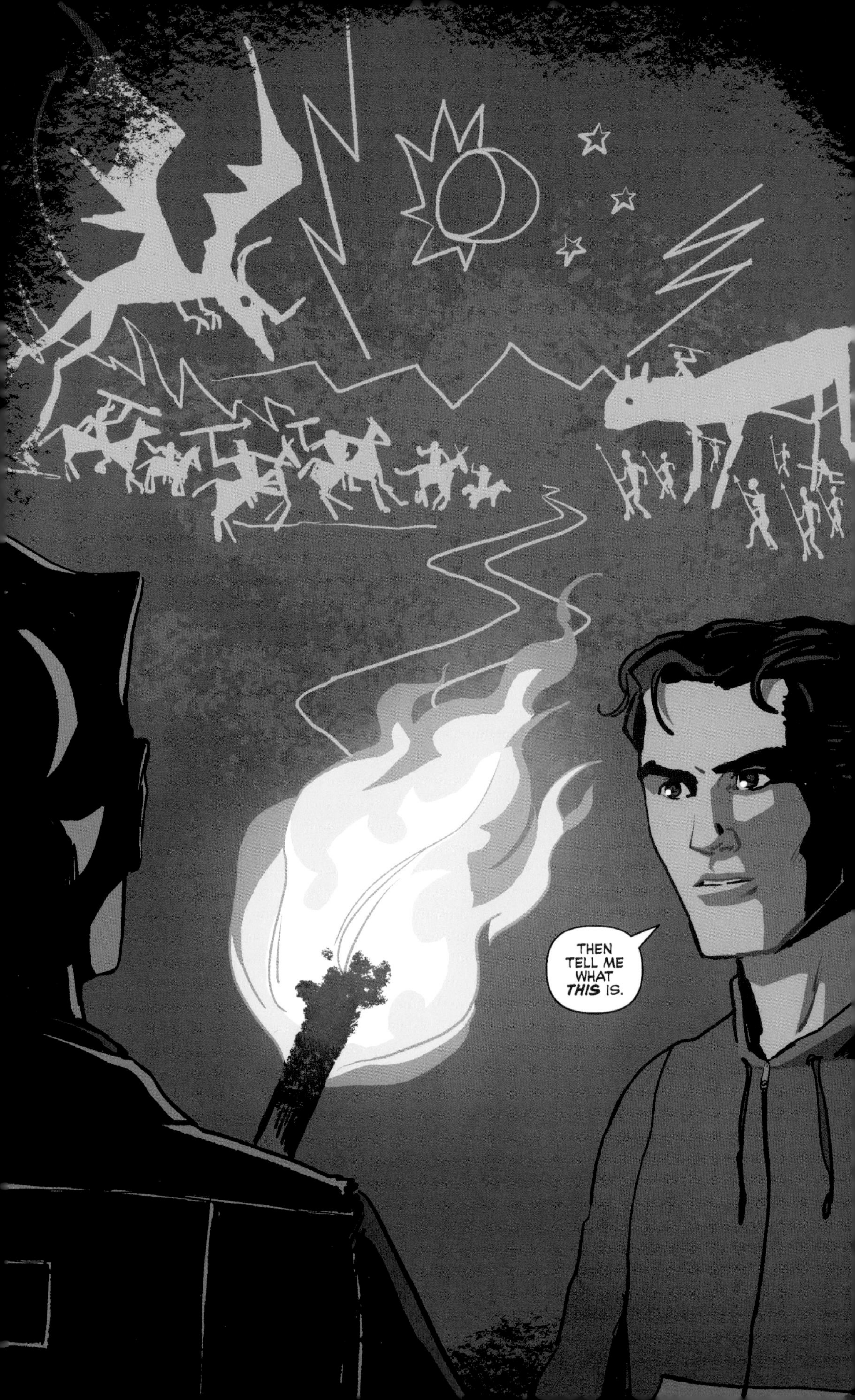
THEN TELL ME WHAT THIS IS.

TO BE CONTINUED...

704

STORY BY
NICK SPENCER

ART BY
SANDY JARRELL

LETTERING BY
JACK MORELLI

COLORS BY
MATT HERMS

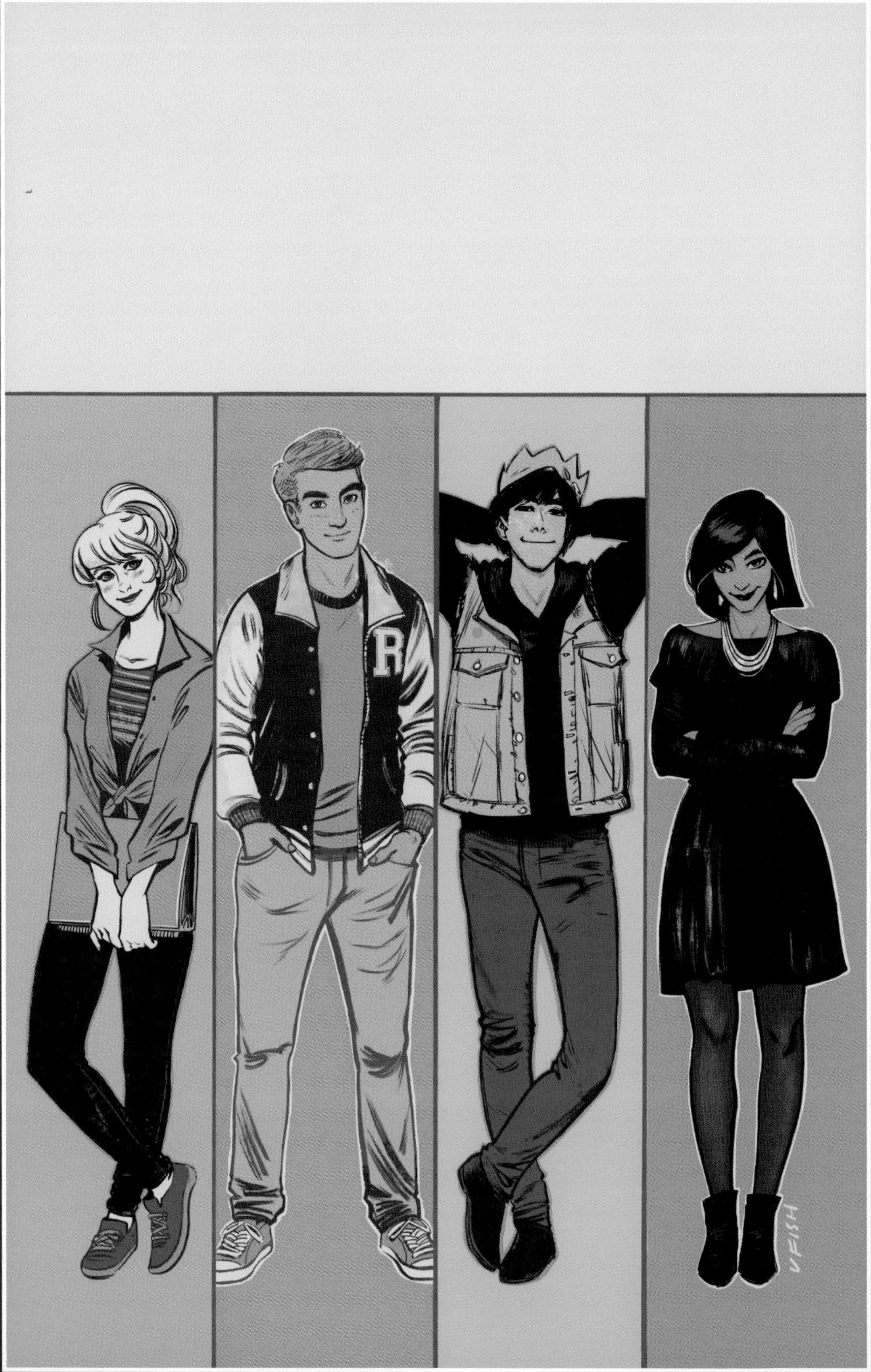

R
VFISH

COVER ART: VERONICA FISH

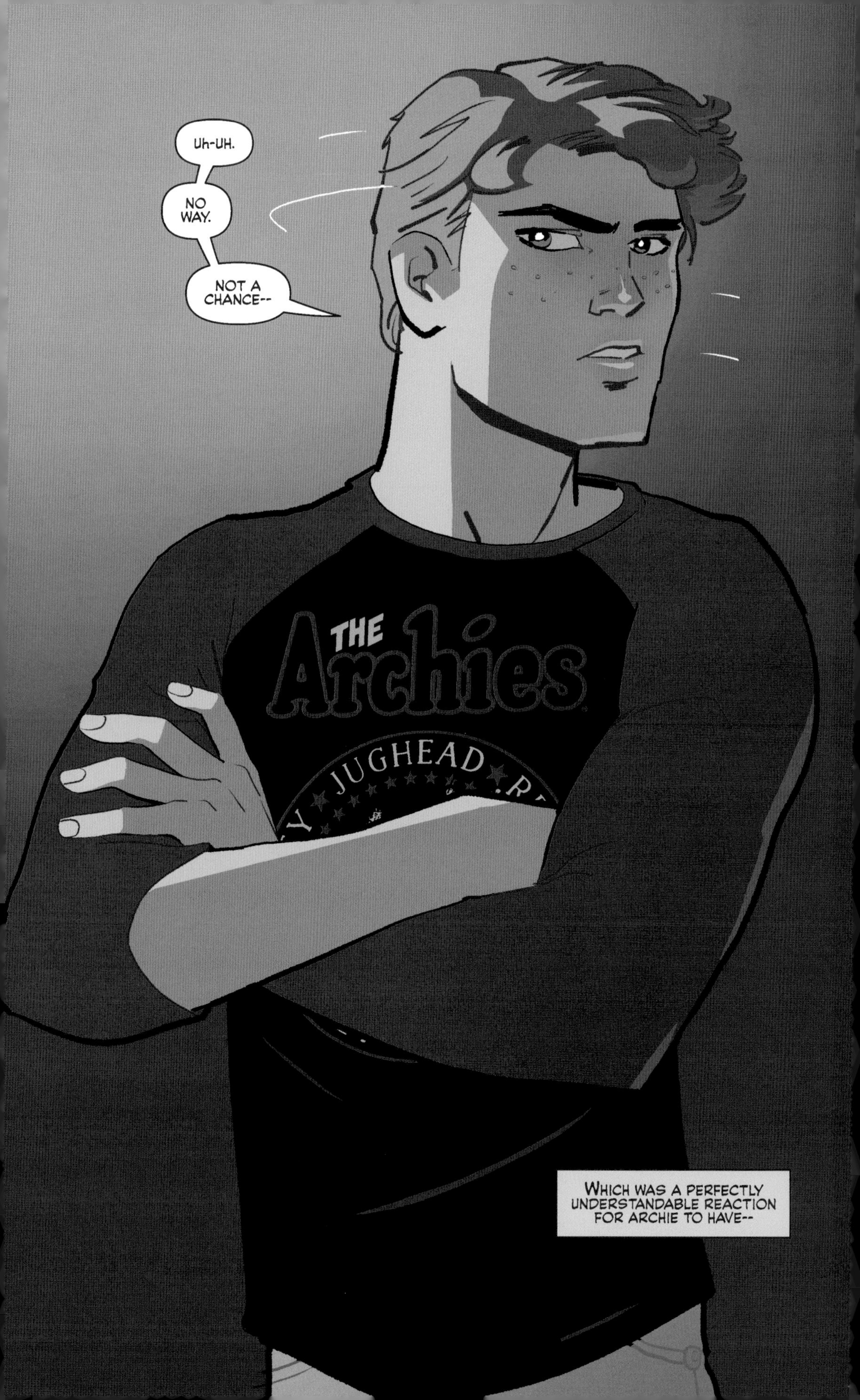
UH-UH.
NO WAY.
NOT A CHANCE--
THE Archies
JUGHEAD
WHICH WAS A PERFECTLY UNDERSTANDABLE REACTION FOR ARCHIE TO HAVE--

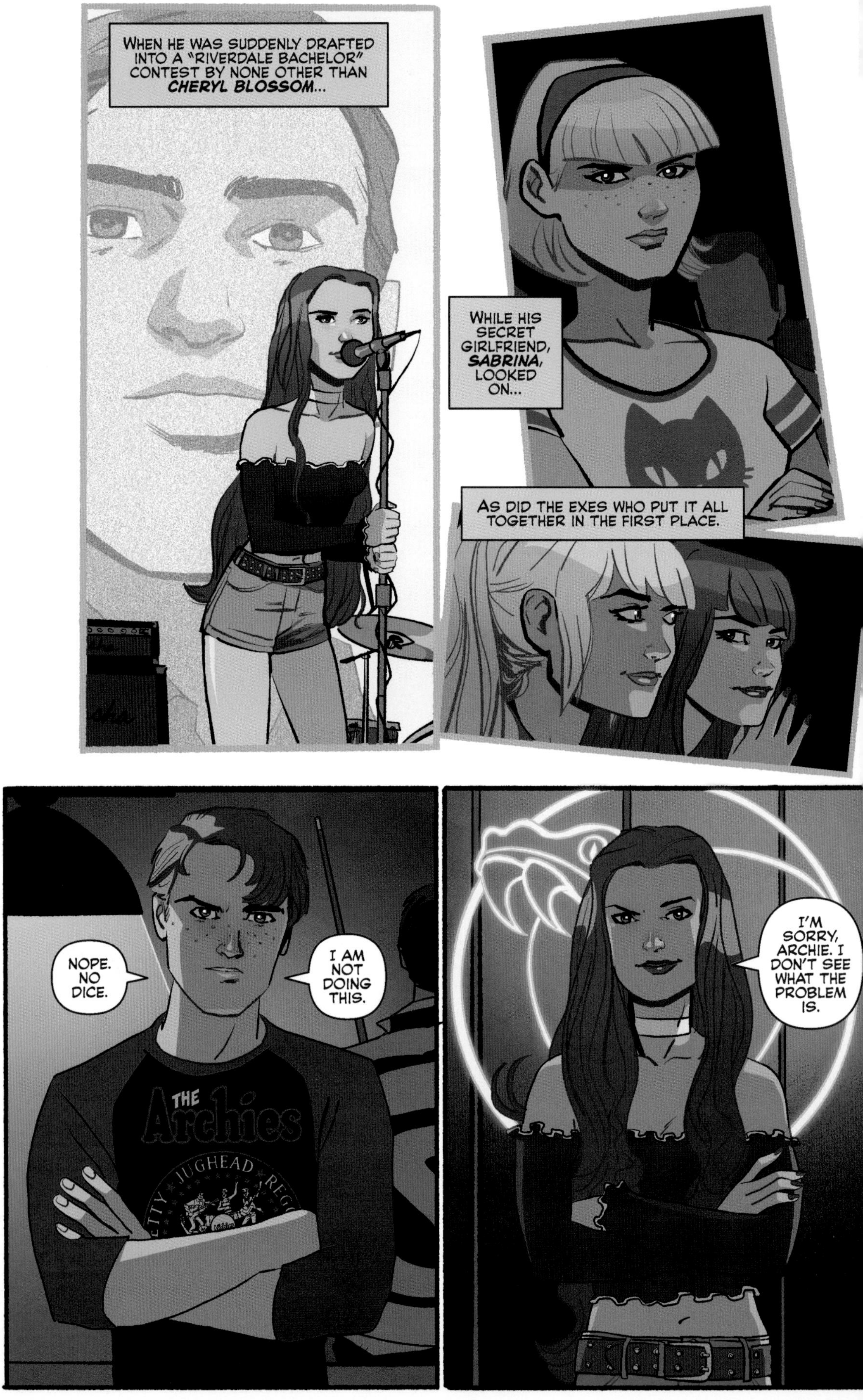
WHEN HE WAS SUDDENLY DRAFTED INTO A "RIVERDALE BACHELOR" CONTEST BY NONE OTHER THAN CHERYL BLOSSOM...
WHILE HIS SECRET GIRLFRIEND, SABRINA, LOOKED ON...
AS DID THE EXES WHO PUT IT ALL TOGETHER IN THE FIRST PLACE.
I AM NOT DOING THIS.
NOPE. NO DICE.
THE Archies
JUGHEAD
I'M SORRY, ARCHIE. I DON'T SEE WHAT THE PROBLEM IS.

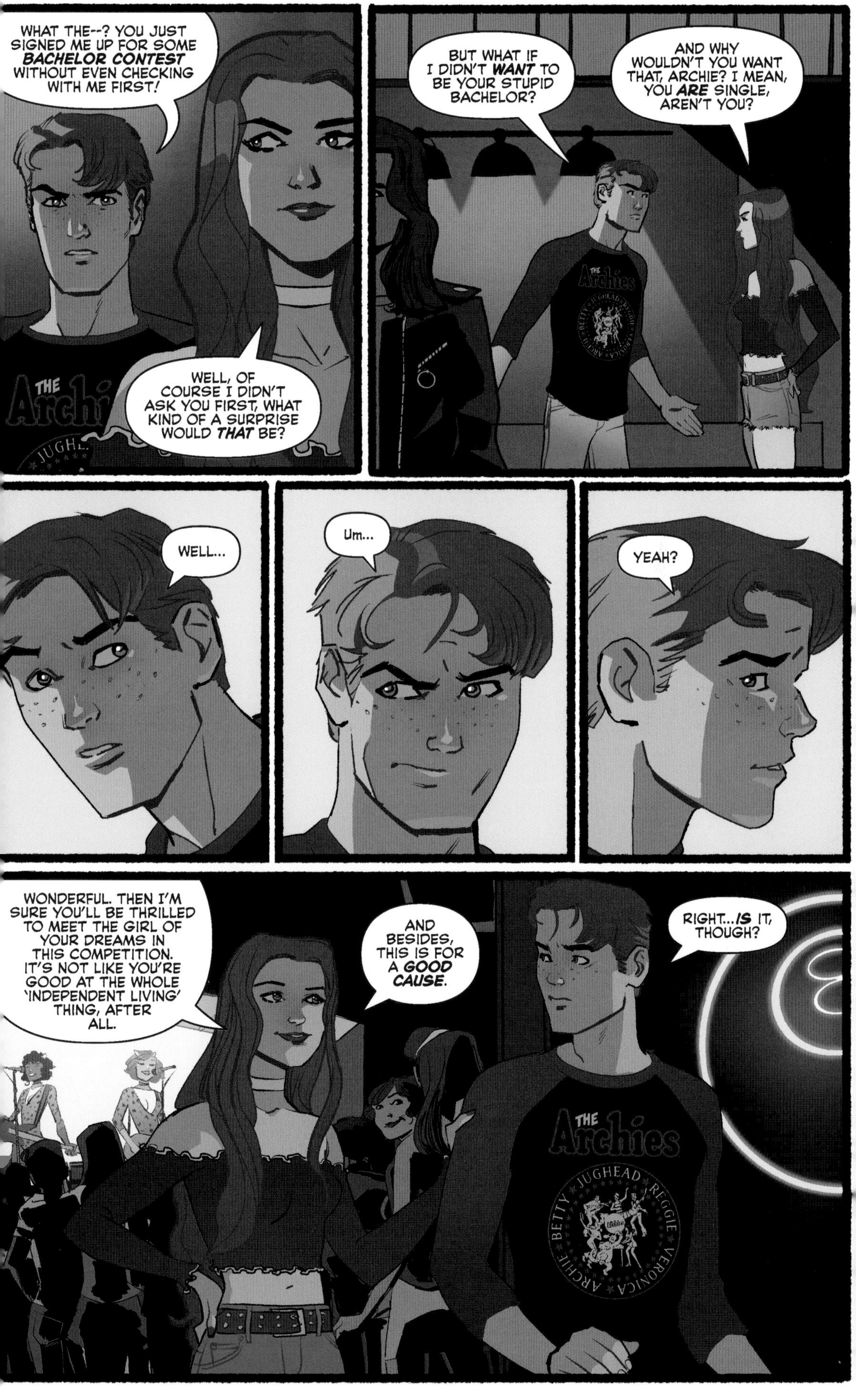
WHAT THE--? YOU JUST SIGNED ME UP FOR SOME ***BACHELOR CONTEST*** WITHOUT EVEN CHECKING WITH ME FIRST!
WELL, OF COURSE I DIDN'T ASK YOU FIRST, WHAT KIND OF A SURPRISE WOULD ***THAT*** BE?
THE Archies
JUGHEAD
BUT WHAT IF I DIDN'T ***WANT*** TO BE YOUR STUPID BACHELOR?
AND WHY WOULDN'T YOU WANT THAT, ARCHIE? I MEAN, YOU ***ARE*** SINGLE, AREN'T YOU?
WELL...
Um...
YEAH?
WONDERFUL. THEN I'M SURE YOU'LL BE THRILLED TO MEET THE GIRL OF YOUR DREAMS IN THIS COMPETITION. IT'S NOT LIKE YOU'RE GOOD AT THE WHOLE 'INDEPENDENT LIVING' THING, AFTER ALL.
AND BESIDES, THIS IS FOR A ***GOOD CAUSE***.
RIGHT...***IS*** IT, THOUGH?
THE Archies
JUGHEAD REGGIE VERONICA ARCHIE BETTY

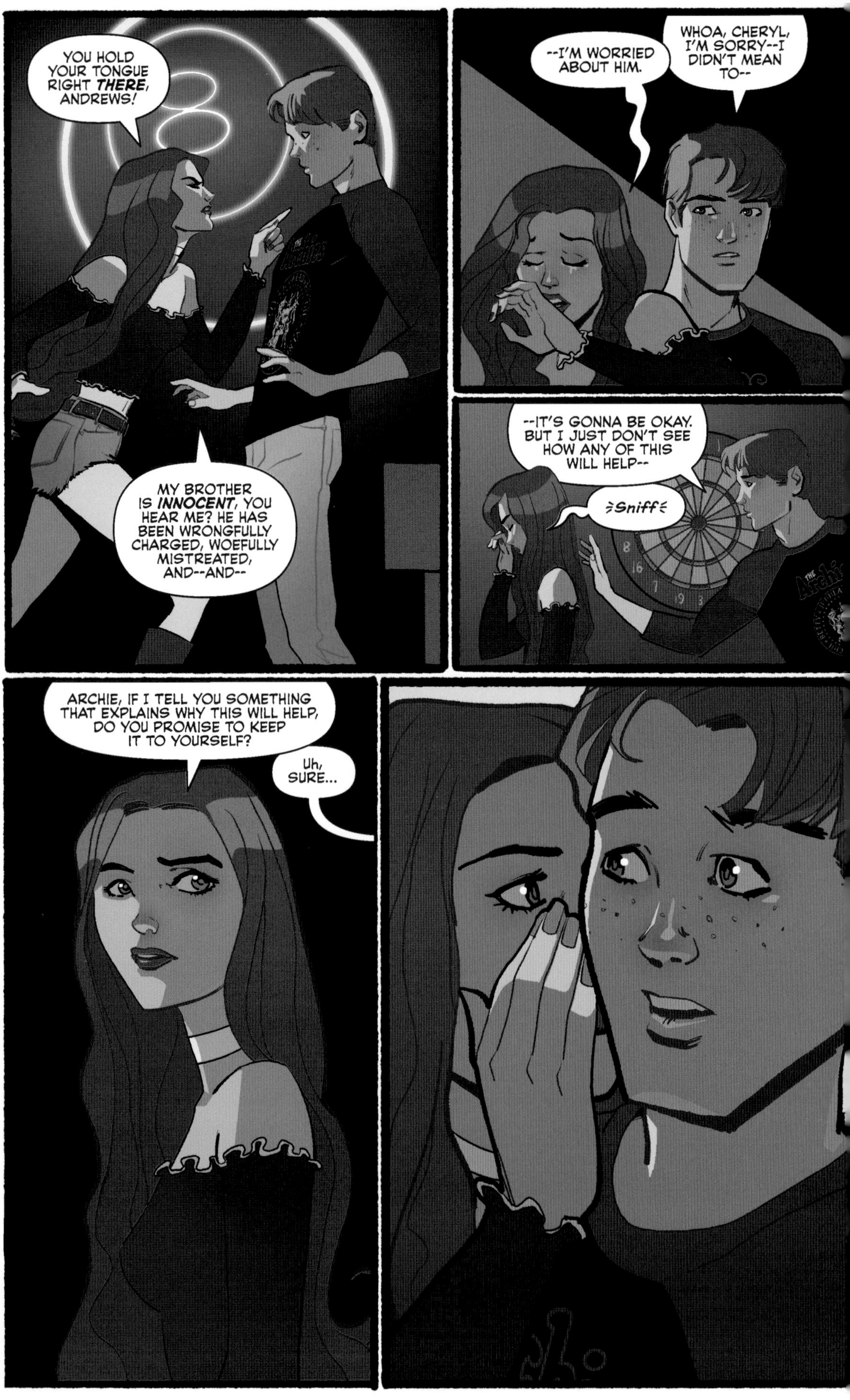
YOU HOLD YOUR TONGUE RIGHT *THERE*, ANDREWS!
MY BROTHER IS *INNOCENT*, YOU HEAR ME? HE HAS BEEN WRONGFULLY CHARGED, WOEFULLY MISTREATED, AND--AND--
WHOA, CHERYL, I'M SORRY--I DIDN'T MEAN TO--
--I'M WORRIED ABOUT HIM.
--IT'S GONNA BE OKAY. BUT I JUST DON'T SEE HOW ANY OF THIS WILL HELP--
Sniff
ARCHIE, IF I TELL YOU SOMETHING THAT EXPLAINS WHY THIS WILL HELP, DO YOU PROMISE TO KEEP IT TO YOURSELF?
Uh, SURE...

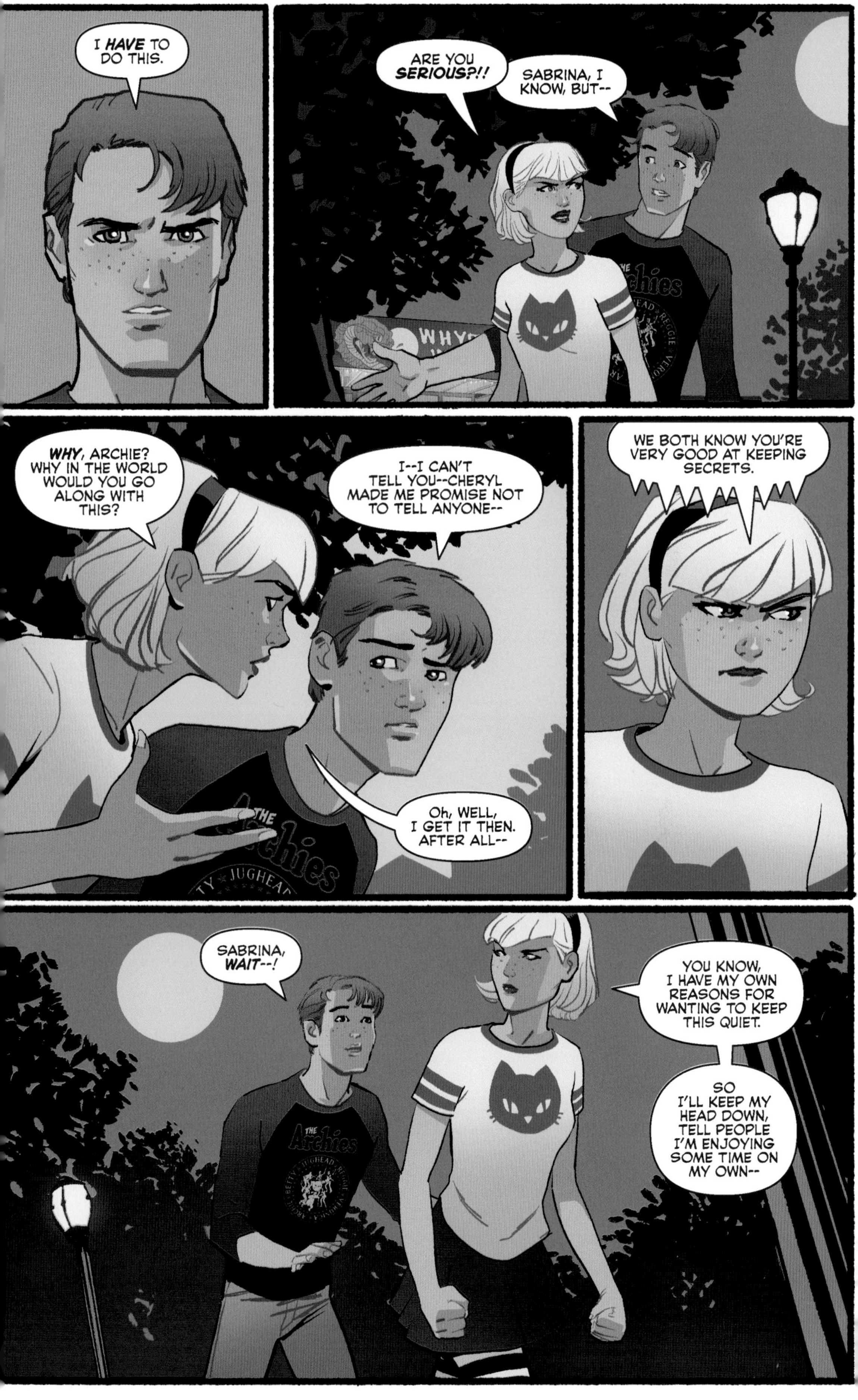
I HAVE TO DO THIS.
ARE YOU SERIOUS?!!
SABRINA, I KNOW, BUT--
WHY, ARCHIE? WHY IN THE WORLD WOULD YOU GO ALONG WITH THIS?
I--I CAN'T TELL YOU--CHERYL MADE ME PROMISE NOT TO TELL ANYONE--
Oh, WELL, I GET IT THEN. AFTER ALL--
WE BOTH KNOW YOU'RE VERY GOOD AT KEEPING SECRETS.
SABRINA, WAIT--!
YOU KNOW, I HAVE MY OWN REASONS FOR WANTING TO KEEP THIS QUIET.
SO I'LL KEEP MY HEAD DOWN, TELL PEOPLE I'M ENJOYING SOME TIME ON MY OWN--

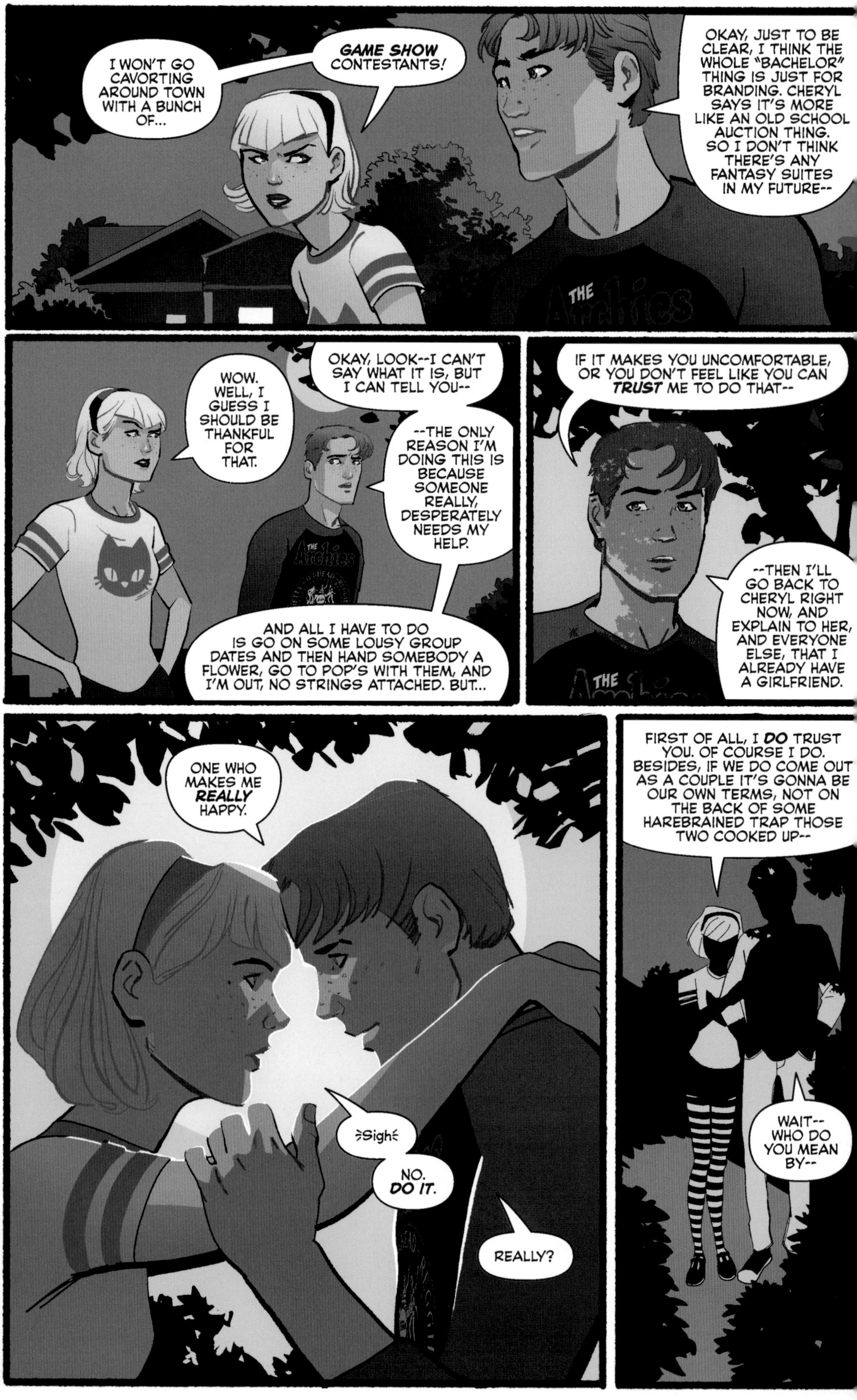
I WON'T GO CAVORTING AROUND TOWN WITH A BUNCH OF...
GAME SHOW CONTESTANTS!
OKAY, JUST TO BE CLEAR, I THINK THE WHOLE "BACHELOR" THING IS JUST FOR BRANDING. CHERYL SAYS IT'S MORE LIKE AN OLD SCHOOL AUCTION THING. SO I DON'T THINK THERE'S ANY FANTASY SUITES IN MY FUTURE--
WOW. WELL, I GUESS I SHOULD BE THANKFUL FOR THAT.
OKAY, LOOK--I CAN'T SAY WHAT IT IS, BUT I CAN TELL YOU--
--THE ONLY REASON I'M DOING THIS IS BECAUSE SOMEONE REALLY, DESPERATELY NEEDS MY HELP.
AND ALL I HAVE TO DO IS GO ON SOME LOUSY GROUP DATES AND THEN HAND SOMEBODY A FLOWER, GO TO POP'S WITH THEM, AND I'M OUT, NO STRINGS ATTACHED. BUT...
IF IT MAKES YOU UNCOMFORTABLE, OR YOU DON'T FEEL LIKE YOU CAN TRUST ME TO DO THAT--
--THEN I'LL GO BACK TO CHERYL RIGHT NOW, AND EXPLAIN TO HER, AND EVERYONE ELSE, THAT I ALREADY HAVE A GIRLFRIEND.
ONE WHO MAKES ME REALLY HAPPY.
Sigh
NO. DO IT.
REALLY?
FIRST OF ALL, I DO TRUST YOU. OF COURSE I DO. BESIDES, IF WE DO COME OUT AS A COUPLE IT'S GONNA BE OUR OWN TERMS, NOT ON THE BACK OF SOME HAREBRAINED TRAP THOSE TWO COOKED UP--
WAIT-- WHO DO YOU MEAN BY--

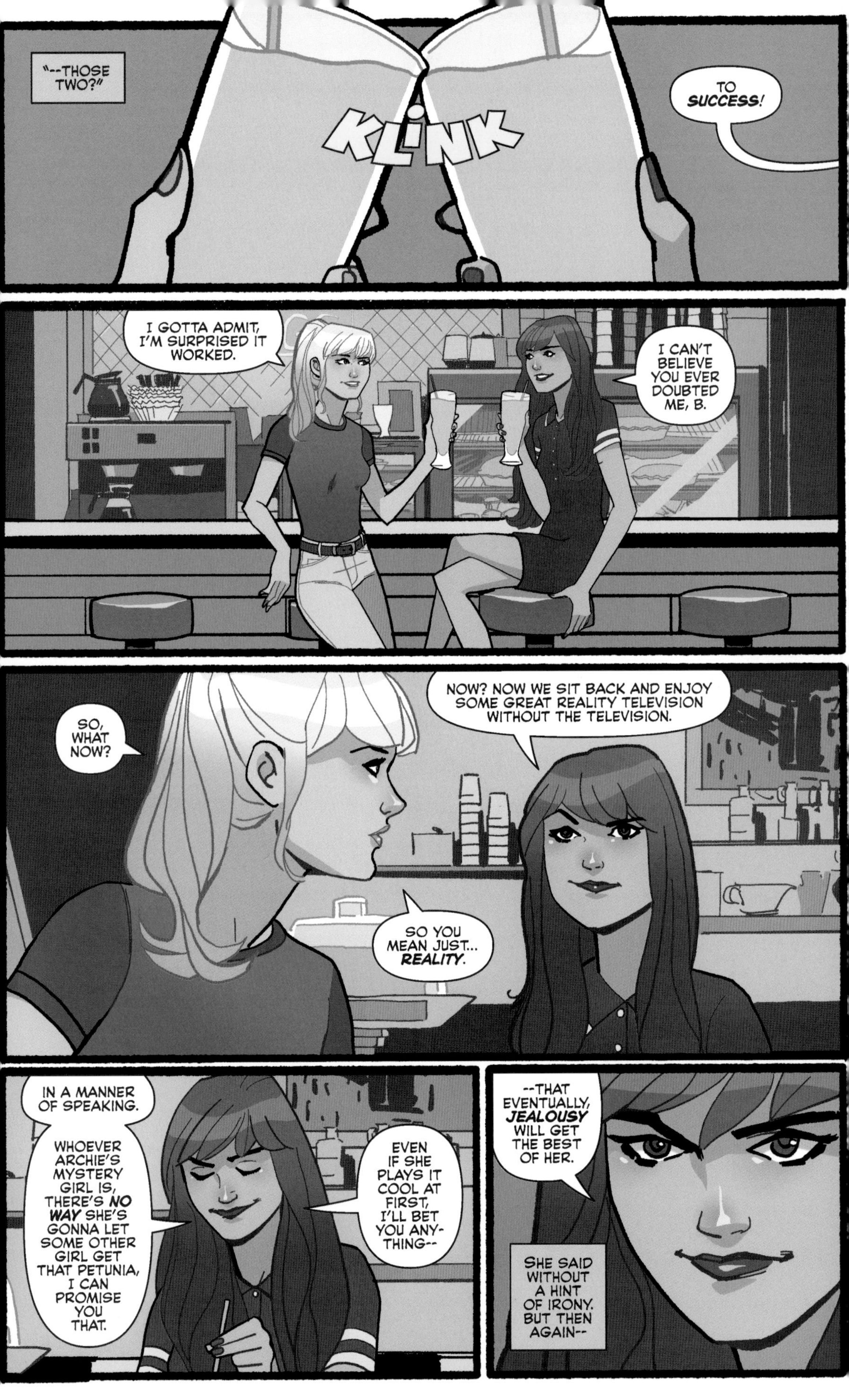
"--THOSE TWO?"
KLINK
TO SUCCESS!
I GOTTA ADMIT, I'M SURPRISED IT WORKED.
I CAN'T BELIEVE YOU EVER DOUBTED ME, B.
SO, WHAT NOW?
NOW? NOW WE SIT BACK AND ENJOY SOME GREAT REALITY TELEVISION WITHOUT THE TELEVISION.
SO YOU MEAN JUST... ***REALITY***.
IN A MANNER OF SPEAKING.
WHOEVER ARCHIE'S MYSTERY GIRL IS, THERE'S ***NO WAY*** SHE'S GONNA LET SOME OTHER GIRL GET THAT PETUNIA, I CAN PROMISE YOU THAT.
EVEN IF SHE PLAYS IT COOL AT FIRST, I'LL BET YOU ANY-THING--
--THAT EVENTUALLY, ***JEALOUSY*** WILL GET THE BEST OF HER.
SHE SAID WITHOUT A HINT OF IRONY. BUT THEN AGAIN--

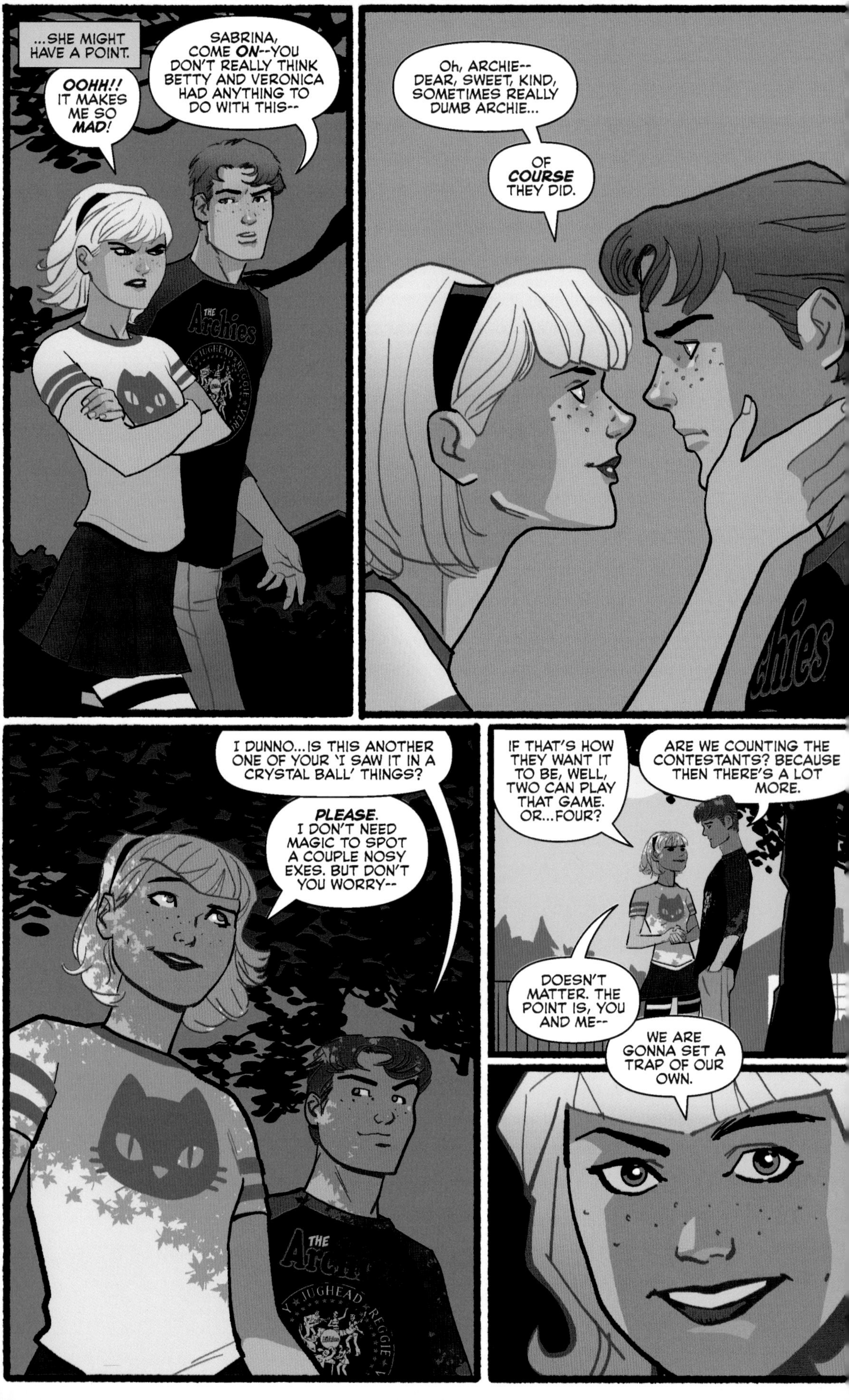
...SHE MIGHT HAVE A POINT.
SABRINA, COME ON--YOU DON'T REALLY THINK BETTY AND VERONICA HAD ANYTHING TO DO WITH THIS--
OOHH!! IT MAKES ME SO MAD!
Oh, ARCHIE-- DEAR, SWEET, KIND, SOMETIMES REALLY DUMB ARCHIE...
OF COURSE THEY DID.
THE Archies
I DUNNO...IS THIS ANOTHER ONE OF YOUR 'I SAW IT IN A CRYSTAL BALL' THINGS?
PLEASE. I DON'T NEED MAGIC TO SPOT A COUPLE NOSY EXES. BUT DON'T YOU WORRY--
IF THAT'S HOW THEY WANT IT TO BE, WELL, TWO CAN PLAY THAT GAME. OR...FOUR?
ARE WE COUNTING THE CONTESTANTS? BECAUSE THEN THERE'S A LOT MORE.
DOESN'T MATTER. THE POINT IS, YOU AND ME--
WE ARE GONNA SET A TRAP OF OUR OWN.

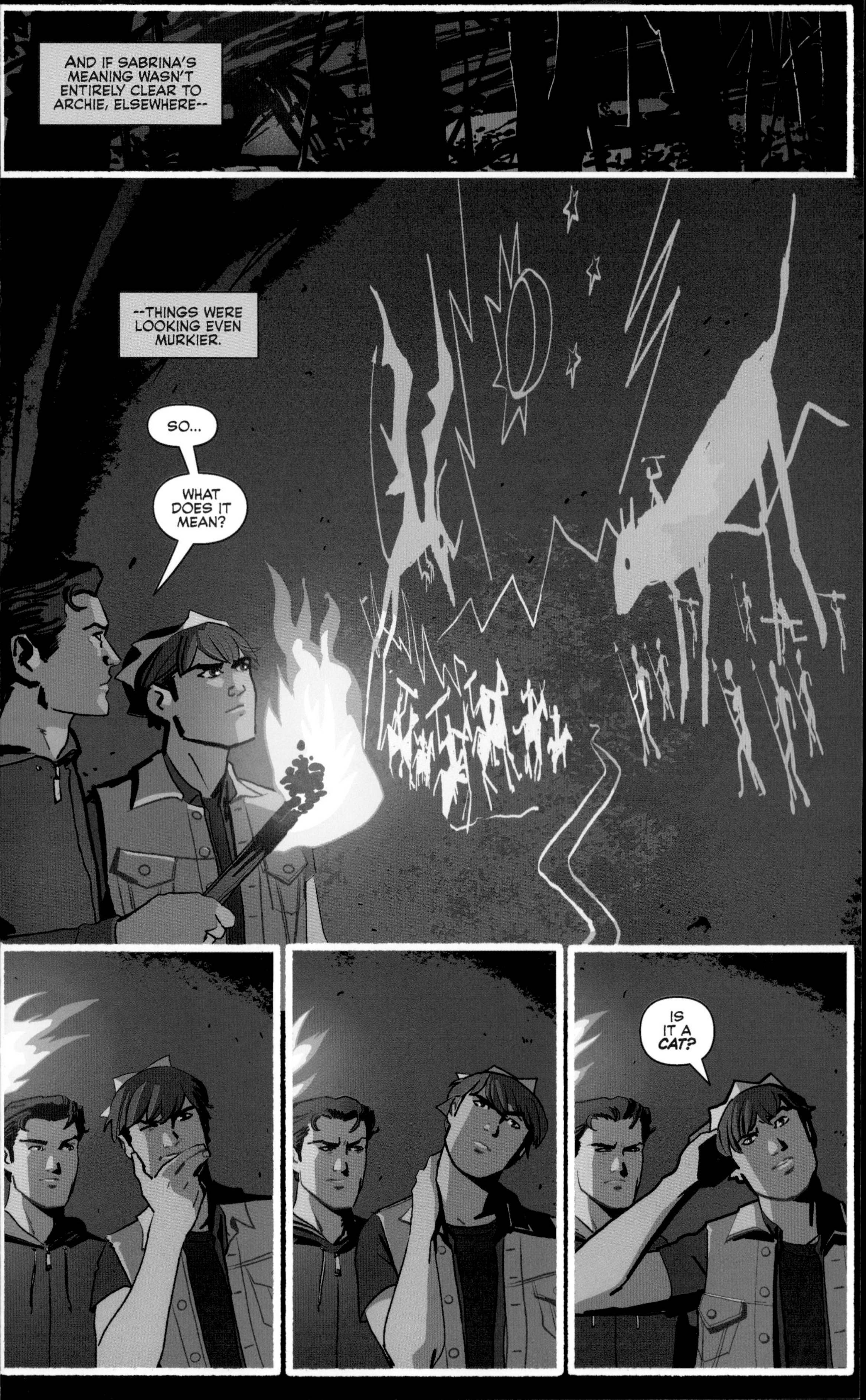
AND IF SABRINA'S MEANING WASN'T ENTIRELY CLEAR TO ARCHIE, ELSEWHERE--
--THINGS WERE LOOKING EVEN MURKIER.
SO...
WHAT DOES IT MEAN?
IS IT A CAT?

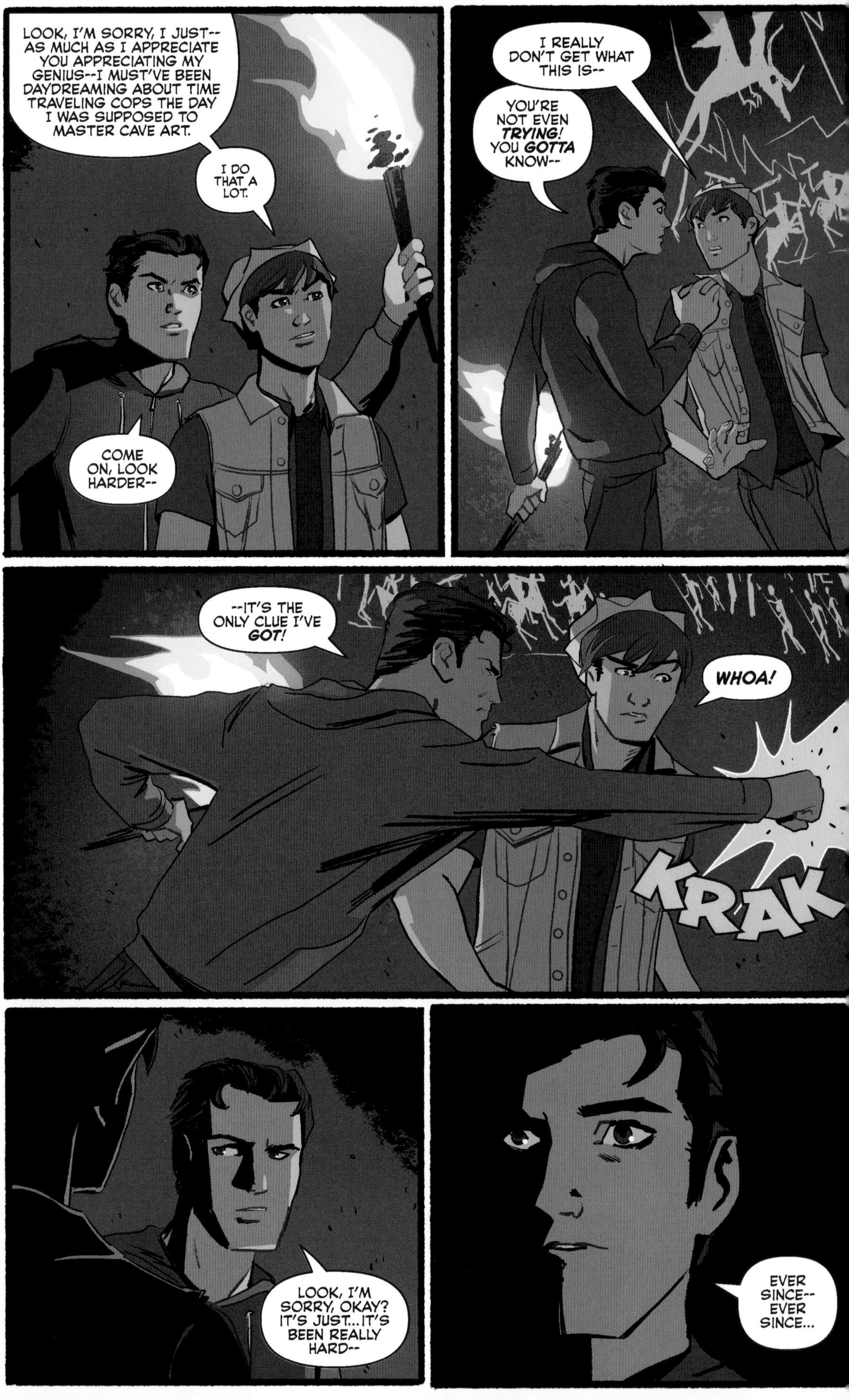

LOOK, I'M SORRY, I JUST--AS MUCH AS I APPRECIATE YOU APPRECIATING MY GENIUS--I MUST'VE BEEN DAYDREAMING ABOUT TIME TRAVELING COPS THE DAY I WAS SUPPOSED TO MASTER CAVE ART.
I DO THAT A LOT.
COME ON, LOOK HARDER--
I REALLY DON'T GET WHAT THIS IS--
YOU'RE NOT EVEN TRYING! YOU GOTTA KNOW--
--IT'S THE ONLY CLUE I'VE GOT!
WHOA!
KRAK
LOOK, I'M SORRY, OKAY? IT'S JUST...IT'S BEEN REALLY HARD--
EVER SINCE--EVER SINCE...

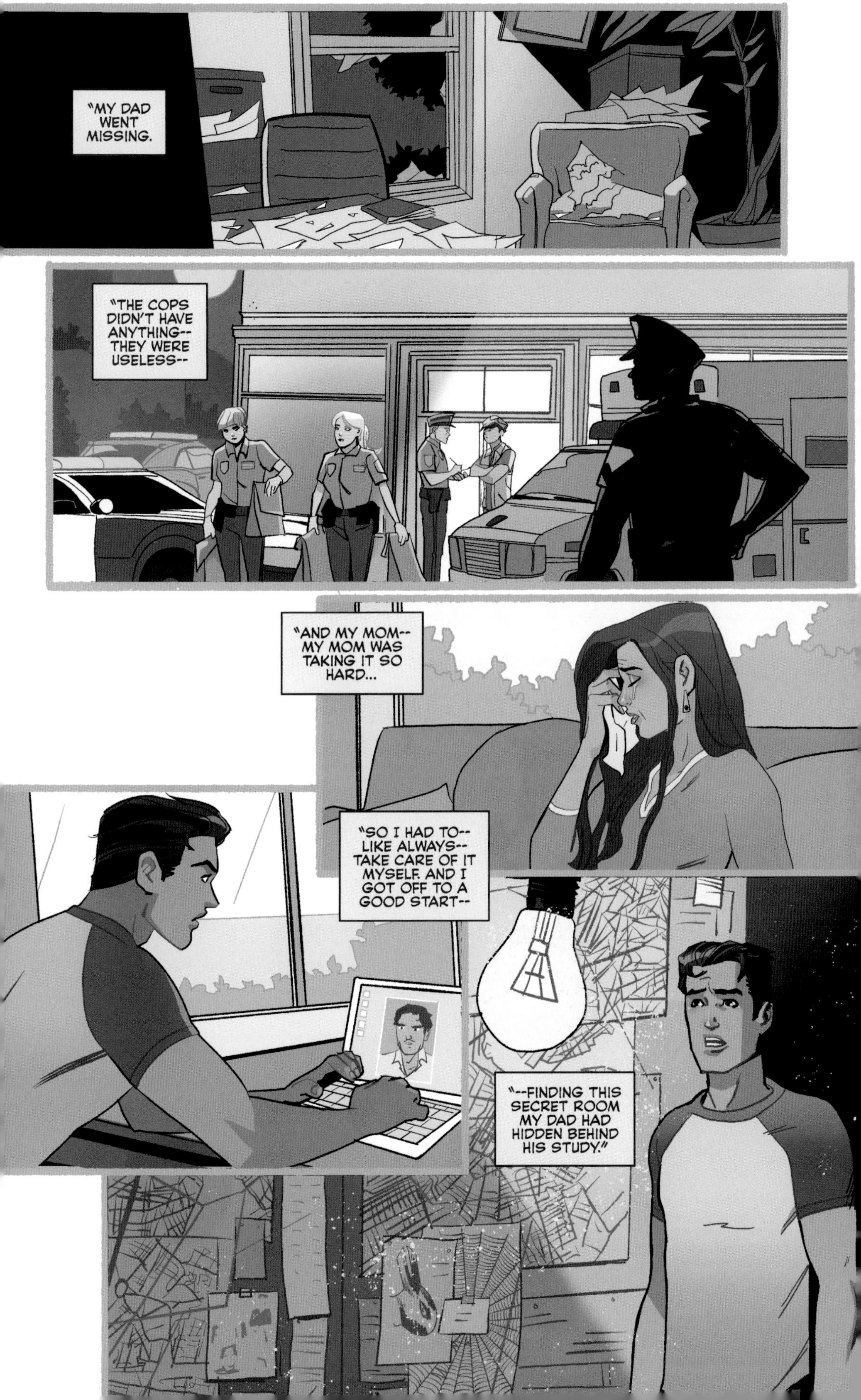
"MY DAD WENT MISSING.
"THE COPS DIDN'T HAVE ANYTHING-- THEY WERE USELESS--
"AND MY MOM-- MY MOM WAS TAKING IT SO HARD...
"SO I HAD TO-- LIKE ALWAYS-- TAKE CARE OF IT MYSELF. AND I GOT OFF TO A GOOD START--
"--FINDING THIS SECRET ROOM MY DAD HAD HIDDEN BEHIND HIS STUDY."

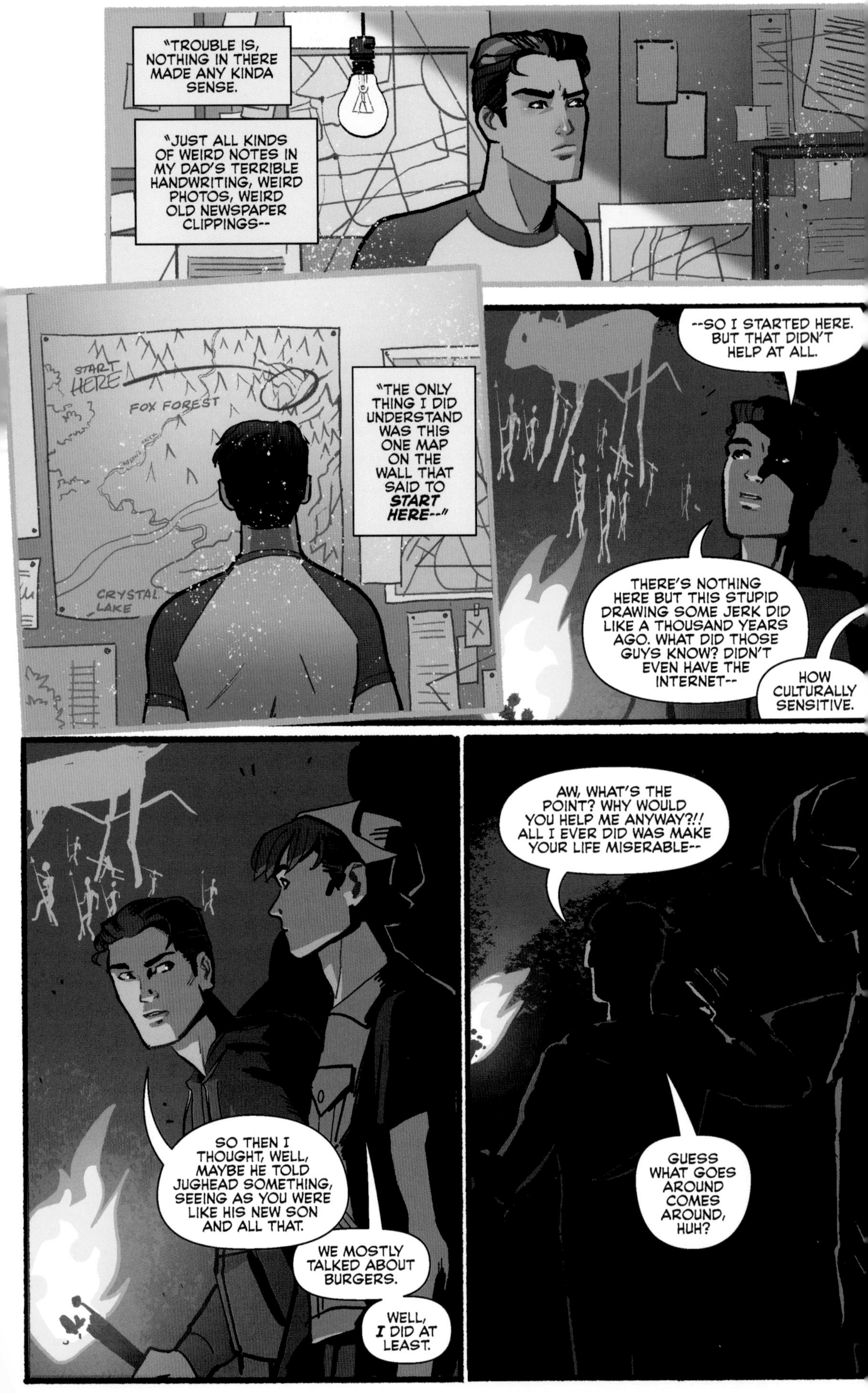
"TROUBLE IS, NOTHING IN THERE MADE ANY KINDA SENSE.
"JUST ALL KINDS OF WEIRD NOTES IN MY DAD'S TERRIBLE HANDWRITING, WEIRD PHOTOS, WEIRD OLD NEWSPAPER CLIPPINGS--
START HERE
FOX FOREST
CRYSTAL LAKE
"THE ONLY THING I DID UNDERSTAND WAS THIS ONE MAP ON THE WALL THAT SAID TO ***START HERE***--"
--SO I STARTED HERE. BUT THAT DIDN'T HELP AT ALL.
THERE'S NOTHING HERE BUT THIS STUPID DRAWING SOME JERK DID LIKE A THOUSAND YEARS AGO. WHAT DID THOSE GUYS KNOW? DIDN'T EVEN HAVE THE INTERNET--
HOW CULTURALLY SENSITIVE.
SO THEN I THOUGHT, WELL, MAYBE HE TOLD JUGHEAD SOMETHING, SEEING AS YOU WERE LIKE HIS NEW SON AND ALL THAT.
WE MOSTLY TALKED ABOUT BURGERS.
WELL, ***I*** DID AT LEAST.
AW, WHAT'S THE POINT? WHY WOULD YOU HELP ME ANYWAY?!! ALL I EVER DID WAS MAKE YOUR LIFE MISERABLE--
GUESS WHAT GOES AROUND COMES AROUND, HUH?

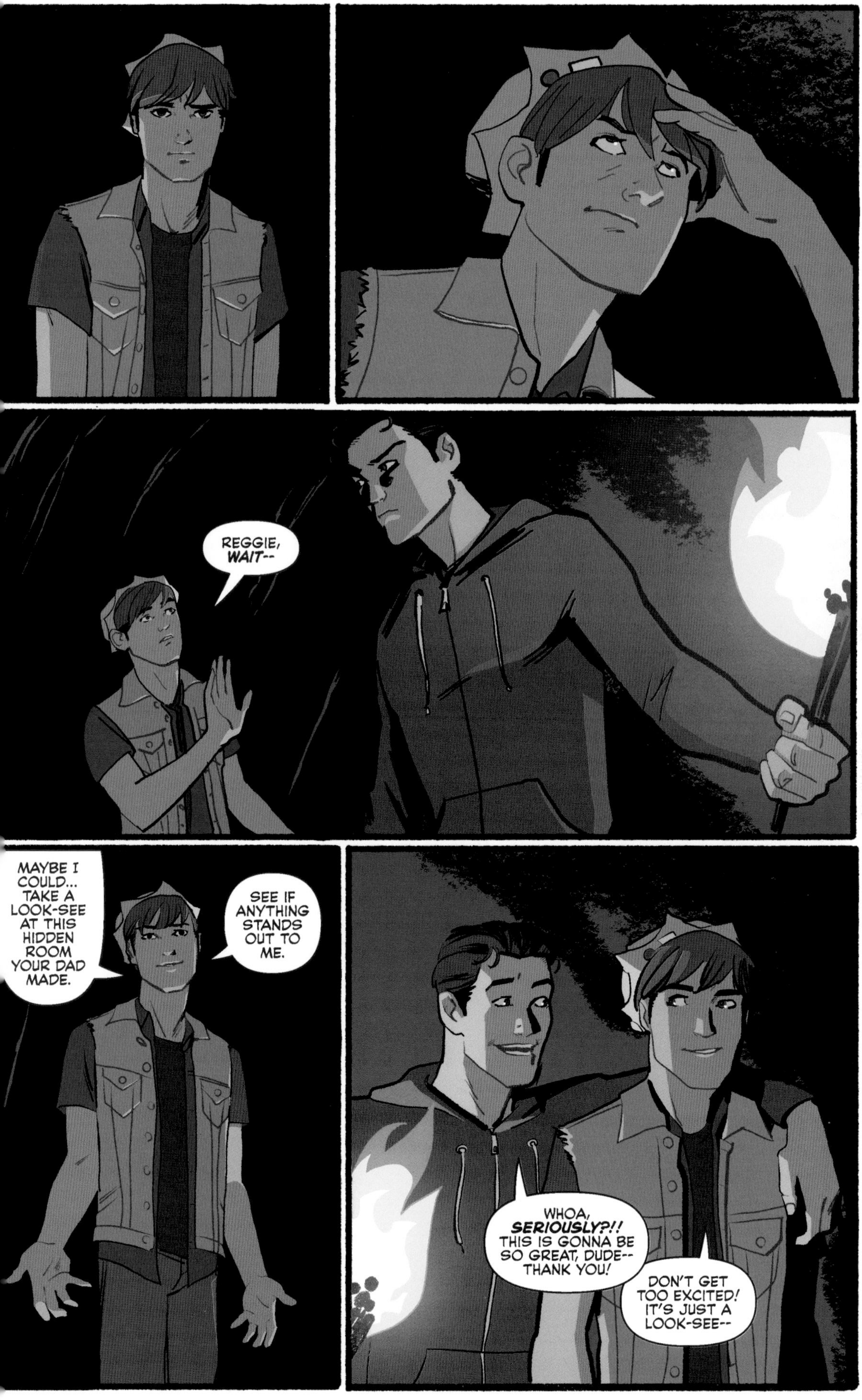
REGGIE, WAIT--
MAYBE I COULD... TAKE A LOOK-SEE AT THIS HIDDEN ROOM YOUR DAD MADE.
SEE IF ANYTHING STANDS OUT TO ME.
WHOA, SERIOUSLY?!! THIS IS GONNA BE SO GREAT, DUDE-- THANK YOU!
DON'T GET TOO EXCITED! IT'S JUST A LOOK-SEE--

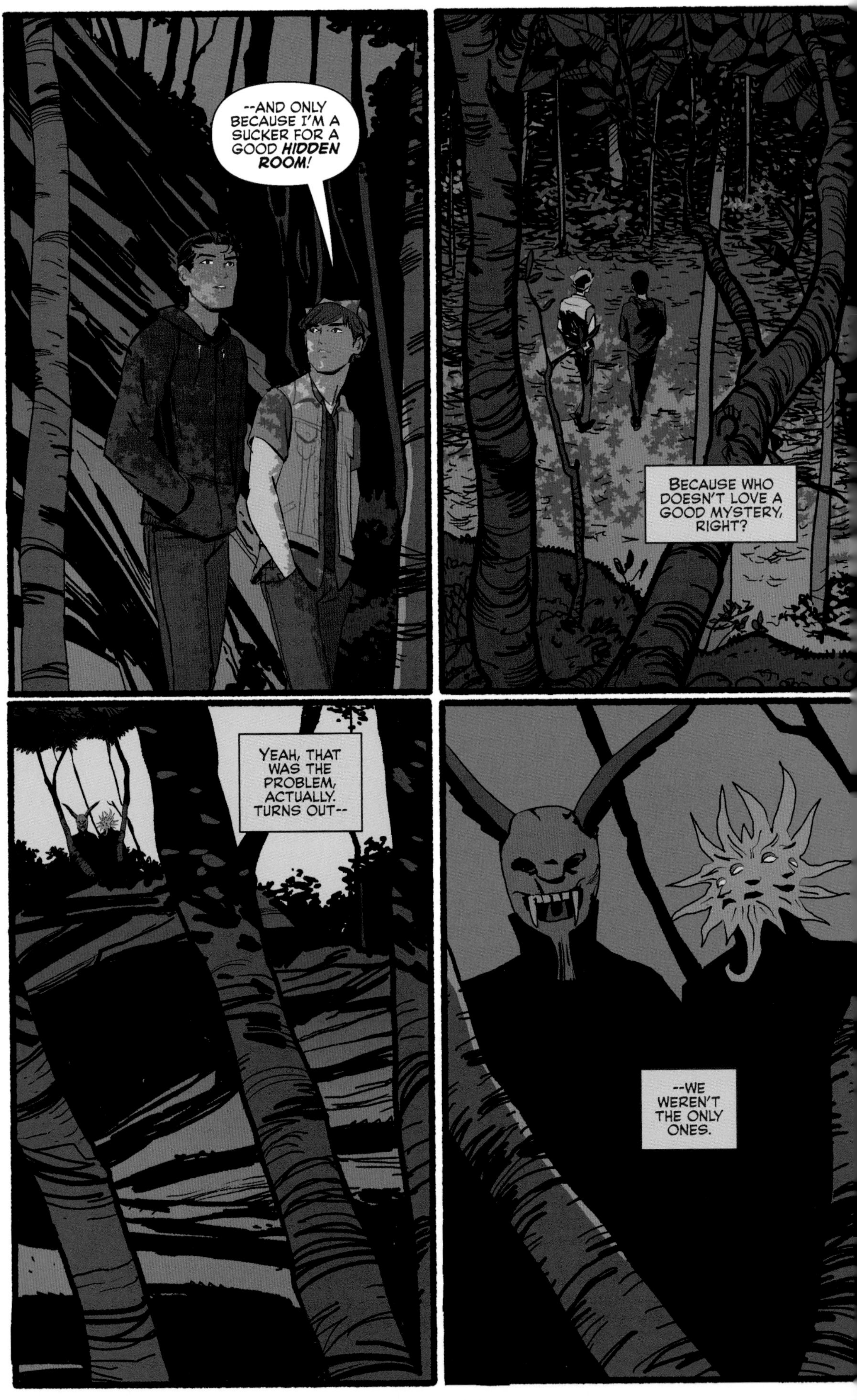
--AND ONLY BECAUSE I'M A SUCKER FOR A GOOD *HIDDEN ROOM*!
BECAUSE WHO DOESN'T LOVE A GOOD MYSTERY, RIGHT?
YEAH, THAT WAS THE PROBLEM, ACTUALLY. TURNS OUT--
--WE WEREN'T THE ONLY ONES.

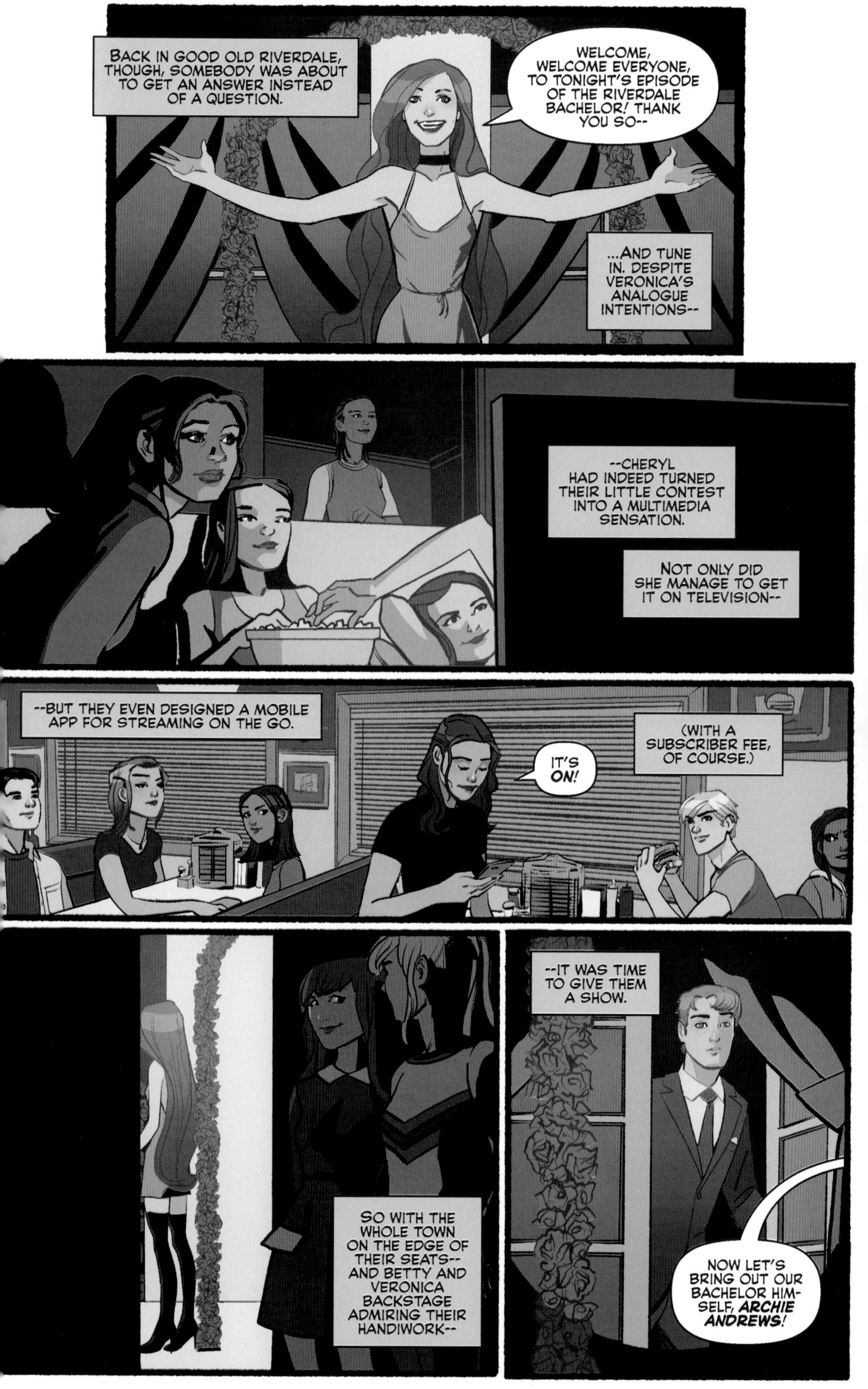
BACK IN GOOD OLD RIVERDALE, THOUGH, SOMEBODY WAS ABOUT TO GET AN ANSWER INSTEAD OF A QUESTION.
WELCOME, WELCOME EVERYONE, TO TONIGHT'S EPISODE OF THE RIVERDALE BACHELOR! THANK YOU SO--
...AND TUNE IN. DESPITE VERONICA'S ANALOGUE INTENTIONS--
--CHERYL HAD INDEED TURNED THEIR LITTLE CONTEST INTO A MULTIMEDIA SENSATION.
NOT ONLY DID SHE MANAGE TO GET IT ON TELEVISION--
--BUT THEY EVEN DESIGNED A MOBILE APP FOR STREAMING ON THE GO.
IT'S ON!
(WITH A SUBSCRIBER FEE, OF COURSE.)
SO WITH THE WHOLE TOWN ON THE EDGE OF THEIR SEATS--AND BETTY AND VERONICA BACKSTAGE ADMIRING THEIR HANDIWORK--
--IT WAS TIME TO GIVE THEM A SHOW.
NOW LET'S BRING OUT OUR BACHELOR HIMSELF, ARCHIE ANDREWS!

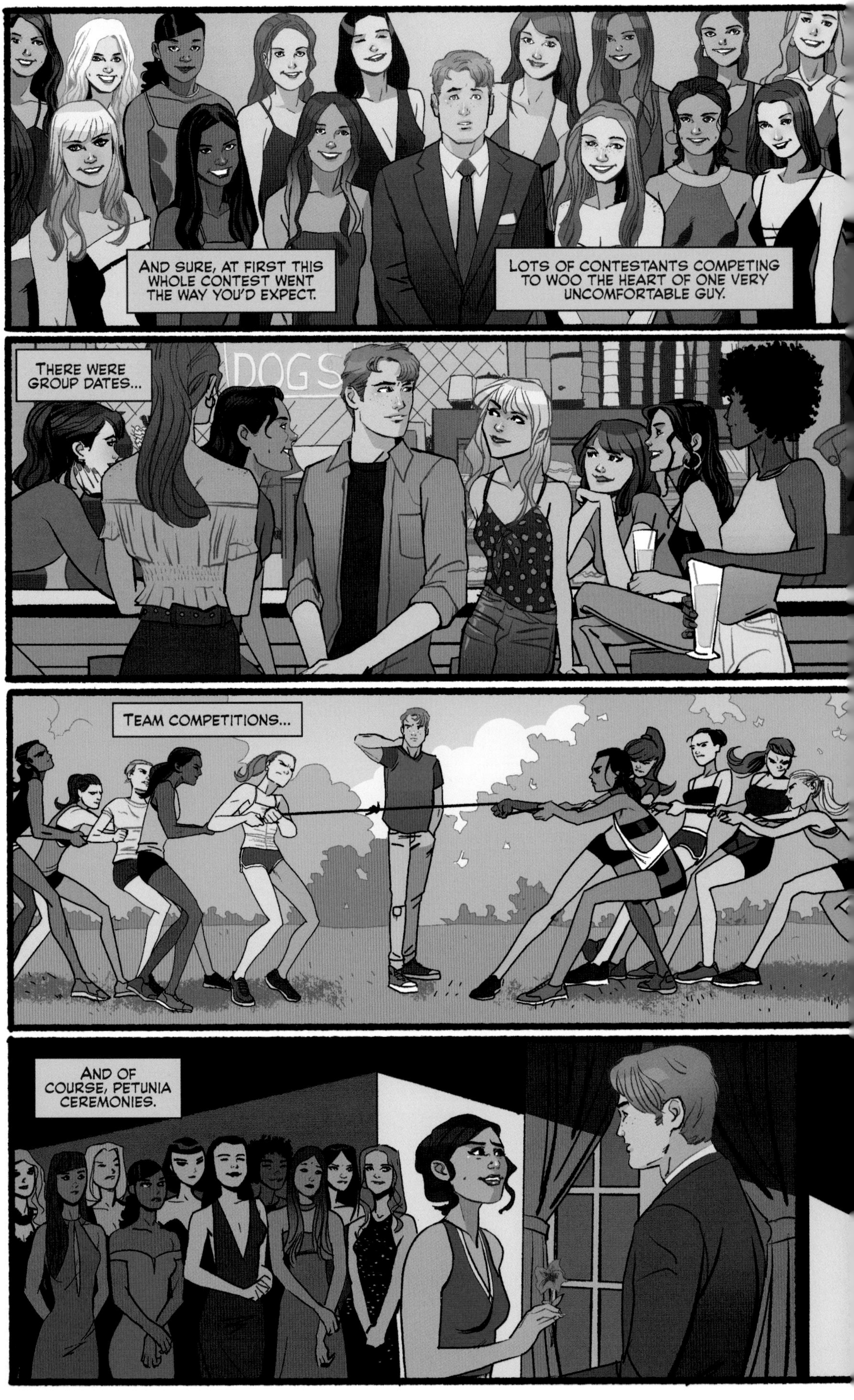
AND SURE, AT FIRST THIS WHOLE CONTEST WENT THE WAY YOU'D EXPECT.
LOTS OF CONTESTANTS COMPETING TO WOO THE HEART OF ONE VERY UNCOMFORTABLE GUY.
THERE WERE GROUP DATES...
DOGS
TEAM COMPETITIONS...
AND OF COURSE, PETUNIA CEREMONIES.

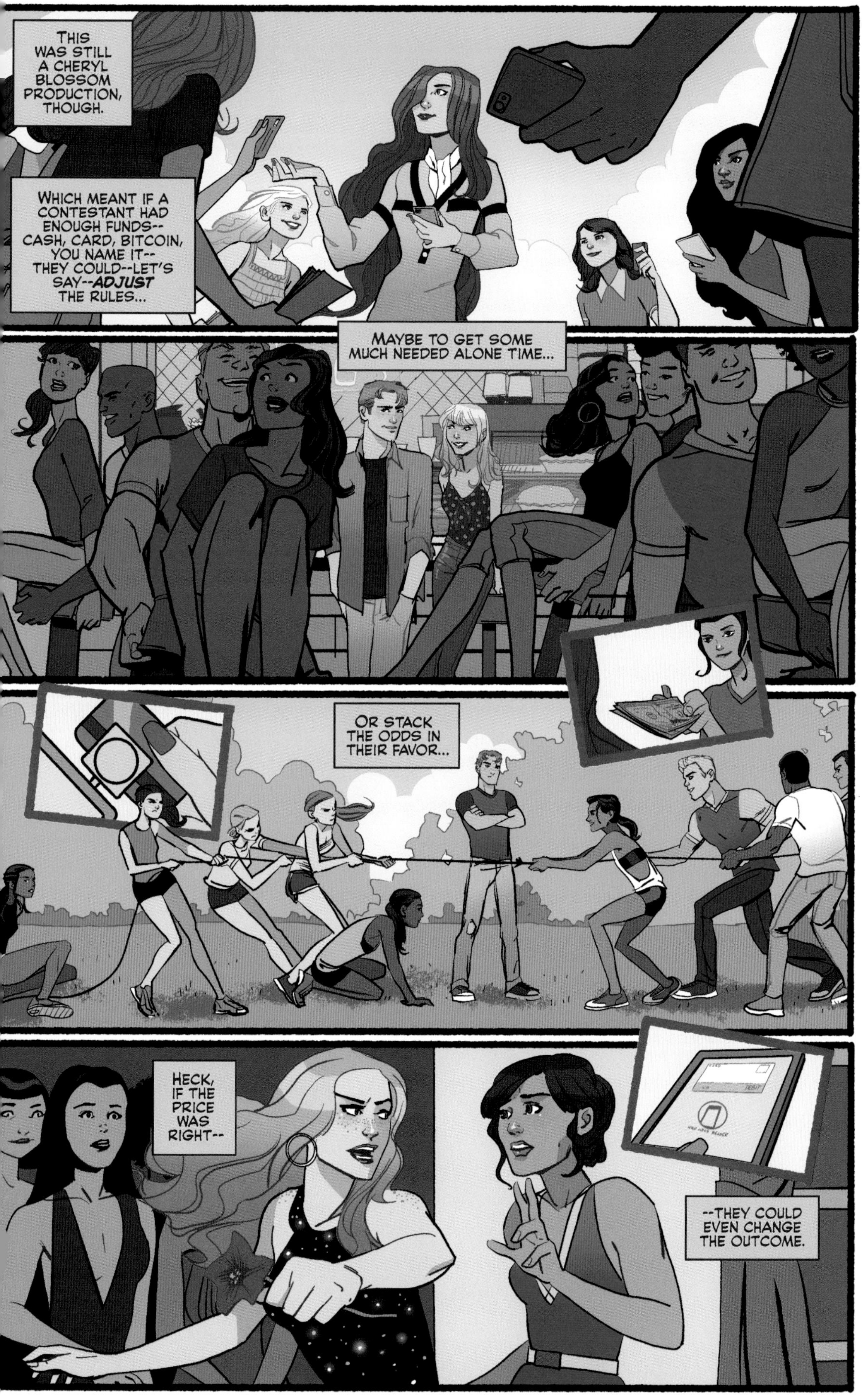
THIS WAS STILL A CHERYL BLOSSOM PRODUCTION, THOUGH.
WHICH MEANT IF A CONTESTANT HAD ENOUGH FUNDS-- CASH, CARD, BITCOIN, YOU NAME IT-- THEY COULD--LET'S SAY--ADJUST THE RULES...
MAYBE TO GET SOME MUCH NEEDED ALONE TIME...
OR STACK THE ODDS IN THEIR FAVOR...
HECK, IF THE PRICE WAS RIGHT--
--THEY COULD EVEN CHANGE THE OUTCOME.

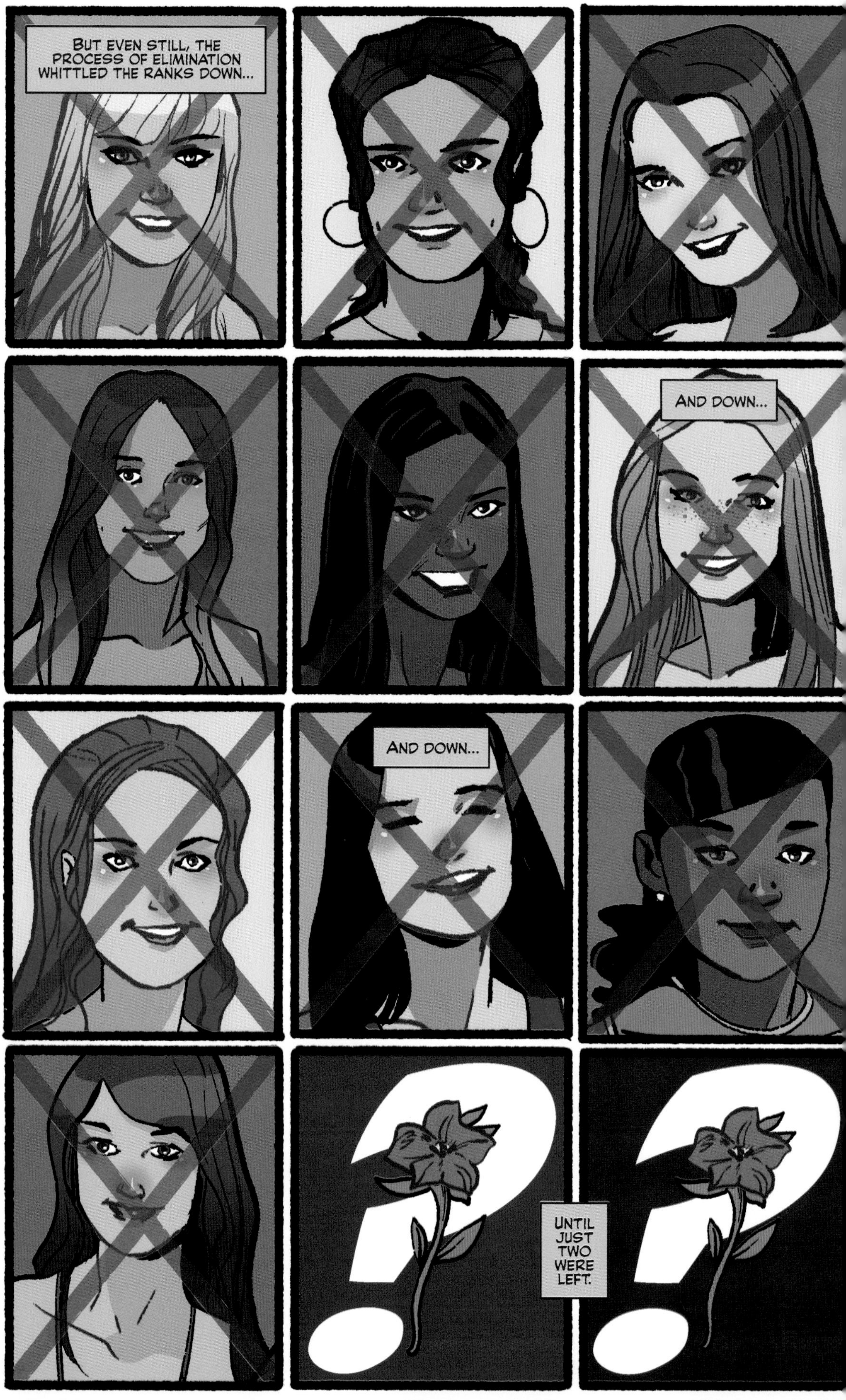
BUT EVEN STILL, THE PROCESS OF ELIMINATION WHITTLED THE RANKS DOWN...
AND DOWN...
AND DOWN...
UNTIL JUST TWO WERE LEFT.

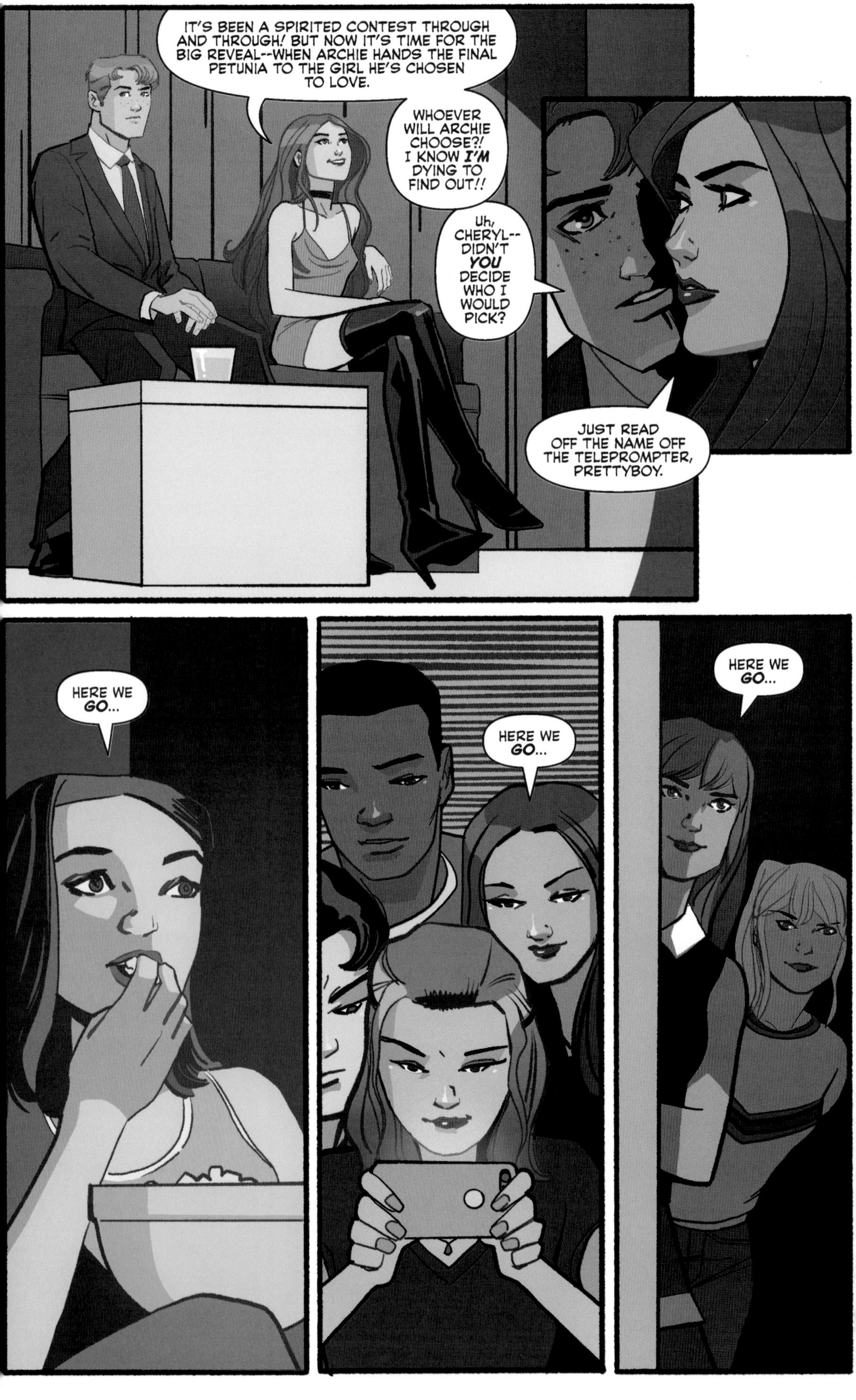
IT'S BEEN A SPIRITED CONTEST THROUGH AND THROUGH! BUT NOW IT'S TIME FOR THE BIG REVEAL--WHEN ARCHIE HANDS THE FINAL PETUNIA TO THE GIRL HE'S CHOSEN TO LOVE.
WHOEVER WILL ARCHIE CHOOSE?! I KNOW I'M DYING TO FIND OUT!!
Uh, CHERYL--DIDN'T YOU DECIDE WHO I WOULD PICK?
JUST READ OFF THE NAME OFF THE TELEPROMPTER, PRETTYBOY.
HERE WE GO...
HERE WE GO...
HERE WE GO...

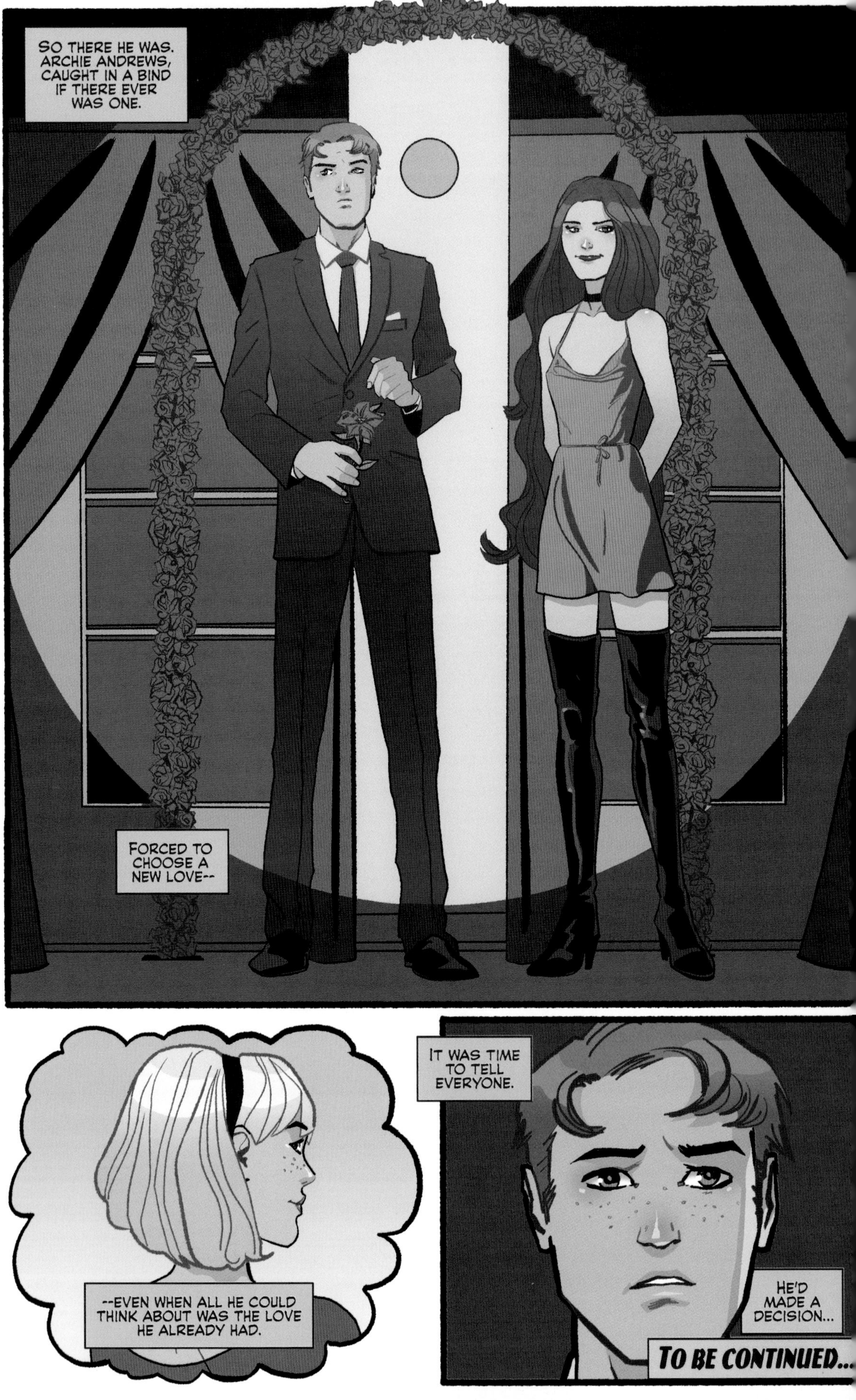
SO THERE HE WAS. ARCHIE ANDREWS, CAUGHT IN A BIND IF THERE EVER WAS ONE.
FORCED TO CHOOSE A NEW LOVE--
--EVEN WHEN ALL HE COULD THINK ABOUT WAS THE LOVE HE ALREADY HAD.
IT WAS TIME TO TELL EVERYONE.
HE'D MADE A DECISION...
TO BE CONTINUED...

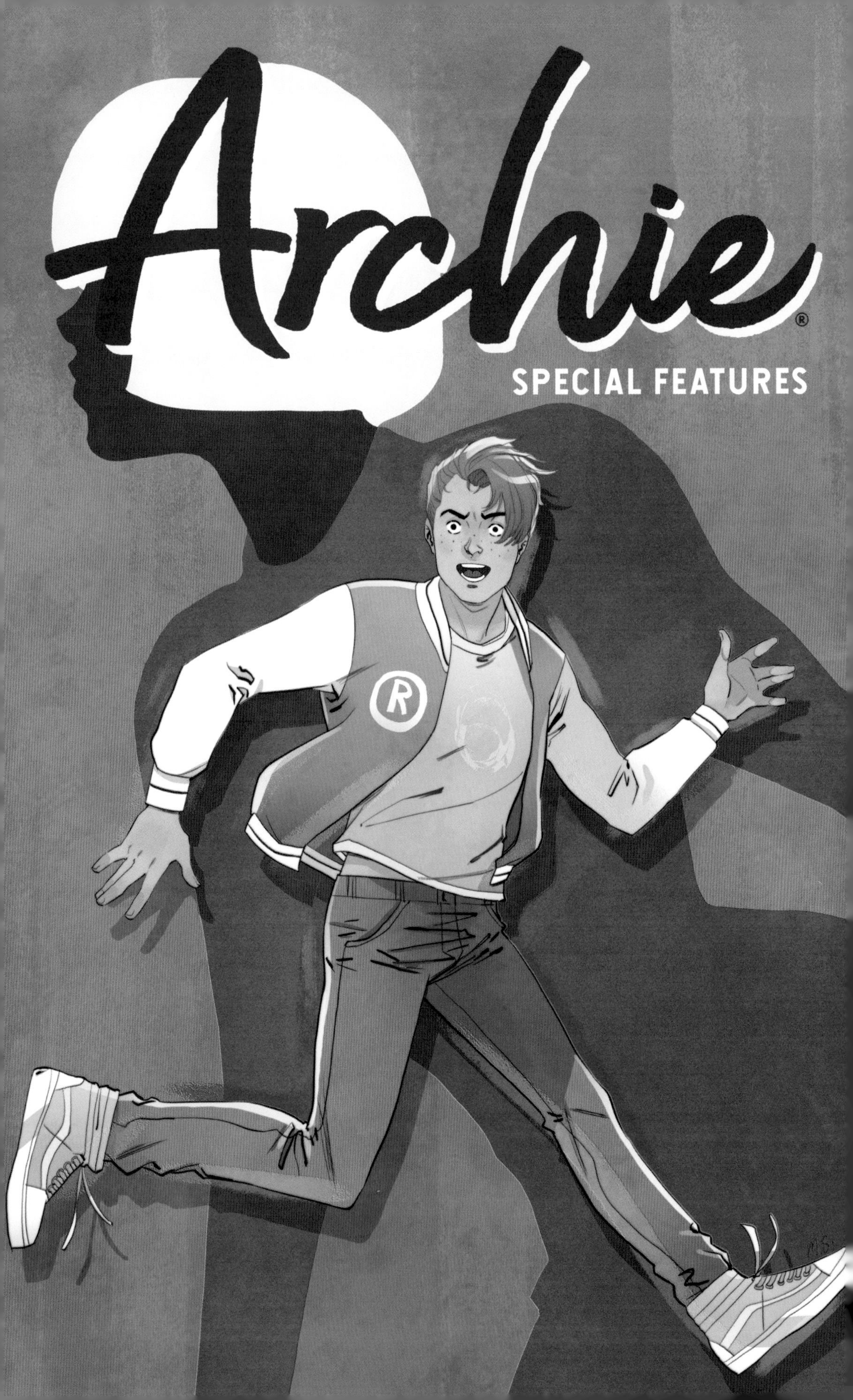
Archie®
SPECIAL FEATURES

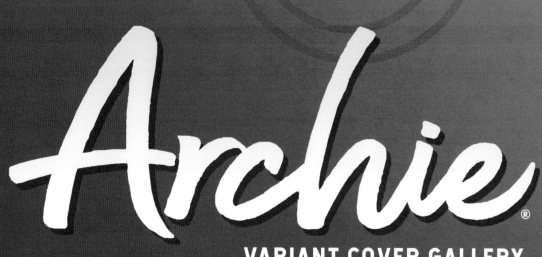

Archie®

VARIANT COVER GALLERY

THAT REGGIE IS A MEATBALL!

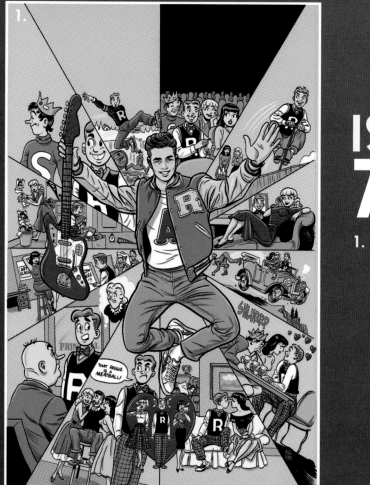

ISSUE 700

1. MIKE & LAURA ALLRED

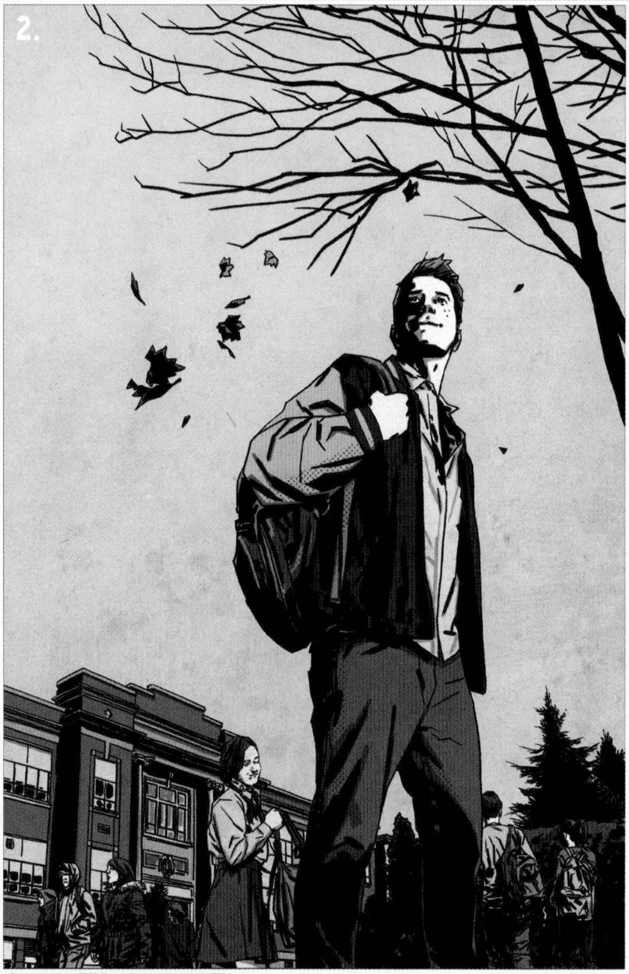
2.

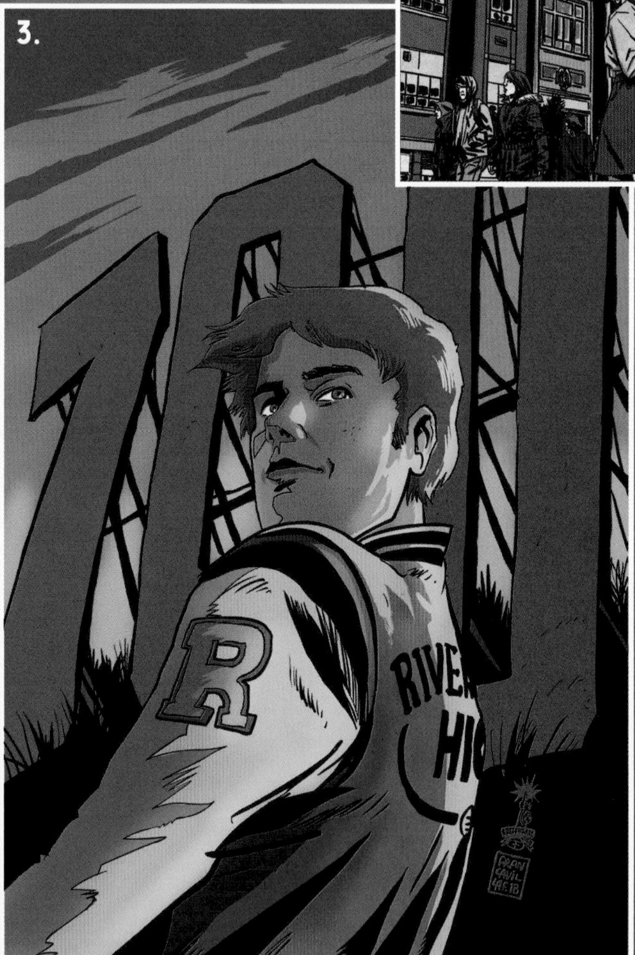
3.
R
RIVER
HIG

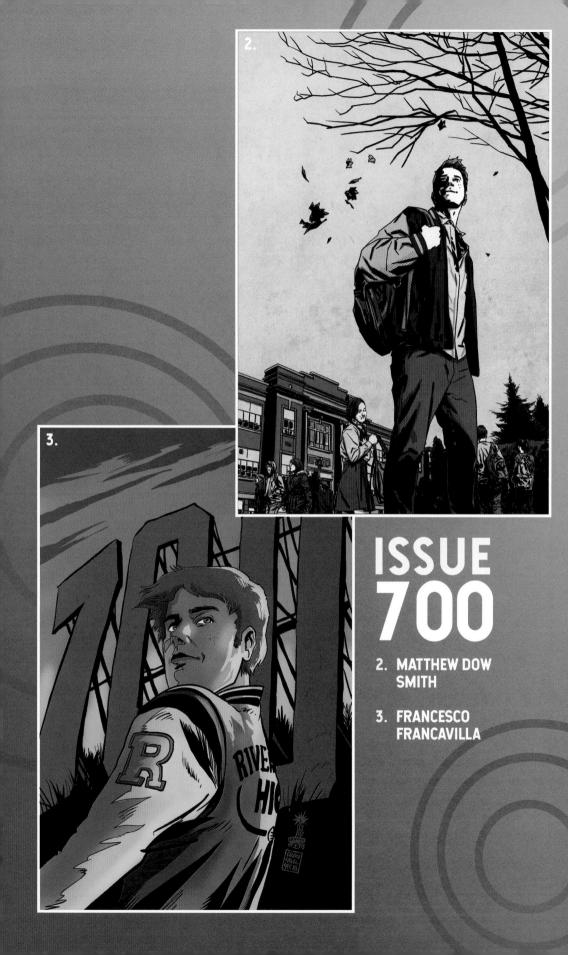

ISSUE 700

2. MATTHEW DOW SMITH

3. FRANCESCO FRANCAVILLA

ISSUE 700

4. ROBERT HACK

5. DAVID MACK

4.

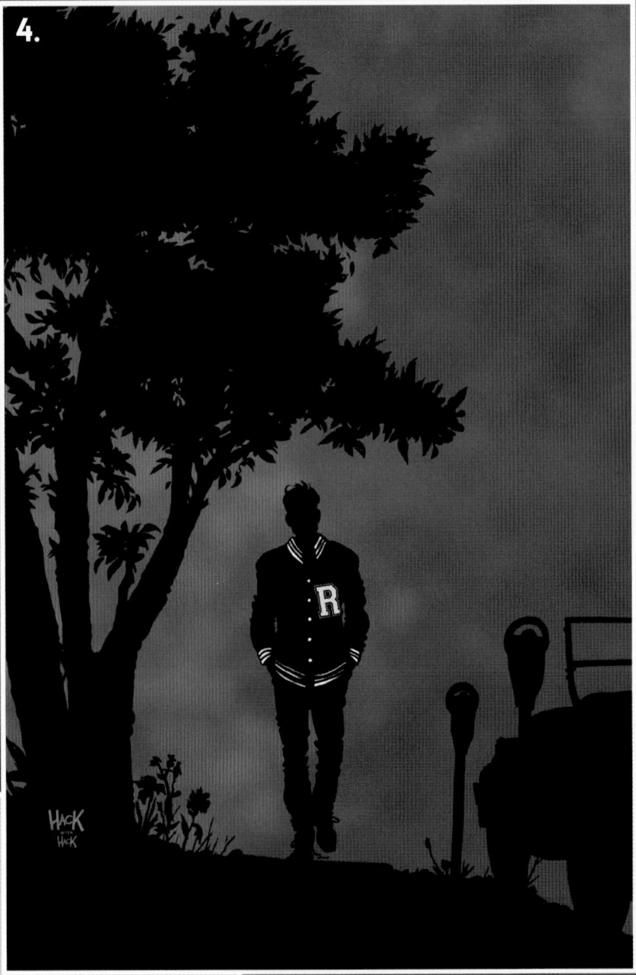
R
HACK

5.

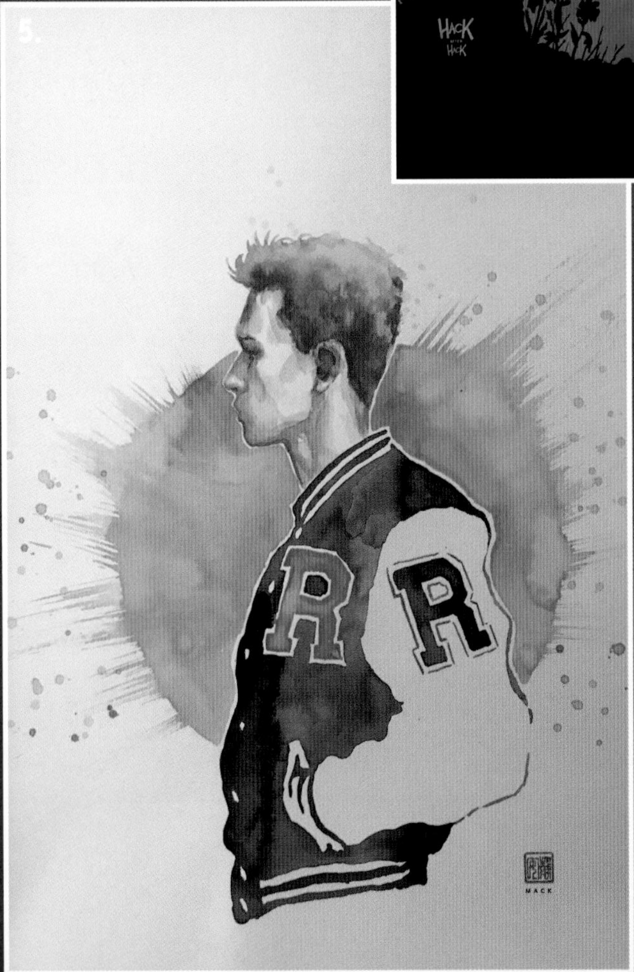
R
R
MACK

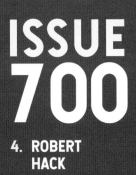

6.

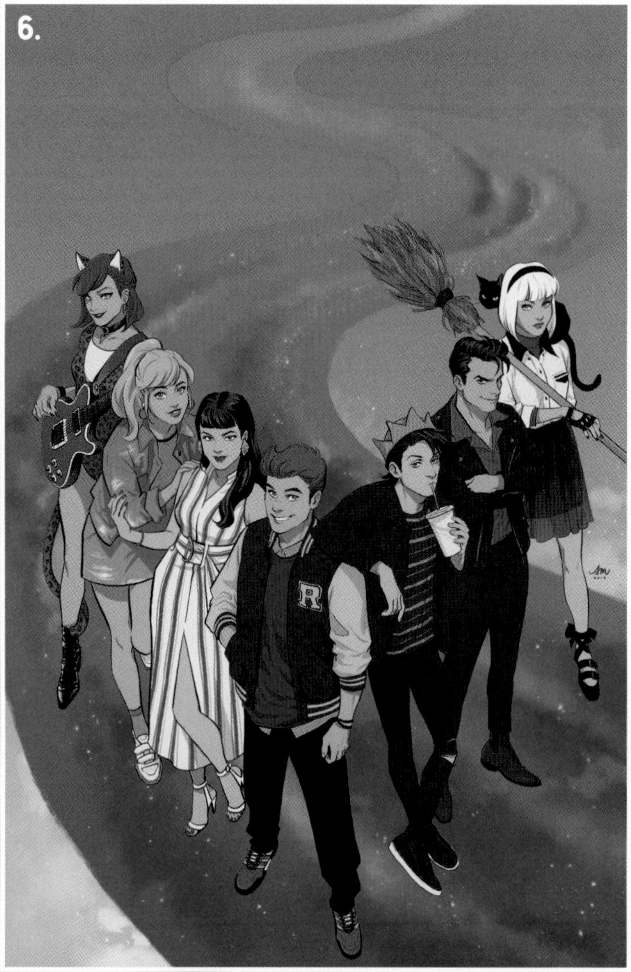

7.

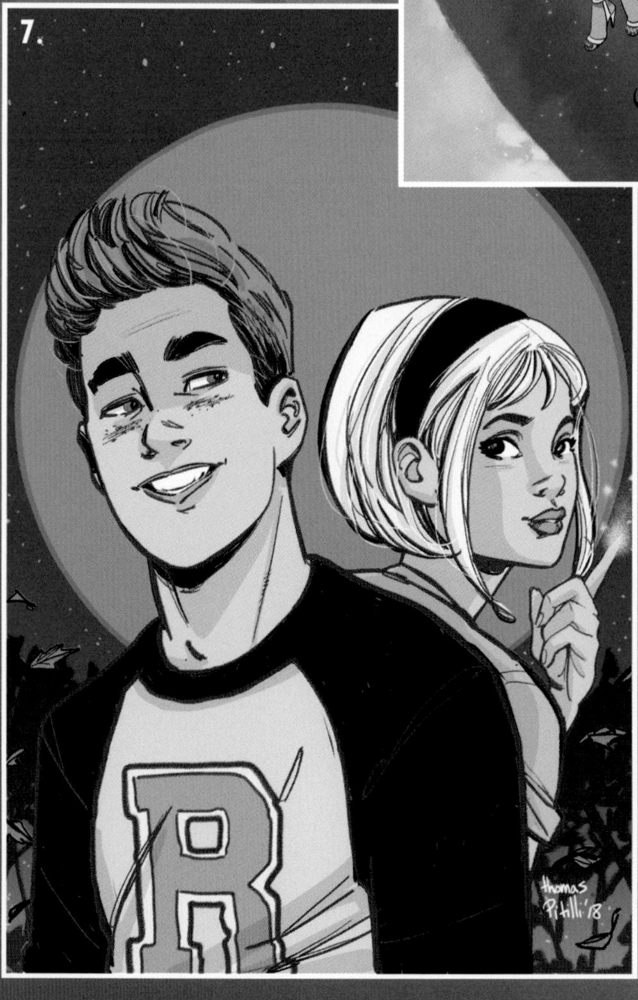
thomas
Pitilli '18

ISSUE 700

6. AUDREY MOK

7. THOMAS PITILLI

ISSUE 700

8. PAUL RENAUD

9. MICHAEL WALSH

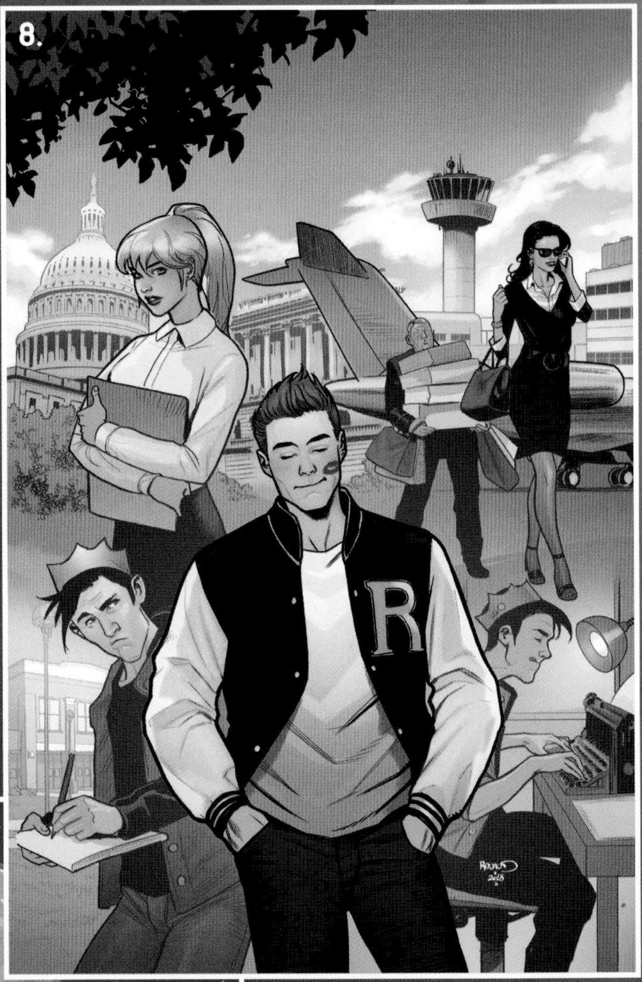
8.

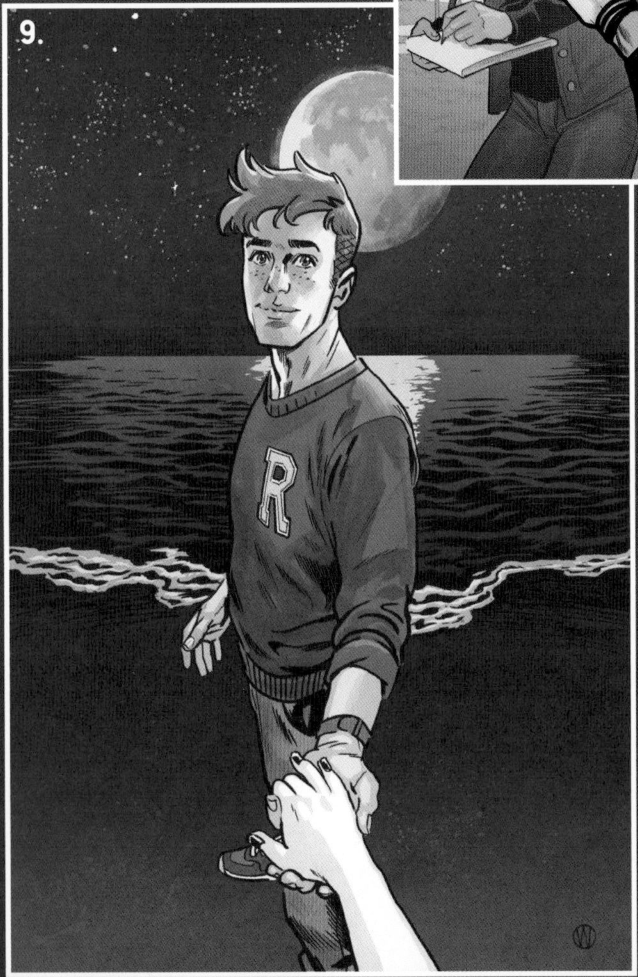
9.

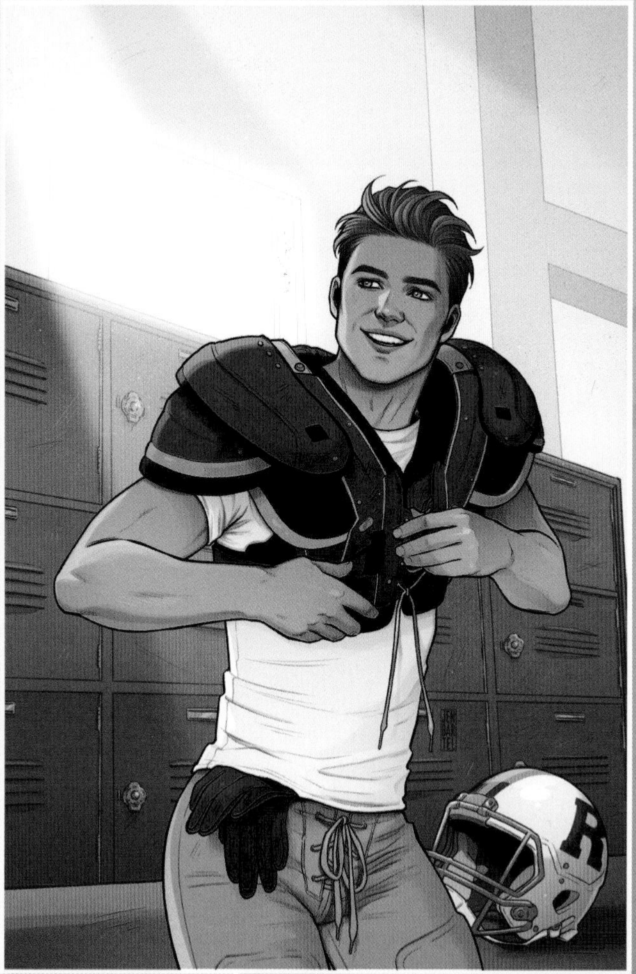

2.

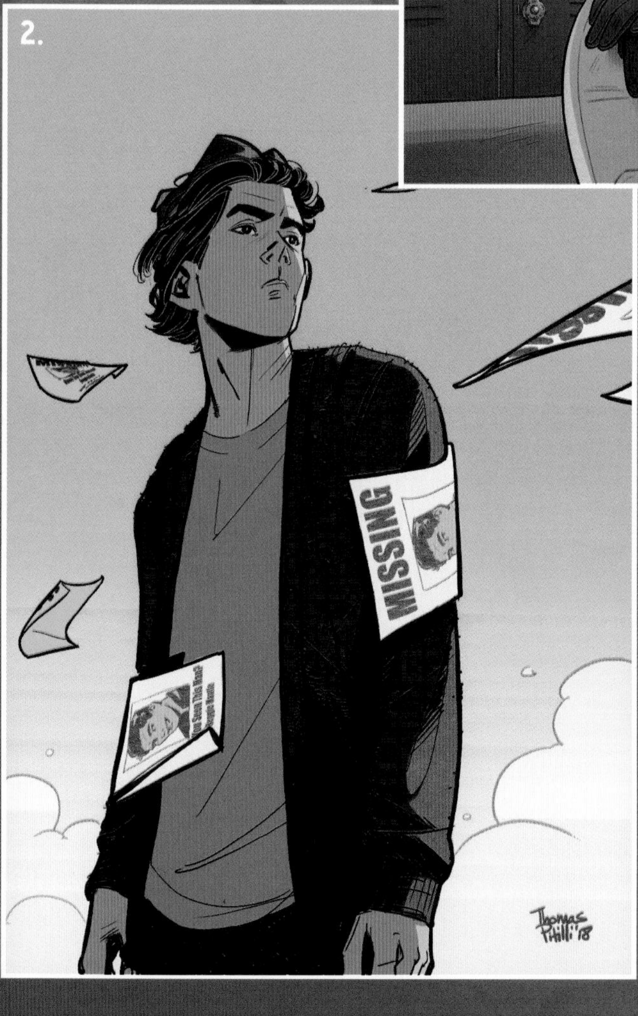
MISSING

ISSUE 701

1. JEN BARTEL
2. THOMAS PITILLI

ISSUE 702

1. JOE QUINONES

2. MICHAEL WALSH

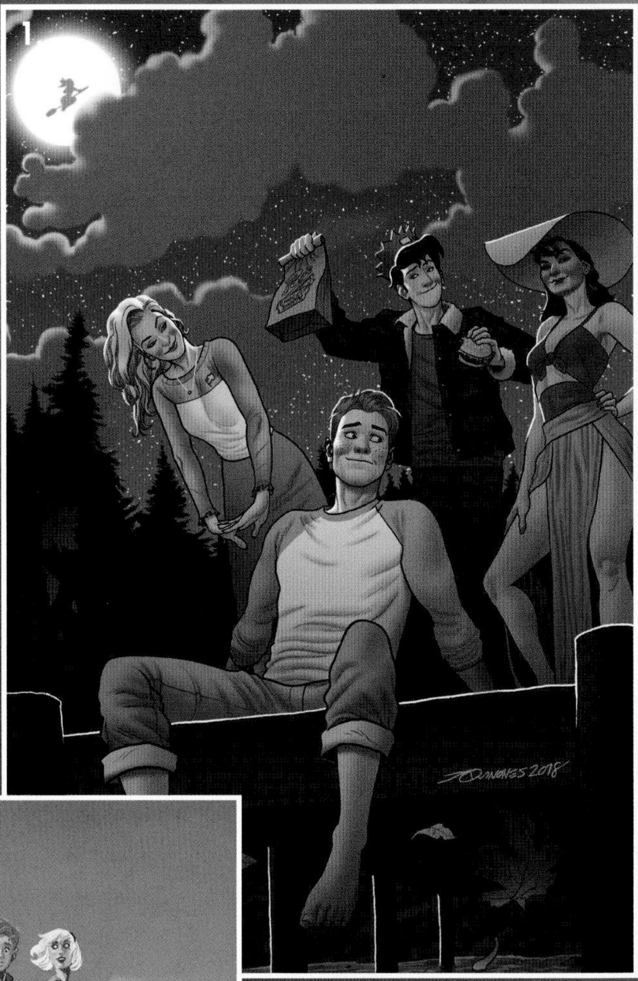
1.
JQUINONES 2018

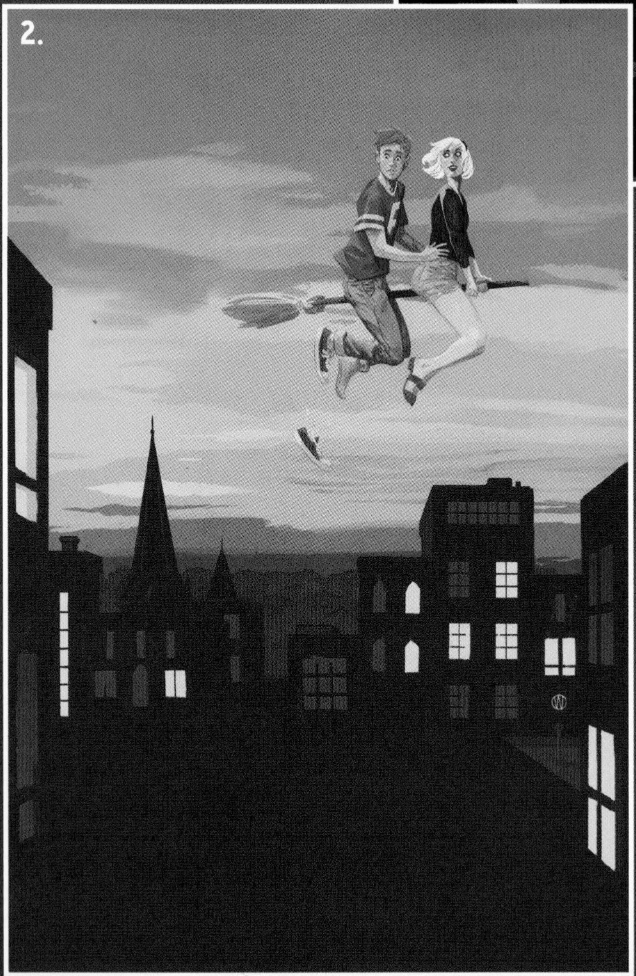
2.

1.

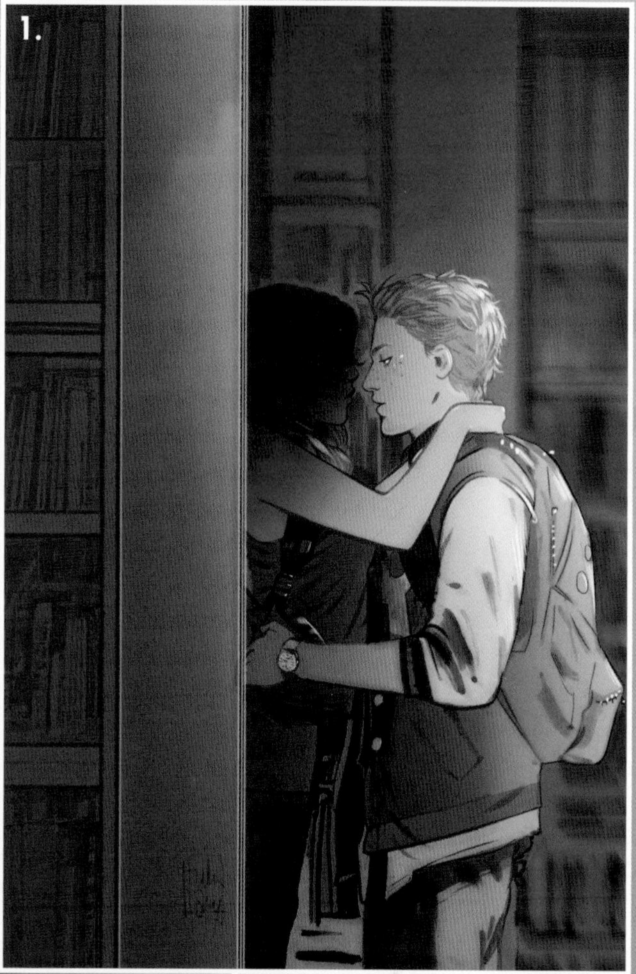

2.

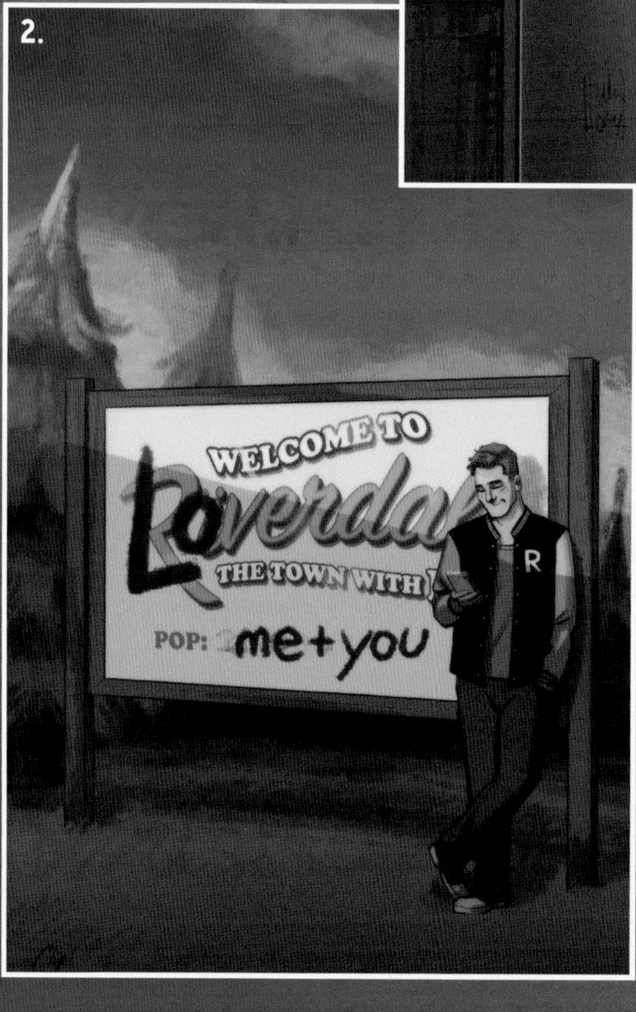
WELCOME TO
Riverdale
THE TOWN WITH
POP: me+you
R

ISSUE 703

1. TULA LOTAY
2. CHIP ZDARSKY

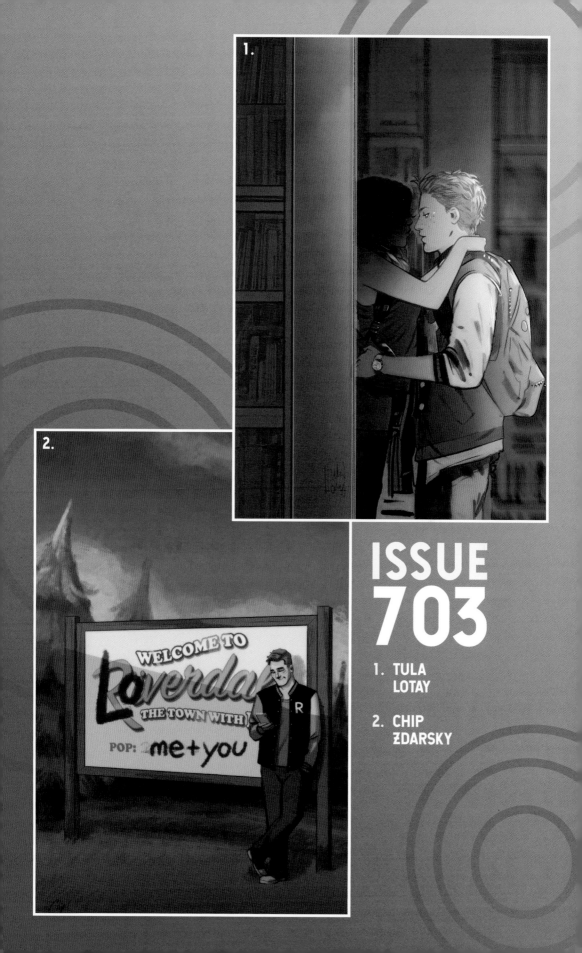

ISSUE 704

1. SANDY JARRELL
2. MATTHEW DOW SMITH

1.

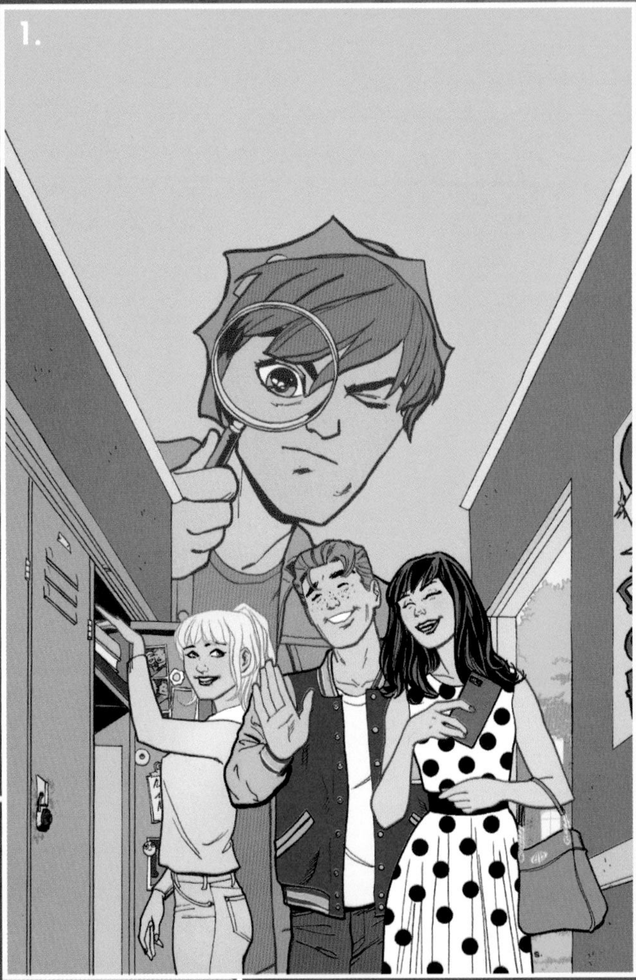

2.

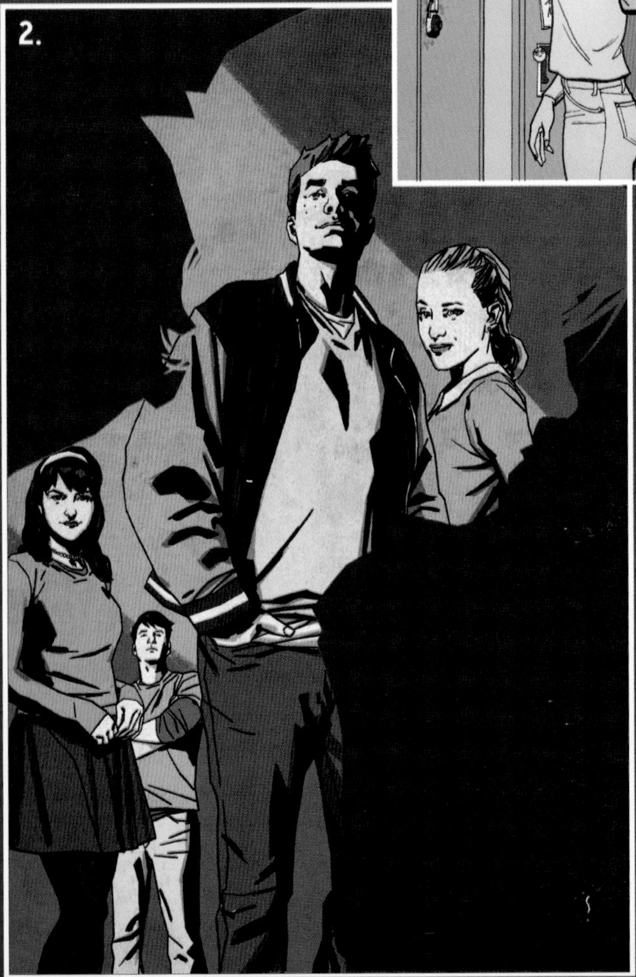

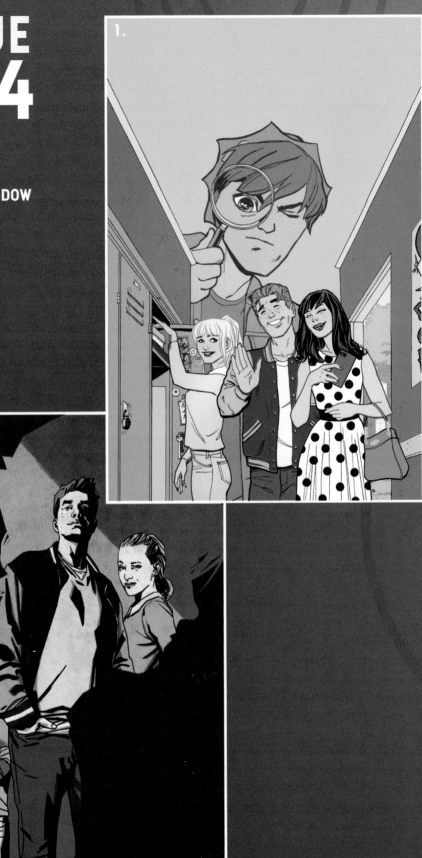

699

Before the release of *Archie* #700 Archie Comics released a special bonus issue to catch people up on the story so far. Here's the cover for that issue!

COVER ART: MARGUERITE SAUVAGE

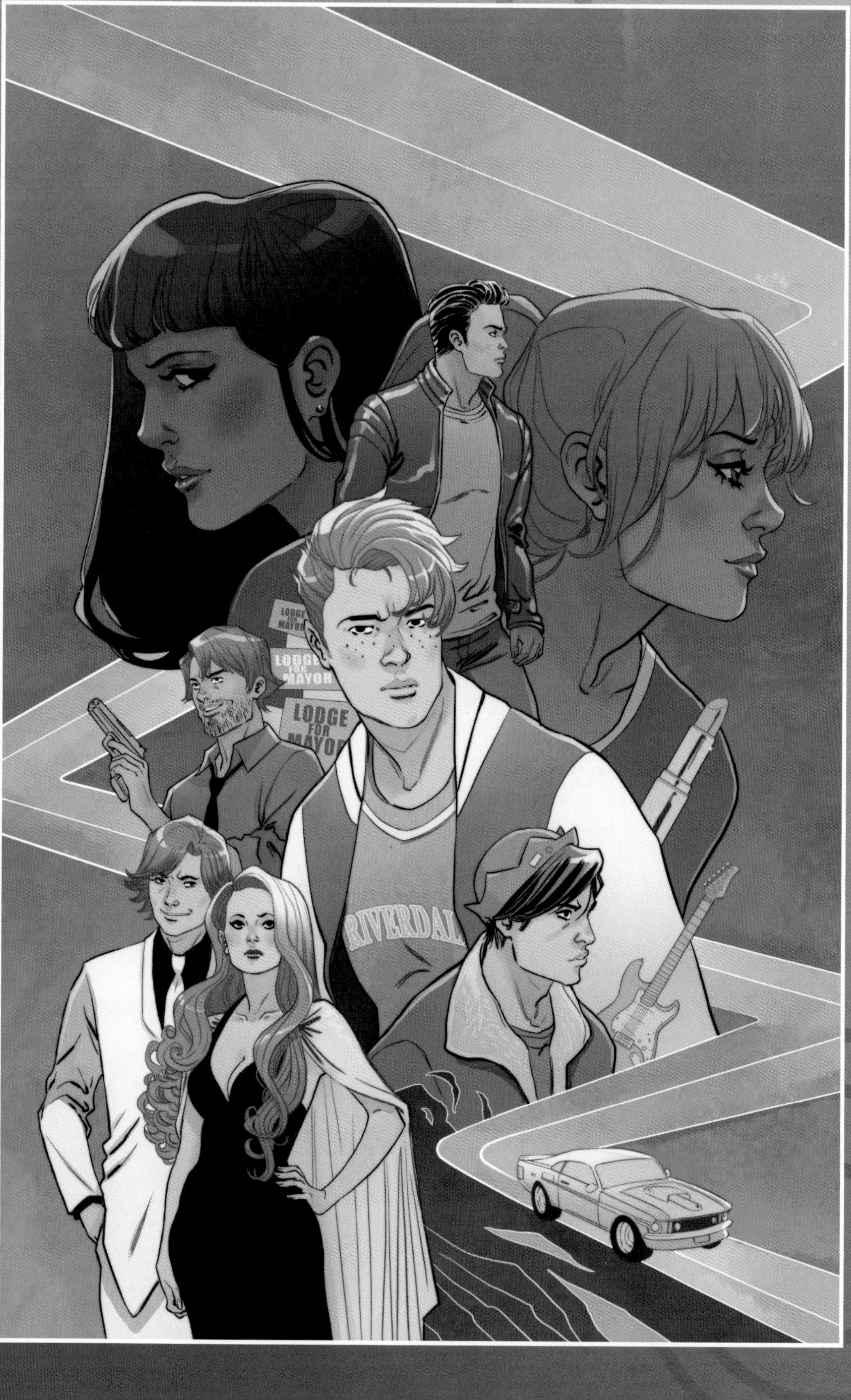
LODGE FOR MAYOR
LODGE FOR MAYOR
LODGE FOR MAYOR
RIVERDALE

COVER SKETCHES

COVER SKETCHES AND FINAL ART BY **MARGUERITE SAUVAGE**

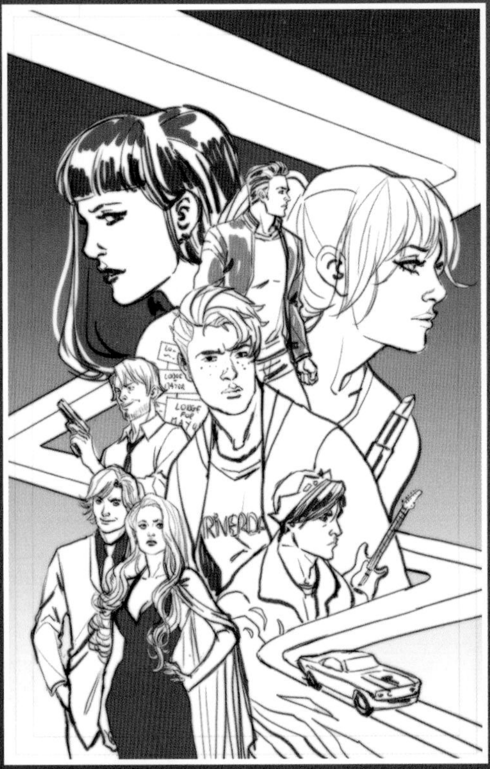
RIVERDA

ARCHIE 699: **SKETCH**

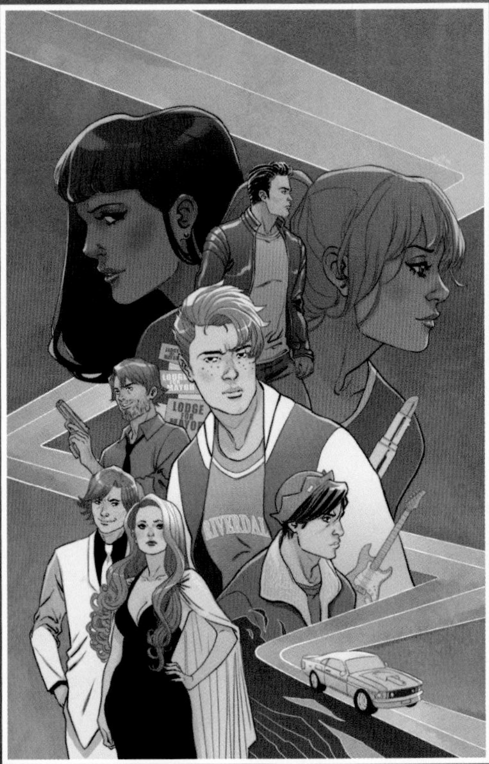
LODGE FOR MAYOR
RIVERDAL

ARCHIE 699: **FINAL ART**

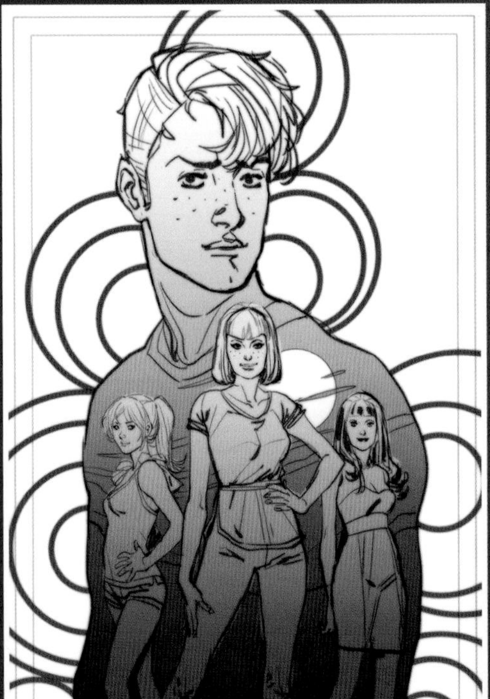

ARCHIE 700: **SKETCH**

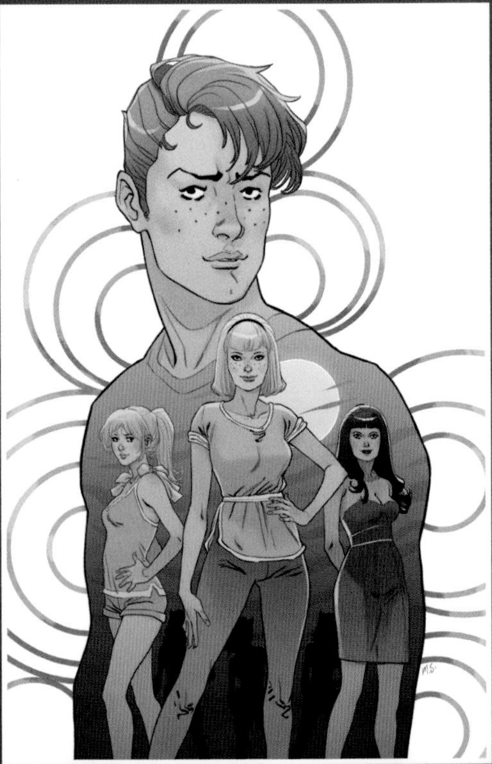
M.S.

ARCHIE 700: **FINAL ART**

INTERIOR PENCILS

INTERIOR SKETCHES AND FINAL ART BY **MARGUERITE SAUVAGE**

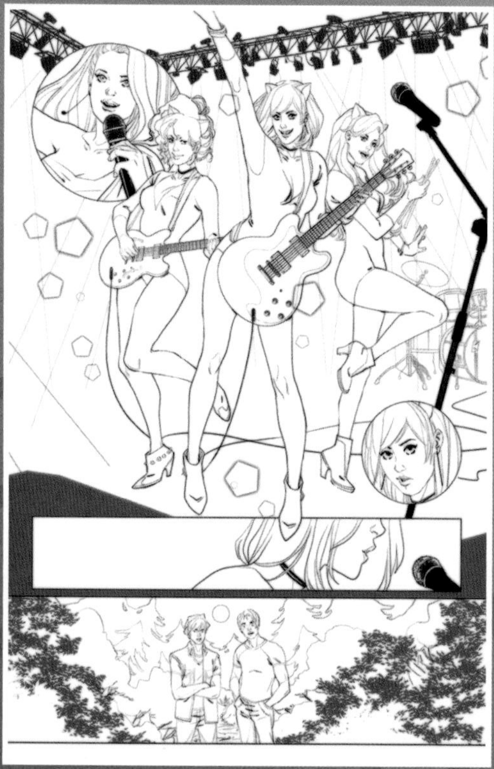

ARCHIE 700 PAGE 17: **SKETCH**

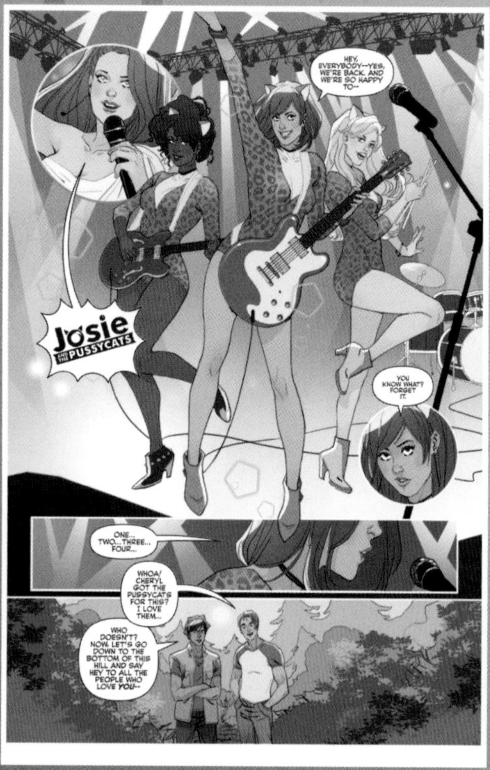
HEY, EVERYBODY--YES, WE'RE BACK. AND WE'RE SO HAPPY TO--
Josie AND THE PUSSYCATS
YOU KNOW WHAT? FORGET IT.
ONE... TWO... THREE... FOUR...
WHOA! CHERYL GOT THE PUSSYCATS FOR THIS? I LOVE THEM...
WHO DOESN'T? NOW, LET'S GO DOWN TO THE BOTTOM OF THIS HILL AND SAY HEY TO ALL THE PEOPLE WHO LOVE YOU--

ARCHIE 700 PAGE 17: **FINAL ART**

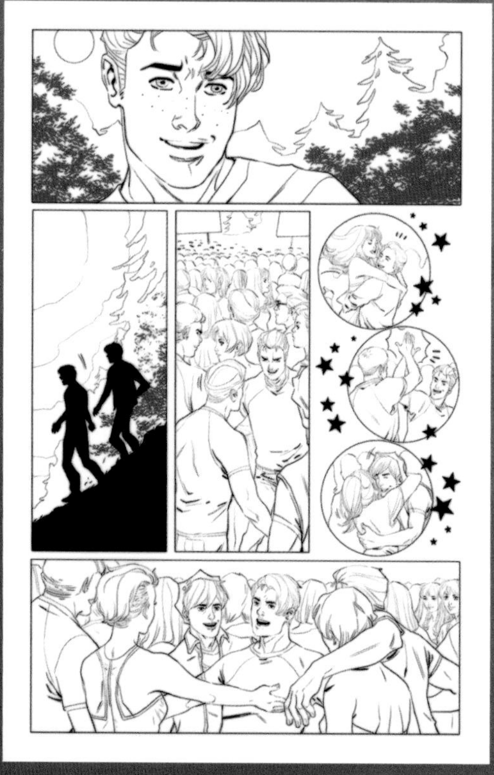

ARCHIE 700 PAGE 18: **SKETCH**

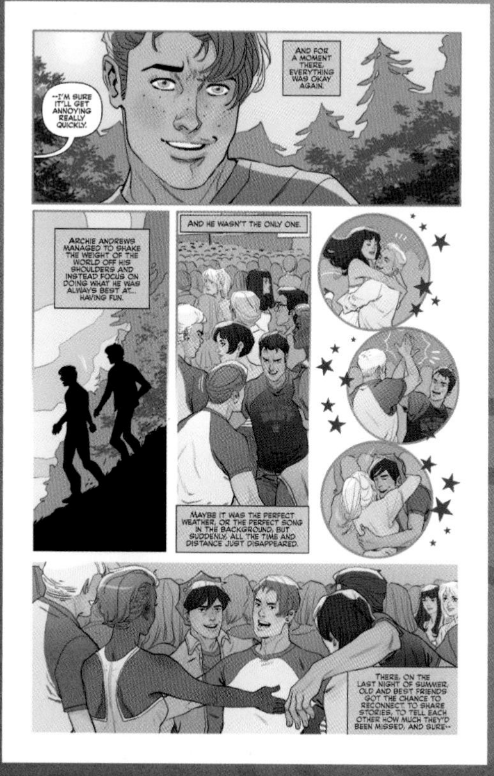
--I'M SURE IT'LL GET ANNOYING REALLY QUICKLY.
AND FOR A MOMENT THERE, EVERYTHING WAS OKAY AGAIN.
ARCHIE ANDREWS MANAGED TO SHAKE THE WEIGHT OF THE WORLD OFF HIS SHOULDERS AND INSTEAD FOCUS ON DOING WHAT HE WAS ALWAYS BEST AT... HAVING FUN.
AND HE WASN'T THE ONLY ONE.
MAYBE IT WAS THE PERFECT WEATHER, OR THE PERFECT SONG IN THE BACKGROUND, BUT SUDDENLY, ALL THE TIME AND DISTANCE JUST DISAPPEARED.
THERE, ON THE LAST NIGHT OF SUMMER, OLD AND BEST FRIENDS GOT THE CHANCE TO RECONNECT, TO SHARE STORIES, TO TELL EACH OTHER HOW MUCH THEY'D BEEN MISSED, AND SURE--

ARCHIE 700 PAGE 18: **FINAL ART**

INTERIOR PENCILS

INTERIOR SKETCHES AND FINAL ART BY **MARGUERITE SAUVAGE**

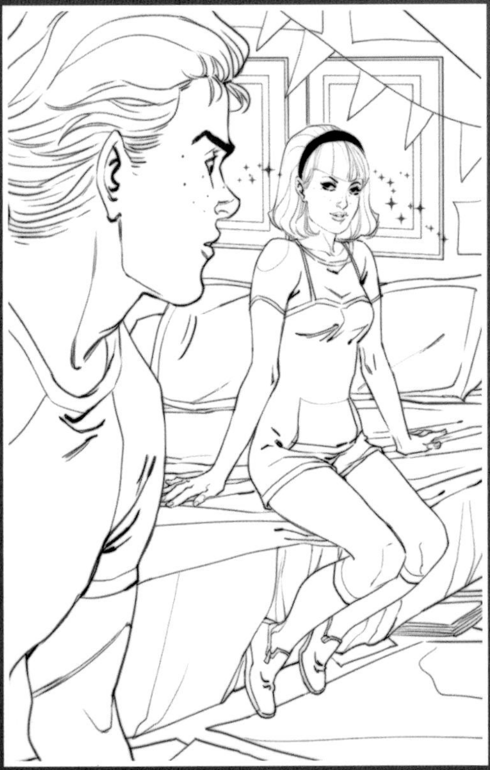

ARCHIE 700 PAGE 24: **SKETCH**

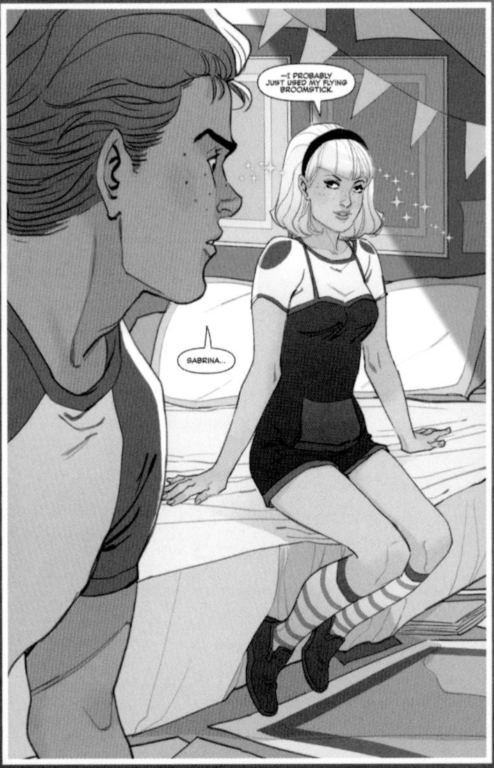

--I PROBABLY JUST USED MY FLYING BROOMSTICK.
SABRINA...

ARCHIE 700 PAGE 24: **FINAL ART**

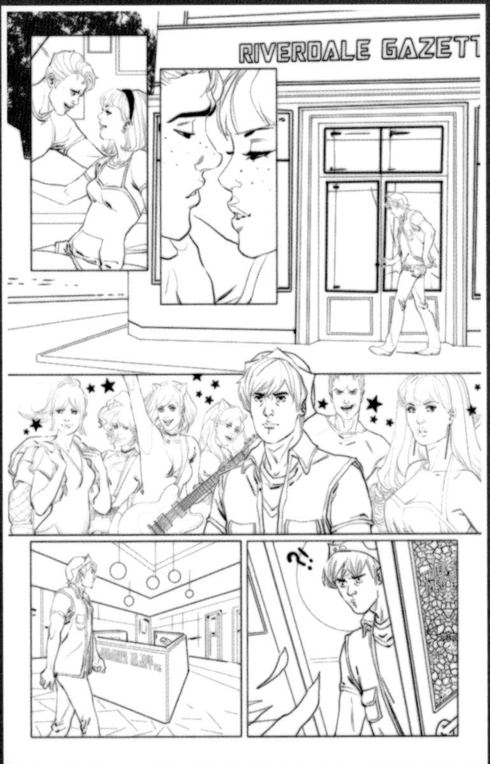

RIVERDALE GAZETT

ARCHIE 700 PAGE 25: **SKETCH**

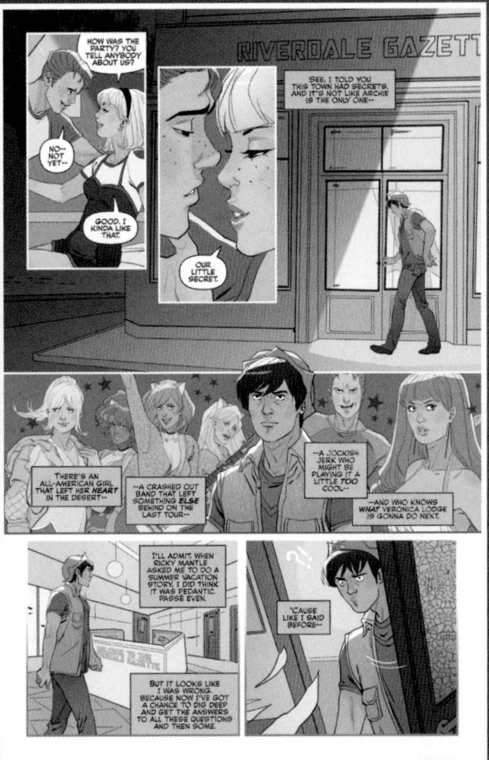

HOW WAS THE PARTY? YOU TELL ANYBODY ABOUT US?
NO-- NOT YET--
GOOD. I KINDA LIKE THAT.
OUR LITTLE SECRET.
RIVERDALE GAZETT
SEE, I TOLD YOU THIS TOWN HAD SECRETS. AND IT'S NOT LIKE ARCHIE IS THE ONLY ONE--
THERE'S AN ALL-AMERICAN GIRL THAT LEFT HER *HEART* IN THE DESERT--
--A CRASHED OUT BAND THAT LEFT SOMETHING *ELSE* BEHIND ON THE LAST TOUR--
--A JOCKISH JERK WHO MIGHT BE PLAYING IT A LITTLE *TOO* COOL--
--AND WHO KNOWS *WHAT* VERONICA LODGE IS GONNA DO NEXT.
I'LL ADMIT, WHEN RICKY MANTLE ASKED ME TO DO A SUMMER VACATION STORY, I DID THINK IT WAS PEDANTIC. PASSÉ EVEN.
BUT IT LOOKS LIKE I WAS WRONG. BECAUSE NOW I'VE GOT A CHANCE TO DIG DEEP AND GET THE ANSWERS TO ALL THESE QUESTIONS AND THEN SOME.
?!
'CAUSE LIKE I SAID BEFORE--

ARCHIE 700 PAGE 25: **FINAL ART**

BONUS COMIC

Take a deeper dive into some of the skeletons buried in and around Riverdale as well as hidden and unexpected connections to the Farm and the Game. Everyone is hiding something in this companion to the third season of the massive hit CW series RIVERDALE.

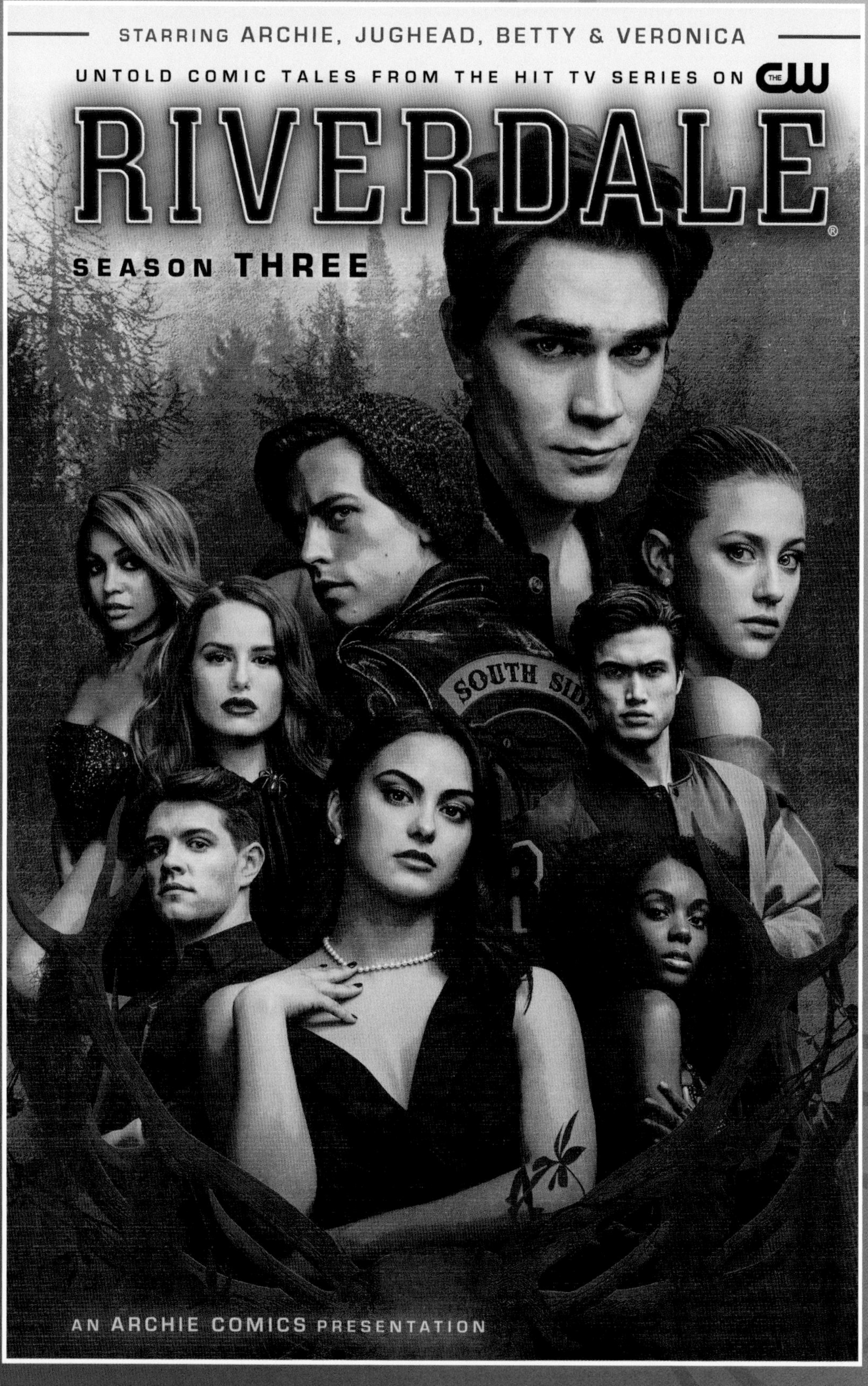

STARRING ARCHIE, JUGHEAD, BETTY & VERONICA
UNTOLD COMIC TALES FROM THE HIT TV SERIES ON THE CW
RIVERDALE®
SEASON THREE
SOUTH SIDE
AN ARCHIE COMICS PRESENTATION

001

STORY BY
MICOL OSTOW

ART BY
THOMAS PITILLI

LETTERING BY
JOHN WORKMAN

COLORS BY
ANDRE SZYMANOWICZ

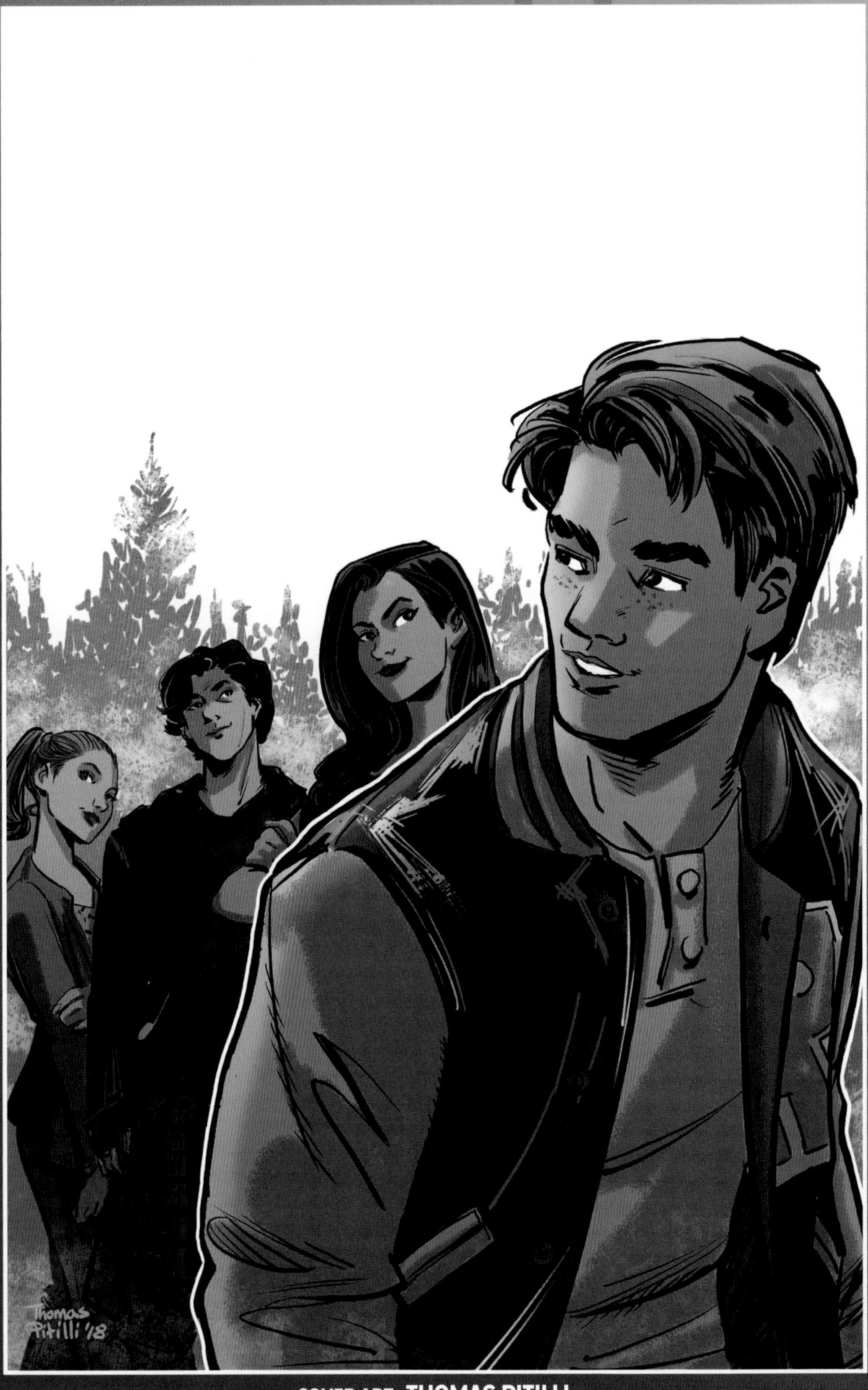
Thomas Pitilli '18

COVER ART: THOMAS PITILLI

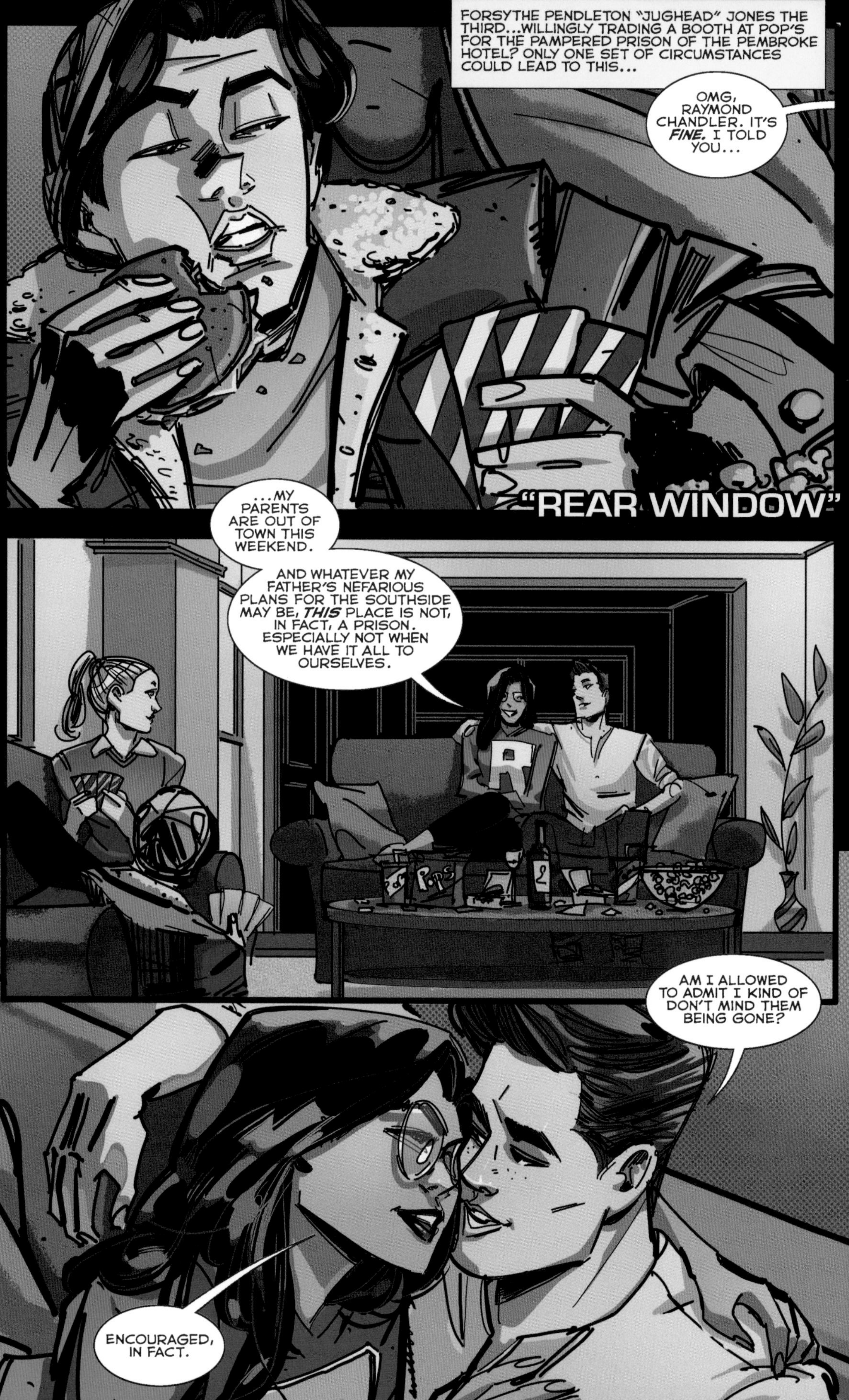
FORSYTHE PENDLETON "JUGHEAD" JONES THE THIRD...WILLINGLY TRADING A BOOTH AT POP'S FOR THE PAMPERED PRISON OF THE PEMBROKE HOTEL? ONLY ONE SET OF CIRCUMSTANCES COULD LEAD TO THIS...
OMG, RAYMOND CHANDLER. IT'S *FINE.* I TOLD YOU...
"REAR WINDOW"
...MY PARENTS ARE OUT OF TOWN THIS WEEKEND.
AND WHATEVER MY FATHER'S NEFARIOUS PLANS FOR THE SOUTHSIDE MAY BE, *THIS* PLACE IS NOT, IN FACT, A PRISON. ESPECIALLY NOT WHEN WE HAVE IT ALL TO OURSELVES.
AM I ALLOWED TO ADMIT I KIND OF DON'T MIND THEM BEING GONE?
ENCOURAGED, IN FACT.

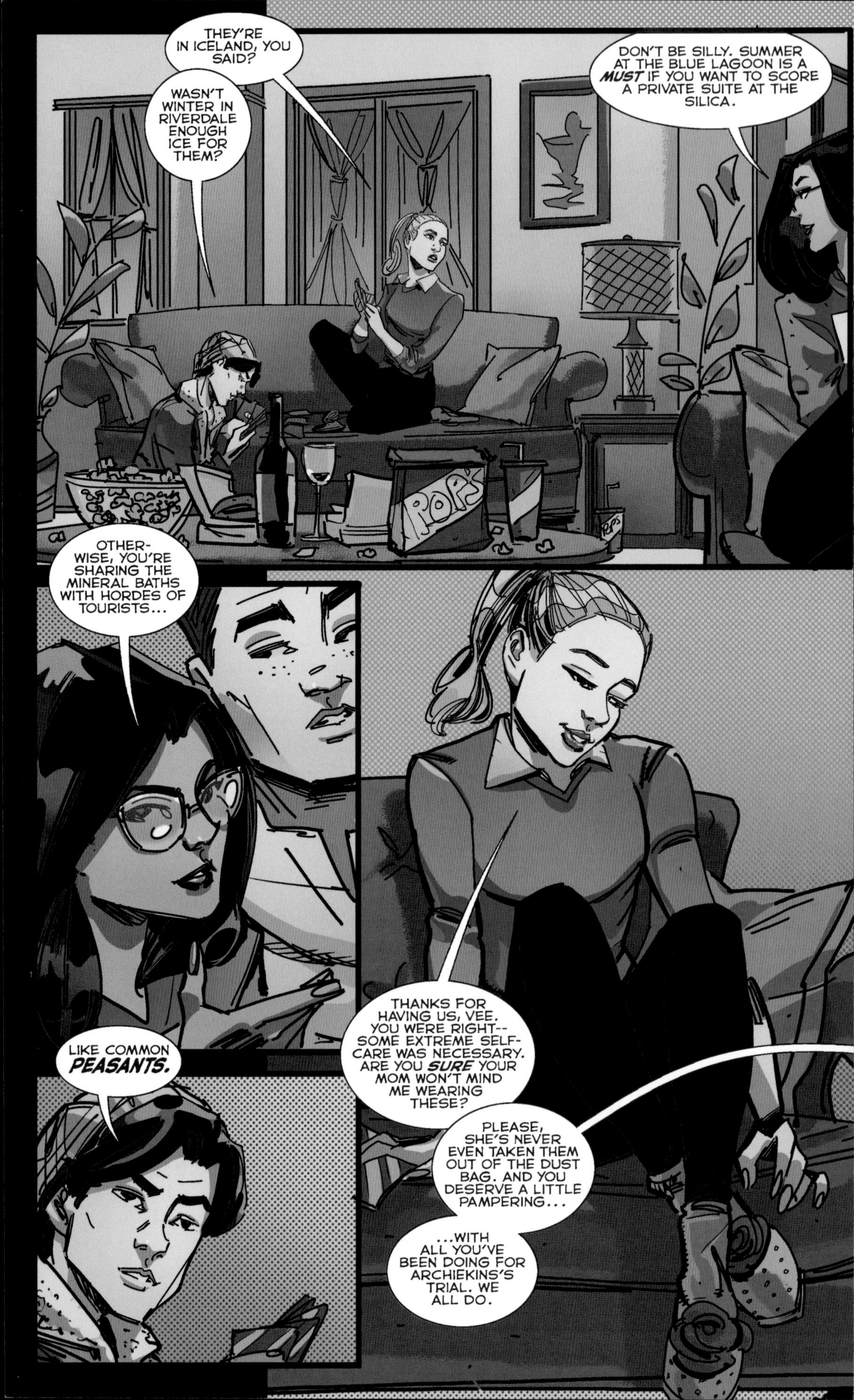
THEY'RE IN ICELAND, YOU SAID?
WASN'T WINTER IN RIVERDALE ENOUGH ICE FOR THEM?
DON'T BE SILLY. SUMMER AT THE BLUE LAGOON IS A *MUST* IF YOU WANT TO SCORE A PRIVATE SUITE AT THE SILICA.
POP'S
OTHER-WISE, YOU'RE SHARING THE MINERAL BATHS WITH HORDES OF TOURISTS...
LIKE COMMON **PEASANTS.**
THANKS FOR HAVING US, VEE. YOU WERE RIGHT--SOME EXTREME SELF-CARE WAS NECESSARY. ARE YOU *SURE* YOUR MOM WON'T MIND ME WEARING THESE?
PLEASE, SHE'S NEVER EVEN TAKEN THEM OUT OF THE DUST BAG. AND YOU DESERVE A LITTLE PAMPERING...
...WITH ALL YOU'VE BEEN DOING FOR ARCHIEKINS'S TRIAL. WE ALL DO.

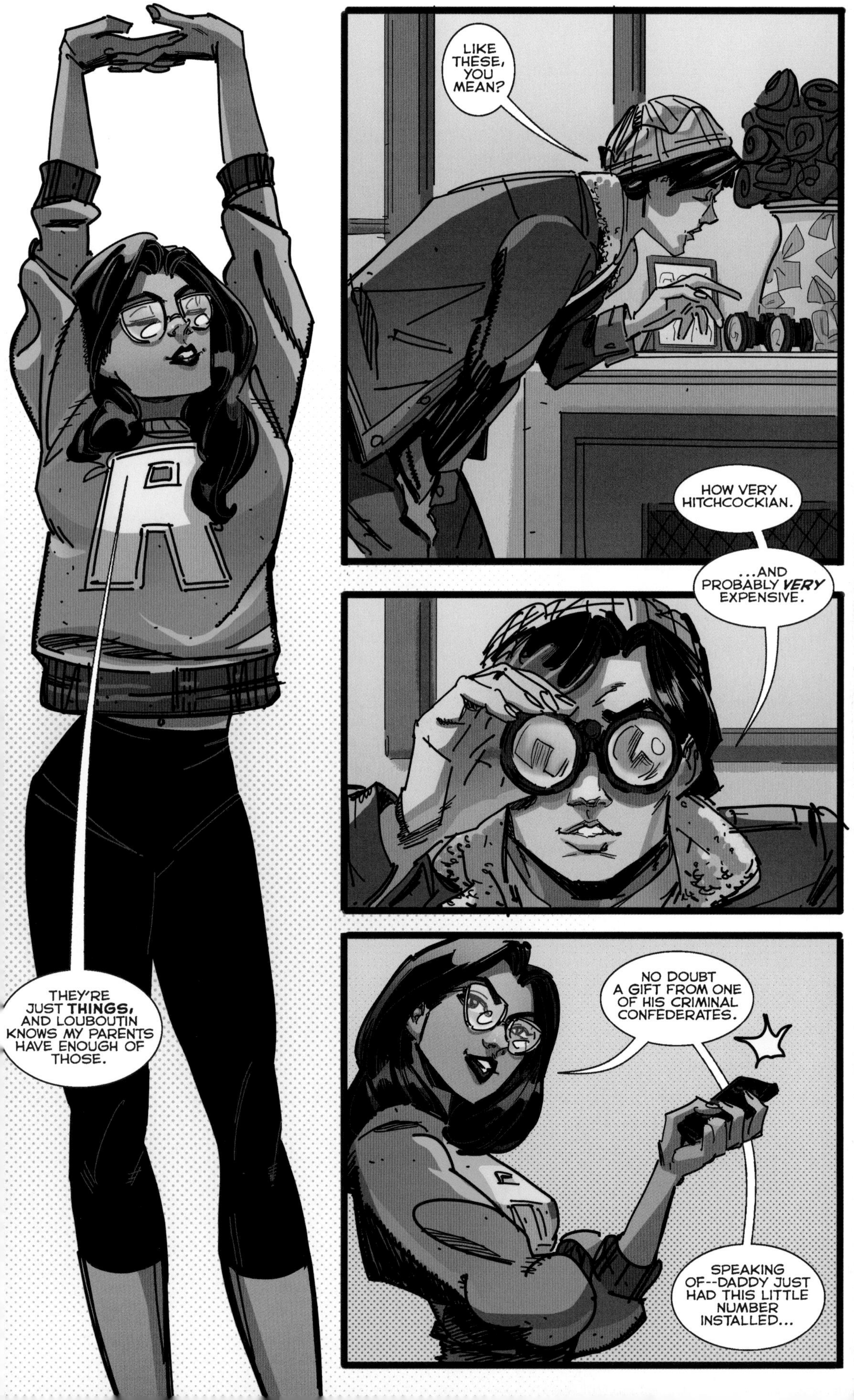
LIKE THESE, YOU MEAN?
HOW VERY HITCHCOCKIAN.
...AND PROBABLY VERY EXPENSIVE.
THEY'RE JUST THINGS, AND LOUBOUTIN KNOWS MY PARENTS HAVE ENOUGH OF THOSE.
NO DOUBT A GIFT FROM ONE OF HIS CRIMINAL CONFEDERATES.
SPEAKING OF--DADDY JUST HAD THIS LITTLE NUMBER INSTALLED...

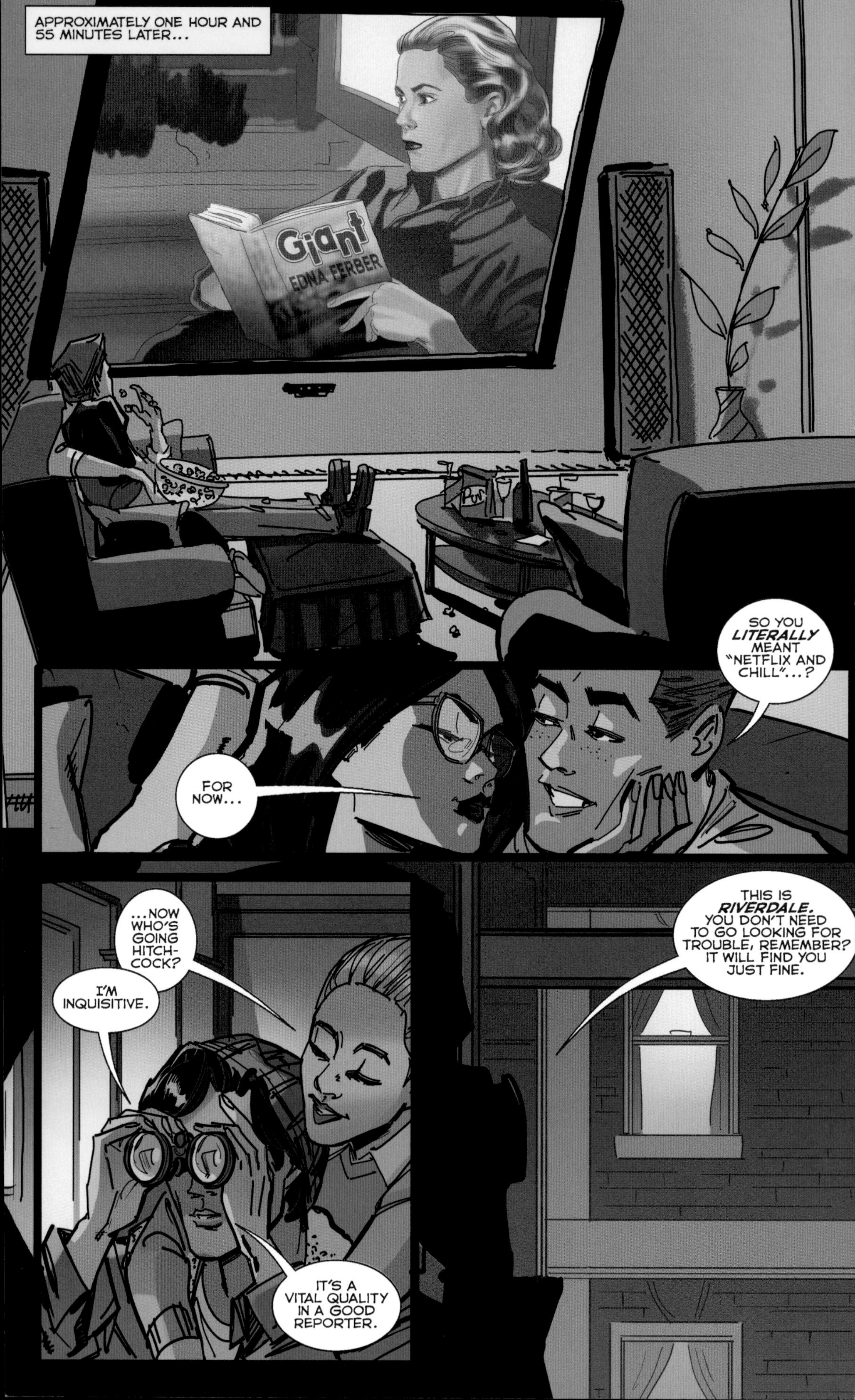
APPROXIMATELY ONE HOUR AND 55 MINUTES LATER...
Giant
EDNA FERBER
SO YOU *LITERALLY* MEANT "NETFLIX AND CHILL"...?
FOR NOW...
...NOW WHO'S GOING HITCH-COCK?
I'M INQUISITIVE.
IT'S A VITAL QUALITY IN A GOOD REPORTER.
THIS IS *RIVERDALE.* YOU DON'T NEED TO GO LOOKING FOR TROUBLE, REMEMBER? IT WILL FIND YOU JUST FINE.

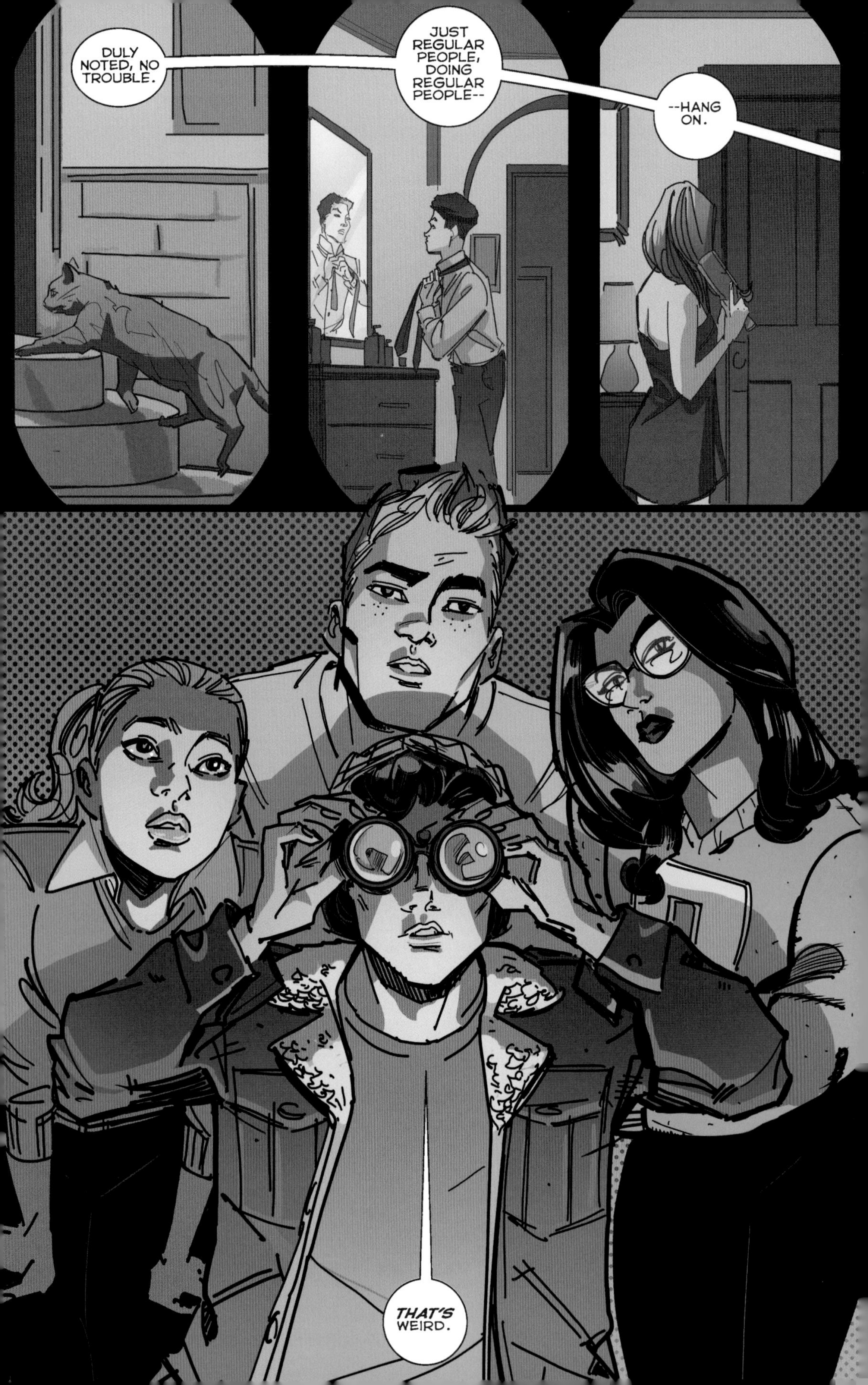
DULY NOTED, NO TROUBLE.
JUST REGULAR PEOPLE, DOING REGULAR PEOPLE--
--HANG ON.
THAT'S WEIRD.

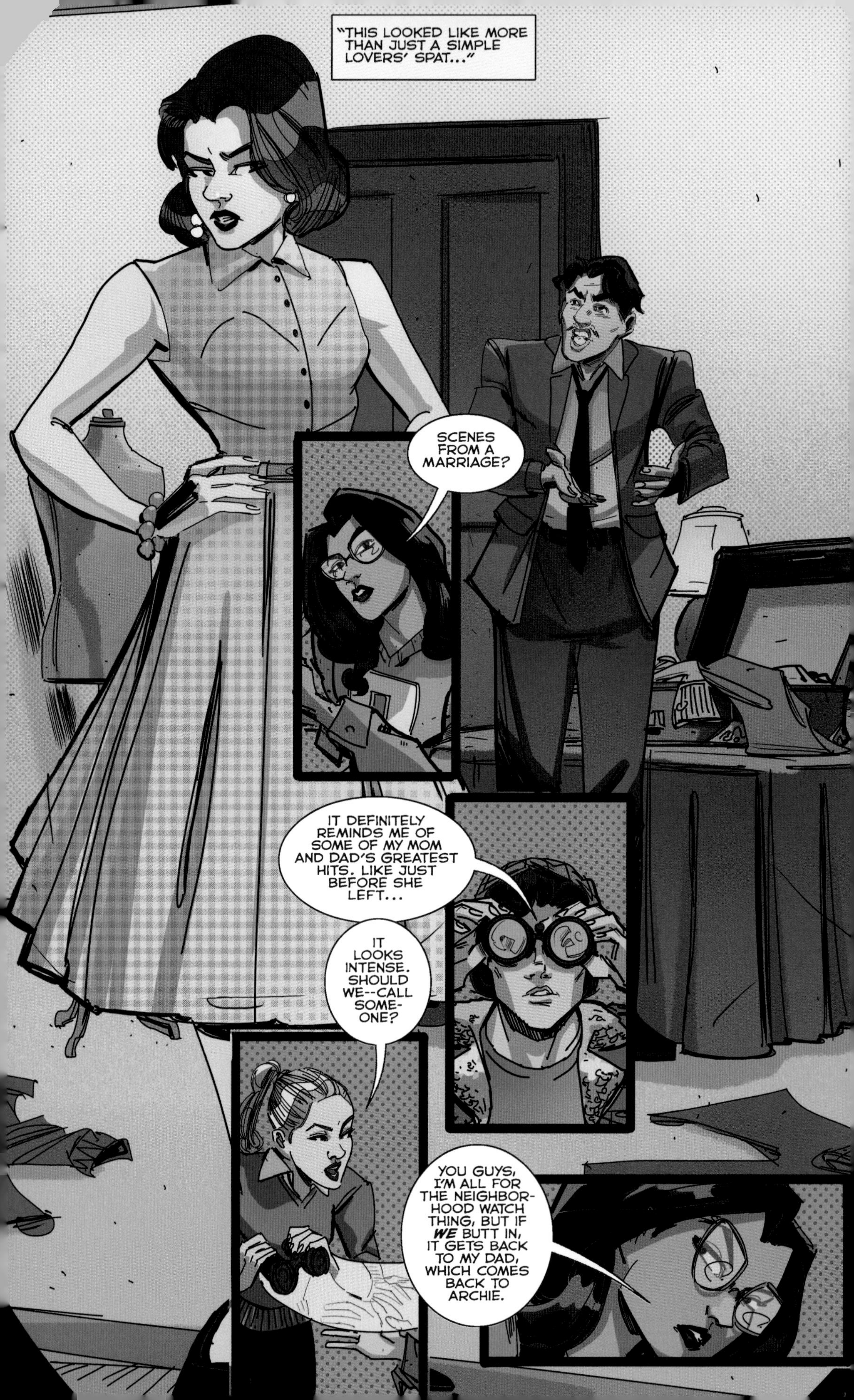
"THIS LOOKED LIKE MORE THAN JUST A SIMPLE LOVERS' SPAT..."
SCENES FROM A MARRIAGE?
IT DEFINITELY REMINDS ME OF SOME OF MY MOM AND DAD'S GREATEST HITS. LIKE JUST BEFORE SHE LEFT...
IT LOOKS INTENSE. SHOULD WE--CALL SOME-ONE?
YOU GUYS, I'M ALL FOR THE NEIGHBOR-HOOD WATCH THING, BUT IF *WE* BUTT IN, IT GETS BACK TO MY DAD, WHICH COMES BACK TO ARCHIE.

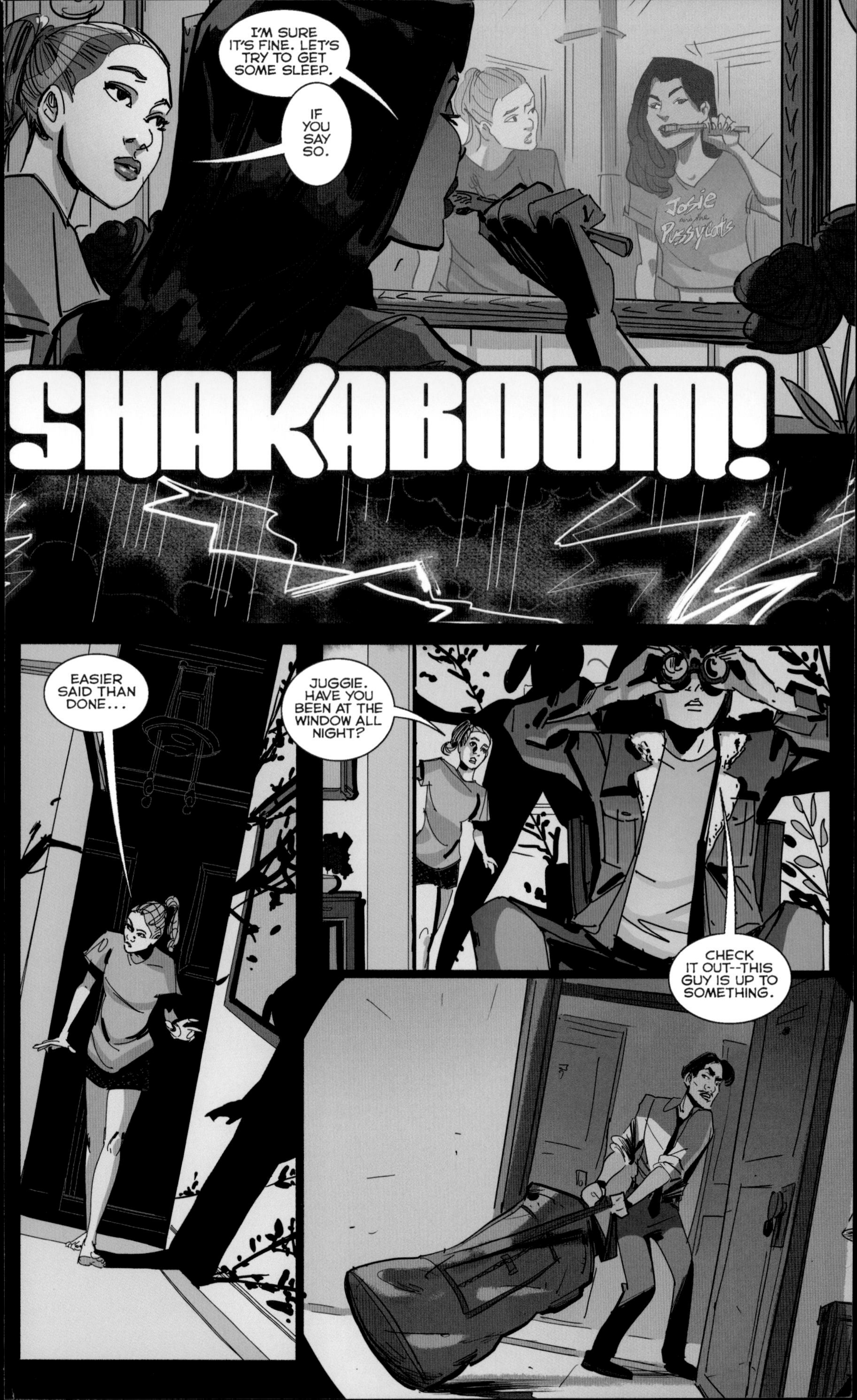
I'M SURE IT'S FINE. LET'S TRY TO GET SOME SLEEP.
IF YOU SAY SO.
Josie and the Pussycats
SHAKABOOM!
EASIER SAID THAN DONE...
JUGGIE. HAVE YOU BEEN AT THE WINDOW ALL NIGHT?
CHECK IT OUT--THIS GUY IS UP TO SOMETHING.

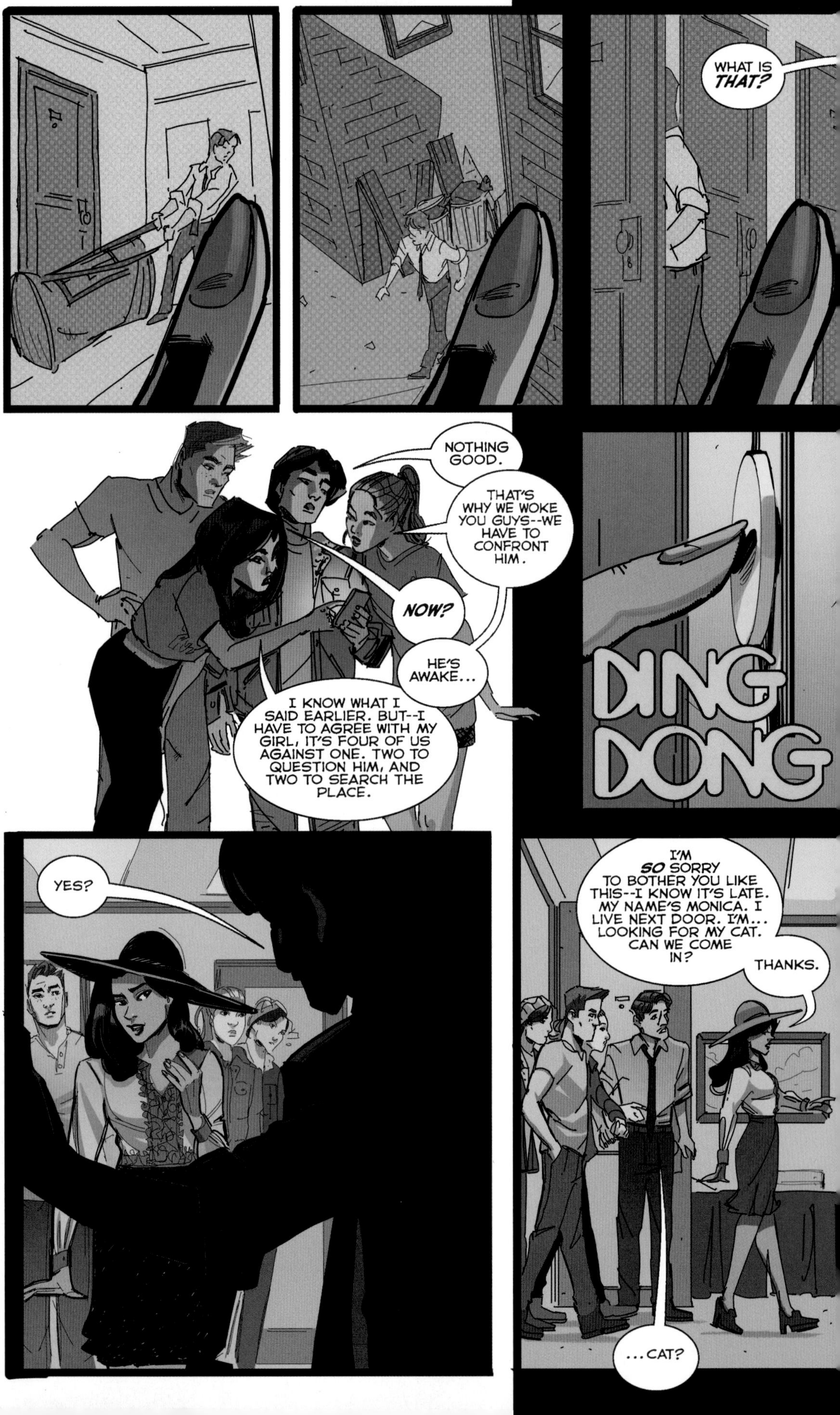
WHAT IS THAT?
NOTHING GOOD.
THAT'S WHY WE WOKE YOU GUYS--WE HAVE TO CONFRONT HIM.
NOW?
HE'S AWAKE...
I KNOW WHAT I SAID EARLIER. BUT--I HAVE TO AGREE WITH MY GIRL, IT'S FOUR OF US AGAINST ONE. TWO TO QUESTION HIM, AND TWO TO SEARCH THE PLACE.
DING DONG
YES?
I'M SO SORRY TO BOTHER YOU LIKE THIS--I KNOW IT'S LATE. MY NAME'S MONICA. I LIVE NEXT DOOR. I'M... LOOKING FOR MY CAT. CAN WE COME IN?
THANKS.
...CAT?

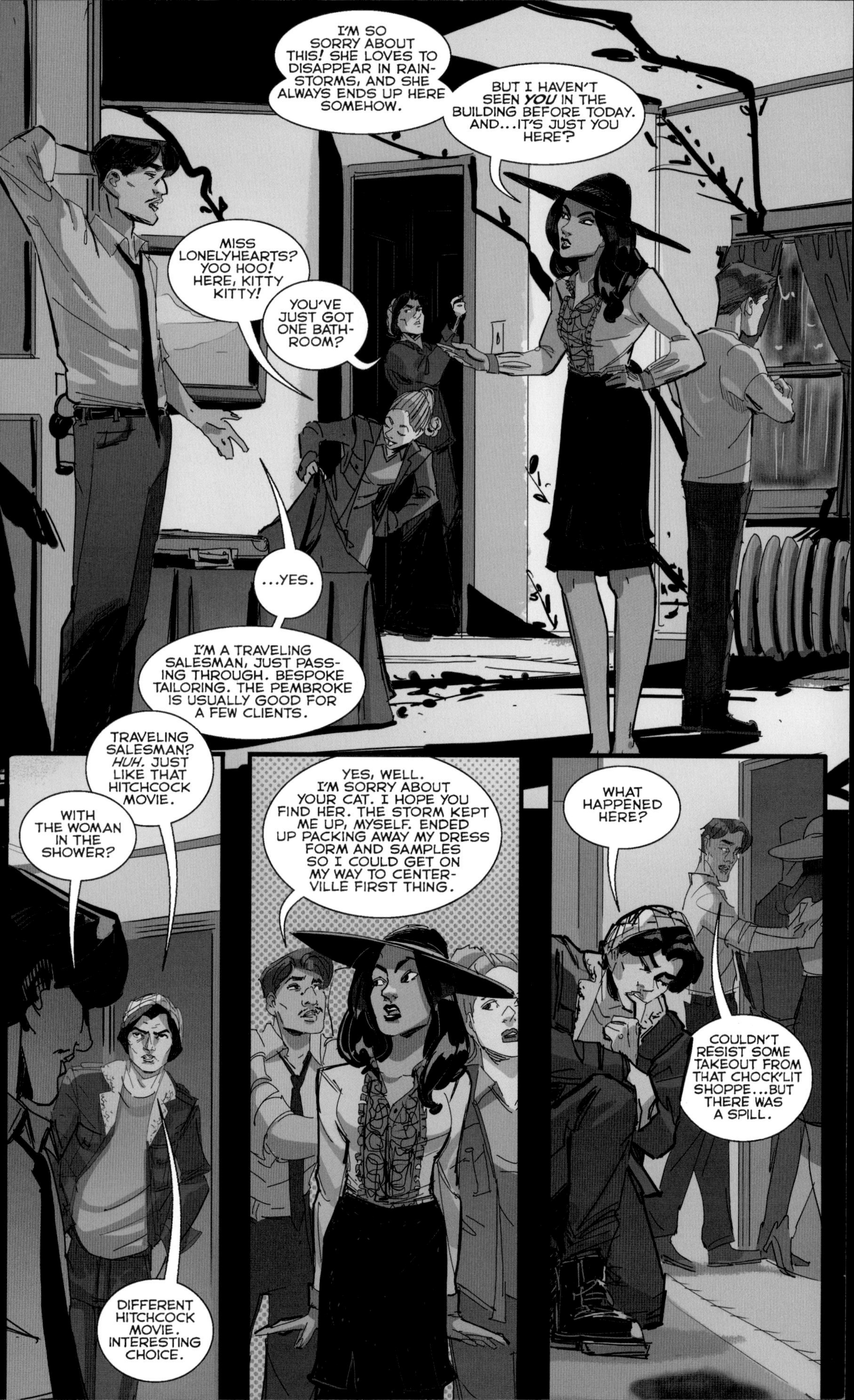
I'M SO SORRY ABOUT THIS! SHE LOVES TO DISAPPEAR IN RAIN-STORMS, AND SHE ALWAYS ENDS UP HERE SOMEHOW.
BUT I HAVEN'T SEEN YOU IN THE BUILDING BEFORE TODAY. AND...IT'S JUST YOU HERE?
MISS LONELYHEARTS? YOO HOO! HERE, KITTY KITTY!
YOU'VE JUST GOT ONE BATH-ROOM?
...YES.
I'M A TRAVELING SALESMAN, JUST PASS-ING THROUGH. BESPOKE TAILORING. THE PEMBROKE IS USUALLY GOOD FOR A FEW CLIENTS.
TRAVELING SALESMAN? HUH. JUST LIKE THAT HITCHCOCK MOVIE.
WITH THE WOMAN IN THE SHOWER?
DIFFERENT HITCHCOCK MOVIE. INTERESTING CHOICE.
YES, WELL. I'M SORRY ABOUT YOUR CAT. I HOPE YOU FIND HER. THE STORM KEPT ME UP, MYSELF. ENDED UP PACKING AWAY MY DRESS FORM AND SAMPLES SO I COULD GET ON MY WAY TO CENTER-VILLE FIRST THING.
WHAT HAPPENED HERE?
COULDN'T RESIST SOME TAKEOUT FROM THAT CHOCK'LIT SHOPPE...BUT THERE WAS A SPILL.

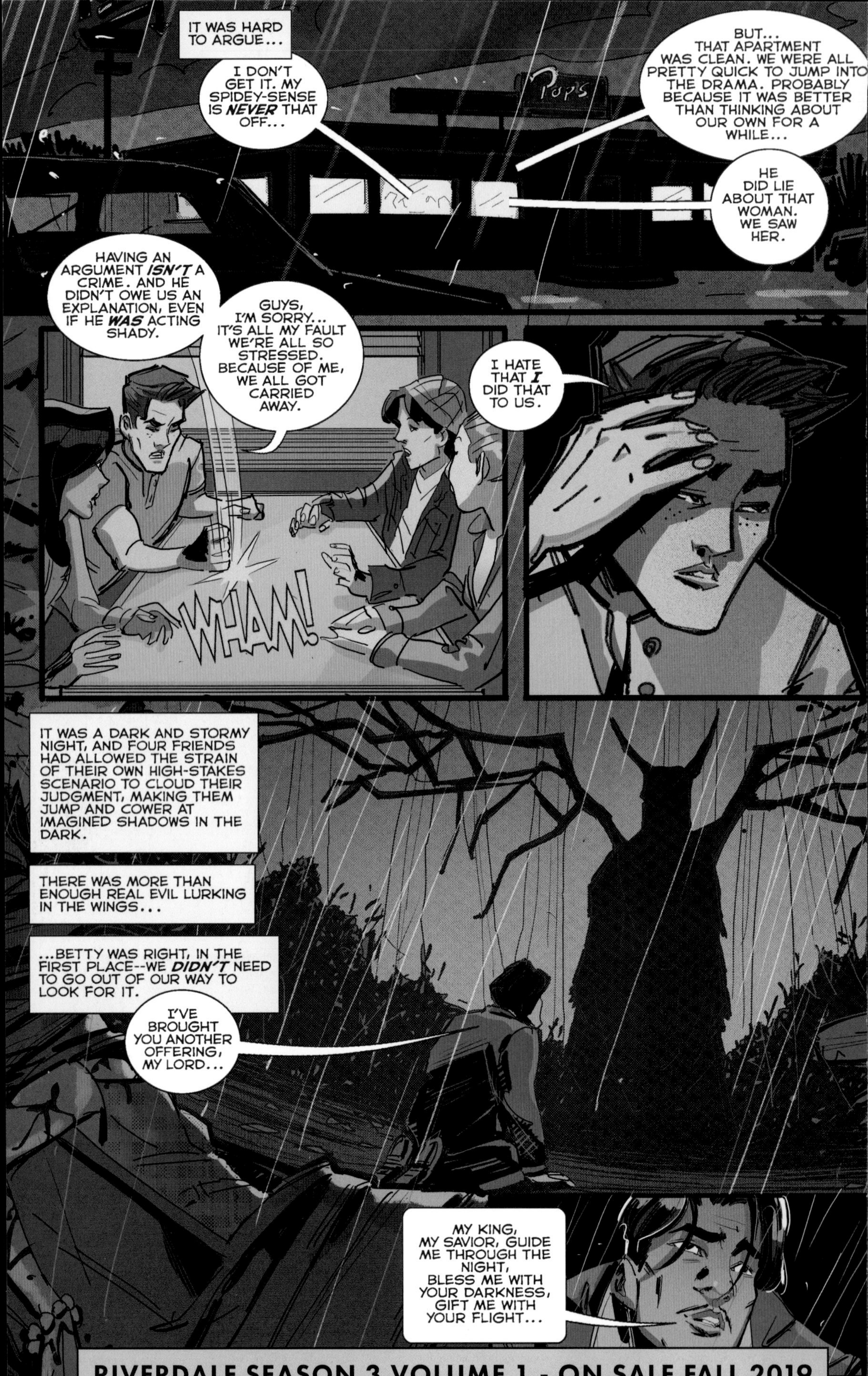
IT WAS HARD TO ARGUE...
I DON'T GET IT. MY SPIDEY-SENSE IS NEVER THAT OFF...
BUT... THAT APARTMENT WAS CLEAN. WE WERE ALL PRETTY QUICK TO JUMP INTO THE DRAMA. PROBABLY BECAUSE IT WAS BETTER THAN THINKING ABOUT OUR OWN FOR A WHILE...
HE DID LIE ABOUT THAT WOMAN. WE SAW HER.
HAVING AN ARGUMENT ISN'T A CRIME. AND HE DIDN'T OWE US AN EXPLANATION, EVEN IF HE WAS ACTING SHADY.
GUYS, I'M SORRY... IT'S ALL MY FAULT WE'RE ALL SO STRESSED. BECAUSE OF ME, WE ALL GOT CARRIED AWAY.
WHAM!
I HATE THAT I DID THAT TO US.
IT WAS A DARK AND STORMY NIGHT, AND FOUR FRIENDS HAD ALLOWED THE STRAIN OF THEIR OWN HIGH-STAKES SCENARIO TO CLOUD THEIR JUDGMENT, MAKING THEM JUMP AND COWER AT IMAGINED SHADOWS IN THE DARK.
THERE WAS MORE THAN ENOUGH REAL EVIL LURKING IN THE WINGS...
...BETTY WAS RIGHT, IN THE FIRST PLACE--WE DIDN'T NEED TO GO OUT OF OUR WAY TO LOOK FOR IT.
I'VE BROUGHT YOU ANOTHER OFFERING, MY LORD...
MY KING, MY SAVIOR, GUIDE ME THROUGH THE NIGHT, BLESS ME WITH YOUR DARKNESS, GIFT ME WITH YOUR FLIGHT...